BADAR MUNIR

325- 8024.

IE 5263

Expert Systems Applications in Engineering and Manufacturing

Adedeji B. Badiru
Expert Systems Laboratory
School of Industrial Engineering
University of Oklahoma

PRENTICE HALL
Englewood Cliffs, New Jersey 07632

Library of Congress Cataloging-in-Publication Data

Badiru, Adedeji Bodunde
    Expert systems applications in engineering and manufacturing /
Adedeji Bodunde Badiru.
        p.   cm. -- (Prentice-Hall international series in industrial
and systems engineering)
    Includes bibliographical references and index.
    ISBN 0-13-278219-7
    1. Production engineering--Automation.   2. Expert systems
(Computer science)--Industrial applications.   3. Artificial
intelligence--Industrial applications.   I. Title.   II. Series.
TS176.B3   1992
670.42'7--dc20   91-36421
                                                             CIP

Acquisitions Editor: Elizabeth Kaster
Editorial/production supervision: Cyndy Lyle Rymer
Cover Designer: Wanda Lubelska
Prepress Buyer: Linda Behrens
Manufacturing Buyer: David Dickey
Editorial Assistant: Jamie Zampino
Supplements Editor: Alice Dworkin

 © 1992 by Prentice-Hall, Inc.
A Simon & Schuster Company
Englewood Cliffs, New Jersey 07632

To Iswat, Abidemi, Adetokunboh, and Omotunji

Printed in the United States of America
10 9 8 7 6 5 4 3 2 1

ISBN 0-13-278219-7

Prentice-Hall International (UK) Limited, *London*
Prentice-Hall of Australia Pty. Limited, *Sydney*
Prentice-Hall Canada Inc., *Toronto*
Prentice-Hall Hispanoamericana, S.A., *Mexico*
Prentice-Hall of India Private Limited, *New Delhi*
Prentice-Hall of Japan, Inc., *Tokyo*
Simon & Schuster Asia Pte. Ltd., *Singapore*
Editora Prentice-Hall do Brasil, Ltda., *Rio de Janeiro*

PRENTICE HALL INTERNATIONAL SERIES
IN INDUSTRIAL AND SYSTEMS ENGINEERING

W. J. Fabrycky and J. H. Mize, Editors

Contents

CHAPTER 11

SURVEY OF ENGINEERING AND MANUFACTURING APPLICATIONS, 285

CHAPTER 12

CASE STUDIES: SAMPLES OF EXPERT SYSTEM DEVELOPMENTS, 305

Preface

Expert systems are rapidly becoming one of the major approaches to solving engineering and manufacturing problems. Expert systems have been implemented for several practical applications in many decision problems. The growing interst in the technology of expert systems has surpassed anything previously witnessed in the scientific community.

Expert systems are helping major companies to diagnose processes in real time, schedule operations, troubleshoot equipment, maintain machinery, and design service and production facilities. With the implementation of expert systems in industrial environments, companies are finding that real-world problems are best solved by an integrated strategy involving the management of personnel, software, and hardware systems.

Solutions to most engineering and manufacturing problems involve not only heuristics, but also mathematical calculations, large data manipulations, statistical analysis, real-time information management, system optimization, and man-machine interfaces. These issues and other related topics are addressed in this book. In addition to the basic concepts of expert systems, guidelines are presented on various items ranging from problem selection, data analysis, knowledge acquisition, and system development to verification, validation, integration, implementation, and maintenance.

The book takes an integrated and comprehensive view of expert system development process. The peculiar aspects of engineering and manufacturing problems are addressed in various sections of the book.

This book adds to the growing collection of literature on expert systems. It presents the basic concepts and practical procedures for students and practitioners in the engineering and manufacturing communities. The topics have been carefully selected to illustrate how to select, initiate, and implement expert system projects. The "how-to" approach of the book should be very helpful to readers in getting started with the expert systems development process. The book is suitable as a textbook in upper level undergraduate courses or first-year graduate level courses in engineering and manufacturing.

Because the basic technology of artificial intelligence has gradually improved over the past decade, the issue is not whether the technology is useful, but how to implement it. This is why the integrated approach of this book is very useful. The book focuses not only on the technology of expert systems, but also on how to implement and manage the technology. The expert systems presented as examples throughout the book were developed in the Expert Systems Laboratory in the School of Industrial Engineering, University of Oklahoma. The examples illustrate the practicality of solving engineering and manufacturing problems with expert systems. One hundred and thirty-one figures and eighteen tables are used to illustrate and clarify the concepts presented in the book.

Chapter 1 covers the historical background of artificial intelligence (AI). The origin of AI, comparison of human intelligence to artificial intelligence, and the evolution of expert systems are presented in the chapter.

Chapter 2 presents the basic concepts of expert systems. The characteristics, structure, benefits, and user interface of expert systems are presented. A model for the interaction of academia and industry for expert system projects is presented.

Chapter 3 deals with problem analysis and selection. A major determinant of expert systems success is the suitability of the problem domain. Topics covered include problem identification, and data requirement analysis.

Chapter 4 presents guidelines for knowledge acquisition. Guidelines for selecting the knowledge engineer and the domain expert are discussed. The various methods of extracting knowledge from experts are presented.

Chapter 5 discusses knowledge representation techniques. Characteristics and types of knowledge are presented. The standard formal representation techniques are presented with examples. New concepts are also presented to enhance the search process during consultation.

Chapter 6 covers the management of uncertainty in expert systems. Conventional techniques such as Bayesian reasoning and certainty factors are presented.

Chapter 7 presents guidelines for selecting an expert system development tool.

Chapter 8 presents a practical procedure for constructing expert systems. Components of the development process are defined.

Chapter 9 covers verification, validation, and integration processes. Expert systems quality management is also presented.

Chapter 10 deals with implementation and management strategies. A model for expert system technology transfer is also presented. A conceptual model for using expert systems to aid project management functions is presented.

Chapter 11 presents a survey of engineering and manufacturing applications of expert systems. Most of the examples presented in the chapter are commercial systems that have proven their practicality and effectiveness in solving problems.

Chapter 12 presents case studies of expert system developments. The cases represent expert systems developed in the Expert Systems Laboratory in the School of Industrial Engineering at the University of Oklahoma.

A brief guide to using VP-Expert is presented in Appendix A. A tabulated guide to expert systems development tools is presented in Appendix B. Appendix C presents the names and addresses of selected companies involved in expert system products and services. A glossary of artificial intelligence and expert systems terms is presented in Appendix D. Standard conversion factors applicable to engineering and manufacturing problems are contained in Appendix E. Listings of sample knowledge bases are presented in Appendix F. A comprehensive bibliography is presented at the end of the book for further reference by interested readers.

Through the innovative implementation of expert systems, computers are now helping to solve problems that were previously thought to be impossible to solve. The investment of time, money, and effort in expert systems is a worthwhile venture. I encourage readers to keep the following pronouncement in mind as they explore the technology of expert systems:

A good knowledge base is an everlasting capital!

ACKNOWLEDGMENTS

I sincerely thank everyone who contributed to making this book a reality. Particular thanks go to my wife, Iswat, for continuing to give me her full support in all my professional endeavors. I thank Elizabeth Kaster, Industrial and Systems Engineering editor for Prentice Hall, for her perseverance with this project. Her positive attitude was a good source of motivation throughout the preparation of this book. I thank all my colleagues in the School of Industrial Engineering for their continuing positive collegiality. Special thanks go to Dr. Bob Foote and Dr. Simin Pulat. I should also thank my computer for not failing me at the most crucial times of need. Though it beeped and fussed several times, it kept on cranking out pages of the manuscript.

Above all, I thank God for giving me the strength to continue even when I think I should stop.

A.B.B.

1

Artificial Intelligence Background

The background of Artificial Intelligence (AI) has been characterized by controversial opinions and diverse approaches. The controversies have ranged from the basic definition of intelligence to questions about the moral and ethical aspects of pursuing AI. However, despite the unsettled controversies, the technology continues to generate practical results. With increasing efforts in AI research, many of the prevailing arguments are being resolved with proven technical approaches. Expert systems, the main subject of this book, is the most promising branch of AI.

"Artificial intelligence" is a controversial name for a technology that promises much potential for improving human productivity. The phrase seems to challenge human pride in being the sole creation capable of possessing real intelligence. All kinds of anecdotal jokes about AI have been offered by casual observers. A speaker once recounted his wife's response when he told her that he was venturing into the new technology of artificial intelligence. "Thank God, you are finally realizing how dumb I have been saying you were all these years," was alleged to have been the wife's words of encouragement. One whimsical definition of AI refers to it as the "Artificial Insemination of knowledge into a machine." Despite the deriding remarks, serious embracers of AI may yet have the last laugh. It is being shown again and again that AI may hold the key to improving operational effectiveness in many areas of application. Some observers have suggested changing the term "Artificial Intelligence" to a less controversial one such as "Intelligent Applications (IA)." This refers more to the way that computer and software are used innovatively to solve complex decision problems.

1

Natural Intelligence involves the capability of humans to acquire knowledge, reason with the knowledge, and use it to solve problems effectively. It also refers to the ability to develop new knowledge based on existing knowledge. By contrast, *Artificial Intelligence* is defined as the ability of a machine to use simulated knowledge in solving problems.

1.1 ORIGIN OF ARTIFICIAL INTELLIGENCE

The definition of intelligence had been sought by many ancient philosophers and mathematicians including Aristotle, Plato, Copernicus, and Galileo. These great philosophers attempted to explain the process of thought and understanding. The real key that started the quest for the simulation of intelligence did not occur, however, until the English philosopher Thomas Hobbes put forth an interesting concept in the 1650s. Hobbes believed that thinking consists of symbolic operations and that everything in life can be represented mathematically. These beliefs directly led to the notion that a machine capable of carrying out mathematical operations on symbols could imitate human thinking. This is the basic driving force behind the AI effort. For that reason Hobbes is sometimes referred to as the grandfather of Artificial Intelligence.

While the term "Artificial Intelligence" was coined by John McCarthy relatively recently (1956), the idea had been considered centuries before. As early as 1637 Rene Descartes was conceptually exploring the ability of a machine to have intelligence when he said:

> For we can well imagine a machine so made that it utters words and even, in a few cases, words pertaining specifically to some actions that affect it physically. However, no such machine could ever arrange its words in various different ways so as to respond to the sense of whatever is said in its presence—as even the dullest people can do.

Descartes believed that the mind and the physical world are on parallel planes that cannot be equated. They are of different substances following entirely different rules and can, thus, not be successfully compared. The physical world (i.e. machines) cannot imitate the mind because there is no common reference point.

Hobbes proposed the idea that thinking could be reduced to mathematical operations. On the other hand Descartes had the insight into functions that machines might someday be able to perform. But he had reservations about the concept that thinking could be simply a mathematical process.

The 1800s was an era that saw some advancement in the conceptualization of the computer. Charles Babbage, a British mathematician, laid the foundation for the construction of the computer, a machine defined as being capable of performing mathematical computations. In 1833, Babbage introduced an Analytical Engine. This computational machine incorporated two unprecedented ideas that were to become crucial elements in the modern computer. First, it had operations that were fully programmable and second, the engine could contain conditional branches. Without these two abilities the power of today's computers would be inconceivable. Babbage was never able to realize his dream of building the analytic engine due to a lack of financial support. However, his dream was revived through the efforts of later researchers. Babbage's basic concepts could be observed in the way that most computers operate today.

Another British mathematician, George Boole, worked on issues that were to become equally important. Boole formulated the "laws of thought" that set up rules of logic for representing thought. The rules contained only two-valued variables. By this, any variable in a logical operation could be in one of only two states: yes or no, true or false, all or nothing, 0 or 1, on or off, and so on. This was the birth of digital logic, a key component of the artificial intelligence effort.

In the early 1900s Alfred North Whitehead and Bertrand Russell extended Boole's logic to include mathematical operations. This not only led to the formulation of digital computers but also made possible one of the first ties between computers and thought process.

However, there was still a lack of an acceptable way to construct such a computer. In 1938 Claude Shannon published "A Symbolic Analysis of Relay and Switching Circuits." This work demonstrated that Boolean logic consisting of only two-variable states (e.g. on-off switching of circuits) can be used to perform logic operations. Based on this premise, the ENIAC (Electronic Numerical Integrator And Computer) was built in 1946 at the University of Pennsylvania. The ENIAC was a large-scale fully operational electronic computer that signaled the beginning of the first generation of computers. It could perform calculations 1,000 times faster than its electro-mechanical predecessors. It weighed 30 tons, stood two stories high, and occupied 1500 square feet of floor space. Unlike today's computers that operate in binary codes (0s and 1s), the ENIAC operated in decimal (0, 1, 2, . . ., 9) and it required 10 vacuum tubes to represent one decimal digit. With over 18,000 vacuum tubes, the ENIAC needed a great amount of electrical power; so much that it was said that it dimmed the lights in Philadelphia whenever it operated.

1.2 HUMAN INTELLIGENCE VERSUS MACHINE INTELLIGENCE

Two of the leading mathematicians and computer enthusiasts during the 1900 to 1950 time frame were Alan Turing and John Von Neumann. In 1945, Von Neumann insisted that computers should not be built as glorified adding machines, with all their operations specified in advance. Rather, he suggested, computers should be built as general purpose logic machines capable of executing a wide variety of programs. Such machines, Von Neumann proclaimed, would be highly flexible and capable of being readily shifted from one task to another. They could react intelligently to the results of their calculations, could choose among alternatives, and could even play checkers or chess. This represented something unheard of at that time: a machine with built-in intelligence, able to operate on internal instructions.

Prior to Von Neumann's concept, even the most complex mechanical devices had always been controlled from the outside, for example, by setting dials and knobs. Von Neumann did not invent the computer, but what he introduced was equally significant: computing by use of computer programs, the way it is done today. His work paved the way for what would later be called artificial intelligence in computers.

Alan Turing also made major contributions to the conceptualization of a machine that can be universally used for all problems based only on variable instructions fed into it. Turing's universal machine concept, along with Von Neumann's concept of a storage area containing multiple instructions that can be accessed in any sequence, solidified the ideas needed to develop the programmable computer. Thus, a machine was developed that could perform logical operations and could do them in varying orders by changing the set of instructions that were executed.

Due to the fact that operational machines were now being realized, questions about the "intelligence" of the machines began to surface. Turing's other contribution to the world of AI came in the area of defining what constitutes intelligence. In 1950, he designed the Turing test for determining the intelligence of a system. The test utilized the conversational interaction between three players to try and verify computer intelligence.

The test is conducted by having a person (the interrogator) in a room that contains only a computer terminal. In an adjoining room, hidden from view, a man (Person A) and a woman (Person B) are located with another computer terminal. The interrogator communicates with the couple in the other room by typing questions on the keyboard. The questions appear on the couple's computer screen and they respond by typing on their own keyboard. The interrogator can direct questions to either Person A or Person B, but without knowing which is the man and which is the woman.

The purpose of the test is to distinguish between the man and the woman merely by analyzing their responses. In the test, only one of the people is obligated to give truthful responses. The other person deliberately attempts to fool and confuse the interrogator by giving responses that may lead to an incorrect guess. The second stage of the test is to substitute a computer for one of the two persons in the other room. Now, the human is obligated to give truthful responses to the interrogator while the computer tries to fool the interrogator into thinking that it is human. Turing's contention is that if the interrogator's success rate in the human/computer version of the game is not better than his success rate in the man/woman version, then the computer can be said to be "thinking." That is, the computer possesses "intelligence." Turing's test has served as a classical example for artificial intelligence proponents for many years.

By 1952 computer hardware had advanced far enough that actual experiments in writing programs to imitate thought processes could be conducted. The team of Herbert Simon, Allen Newell, and Cliff Shaw organized to conduct such an experiment. They set out to establish what kinds of problems a computer could solve with the right programming. Proving theorems in symbolic logic such as those set forth by Whitehead and Russell in the early 1900s fit the concept of what they felt an intelligent computer should be able to handle.

It quickly became apparent that there was a need for a new, higher level computer language than was currently available. First, they needed a language that was more user-friendly and could take program instructions that are easily understood by a human programmer and automatically convert them into machine language that could be understood by the computer. Second, they needed a programming language that changed the way in which computer memory was allocated. All previous languages would pre-assign memory at the start of a program. The team found that the type of programs they were writing would require large amounts of memory and would function unpredictably.

To solve the problem, they developed a list processing language. This type of language would label each area of memory and then maintain a list of all available memory. As memory became available it would update the list and when more memory was needed it would allocate the amount necessary. This type of programming also allowed the programmer to be able to structure his or her data so that any information that was to be used for a particular problem could be easily accessed.

The end result of their effort was a program called Logic Theorist. This program had rules consisting of axioms already proved. When it was given a new logical expression, it would search through all of the possible operations in an effort to discover a proof of the new expression. Instead of using a brute force search method, they pioneered the use of heuristics in the search method.

The Logic Theorist that they developed in 1955 was capable of solving thirty-eight of fifty-two theorems that Whitehead and Russell had devised. It was not only capable of the proofs but did them very quickly. What took Logic Theorist a matter of minutes to prove would have taken years to do if it had been done by simple brute force on a computer. By comparing the steps which it went through to arrive at a proof to those that human subjects went through, it was also found that it had a remarkable imitation of the human thought process.

Despite the various successful experiments, many observers still believe that AI does not have much potential for practical applications. There is a popular joke in the AI community that points out the deficiency of AI in natural language applications. It is said that a computer was asked to translate the following English statement into Russian and back to English: "*The spirit is willing but the flesh is weak.*" The reverse translation from Russian to English yielded: "*The vodka is good but the meat is rotten.*"

1.3 THE FIRST AI CONFERENCE

The summer of 1956 signified the first attempt to establish the field of machine intelligence into an organized effort. The Dartmouth Summer Conference, organized by John McCarthy, Marvin Minsky, Nathaniel Rochester, and Claude Shannon, brought together people whose work and interest formally founded the field of AI. The conference, held at Dartmouth College in New Hampshire, was funded by a grant from the Rockefeller foundation. It was at that conference that John McCarthy coined the term "artificial intelligence". It was the same John McCarthy who developed the LISP programming language that has become a standard tool for AI development. In attendance at the meeting, in addition to the organizers, were Herbert Simon, Allen Newell, Arthur Samuel, Trenchard More, Oliver Selfridge, and Ray Solomonoff.

The Logic Theorist (LT), developed by Newell, Shaw, and Simon, was discussed at the conference. The system, considered the first AI program, used heuristic search to solve mathematical problems in *Principia Mathematica*, written by Whitehead and Russell (Newell and Simon 1972). Newell and Simon were far ahead of others in actually implementing AI ideas with their Logic Theorist. The Dartmouth meeting served mostly as an avenue for the exchange of information and, more importantly, as a turning point in the main emphasis of work in the AI endeavor. Instead of concentrating so much on the hardware to imitate intelligence, the meeting set the course for examining the structure of the data being processed by computers, the use of computers to process symbols, the need for new languages, and the role of computers for testing theories.

1.4 EVOLUTION OF SMART PROGRAMS

The next major step in software technology came from Newell, Shaw, and Simon in 1959. The program they introduced was called General Problem Solver (GPS). GPS was intended to be a program that could solve many types of problems. It was capable of solving theorems, playing chess, or doing various complex puzzles. GPS was a significant step forward in AI. It incorporates several new ideas to facilitate problem solving. The nucleus of the system was the use of means-end analysis. **Means-end analysis** involves comparing a present state with a goal state. The difference between the two states is determined and a search is done to find a method to reduce this difference. This process is continued until there is no difference between the current state and the goal state.

In order to further improve the search, GPS contained two other features. The first is that, if while trying to reduce the deviation from the goal state, it finds that it has actually complicated the search process, it was capable of backtracking to an earlier state and exploring alternate solution paths. The second is that it was capable of defining sub-goal states that, if satisfied, would permit the solution process to continue. In formulating GPS, Newell and Simon had done extensive work studying human subjects and the way they solved problems. They felt that GPS did a good job of imitating the human subjects. They commented on the effort by saying (Newell and Simon 1961):

> The fragmentary evidence we have obtained to date encourages us to think that the General Problem Solver provides a rather good first approximation to an information processing theory of certain kinds of thinking and problem-solving behavior. The processes of 'thinking' can no longer be regarded as completely mysterious.

GPS was not without critics. One of the criticisms was that the only way the program obtained any information was to get it from human input. The way and order in which the problems were presented was controlled by humans, thus, the program was doing only what it was told to do. Newell and Simon argued that the fact that the program was not just repeating steps and sequences but was actually applying rules to solve problems it had not previously encountered, is indicative of intelligent behavior.

There were other criticisms also. Humans are able to devise new shortcuts and improvise. GPS would always go down the same path to solve the same problem, making the same mistakes as before. It could not learn. Another problem was that GPS was good when given a certain area or a specific search space to solve. The problem with this limitation was that in the solution of problems, it was difficult to determine what search space to use. Sometimes solving the problem is trivial compared to finding the search space. The problems posed to GPS were all of a specific nature. They were all puzzles or logical challenges: problems that could easily be expressed in symbolic form and operated on in a pseudo-mathematical approach. There are many problems that humans face that are not so easily expressed in symbolic form.

Also during the year 1959, John McCarthy came out with a tool that was to greatly improve the ability of researchers to develop AI programs. He developed a new computer programming language called LISP (list processing). It was to become one of the most widely used languages in the field.

LISP is distinctive in two areas: memory organization and control structure. The memory organization is done in a tree fashion with interconnections between memory groups. Thus, it permits a programmer to keep track of complex structural relationships. The other distinction is the way the control of the program is done. Instead of working from the prerequisites to a goal, it starts with the goal and works backwards to determine what prerequisites are required to achieve the goal.

In 1960, Frank Rosenblatt did some work in the area of pattern recognition. He introduced a device called PERCEPTRON that was supposed to be capable of recognizing letters and other patterns. It consisted of a grid of four hundred photo cells connected with wires to a response unit that would produce a signal only if the light coming off the subject to be recognized crossed a certain threshold.

During the latter part of the 1960s, there were two efforts in another area of simulating human reasoning. Kenneth Colby at Stanford University and Joseph Weizenbaum at MIT wrote separate programs that were capable of interacting in a two-way conversation. Weizenbaum's program was called ELIZA. The programs were able to sustain very realistic conversations by using very clever techniques. For example, ELIZA used a pattern-matching method that would scan for keywords like 'I', 'you', 'like', and so on. If one of these words was found, it would execute rules associated with it. If there was no match found the program would respond with a request for more information or with some noncommittal response.

It was also during the 1960s that Marvin Minsky and his students at MIT made significant contributions towards the progress of AI. One student, T. G. Evans, wrote a program that could perform visual analogies. The program was shown two figures that had some relationship to each other and was then asked to find another set of figures from a set that matched the same relationship. The input to the computer was not done by a visual sensor (like the one worked on by Rosenblatt), but instead the figures were described to the system.

In 1968 another student of Minsky's, Daniel Bobrow, introduced a linguistic problem solver called STUDENT. It was designed to solve problems that were presented to it in a word problem format. The key to the program was the assumption that every sentence was an equation. It would take certain words and turn them into mathematical operations. For example, it would convert "is" into "=" and "per" into "÷".

Even though STUDENT responded very much the same way that a real student would, there was a major difference in depth of understanding. While the program was capable of calculating the time two trains would collide given the starting points and speeds of both, it had no real understanding or even cared what a "train" or "time" was. Expressions like "per chance" and "this is it" could mean totally different things than what the program would assume. A human student would be able to discern the intended meaning from the context in which the terms were used.

In an attempt to answer the criticisms about understanding, another student at MIT, Terry Winograd, developed a significant program named SHRDLU. In setting up his program, he utilized what was referred to as a micro-world or blocks-world. This limited the scope of the world that the program had to try to understand. The program communicated in what appeared to be natural language.

The operation of SHRDLU consisted of a set of blocks of varying shapes (cubes, pyramids, etc), sizes, and colors. These blocks were all set on an imaginary table. Upon request, SHRDLU would rearrange the blocks to any requested configuration. The program was capable of knowing when a request was unclear or impossible. For instance, if it was requested to put a block on top of the pyramid it would request that the user specify more clearly what block and what pyramid. It could also recognize that the block would not sit on top of the pyramid.

Two other approaches that the program took that were new to programs were the ability to make assumptions and the ability to learn. If asked to pick up a larger block, it would assume a larger block than the one it was currently working on. If asked to build a figure that it did not know it would ask for an explanation of what it was and, thereafter, it would recognize the object. One major sophistication that SHRDLU added to the science of AI programming was its use of a series of expert modules or specialists. There was one segment of the program that specialized in segmenting sentences into meaningful word groups, a sentence specialist to determine the relationship between nouns and verbs, and a scenario specialist that understood how individual scenes related to one another. This sophistication added much enhancement to the method in which instructions were analyzed.

As sophisticated as SHRDLU was at that time, it did not escape criticism. Other scholars were quick to point out its deficiencies. One of the shortcomings was that SHRDLU only responded to requests; it could not initiate conversations. It also had no sense of conversational flow. It would jump from performing one type of task to a totally different one if so requested. While SHRDLU had an understanding of the tasks it was to perform and the physical world in which it operated, it still could not understand very abstract concepts.

1.5 BRANCHES OF ARTIFICIAL INTELLIGENCE

The various attempts to formally define the use of machines to simulate human intelligence led to the development of several branches of AI. Current sub-specialities of artificial intelligence include:

(1). *Natural language processing:* This deals with various areas of research such as data base inquiry systems, story understanders, automatic text indexing, grammar and style analysis of text, automatic text generation, machine translation, speech analysis, and speech synthesis.

(2). *Computer vision:* This deals with research efforts involving scene analysis, image understanding, and motion derivation.

(3). *Robotics:* This involves the control of effectors on robots to manipulate or grasp objects, locomotion of independent machines, and use of sensory input to guide actions.

(4). *Problem solving and planning:* This involves applications such as refinement of high-level goals into lower-level ones, determination of actions needed to achieve goals, revision of plans based on intermediate results, and focused search of important goals.

(5). *Learning:* This area of AI deals with research into various forms of learning including rote learning, learning through advice, learning by example, learning by task performance, and learning by following concepts.

(6). *Expert systems:* This deals with the processing of knowledge as opposed to the processing of data. It involves the development of computer software to solve complex decision problems.

1.6 NEURAL NETWORKS

Neural networks, sometimes called connectionist systems, represent networks of simple processing elements or nodes capable of processing information in response to external inputs. Neural networks were originally presented as being models of the human nervous system. Just after World War II, scientists found out that the physiology of the brain was similar to the electronic processing mode used by computers. In both cases, large amounts of data are manipulated. In the case of computers, the elementary unit of processing is the *bit*, which is in either an "on" or "off" state. In the case of the brain, *neurons* perform the basic data processing. Neurons are tiny cells that follow a binary principle of being either in a state of firing (on) or not firing (off). When a neuron is on, it fires a signal to other neurons across a network of synapses.

In the late 1940s, Donald Hebb, a researcher, hypothesized that biological memory results when two neurons are active simultaneously. The synaptic connection of synchronous neurons is reinforced and given preference over connections made by neurons that are not active simultaneously. The level of preference is measured as a weighted value. Pattern recognition, a major strength of human intelligence, is based on the weighted strengths of the reinforced connections between various pairs of simultaneously active neurons.

The idea presented by Hebb was to develop a computer model based on the way in which neurons form connections in the human brain. But the idea was considered to be preposterous at that time since the human brain contains 100 billion neurons and each neuron is connected to 10,000 others by a synapse. Even by today's computing capability, it is still difficult to duplicate the activities of neurons. In 1969, Marvin Minsky and Seymour Pappert wrote the book entitled *Perceptrons*, in which they criticized existing neural network research as being worthless. It has been claimed that the pessimistic views presented by the book discouraged further funding for neural network research for several years. Funding was, instead, diverted to further research of expert systems, which Minsky and Pappert favored. It is only recently that neural networks are beginning to make a strong comeback.

Because neural networks are modeled after the operations of the brain, they hold considerable promise as building blocks for achieving the ultimate aim of artificial intelligence. The present generation of neural networks use artificial neurons. Each neuron is connected to at least one other neuron in a synapse-like fashion. The networks are based on some form of learning model. Neural networks learn by evaluating changes in input. Learning can be either supervised or unsupervised. In supervised learning, each response is guided by given parameters. The computer is instructed to compare any inputs to ideal responses, and any discrepancy between the new inputs and ideal responses is recorded. The system then uses this data bank to guess how much the newly gathered data is similar to or different from the ideal responses. That is, how closely the pattern matches. Supervised learning networks are now commercially used for control systems and for handwriting and speech recognition.

In unsupervised learning, input is evaluated independently and stored as patterns. The system evaluates a range of patterns and identifies similarities and dissimilarities among them. However, the system cannot derive any meaning from the information without human assignment of values to the patterns. Comparisons are relative to other results, rather than to an ideal result. Unsupervised learning networks are used to discover patterns where a particular outcome is not known in advance, such as in physics research and the analysis of financial data. Several commercial neural network products are now available. An example is NeuroShell from Ward Systems Group. The software is expensive but it is relatively easy to use. It interfaces well with other software such as Lotus 1-2-3 and dBASE, as well as with C, Pascal, FORTRAN, and BASIC programming languages.

Despite the proven potential of neural networks, they drastically oversimplify the operations of the brain. The existing systems can undertake only elementary pattern-recognition tasks, and are weak at deductive reasoning, math calculations, and other computations that are easily handled by conventional computer processing. The difficulty in achieving the promise of neural networks lies in our limited understanding of how the human brain functions. Undoubtedly, to accurately model the brain, we must know more about it. But a complete knowledge of the brain is still many years away.

1.7 EMERGENCE OF EXPERT SYSTEMS

In the late 1960s to early 1970s, a special branch of AI began to emerge. The branch, known as expert systems, has grown dramatically in the past few years and it represents the most successful demonstration of the capabilities of AI. Expert systems are the first truly commercial application of work done in the AI field and as such have received considerable publicity. Due to the potential benefits, there is currently a major concentration in the research and development of expert systems compared to other efforts in AI.

Not driven by the desire to develop general problem solving techniques that had characterized AI before, expert systems address problems that are focused. When Edward Feigenbaum developed the first successful expert system, DENDRAL, he had a specific type of problem that he wanted to be able to solve. The problem involved determining which organic compound was being analyzed in a mass spectrograph. The program was intended to simulate the work that an expert chemist would do in analyzing the data. This led to the term expert system.

The period of time from 1970 to 1980 saw the introduction of numerous expert systems to handle several functions from diagnosing diseases to analyzing geological exploration information. Of course, expert systems have not escaped the critics. Given the nature of the system, critics argue that it does not fit the true structure of artificial intelligence. Because of the use of only specific knowledge and the ability to solve only specific problems, some critics are apprehensive about referring to an expert system as being intelligent. Proponents argue that if the system produces the desired results, it is of little concern whether it is intelligent or not.

A controversy of interest surfaced in 1972 with a book published by Hubert Dreyfus called *What Computers Can't Do: A Critique of Artificial Reason*. Views similar to those contained in the book were presented in 1976 by Joseph Weizenbaum. The issues that both authors raised touched on some of the basic questions that prevailed way back in the days of Descartes. One of Weizenbaum's reservations concerned what should ethically and morally be handed over to machines. He maintained that the path that AI was pursuing was headed in a dangerous direction. There are some aspects of human experience, such as love and morality, that could not adequately be imitated by machines.

While the debates were going on over how much AI could do, the work on getting AI to do more continued. In 1972, Roger Shrank introduced the notion of script; the set of familiar events that can be expected from an often encountered setting. This enables a program to quickly assimilate facts. In 1975, Marvin Minsky presented the idea of frames. Even though both concepts did not drastically advance the theory of AI, they did help expedite research in the field.

In 1979, Minsky suggested a method that could lead to a better simulation of intelligence. He presented the "society of minds" view, in which the execution of knowledge is performed by several programs working in conjunction simultaneously. This concept helped to encourage interesting developments such as present day parallel processing.

As time proceeded through the 1980s, AI gained significant exposure and interest. Artificial Intelligence, once a phrase restricted to the domain of esoteric research, has now become a practical tool for solving real problems. While AI is enjoying its most prosperous period, it is still plagued with disagreements and criticisms. The emergence of commercial expert systems on the market has created both enthusiasm and skepticism. There is no doubt that more research and successful applications developments will help prove the potential of expert systems. It should be recalled that new technologies sometimes fail to convince all initial observers. IBM, which later became a giant in the personal computer business, hesitated for several years before getting into the market because the company never thought that those *little boxes* called personal computers would ever have any significant impact on the society. How wrong they were!

The effort in AI is a worthwhile endeavor as long as it increases the understanding that we have of intelligence and as long as it enables us to do things that we previously could not do. Due to the discoveries made in AI research, computers are now capable of things that were once beyond imagination.

EMBEDDED EXPERT SYSTEMS   More expert systems are beginning to show up, not as stand-alone systems, but as software applications in large software systems. This trend is bound to continue as systems integration takes hold in many software applications. Many conventional commercial packages such as statistical analysis systems, data management systems, information management systems, project management systems, and data analysis systems now contain embedded heuristics that constitute expert systems components of the packages. Even some computer operating systems now contain embedded expert systems designed to provide real-time systems monitoring and troubleshooting. With the success of embedded expert systems, the long-awaited payoffs from the technology are now beginning to be realized.

Because the technology behind expert systems has changed little over the past decade, the issue is not whether the technology is useful, but how to implement it. This is why the integrated approach of this book is very useful. The book focuses not only on the technology of expert systems, but also on how to implement and manage the technology. Combining neural network technology with expert systems, for example, will become more prevalent. In combination, the neural network might be implemented as a tool for scanning and selecting data while the expert system would evaluate the data and present recommendations.

1.8 APPLICATIONS IN ENGINEERING AND MANUFACTURING

Over the past several years, expert systems have begun to prove their potential for solving important problems in engineering and manufacturing environments. Expert systems are helping major companies to diagnose processes in real time, schedule operations, troubleshoot equipment, maintain machinery, and design service and production facilities. With the implementation of expert systems in industrial environments, companies are finding that real-world problems are best solved by an integrated strategy involving the management of personnel, software, and hardware systems.

Solutions to most engineering and manufacturing problems involve not only heuristics, but also mathematical calculations, large data manipulations, statistical analysis, real-time information management, system optimization, and man-machine interfaces. These issues and other related topics are addressed in detail in this book. In addition to the basic concepts of expert systems, guidelines are presented on various items ranging from problem selection, data analysis, knowledge acquisition, and system development to verification, validation, integration, implementation, and maintenance.

The book takes an integrated and comprehensive view of the expert system development process. The peculiar aspects of engineering and manufacturing problems are addressed in various sections throughout the book. Chapter 11 presents a survey of existing applications of expert systems in engineering and manufacturing operations.

1.9 EXERCISES

1.1 Discuss the ways in which computers have made life easier.

1.2 Discuss the ways in which computers have made life more difficult.

1.3 Do you feel any reservation about the pursuit of artificial intelligence?

1.4 Discuss your own perspectives of how expert systems might revolutionize the way people solve decision problems.

1.5 Develop a taxonomy of the pioneering works in artificial intelligence and expert systems. Indicate who did what and when.

1.6 Compare and contrast the information processing capabilities of human beings to that of computers with respect to speed, accuracy, reliability, adaptability, intelligent reasoning, and memory.

1.7 Discuss the potential threat to job security posed by artificial intelligence applications.

1.8 Discuss the potential of artificial intelligence in creating new jobs.

1.9 List the ten most important engineering problems suitable for expert systems applications.

1.10 List the ten most important manufacturing problems suitable for expert systems applications.

1.11 Propose a definition of artificial intelligence with reference to its applications to engineering problems.

1.12 Develop a critical review of Turing's test. Can machines really become intelligent?

1.13 Propose a set of criteria that must be met for machine or software to be considered intelligent.

1.14 Discuss the differences between knowledge and ignorance with respect to artificial intelligence applications.

1.15 Does having "knowledge" imply having "intelligence"? Explain.

1.16 Develop definitions that indicate the differences and/or similarities between knowledge, data, information, and belief.

1.17 Draw a graphical representation that shows the interrelationships between the various branches of AI.

1.18 Epistemology is sometimes said to be a branch of AI. Look up the meaning of epistemology in a good encyclopedia. Does the meaning indicate any relationship to artificial intelligence concepts?

1.19 Artificial intelligence is now being applied to unique problems such as music composition. What similarities exist between music and engineering in terms of AI applications?

1.20 Suggest how neural networks and expert systems may be interfaced to enhance the effectiveness of both.

2

Basic Concepts
of Expert Systems

This chapter introduces the basic concepts of expert systems. The hierarchical process of developing expert systems is presented. The essential characteristics of expert systems are presented. More specific details of the concepts introduced in this chapter are covered in subsequent chapters.

2.1 EXPERT SYSTEMS PROCESS

This book is organized in the structure of a strategic process for developing successful expert systems. Figure 2.1 presents the hierarchy of topics as they are presented here and in the subsequent chapters. The strategic process is recommended for anyone venturing into the technology of expert systems from the standpoint of training, research, or applications. This chapter covers the basic concepts of expert systems technology. A basic understanding of these concepts is essential to getting the most out of expert systems. More specific details of the concepts presented in this chapter are discussed in appropriate sections of the subsequent chapters. Chapter 3 covers the problem selection process. To be effective, the right problems must be selected for expert systems implementation. The principle of "garbage in, garbage out" is also applicable here. Wrong problems lead to incorrect implementation of expert systems.

Chapter 4 covers the knowledge acquisition process. Knowledge acquisition is a critical aspect of the expert systems effort. If garbage of a knowledge is collected, the best that can be expected is garbage of a system. Chapter 5 presents the

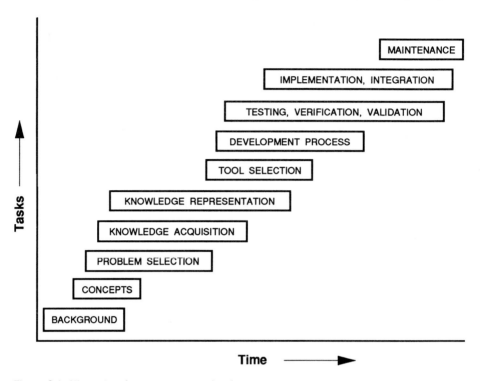

Figure 2.1. Hierarchy of expert systems development process

various techniques for representing knowledge. Once knowledge is acquired, it must be represented in the proper format to preserve its integrity and assure effective retrieval and usage. Chapter 6 presents some techniques for handling uncertainty in expert systems. Chapter 7 presents guidelines for selecting expert systems development tools. The development tool must be selected on the basis of the problem to be addressed, the nature of the knowledge to solve the problem, and the technique needed to represent that type of knowledge. If the tool is selected before the problem, the knowledge, and the representation technique are fully understood, then the problem of forcing the application to fit the tool may develop. This, of course, is a wrong approach to problem solving. The proper approach is to select a tool that fits the application rather than the other way around.

Chapter 8 covers the actual development process going from the prototype stage all the way to a final delivery system. Chapter 9 covers the testing, verification, and validation requirements of expert systems. Chapter 10 presents implementation and maintenance strategies. Chapter 11 presents a survey of engineering and manufacturing applications. Chapter 12 presents case samples of expert system development. Appendices provide a discussion of the VP-Expert development tool, a guide to expert systems tools, names and addresses of vendors, a glossary of expert systems and computer terms, and conversion factors.

2.2 EXPERT SYSTEMS CHARACTERISTICS

By definition, an expert system is a computer program that simulates the thought process of a human expert to solve complex decision problems in a specific domain. This chapter addresses the characteristics of expert systems that make them different from conventional programming and traditional decision support tools. The growth of expert systems is expected to continue for several years. With the continuing growth, many new and exciting applications will emerge. An expert system operates as an interactive system that responds to questions, asks for clarification, makes recommendation and generally aids the decision making process. Expert systems provide "expert" advice and guidance in a wide variety of activities, from computer diagnosis to delicate medical surgery.

Various definitions of expert systems have been offered by several authors. A general definition which is representative of the intended functions of expert systems is presented below:

An *expert system* is an interactive computer-based decision tool that uses both facts and heuristics to solve difficult decision problems based on knowledge acquired from an expert.

An expert system may be viewed as a computer simulation of a human expert. Expert systems are an emerging technology with many areas for potential applications. Past applications range from MYCIN, used in the medical field to diagnose infectious blood diseases, to XCON, used to configure computer systems. These expert systems have proven to be quite successful. Most applications of expert systems will fall into one of the following categories:

- Interpreting and identifying
- Predicting
- Diagnosing
- Designing
- Planning
- Monitoring
- Debugging and testing
- Instructing and training
- Controlling

Applications that are computational or deterministic in nature are not good candidates for expert systems. Traditional decision support systems such as spreadsheets are very mechanistic in the way they solve problems. They operate under mathematical and Boolean operators in their execution and arrive at one and only one static solution for a given set of data. Calculation-intensive applications with very exacting requirements are better handled by traditional decision support tools or conventional programming. The best application candidates for expert systems are those dealing with expert heuristics for solving problems. Conventional computer programs are based on factual knowledge; an indisputable strength of computers. Humans, by contrast, solve problems on the basis of a mixture of factual and heuristic knowledge. Heuristic knowledge, composed of intuition, judgment, and logical inferences, is an indisputable strength of humans. Successful expert systems will be those that combine facts and heuristics and, thus, merge human knowledge with computer power in solving problems. To be effective, an expert system must focus on a particular problem domain as discussed below.

DOMAIN SPECIFICITY   Expert systems are typically very domain specific. For example, a diagnostic expert system for troubleshooting computers must perform all the necessary data manipulation as a human expert would. The developer of such a system must limit his or her scope of the system to just what is needed to solve the target problem. Special tools or programming languages are often needed to accomplish the specific objectives of the system.

SPECIAL PROGRAMMING LANGUAGES   Expert systems are typically written in special programming languages. The use of languages like LISP and PROLOG in the development of an expert system "simplifies" the coding process. The major advantage of these languages, as compared to conventional programming languages, is the simplicity of the addition, elimination, or substitution of new rules and memory management capabilities. Presented below are some of the distinguishing characteristics of programming languages needed for expert systems work:

- Efficient mix of integer and real variables.
- Good memory management procedures.
- Extensive data manipulation routines.
- Incremental compilation.
- Tagged memory architecture.
- Optimization of the systems environment.
- Efficient search procedures.

2.3 EXPERT SYSTEMS STRUCTURE

Complex decisions involve intricate combinations of factual and heuristic knowledge. In order for the computer to be able to retrieve and effectively use heuristic knowledge, the knowledge must be organized in an easily-accessible format that distinguishes between data, knowledge, and control structures. For this reason, expert systems are organized in three distinct levels:

(1). *Knowledge base:* This consists of problem solving rules, procedures, and intrinsic data relevant to the problem domain.

(2). *Working memory:* This refers to task specific data for the problem under consideration.

(3). *Inference engine:* This is a generic control mechanism that applies the axiomatic knowledge in the knowledge base to the task-specific data to arrive at some solution or conclusion.

These three distinct levels are unique in that the three pieces may very well come from different sources. The inference engine, such as VP-Expert, may come from a commercial vendor. The knowledge base may be a specific diagnostic knowledge base compiled by a consulting firm, and the problem data may be supplied by the end user. A knowledge base is the nucleus of the expert system structure. A knowledge base is not a data base. The traditional data base environment deals with data that have a static relationship between the elements in the problem domain. A knowledge base is created by knowledge engineers, who translate the knowledge of real human experts into rules and strategies. These rules and strategies can change depending on the prevailing problem scenario. The knowledge base provides the expert system with the capability to recommend directions for user inquiry. The system also instigates further investigation into areas that may be important to a certain line of reasoning, but not apparent to the user.

The modularity of an expert system is an important distinguishing characteristic compared to a conventional computer program. Modularity is effected in an expert system by the use of three distinct components as shown in Figure 2.2.

The knowledge base constitutes the problem-solving rules, facts, or intuition that a human expert might use in solving problems in a given problem domain. The knowledge base is usually stored in terms of *If-Then rules*. The working memory represents relevant data for the current problem being solved. The inference engine is the control mechanism that organizes the problem data and searches through the knowledge base for applicable rules. With the increasing popularity of expert systems, many commercial inference engines are coming into the market. A survey of selected commercial inference engines is presented in the Appendix at the end of this book. The development of a functional expert system usually centers around the organization of the knowledge base. A functional integration of expert systems components is shown in Figure 2.3.

A good expert system is expected to grow as it "learns" from user feedback. Feedback is incorporated into the knowledge base as appropriate to make the expert system "smarter." The dynamism of the application environment for expert systems is based on the individual dynamism of the components. This can be classified as follows:

Most Dynamic: Working Memory

The contents of the working memory, sometimes called the data structure, change with each problem situation. Consequently, it is the most dynamic component of an expert system, assuming, of course, that it is kept current.

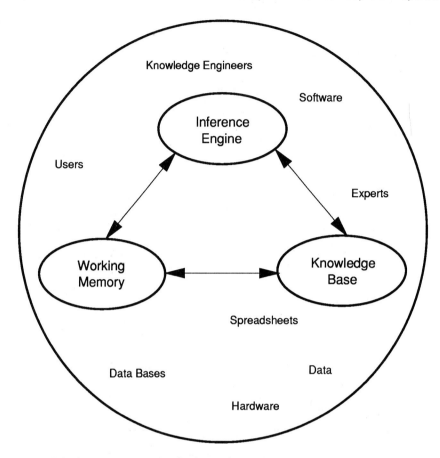

Figure 2.2. Expert systems organization and operating environment

Moderately Dynamic: Knowledge Base

The knowledge base need not change unless there is a new piece of information that indicates a change in the problem solution procedure. Changes in the knowledge base should be carefully evaluated before being implemented. In effect, changes should not be based on just one consultation experience. For example, a rule that is found to be irrelevant under one problem situation may turn out to be crucial in solving other problems.

Least Dynamic: Inference Engine

Because of the strict control and coding structure of an inference engine, changes are made only if absolutely necessary to correct a bug or to enhance the inferential process. Commercial inference engines, in particular, change only at the discretion of the developer. Since frequent updates can be disrupting and costly to clients, most commercial software developers try to minimize the frequency of updates.

2.3.1   The Need for Expert Systems

Expert systems are necessitated by the limitations associated with conventional human decision-making processes. These limitations include:

(1). Human expertise is very scarce.

(2). Humans get tired from physical or mental workload.

(3). Humans forget crucial details of a problem.

(4). Humans are inconsistent in their day-to-day decisions.

(5). Humans have limited working memory.

(6). Humans are unable to quickly comprehend large amounts of data.

(7). Humans are unable to retain large amounts of data in memory.

(8). Humans are slow in recalling information stored in memory.

(9). Humans are subject to deliberate or inadvertent bias in their actions.

(10). Humans can deliberately avoid decision responsibilities.

(11). Humans *lie*, *hide*, and *die*.

Figure 2.3. Integration of expert systems components

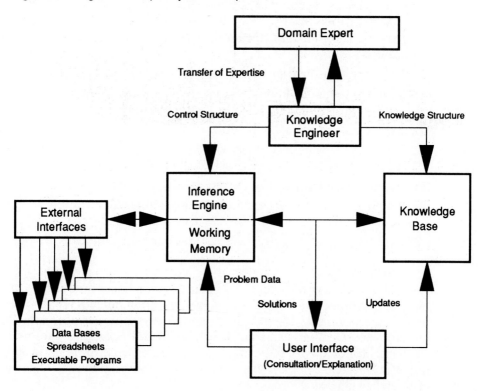

Coupled with the above human limitations are the weaknesses inherent in conventional programming and traditional decision support tools. Despite the mechanistic power of computers, they have certain limitations that impair their effectiveness in implementing human-like decision processes. Some of the limitations of conventional decision support tools are:

(1). Conventional programs are algorithmic in nature and depend only on raw machine power.

(2). Conventional programs depend on facts that may be difficult to obtain.

(3). Conventional programs do not make use of the effective heuristic approaches used by human experts.

(4). Conventional programs are not easily adaptable to changing problem environments.

(5). Conventional programs seek explicit and factual solutions that may not be possible.

2.3.2 Benefits of Expert Systems

Expert systems offer an environment where the good capabilities of humans and the power of computers can be incorporated to overcome many of the limitations discussed in the previous section. Presented below are some of the most obvious benefits that are offered by expert systems:

(1). Expert systems increase the probability, frequency, and consistency of making good decisions.

(2). Expert systems help distribute human expertise.

(3). Expert systems facilitate real-time, low-cost, expert-level decisions by the nonexpert.

(4). Expert systems enhance the utilization of most of the available data.

(5). Expert systems permit objectivity by weighing evidence without bias and without regard for the user's personal and emotional reactions.

(6). Expert systems permit dynamism through modularity of structure.

(7). Expert systems free up the mind and time of the human expert to enable him or her to concentrate on more creative activities.

(8). Expert systems encourage investigations into the subtle areas of a problem.

EXPERT SYSTEMS ARE FOR EVERYONE   No matter which area of business one is engaged in, expert systems could fulfill the need for higher productivity and reliability of decisions. Everyone can find an application potential in the field of expert systems. Contrary to the belief that expert systems may pose a threat to job security, expert systems can actually help to create opportunities for new job areas. Presented below are some areas which hold promise for new job opportunities. A prospective embracer of expert systems can engage himself in one or more of the following areas:

- Basic research
- Applied research
- Knowledge engineering
- Inference engine development
- Consulting (development and implementation)
- Training
- Sales and marketing
- Passive or active end user

An active user is one who directly uses expert systems consultations to obtain recommendations. A passive user is one who trusts the results obtained from expert systems and supports the implementation of those results.

2.3.3   Transition from Data Processing to Knowledge Processing

What data has been to the previous generations of computing, knowledge is to the present generation of computing. Expert systems represent a revolutionary transition from the traditional data processing to knowledge processing. Figure 2.4 illustrates the relationships between the procedures for data processing and knowledge processing to make decisions. In traditional data processing, the decision maker obtains the information generated and performs an explicit analysis of the information before making his or her decision. In an expert system, knowledge is processed by using available data as the processing fuel. Conclusions are reached and recommendations are derived implicitly. The expert system offers the recommendation to the decision maker, who makes the final decision and implements it as appropriate. Conventional data can now be manipulated to work with durable knowledge, which can be processed to generate timely information, which is then used to enhance human decisions.

2.4 HEURISTIC REASONING

Human experts use a type of problem-solving technique called heuristic reasoning. This reasoning type, commonly called "rules of thumb" or "expert heuristics," allows the expert to quickly and efficiently arrive at a good solution. Expert systems base their reasoning process on symbolic manipulation and heuristic inference procedures that closely match the human thinking process. Conventional programs can only recognize numeric or alphabetic strings and manipulate them only in a pre-programmed manner.

SEARCH CONTROL METHODS   All expert systems are search intensive. Many techniques have been employed to make these intensive searches more efficient. Branch and bound, pruning, depth first search, and breadth first search are some of the search techniques that have been explored. Because of the intensity of the search process, it is important that good search control strategies be used in expert systems inference process.

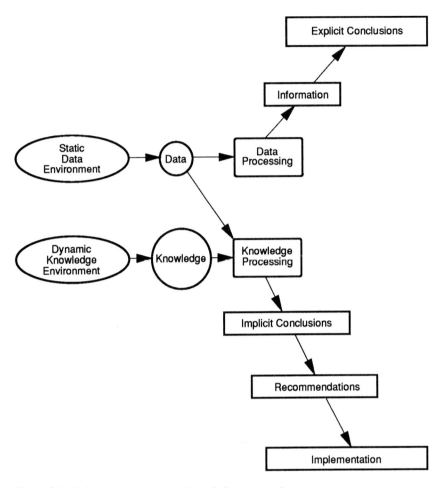

Figure 2.4. Data processing versus knowledge processing

FORWARD CHAINING   This method involves checking the condition part of a rule to determine whether it is true or false. If the condition is true, then the action part of the rule is also true. This procedure continues until a solution is found or a dead end is reached. Forward chaining is commonly referred to as data-driven reasoning. Further discussions of forward chaining are presented in subsequent chapters.

BACKWARD CHAINING   Backward chaining is used to backtrack from a goal to the paths that lead to the goal. It is the reverse of forward chaining. Backward chaining is very good when all outcomes are known and the number of possible outcomes are not large. In this case, a goal is specified and the expert system tries to determine what conditions are needed to arrive at the specified goal. Backward chaining is also called goal-driven reasoning. More details are provided on the backward chaining process in Chapter 5.

2.5 USER INTERFACE

The initial development of an expert system is performed by the expert and the knowledge engineer. Unlike most conventional programs in which only programmers can make program design decisions, the design of large expert systems is implemented through a team effort. A consideration of the needs of the end user is very important in designing the contents and user interface of expert systems.

NATURAL LANGUAGE   The programming languages used for expert systems tend to operate in a manner similar to ordinary conversation. We usually state the premise of a problem in the form of a question with actions being stated much as we would verbally answer the question—that is, in a "natural language" format. If during or after a consultation, an expert system determines that a piece of its data or knowledge base is incorrect, or is no longer applicable because the problem environment has changed, it should be able to update the knowledge base accordingly. This capability would allow the expert system to converse in a natural language format with either the developers or users.

Expert systems not only arrive at solutions or recommendations, but can give the user a level of confidence about the solution. In this manner, an expert system can handle both quantitative and qualitative factors when analyzing problems. This aspect is very important when we consider how inexact most input data is for day-to-day decision-making. For example, the problems addressed by an expert system can have more than one solution or, in some cases, no definite solution at all. Yet, the expert system can provide useful recommendations to the user just as a human consultant might do.

EXPLANATIONS FACILITY IN EXPERT SYSTEMS   One of the key characteristics of an expert system is the explanation facility. With this capability, an expert system can explain how it arrives at its conclusions. The user can ask questions dealing with the what, how, and why aspects of a problem. The expert system will then provide the user with a trace of the consultation process; pointing out the key reasoning paths followed during the consultation. Sometimes, an expert system is required to solve other problems, possibly not directly related to the specific problem at hand, but whose solution will have an impact on the total problem-solving process. The explanation facility helps the expert system to clarify and justify why such a digression might be needed.

DATA UNCERTAINTIES   Expert systems are capable of working with inexact data. An expert system allows the user to assign probabilities, certainty factors, or confidence levels to any or all input data. This feature closely represents how most problems are handled in the real world. An expert system can take all relevant factors into account and make a recommendation based on the "best" possible solution rather than the only exact solution.

2.5.1 Application Roadmap

The symbolic processing capabilities of AI technology lead to many potential applications in engineering and manufacturing. With the increasing sophistication of AI techniques, analysts are now able to use innovative methods to provide viable solutions to complex problems in everyday applications. Figure 2.5 presents a structural representation of the application paths for artificial intelligence and expert systems.

Figure 2.5. Application roadmap for expert systems

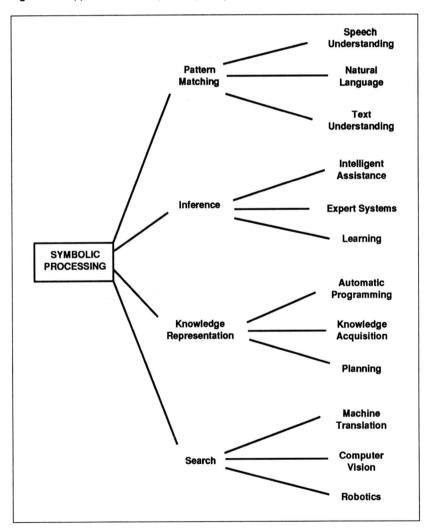

2.5.2 Symbolic Processing

Contrary to the practice in conventional programming, expert systems can manipulate objects symbolically to arrive at reasonable conclusions to a problem scenario. The object drawings in this section are used to illustrate the versatility of symbolic processing by using the manipulation of objects to convey information. Let us assume that we are given the collection of five common objects as shown in Figure 2.6. The objects are Head, Hammer, Bucket, Foot, and Bill (as in doctor's bill). We can logically arrange a subset of the set of given objects to convey specific inferences. In Figure 2.7, four of the five objects are arranged in the order Hammer, Head, Foot, and Bucket. This unique arrangement may be represented by the equation presented below:

$$\text{Hammer} \sim \text{Head} = \text{Foot} \sim \text{Bucket}$$

It is desired to infer a reasonable statement of the information being conveyed by the symbolic arrangement of objects in Figure 2.7. Figure 2.8 presents

Figure 2.6. Collection of common objects

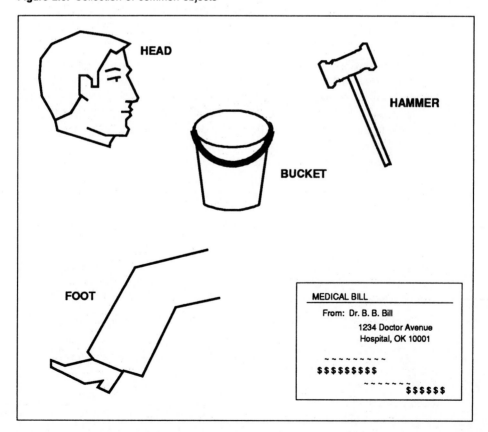

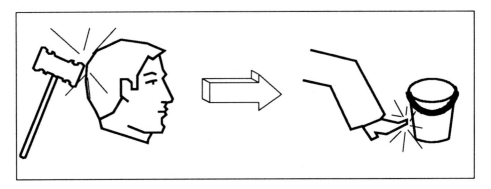

Figure 2.7. Arrangement of common objects

an alternate arrangement of another subset (Hammer, Foot, Foot, and Bill) of the given objects. This alternate arrangement may be represented by the equation shown below:

$$\text{Hammer} \sim \text{Foot} = \text{Foot} \sim \text{Bill}$$

It is desired to infer a reasonable statement from Figure 2.8. It should be noted that ordinary mathematical reasoning concerning the equation, Hammer~Foot = Foot~Bill, might lead to Hammer = Bill. However, in artificial intelligence symbolic reasoning, the context of the arrangement of the objects will determine the proper implication. The reader should attempt to draw the appropriate inferences from the object arrangements before referring to the solutions presented at the end of this chapter.

Figure 2.8. Alternate arrangement of objects

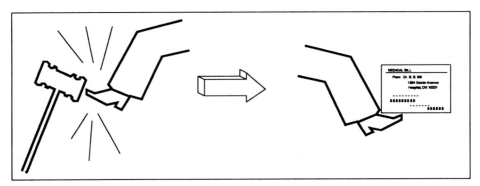

2.6 FUTURE DIRECTIONS FOR EXPERT SYSTEMS

The intensity of the ongoing efforts in the area of expert systems has created unique opportunities in many spheres of human endeavor. Listed below are some emerging areas:

(1). Large-scale research into natural language systems.

(2). Further research in knowledge base organization.

(3). Development of more efficient search techniques.

(4). Insatiable demand for expert systems–related consulting services.

(5). Commercial knowledge bases.

(6). More commercial inference engines and development tools.

(7). Drive for advanced hardware and software capabilities.

(8). Increased need for expert systems training facilities.

(9). Continuing growth in the market for expert systems products and services.

The current generation of expert systems represents only the first step in the technology. Not only are there several areas that are yet to be explored, there are also constant improvements to the systems currently in use. With each change in the development of expert systems, the information required from the human expert changes as well. The emerging generation of expert systems are combining shallow or surface knowledge with deep knowledge, with the former being used for routine problem solving for the purpose of improving efficiency while the latter is used for very difficult problems.

2.7 ACADEMIA-INDUSTRY COOPERATION
FOR EXPERT SYSTEMS

The interest in artificial intelligence and expert systems from the standpoints of both research and applications continues to grow widely. A couple of years ago, only a handful of schools offered formal courses in expert systems. But now, several schools have instituted formal expert systems training programs in academic disciplines ranging from industrial engineering, computer science, chemistry, and medicine to psychology. The potential for applying expert systems to a large variety of problems has made the technology very appealing to both practitioners and educators in all areas of applications.

UNIQUE CAPABILITY OF ACADEMIC INSTITUTIONS   Academic institutions, because of their educational setup, are in a better position to generate, learn, and transfer expert systems knowledge than industry establishments. In fact, most of the significant early developments in expert systems emanated from academic institutions. The insatiable quest for knowledge in academia can fuel the search for innovative solutions to specific industry problems.

UNIQUE CAPABILITY OF INDUSTRY   Industrial establishments are well versed in practical implementation of technology. The commercialization of technology is one impetus that drives further efforts to develop new technology. Technologies that are developed within the academic community mainly for research purposes often languish in laboratories because of the lack of funds or orientation for commercial development. The potentials of these technologies go untapped either because:

(1). The developer does not know which segment of industry may need the technology.
(2). Industry is not aware that the technology to solve their problems is available in some laboratory in some academic institution.
(3). There is no coordinated mechanism for technological interface between industry and academia.

A coordinated marriage between the two bodies (industry and academia) can provide an avenue that facilitates quicker implementation of expert systems technology to solve engineering and manufacturing problems. This will facilitate a smooth relationship between people and technology. Industry has the financial capability, interest, and aggressiveness to bring technologies out of academic laboratories. Also, a cooperative industry is a fertile ground for prototyping new academic ideas. Figure 2.9 shows a conceptual model of the needed cooperative efforts between industry and academia.

INDUSTRY NEED   Many professionals in industry still lack the basic knowledge to successfully take advantage of the capability of expert systems. This is mainly because not many of these professionals had the opportunity to enroll in a formal course in expert systems while they were in school. Many companies are now aggressively urging their employees to attend workshops, conferences, seminars, and formal classes in order to acquire the necessary knowledge. Some companies even organize in-house regular training programs. Despite these efforts, industry professionals still lag behind for three main reasons:

(1). Training programs take them away from their regular job functions. Consequently, not enough time is allocated for comprehensive training.
(2). Since the payoff on expert systems training may not be immediately apparent, managers tend to want the professional to concentrate his/her effort on a prevailing dollar-valued problem and defer the release time for training.
(3). Post-training assignments often do not match the skills acquired from a training. As a result the professional is unable to implement the new technology skill and finds it difficult to keep abreast of the fast-paced developments in the technology. Re-training is, thus, usually needed when an opportunity for an expert system project finally develops.

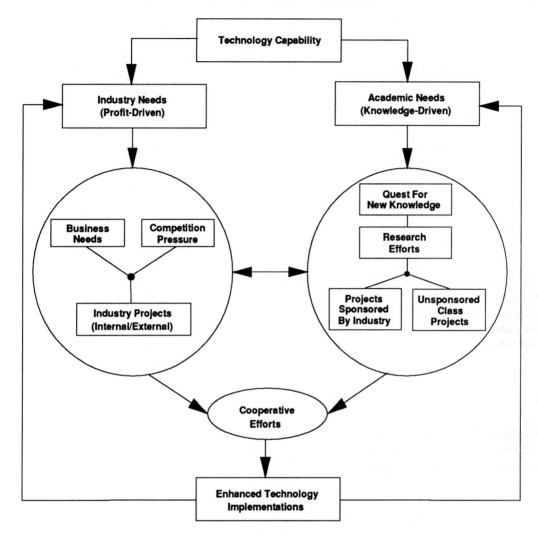

Figure 2.9. Model for academia-industry cooperation

ACADEMIC NEED   Academic institutions interested in expert systems are presently being hampered by the lack of adequate research and training facilities. Industry can help in this regard by providing direct support for selected institutions. The institutions also need real problems to work on as projects or case studies. Industry can provide these under a cooperative arrangement. The development of successful expert systems requires domain experts who are very conversant with the problem environment. Industry professionals can easily fill the role of domain experts for systems developed within the academic environment.

INDUSTRY APPROACH   Because of the limited training opportunity, the industry professional is often caught in a perplexing tangle of requirements that he/she is unable to satisfy. One approach that some companies take in solving this dilemma is to hire fresh graduates who already have the appropriate expert systems training. These younger employees work with experienced professionals who are familiar with companies' operations and problems. This type of arrangement works very well for expert systems projects where the experienced professional serves as the domain expert and the new graduate serves as the knowledge engineer. The problem is that there is still an acute shortage of expert systems graduates to satisfy industry demand.

ACADEMIC APPROACH   Expert systems courses, which are taught in many academic institutions, offer great training opportunities for working professionals who are willing to take courses on a part-time basis. Expert systems courses draw students from many other areas, including engineering, business, mathematics, psychology, meteorology, and music. Many students who graduate with at least one expert systems course listed on their transcripts are aggressively sought by prospective employers. The problem is that these trained students graduate soon after becoming proficient in the new technology. The high turnover rate makes it difficult for schools to maintain a stable team of experienced students to carry on lengthy expert systems projects.

INDUSTRY/ACADEMIC INTERACTION   Expert systems courses offered at convenient times during the day facilitate enrollment of industry professionals. The professionals don't necessarily have to miss much time from work in order to participate in course activities. A key requirement of such courses should be a term project that addresses a real-life problem. The industry professionals should be encouraged to select problems that address a prevailing problem within their company. This helps the professionals to have a focused and rewarding effort for the expert systems endeavor. Class projects developed in the academic environment can be successfully implemented in actual work environments to provide tangible benefits. Those benefits include increased productivity, faster response time to company demands, and annual dollar savings.

CONTINUING INDUSTRY COOPERATION   Industry-based class projects should not end with the termination of the course. The author always urges the industry professionals to continue to dedicate time to the maintenance of the expert system and to explore other potential applications within the company. This requirement facilitates a continuing interaction between academia and industry even after the course is over. The professionals can consult with the faculty in academia on a continuing basis about new expert systems–related problems in industry. With this mutually cooperative interaction, new developments in industry are brought to the attention of academia while new academic research developments are discussed with industry professionals. In addition, on-campus students who have no previous industry exposure are given the opportunity to have a "mentor in the real world" through plant tours and informal consultations.

KNOWLEDGE CLEARINGHOUSE   Academic institutions can serve as convenient locations for knowledge clearinghouses. Such clearinghouses can be implemented under the auspices of expert systems laboratories. Specific expert systems problems in industry can be brought to the laboratories for joint solution not necessarily under a regular class arrangement. This will further enhance the contacts and interactions between professionals in industry and students on campus. The laboratories can serve as repositories for various commercial expert systems tools. These tools will be available to industry professionals to test, learn, and use in the laboratories before deciding to purchase them for in-company implementations. In return, industry could help support the laboratory through the donation of equipment, funds, and personnel time. The services provided by a clearinghouse could include the following:

(1). Providing consulting services on expert systems technology to business and industry.

(2). Conducting in-plant custom short courses with hands-on projects for business and industry.

(3). Serving as a technology library for expert systems information.

(4). Providing software, hardware, and technology information services for prospective expert systems developers.

(5). Facilitating technology transfer by helping business and industry to move expert systems technology from the laboratory to the marketplace. The transfer can be either of direct expert systems products or of services.

(6). Providing technology management guidelines that will enable entrepreneurs to successfully incorporate expert systems products into their existing products and services.

(7). Expanding the training opportunities for students and working professionals.

GOVERNMENT SUPPORT   The government can support the cooperative interactions between industry and university by providing broad-based funding mechanisms. For example, the National Science Foundation (NSF) recently started to provide funds for Industry/University Cooperative Research Centers. Centers for Artificial Intelligence and Expert Systems hold good potentials for funding over the next several years.

2.8 ANSWERS TO SYMBOLIC PROCESSING EXERCISE

Figure 2.7:   If hammer smashes head, then victim kicks the bucket (i.e. dies). In this case the action part of the statement relates to an action (a fatal one) by the victim of the assault.

Figure 2.8:   If hammer smashes foot, then assailant foots the bill.
In this case the action part of the statement relates to a compensatory action (restitution) by the assailant.

Using a finite set of symbolic objects, we can generate different pieces of information with different permutations of the objects. A particularly interesting aspect of symbolic processing is noted in Figure 2.8. The object "Foot" conveys one meaning when concatenated with one given object (hammer) and another totally different meaning when concatenated with another object (Bill). In fact, the identification of the object "Bill" is itself symbolically conveyed by the contents of the medical bill in Figure 2.6. With the illustrated capability of symbolic processing, very powerful AI-based tools can be developed for practical applications. However, more research and development efforts will be needed before many of those practical applications can be realized.

2.9 EXERCISES

2.1   Discuss the basic differences between a knowledge base and a data base.

2.2   Why is the user interface an important consideration in expert systems?

2.3   Discuss the essential functions in each of the components of the expert systems process presented in Figure 2.1.

2.4   Write a definition of expert systems based on your own understanding of the technology.

2.5   Why is it important to restrict an expert system implementation to a narrow problem domain?

2.6   Discuss the relationships between data processing and knowledge processing.

2.7   Using the objects presented in Figure 2.6, attempt to develop a permutation of some or all of the objects to convey a symbolic message. Write a literal interpretation of the object permutation. Write a symbolic interpretation of the object permutation.

2.8   Outline the potential sources of obstacles that may impede the cooperative interaction between academia and industry to further the implementation of expert systems technology.

2.9   Review the hierarchy of expert systems development process presented in this chapter. Does any other element need to be included? Does the order of the elements need to be reorganized?

2.10 Why is domain specificity an important issue in expert systems?

2.11 Engineering problem solving often involves developing a general solution model with liberal tolerance specifications. Does this approach enhance or impede expert systems applications to engineering problems?

2.12 Consider the functional integration of the components of expert systems as presented in Figure 2.3. Suggest how the interface of the components may be improved.

2.13 The inference engine is said to be the least dynamic component of expert systems. List the circumstances that may require that an inference engine be updated more frequently.

2.14 Emotional situations can affect how an expert solves a particular problem. Human emotions can actually improve problem solution strategies (*helpful bias*). Is it possible and does it make sense to try and incorporate emotion into artificial intelligence problem solving approaches? Discuss the pros and cons.

2.15 Eight benefits of expert systems were presented in this chapter. Suggest two additional benefits that were not mentioned in the chapter.

2.16 Discuss the computer technology revolution that made the transition from data processing to knowledge processing possible.

2.17 What future developments can be expected for artificial intelligence in general and expert systems in particular?

2.18 Academia is a major avenue for developing theories of artificial intelligence while industry is a major avenue for practical applications. Suggest a strategy for ensuring that the two groups work together to achieve the benefits of expert systems.

2.19 Someone walks up to you and requests: "Tell me about expert systems." What would your response be?

2.20 Discuss how expert systems differ from conventional computer programs with reference to engineering problem solving.

3

Problem Analysis and Selection

This chapter addresses the problem of selecting an appropriate problem for expert systems application. This is the first step in the expert systems development process and must be carefully investigated.

3.1 PROBLEM IDENTIFICATION

The selection of an appropriate problem is extremely important and is a major factor for determining the success of expert systems. A good problem for expert systems is one that has the following characteristics:

(1). The problem affects many people.
(2). There is enough concern about the problem.
(3). The problem is in a domain where experts are in short supply.
(4). Solving the problem has the potential for significant time and cost savings.
(5). There is a reliable and accessible source of knowledge to be acquired.

Problem identification refers to the recognition of a situation that constitutes a problem to the organization. Problem identification requires the recognition of a window of opportunity to utilize expert systems. Both the problem domain and the specific problem must be identified. A problem domain refers to the general functional area in which the problem is located. For example, the general problem of engineering design constitutes a problem domain that design engineers will be interested in. Within engineering design, the specific problem may be that of designing a flexible manufacturing system. The identification of a problem may originate from any of several factors. Some of the factors are:

(1). Internal needs and pressures.
(2). External motivation such as market competition.
(3). Management requirement.
(4). Need for productivity improvement.
(5). Desire to stay abreast of the technology.
(6). Technological curiosity.
(7). Compliance with prevailing rules and regulations.
(8). Deficiencies in the present process.

Once the general problem area has been identified, the next step is deciding what to do about the problem. Several options may be available in addressing the problem. These include:

(1). Ignoring the problem.
(2). Denying that the problem exists.
(3). Devising an alternative that circumvents the problem.
(4). Deferring a solution to the problem.
(5). Confronting the problem and finding a solution to it.

If the problem is to be confronted and solved, then a thorough analysis of the problem must be performed. The results of the analysis will indicate the specific approach that may be suitable in tackling the problem.

3.2 PROBLEM ANALYSIS

Problem analysis involves the evaluation of the characteristics associated with a given problem. The input-output process of the problem should be examined. Figure 3.1 presents a representation of the interface between inputs and outputs in a problem scenario. An analysis of the problem will reveal whether or not a computer solution is necessary. One should not embark upon a computer approach without first understanding the fundamental issues involved in the prob-

Figure 3.1. Input/output interface in problem scenario

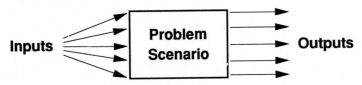

lem. Expert systems should be seen as a tool to solving a problem rather than the focus of the problem. The specific issues to be analyzed are presented below. For example, in engineering applications, there may be a tendency to place too much emphasis on computer applications rather than engineering fundamentals. Expert systems should be used to implement engineering fundamentals after the fundamentals are fully understood in the light of the prevailing problem.

SCOPE OF THE PROBLEM   The problem to be considered for expert systems application should be well-bounded and focused. This is to prevent combinatorial explosion in the solution structure.

SYMBOLIC NATURE OF THE PROBLEM   Problems that are numerically involved and algorithmic in nature may not be suitable for expert systems. The potential for symbolic representation and processing in the given problem should be evaluated. Symbolic processing refers to the use of symbols or strings of characters and data structures to convey problem characteristics. Conventional high-level programming languages such as FORTRAN and BASIC are good for numeric processing, but poor for symbolic processing. Symbolic processing requires special purpose languages such as LISP (List Processing) and PROLOG (Programming in Logic). If a problem does not have the characteristics suitable for symbolic representation, it may not be a suitable candidate for expert systems application.

SOLUTION TIME   The length of time needed to generate a solution to the problem is a major factor in determining the suitability for expert systems application. If a problem requires several weeks to solve, then it may not be suitable for an expert system. In such a large problem, an expert system may help provide intermediate solutions that are needed to arrive at the overall solution. Thus, an expert system can serve as an aid in multistage solution process. On the other hand, if a problem requires very little time to solve, for example a few seconds, it may be too trivial to justify the expense of developing an expert system.

FREQUENCY OF PROBLEM OCCURRENCE   The frequency with which a problem occurs can also determine the approach to addressing the problem. A problem that occurs frequently enough to be a nuisance to regular operations is a good candidate for expert systems. A problem that occurs only once in a long while may not be a good candidate unless it is very difficult to solve when it does occur and it possesses the potential for great catastrophe if it is not solved.

OPTIMIZATION VERSUS SATISFICING   A decision on whether to accept a satisfactory solution in place of the best solution can affect whether or not a problem needs the services of an expert system. Optimization requires the best solution available for a specific problem. Optimal solutions are normally produced by algorithmic models. These models can be implemented conveniently in conventional programming environments and do not need expert systems application. Satisficing models provide trade-off strategies for achieving a satisfactory solution to a problem within given constraints. These models are helpful for cases when time limitation, resource shortage, and performance requirements constrain the solution of a problem or in cases where an optimal solution is not possible. If the trade-off between best and satisfactory solutions is acceptable, then an expert system may be required.

DATA AND KNOWLEDGE AVAILABILITY A complete analysis of a problem will help determine if the data needed to solve the problem can be obtained. A match must be made between data availability, knowledge availability, and problem characteristics as shown in Figure 3.2. The objective is to increase the intersection of the data availability, knowledge availability, and problem requirements as much as possible. Not only must an expert with the right knowledge be available, but the expert must also be willing to make his or her expertise available for solving the problem under consideration.

Most engineering problems have essential elements in common. If these elements are clearly outlined, an engineer can properly perceive, formulate, structure, and analyze the problem environment. The essential elements of engineering problems include problem statement, information, performance measure, solution model, and solution implementation. The steps involved in the solution approach are outlined below:

Step 1. Problem statement:

A problem involves choosing between competing, and probably conflicting, alternatives. The components of problem-solving in engineering include:

- Describing the problem.
- Defining a model to represent the problem.

Figure 3.2. Intersection of data, knowledge, and problem

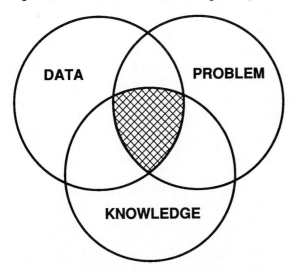

- Solving the model.
- Testing the solution.
- Implementing and maintaining the solution.

Problem definition is not a trivial task. In many cases, we recognize *symptoms* of a problem more readily than we recognize its *cause* and *location*. Even after the problem is accurately identified and defined, a benefit/cost analysis may be needed to determine if the cost of solving the problem is justified.

Step 2. Data and information requirements:

Information is the driving force or fuel for any solution. Information clarifies the relative states of past, present, and future events in the problem scenario. The collection, storage, retrieval, organization, and processing of raw data are important components for generating information. Without data, there can be no information. Without good information, there cannot be any valid solution. The essential requirements for generating information for solving a problem include:

- Ensure that an effective data collection procedure is followed.
- Determine the type and the appropriate amount of data to collect.
- Evaluate the cost of collecting the required data.
- Evaluate the data collected with respect to information potential.

For example: Suppose a manager is presented with a recorded fact that says, *"Sales for the last quarter are 10,000 units."* This constitutes ordinary data. There are many ways of using this data to make a decision depending on the manager's value system. An engineering analyst, with the aid of an expert system, can ensure the proper use of the data by transforming it into information, such as, *"Sales of 10,000 units for last quarter are low."* With this type of information, the manager could develop a more definite course of action.

Step 3. Performance measure:

The decision maker assigns a perceived worth or value to the available alternatives. Setting a measure of performance is crucial to the process of defining and generating recommendations in an expert system environment.

Step 4. Solution model:

A solution model provides the basis for the analysis and synthesis of information, and is the platform over which competing alternatives are compared. To be effective, a solution model must be based on a systematic and logical framework for guiding solution steps. A solution model can be a verbal, graphical, or mathematical representation of the ideas in the solution process. A solution model has the following characteristics:

- It is a simplified representation of an actual situation.
- It explains, simulates, and predicts the actual situation.
- It need not be complete or exact in all respects.
- It emphasizes the most important relationships in the decision process.
- It permits experiments that advance the understanding of the problem.
- It can be used repeatedly for similar problem scenarios.

The formulation of a solution model has three essential components:

(1). *Abstraction:*   Determining the relevant factors in the problem.

(2). *Construction:* Combining the factors into a logical model.

(3.) *Validation:*   Assuring that the model adequately represents the problem.

There are five basic types of solution models applicable to engineering and manufacturing problems. They are:

(1). *Descriptive models:* These are directed at describing a decision scenario and identifying the associated problem. For example, a project analyst might use a Critical Path Method (CPM) network model to identify bottleneck tasks in a project.

(2). *Prescriptive models:* These furnish procedural guidelines for implementing actions. A managerial model for achieving communication, cooperation, and coordination in a problem environment is an example of a prescriptive model.

(3). *Predictive models:* These models are used to predict future events in a problem environment. They are typically based on historical data about the problem situation. For example, a regression model based on past data may be used to predict future productivity gains associated with expected levels of resource allocation in a manufacturing operation.

(4). *Satisficing models:* These are models that provide satisfactory solutions rather than optimized solutions to a problem. The models are needed for cases where an optimal solution may not be achievable.

(5). *Optimizing models:* These models are designed to find the best available solution to a problem subject to a certain set of constraints. For example, a linear programming model can be used to determine the optimal product mix in a production environment.

In many situations, two or more of the above models may be involved in the solution of a problem. For example, a descriptive model might provide insights into the nature of the problem; an optimization model might provide the optimal set of actions to take in solving the problem, a satisficing model might modify the optimal solution based on practicality, a prescriptive model might suggest the procedures for implementing the selected solution, and a predictive model might predict the expected outcome of implementing the solution. A good analysis of the problem to be solved will indicate where an expert system may be suitable in the overall problem scenario.

Step 5. Obtaining the solution:

Using the available data, information, and the solution model, an expert system can determine the real-world actions that are needed to solve the problem at hand. These actions are then presented to the user in terms of recommendations. A sensitivity analysis may be incorporated into the design of the expert system to determine what changes in parameter values might cause a change in the solution.

Step 6. Implementing the solution:

A solution represents the selection of an alternative that satisfies the objective stated in the problem statement. A good solution is useless until it is implemented. Therefore, an important aspect of a solution generated by an expert system is the strategy needed to implement the solution. Some of the factors that may affect the implementation of a solution include:

- Technical aspects of the solution.
- Managerial aspects of the solution.
- Resources required to implement the solution.
- Cost of implementing the solution.
- Time frame needed for implementing the solution.

3.3 DATA REQUIREMENT ANALYSIS

A good problem for an expert system is one in which there is a general agreement on the facts of the problem domain and in which clear boundaries of the problem area and data sets can be determined. Just like human experts, expert systems don't always arrive at the best possible solutions at all times. An expert system will sometimes generate better solutions than a real expert and will sometimes generate inferior solutions based on the prevailing set of data. A problem selected for an expert system implementation should be such that the user is willing to accept imperfect solutions based on whatever imperfection may be associated with the available data. Consequently, a careful analysis of the data requirements for expert systems problems should be performed.

   An expert system knowledge engineer often deals with different types of measurement scales depending on the particular problem being considered. The problem analysis and solution approach will be influenced by the types of data and measurement scales to be used. The symbolic processing approach of expert systems requires an understanding of the different types of data available in a problem. The different types of data measurement scales are as follows:

Nominal scale is the lowest level of measurement scales. It classifies items into categories. The categories are mutually exclusive and collectively exhaustive. That is, the categories do not overlap and they cover all possible categories of the characteristics being observed. Examples of data using the nominal scale are sex, job classification, color, and name.

Ordinal scale is distinguished from a nominal scale by the property of order among the categories. An example is the process of assigning course grades based on the order of student scores. A grade of A is known to be better than a grade of B, but there is no indication of how much better it is. Similarly, first is ahead of second which is ahead of third, but there is no indication of the relative spacings between the categories. Other examples of data on an ordinal scale are high/medium/low, thick/thin, good/bad, and so on.

Interval scale is distinguished from an ordinal scale by having equal intervals between the units of measure. The assignment of scores ranging from 0 to 100 to student projects is an example of a measurement on an interval scale. A score of zero on a project does not imply that the student getting the zero knows absolutely nothing about the subject of the project. Temperature is a good example of an item that is measured on an interval scale. Even though there is a zero point on the temperature scale, it is an arbitrary relative measure. It cannot be determined that an item is zero degrees cold simply by touching it because different people will have different levels of sensitivity to cold. Other examples of interval scale are IQ measurements and aptitude ratings.

Ratio scale has the same properties of an interval scale, but with a true zero point. For example, an estimate of zero processing time for a computer task is a ratio scale measurement. Other examples of items measured on a ratio scale are volume, length, height, weight, and inventory level. In an expert system a mixture of the different types of data scales will be needed in implementing heuristics to arrive at acceptable solutions.

In addition to the measurement scale, data can be classified based on their inherent nature. Examples of the relevant classifications are transient data, recurring data, static data, and dynamic data. *Transient data* is defined as a volatile set of data that is encountered once during an expert system consultation and is not needed again. Transient data need not be stored in a permanent data base record unless it may be needed for future analysis or uses.

Recurring data refers to data that is encountered frequently enough to necessitate storage on a permanent basis. Recurring data may be further categorized into *static data* and *dynamic data*. A recurring data that is static will retain its original parameters and values each time it is encountered during an expert system consultation. A recurring data that is dynamic has the potential for taking on different parameters and values each time it is encountered.

3.4 EXPERT SYSTEM JUSTIFICATION

Expert systems are suitable for knowledge-intensive problems that are typically solved by human experts. Because expert systems depend on human knowledge, if human experts are unable to solve a given problem, then no successful expert system can be developed to solve the problem either. When the demand for human expertise surpasses the availability of experts, then an expert system may be the tool for handling the situation. The justification of using an expert system for a selected problem depends on the primary goal of the organization and the types of alternatives available.

This section presents the use of analytic hierarchy process (AHP) in the justification of expert systems. Expert system justification should be performed after an appropriate problem has been selected and before committing too much time and effort to the development effort. Many of the expert systems now under development for various applications are being developed without any formal attempt to justify the need for them. The lack of proper justification is partly responsible for the cases where some expert systems have not delivered the much advertised benefits. Expert systems may be developed for several reasons including strategic necessity, tactical needs, or economic consideration. A proper justification of expert systems will ensure that the systems are developed and deployed in the most appropriate functions with the greatest potential for success. The potential of expert systems can be best matched with practical applications through formal justification processes.

The justification of an expert system is essentially the same as the justification of any new technological tool where the quantification of the specific cost improvements based on experience may be difficult or impossible. The justification of an expert system will be determined by the system's effectiveness in major and subtle areas of improvement such as reduction in inventories, better raw material management, better control of work in progress, more accurate decisions, better resource utilization, reduction in rework and rehandling, improved employee morale, productivity improvement, better planning, increased consistency, and better service delivery. Robust justification techniques can help in handling both the qualitative and quantitative as well as the subjective aspects of the contribution of an expert system in solving a problem of value to the organization

The consistency, promptness and accuracy of decisions offered by expert systems can facilitate better throughput in a production environment or improved personnel productivity in a service environment. Machine times that previously had been idle could then be put to productive use. The increased capacity and output (subject to market constraints) can generate real economic benefits for the organization. Many production facilities have inherent flexibilities that can be identified only through automated reasoning tools such as expert systems. With its capability to process large amounts of data and resident knowledge, an expert system can point out areas where flexibilities such as equipment substitution or material replacement are possible without jeopardizing the desired product quality. The consistency of decisions and actions provided by expert systems can help in producing products with consistent quality characteristics.

The increased utilization of equipment and resources due to the effect of using expert systems may be quantitatively evaluated as shown below. Every system has an output which has a value per unit. If an expert system reduces the idle time of equipment by reducing down time or forced idle time, then the cost gain may be computed as:

$$V = v\Delta T$$

where

V = value produced per unit time of operation
v = revenue per unit of standard time
ΔT = increased production time (reduction in idle time)

Transition costs can be defined if the value (V) of an employee at a full experience level can be defined. There are some jobs in which job experience and not training is the major determinant of effectiveness. Examples are shipping clerks who must know railroad freight rate systems, insurance clerks, merchandise clerks, inspectors, and so on. A reasonable argument is that an employee value is worth his or her direct cost plus overhead plus profit on total cost. If such an employee is only fifty percent efficient, then one half of this value is lost per day. On the other hand, if the employee is fifty percent more efficient due to the use of expert systems, then one half of his or her cost would be saved. Suppose an employee has a job whose task is difficult. "Difficult" is defined as the fact that a task can be performed with probability p and not performed with probability $1-p$ by a normally effective employee. If an employee increases his probability of performance by δ, then his new real value is $(1 + \delta)V$. This can then be translated to measurable units for inclusion in the justification process. The preceding discussions present some of the factors that may be relevant to the justification process. These factors and other qualitative and quantitative measures can be incorporated into comprehensive multiattribute evaluation methodologies.

To properly evaluate whether the installation of an expert system is justified we must first determine exactly what the system is expected to accomplish. This is why a thorough problem analysis is essential. The specification for an expert system can begin as general statements of the expectations, but it must be reduced to a list of measurable criteria before a justification approach can be implemented. We must determine how the performance or the contribution of the expert system can be measured or estimated. This is the most difficult portion of the justification process and certainly one of the most important. Many of the sources for the data needed for justification will have some subjective nature. For this reason, methodologies that permit the incorporation of subjective data are of utmost importance in the justification of expert systems. Such a methodology is the analytic hierarchy process.

Economic analysis is the process of evaluating alternatives on the basis of cost and revenue implications. The conventional methods of justification are based on quantitative measures of worth of an alternative. In expert systems technology, many tangible and intangible, quantitative and qualitative factors intermingle to compound the justification process. Multiattribute methodologies integrate both objective and subjective factors. Expert systems may be justified on the basis of an integrated evaluation of economic, analytic, and strategic attributes.

Examples of strategic benefits of expert systems include better employee morale, better competitive edge, better insulation against labor uncertainties, better use of information resources, and ability to keep pace with technology. Examples of tactical benefits of expert systems include reduced processing time, higher throughput, better process control, improved quality, improved productivity, better consistency, faster response time, more accurate decisions, and improved data utilization. Examples of economic benefits of expert systems include higher return on investment, better equipment utilization, reduced labor costs, shorter processing times, and lower operating overheads. Analytic hierarchy process is an excellent method for evaluating the potential hierarchical interactions of the several aspects of implementing expert systems.

The analytic hierarchy process (AHP) is a practical approach to solving complex decision problems involving the comparisons of attributes or alternatives. The technique has been used extensively in practice to solve many decision problems. Golden et al (1989) present a comprehensive survey of the technique and its various applications. Based on the previous successful applications of the technique, it can be applied to the comparison of characteristics and attributes involved in the justification of expert systems.

In general, AHP enables decision makers to represent the hierarchical interaction of many factors, attributes, characteristics, or alternatives. For example, in expert systems technology transfer, AHP can be used to identify which attribute should be the determining factor in selecting technology transfer strategies. The general approach to using AHP includes the following steps:

(1). Develop the hierarchical structure for the decision problem.
(2). Determine the relative weights of each alternative with respect to the characteristics and sub-characteristics in the hierarchy.
(3). Determine the overall priority score of each alternative.
(4). Determine the indicators of consistency in making pair-wise comparisons of the characteristics and alternatives.
(5). Make a final decision based on the results.

The hierarchy should be constructed so that elements at the same level are of the same class and must be capable of being related to some elements in the next higher level. In a typical hierarchy, the top level reflects the overall objective or focus of the decision problem. Criteria, factors, or attributes on which the final objective is dependent are listed at intermediate levels in the hierarchy. The lowest level in the hierarchy contains the competing alternatives through which the final objective might be achieved. After the hierarchy has been constructed, the decision maker must undertake a subjective prioritization procedure to determine the weight of each element at each level of the hierarchy. Pair-wise comparisons are performed at each level to determine the relative importance of each element at that level with respect to each element at the next higher level in the hierarchy. Figure 3.3 presents a flowchart of the implementation of AHP.

Figure 3.4 presents an example of a decision hierarchy for decision aid alternatives for productivity improvement. The objective is to select and justify the best overall decision aid to satisfy a specified productivity improvement need in an organization. Three possible systems or alternatives are available. The justification problem is summarized as shown below:

Objective: Select best overall decision aid.
Alternative 1: Manual process.
Alternative 2: Expert systems.
Alternative 3: Conventional program.

The alternatives are to be compared on the basis of factors that the organization considers to be very important. Such factors may be determined based on a combination of objectives relating to productivity improvement, quality improvement, better customer satisfaction, better employee morale, economic feasibility, strategic importance, and so on. For the purpose of this illustration, the following five attributes are used in comparing the alternatives:

Attribute A: Reliability
Attribute B: Consistency
Attribute C: Time savings
Attribute D: Adaptability
Attribute E: Flexibility

The first step in the AHP procedure involves developing relative weights for the five attributes with respect to the objective at the next higher level in the hierarchy. To come up with the relative weights, the attributes are compared pair-wise with respect to their respective contributions to the objective. The pair-wise comparison is done through subjective evaluation by the decision maker(s). Table 3.1 shows the tabulation of the pair-wise comparison of the five attributes. Each of the attributes listed along the rows of the table is compared against each of the attributes listed in the columns. Each number in the body of the table indicates the degree of importance of one attribute over the other on a scale of 1 to 9. A typical question that may be used to arrive at the relative rating is the following:

"Do you consider consistency to be more important than time savings in the selection of a decision aid for productivity improvement?"
"If so, how much more important is it on a scale of 1 to 9?"

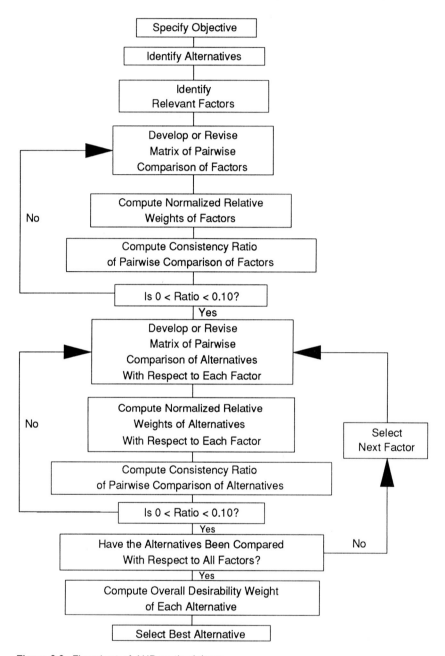

Figure 3.3. Flowchart of AHP methodology

Similar questions are asked iteratively until each attribute has been compared with each of the other attributes. For example, in Table 3.1, attribute B (Consistency) is considered to be more important than attribute C (Time savings) with a degree of 6 with respect to the selection of a decision aid. In general, the

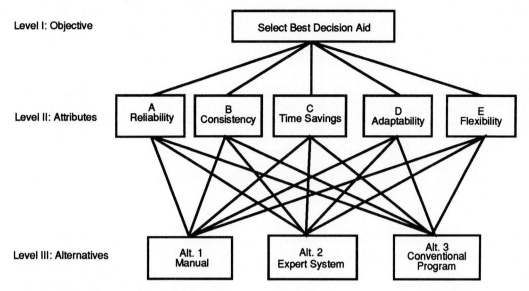

Figure 3.4. Analytic hierarchy process for decision aid alternatives

numbers indicating the relative importance of the attributes are obtained by using the following rules:

Equally important: Degree=1

If attribute A is equally important as attribute B,
Then the importance rating of A over B is 1.

Weakly more important: Degree=3

If attribute A is weakly more important than attribute B,
Then the importance rating of A over B is 3.

Strongly more important: Degree=5

If attribute A is strongly more important than attribute B,
Then the importance rating of A over B is 5.

Very strongly more important: Degree=7

If attribute A is very strongly more important than attribute B,
Then the importance rating of A over B is 7.

Absolutely more important: Degree=9

If attribute A is absolutely more important than attribute B,
Then the importance rating of A over B is 9.

Attributes	Reliability	Consistency	Time Savings	Adaptability	Flexibility
Reliability	1	1/3	5	6	5
Consistency	3	1	6	7	6
Time Savings	1/5	1/6	1	3	1
Adaptability	1/6	1/7	1/3	1	1/4
Flexibility	1/5	1/6	1	4	1

Table 3.1. Pair-wise rating of decision attributes

Intermediate numbers are used as appropriate to indicate intermediate levels of importance. If the comparison order is reversed (e.g., B versus A rather than A versus B), then the reciprocal of the importance rating is entered in the pairwise comparison table. For example, the following statements are equivalent:

Consistency is more important than Time savings with a degree of 6.

Time savings is more important than Consistency with a degree of 1/6.

Because of its fractional rating, the second statement actually implies that Time savings is less important than Consistency. The relative evaluation ratings in Table 3.1 are converted to a matrix of pair-wise comparisons as shown in Table 3.2. The entries in this Table are then normalized to obtain Table 3.3. The normalization is done by dividing each entry in a column by the sum of all the entries in the column. For example, the first cell in Table 3.3 (i.e., 0.219) is obtained by dividing 1.000 by 4.567. Note that the sum of the normalized values in each attribute column is one.

Table 3.2. Matrix of pair-wise comparisons of the five attributes

Attributes	A	B	C	D	E
A	1.000	0.333	5.000	6.000	5.000
B	3.000	1.000	6.000	7.000	6.000
C	0.200	0.167	1.000	3.000	1.000
D	0.167	0.143	0.333	1.000	0.250
E	0.200	0.167	1.000	4.000	1.000
Column Sum	4.567	1.810	13.333	21.000	13.250

The last column in Table 3.3 shows the normalized average rating associated with each attribute. For example, the first entry in that column (i.e., 0.288) is obtained by dividing 1.441 by 5 since there are five attributes. These averages represent the relative weights (between 0.0 and 1.0) of the attributes that are being evaluated. The relative weights show that attribute B (Consistency) has the highest importance rating of 0.489. Thus, consistency is considered to be the most important factor in the selection of a decision aid for productivity improvement. Table 3.4 presents a summary of the relative weights of the attributes. Figure 3.5 presents a graphical representation of the relative weights.

The relative weights of the attributes are denoted as w_i. Thus, if the attributes are numbered from 1 to 5, we would have the following:

$$w_1 = 0.288 \quad w_2 = 0.489 \quad w_3 = 0.086 \quad w_4 = 0.041 \quad w_5 = 0.096$$

These attribute weights are valid only for the particular goal specified in the AHP model for the problem. If another goal is specified, the attributes would need to be reevaluated with respect to that new goal.

Since the initial pair-wise comparisons of the attributes are performed on the basis of subjective opinions of the people involved in the decision making, it is quite possible that there will be some elements of bias and inconsistency in the

Table 3.3. Normalized AHP matrix of paired comparisons

Attributes	A	B	C	D	E	Row Sum	Row Average
A	0.219	0.184	0.375	0.286	0.377	1.441	0.288
B	0.656	0.551	0.450	0.333	0.454	2.444	0.489
C	0.044	0.094	0.075	0.143	0.075	0.431	0.086
D	0.037	0.077	0.025	0.048	0.019	0.206	0.041
E	0.044	0.094	0.075	0.190	0.075	0.478	0.096
Column Sum	1.000	1.000	1.000	1.000	1.000		1.000

Table 3.4. Summary of attribute weights

Attributes	Weights
Reliability	0.288
Consistency	0.489
Time Savings	0.086
Adaptability	0.041
Flexibility	0.096

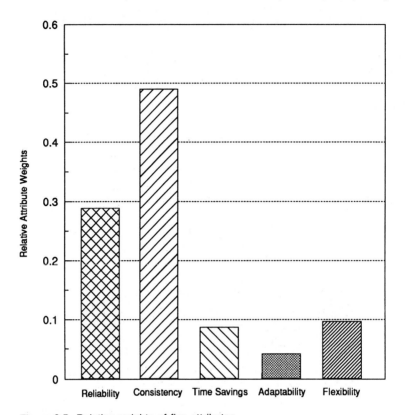

Figure 3.5. Relative weights of five attributes

evaluations. To minimize bias and assure some level of consistency, Saaty (1980) proposed a procedure for calculating the consistency ratio associated with the AHP methodology. The consistency ratio gives a measure of the consistency of the decision maker in comparing attributes and alternatives. All the consistency ratios for the above example fall within the acceptable limit of 0.0 to 0.10.

After the relative weights of the attributes are obtained, the next step is to evaluate the alternatives on the basis of the attributes. In this step, relative evaluation rating is obtained for each alternative with respect to each attribute. The procedure for the pair-wise comparison of the alternatives is similar to the procedure for comparing the attributes. Table 3.5 presents the tabulation of the pair-wise comparisons of the three alternatives with respect to attribute A (Reliability). The table shows that Alternative 1 and Alternative 3 have the same level of importance based on reliability. Examples of questions that may be useful in obtaining the pair-wise rating of the alternatives are:

"Is Alternative 1 better than Alternative 2 with respect to reliability?"
"If so, how much better is it on a scale of 1 to 9?"

Alternatives	Alt 1	Alt 2	Alt 3
Alt 1	1	1/3	1
Alt 2	3	1	2
Alt 3	1	1/2	1

Table 3.5. Pair-wise rating of alternatives on the basis of reliability

It should be noted that the comparisons shown in Table 3.5 are valid only when the reliability values of the alternatives are being considered. Separate pairwise comparisons of the alternatives must be done whenever another attribute is being considered. Consequently, for our example, we would have five separate matrices of pairwise comparisons of the alternatives; one matrix associated with each attribute. Table 3.5 is the first one of the five matrices. The other four are not shown due to space limitation. Each matrix is analyzed and normalized by using the same procedure shown previously for Table 3.1. The normalization of the entries in Table 3.5 yields the following relative weights of the alternatives with respect to reliability:

Alternative 1: 0.21
Alternative 2: 0.55
Alternative 3: 0.24

Table 3.6 shows a summary of the normalized relative ratings of the three alternatives with respect to each of the five attributes. The attribute weights shown earlier in Table 3.4 are now combined with the system weights contained in Table 3.6 to obtain the overall relative weights of the alternatives as shown in the equation on page 54.

Table 3.6. Relative weights of the three alternatives with respect to each attribute

Alternatives	Attributes				
	Reliability	Consistency	Time Savings	Adaptability	Flexibility
Alternative 1	0.21	0.12	0.50	0.63	0.62
Alternative 2	0.55	0.55	0.25	0.30	0.24
Alternative 3	0.24	0.33	0.25	0.07	0.14

$$\alpha_j = \sum_i (w_i k_{ij})$$

where

α_j = *overall* weighted evaluation for Alternative j
w_i = relative weight for attribute i
k_{ij} = evaluation rating for Alternative j with respect to attribute i. This is often referred to as the *local* weight of the alternative.
$w_i k_{ij}$ = a measure representing the *global* weight of alternative j with respect to attribute i. The sum of the global weights associated with an alternative represents the overall weight, α_j, of that alternative.

Table 3.7 shows the summary of the final AHP analysis for the example. The three alternatives have been evaluated on the basis of all five attributes. The question addressed by the AHP approach in this example is to determine which alternative should be selected to satisfy the stated production goal based on weighted evaluation of the relevant attributes. The summary in Table 3.7 shows that Alternative 2 (Expert Systems) should be selected since it has the highest weighted rating of 0.484.

Figure 3.6 presents a bar chart of the relative weights of the three alternatives. The segments in each bar represent the respective rating of each alternative with respect to each of the five attributes. The overall weighted rating of an alternative is sometimes referred to as the alternative's *desirability index* or *weight*. Our illustrative example shows that expert systems are the most desirable of the three alternatives considered.

Table 3.7. Summary of AHP for decision aid alternatives

	Attributes					
	A $i=1$	B $i=2$	C $i=3$	D $i=4$	E $i=5$	
$w_i \Rightarrow$	0.288	0.489	0.086	0.041	0.096	
System j		k_{ij}				α_j
System 1	0.21	0.12	0.50	0.63	0.62	0.248
System 2	0.55	0.55	0.25	0.30	0.24	0.484
System 3	0.24	0.33	0.25	0.07	0.14	0.268
Column Sum	1.000	1.000	1.000	1.000	1.000	1.000

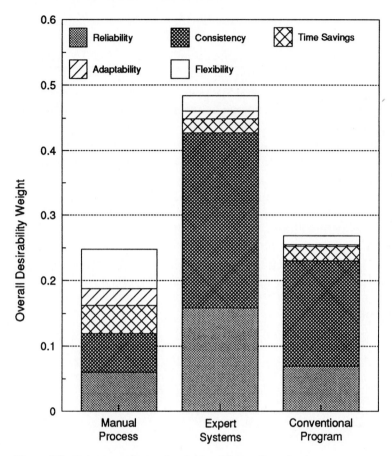

Figure 3.6. Histogram of overall weights of three alternatives

3.4.1   Problem Selection Guidelines

Summarized below are guidelines for selecting expert systems problems. The guidelines are useful as a checklist to be used in conjunction with the other discussions presented earlier in this chapter.

(1). The expert system development effort should not address a problem so difficult that it cannot be solved with the available resources and within the limits of anticipated development time. An experienced knowledge engineer should develop a small prototype system, and then evaluate the results of this effort to decide whether or not to proceed with the full development.

(2). An expert system should alleviate the difficulty that motivated the development, otherwise, the system will end up solving only a subset of the problems that need to be solved. When defining the problems to solve, the development team should consider the needs of both the overall organization and the end users, and try to resolve any basic conflicts between them before seriously undertaking the project.

(3). The expert system should be concise and to the point. The system with the largest number of rules is not necessarily the best system. If a problem appears to be too large, the scope of the project should be reduced.

(4). Choosing a problem that no one has ever solved will create an insurmountable bottleneck in the knowledge acquisition process.

(5). The domain expert should have a collection of real cases readily available. These can be used for the perception of the difficulty of the task and the system's performance.

(6). Avoid problems that require strict structures and those that are numeric in nature. These do not require much of the capabilities of expert systems because they do not require heuristics in their solutions. They can be best handled by algorithmic computer programs.

(7). Make sure the pertinent knowledge in the problem can be represented. For instance, interpretations made from certain sound and visual characteristics are extremely difficult to represent in problems dealing with pattern recognition.

After the expert system has been justified to be suitable for solving the selected problem, the real task of acquiring the required knowledge, coding the knowledge, and developing the expert system can start. The next two chapters discuss knowledge acquisition and representation.

3.5 EXERCISES

3.1 Give an example of each of the five solution models presented in this chapter (prescriptive, predictive, satisficing, optimizing, and descriptive).

3.2 Develop a conceptual framework of how the solution models in Question 1 may be interfaced to enhance the benefits of expert systems.

3.3 List five important factors that may help in identifying a problem situation.

3.4 Select a problem that you are very familiar with and analyze the problem on the basis of the various characteristics presented under problem analysis in this chapter.

3.5 Outline the factors that are important for the justification of expert systems application in engineering design.

3.6 Repeat Question 5 for a problem involving manufacturing planning.

3.7 Give five examples each of the following: transient data, recurring data, static data, and dynamic data.

3.8 Develop an AHP hierarchical structure to compare expert systems implementation to the following alternatives: Conventional MIS, Conventional Algorithmic Program, and Manual Processing. Identify the relevant factors (at least five) to include in the comparison.

3.9 For engineering and manufacturing type of applications, what are some of the other peculiarities that should be considered in selecting a problem for expert systems application?

3.10 Which personnel group should be the most involved in data requirement analysis for an expert system problem selection? Explain.

3.11 Compare the traditional approach of problem justification to the approach of AHP. Discuss the pros and cons of using each approach.

3.12 Propose an engineering problem suitable for expert systems application. Discuss why the problem is justified.

3.13 Propose a manufacturing problem suitable for expert systems application. Discuss why the problem is justified.

3.14 Conduct a survey of journals such as *AI Magazine, AI Expert*, and *IEEE Expert* and develop a taxonomy of the different types of expert systems applications published in the journals over the past two years.

3.15 Discuss why data analysis is an important consideration in problem selection.

3.16 How can performance measures be developed for expert systems based on the specific nature of the problem selected?

3.17 Develop an integrative solution model that links the abstraction, construction, and validation requirements of an expert system problem.

3.18 Discuss the difference between expert system justification and expert system problem justification.

3.19 How does an expert system development tool affect problem selection?

3.20 List ten essential characteristics of a good engineering problem for expert system application.

4

Knowledge Acquisition

Knowledge acquisition is one of the key elements in the development of an expert system. Knowledge acquisition refers to the process by which knowledge engineers acquire and encode the knowledge that domain experts use to solve a given problem. The success of an expert system depends on its ability to accurately represent the problem solving techniques of at least one domain expert. Because of its criticality in the development process, knowledge acquisition is often associated with what is known as the knowledge "acquisition bottleneck."

There has been much research on knowledge acquisition in the last few years. Many differing theories exist on the subject. This chapter discusses the several aspects that must be considered in the knowledge acquisition process and some procedures for enhancing the process. Because of the relative importance of the domain expert, discussions are presented on the desired characteristics of the expert and methods for choosing (and working with) a good one. Several accepted knowledge acquisition techniques are explored. The pros and cons of each technique are presented.

4.1 KNOWLEDGE ACQUISITION PHASES

Knowledge acquisition is implemented in multiple phases. The phases involve finding a good knowledge engineer, establishing the characteristics of the knowledge to be acquired, choosing the domain expert, and transfer/acquisition of knowledge.

4.1.1   The Knowledge Engineer

A knowledge engineer assumes the responsibility of modeling human reasoning and expertise in the form of a computer program. The variety of techniques includes written documentation, past examples of human performance, domain experts, and the knowledge engineer's own expertise.

CHARACTERISTICS OF A GOOD KNOWLEDGE ENGINEER   A good knowledge engineer should have many of the desirable characteristics presented below:

- Patience
- Perseverance
- Attentiveness
- Inquisitiveness
- Result-oriented
- Willingness to learn
- Technical credibility
- Congenial personality
- Good organization skills
- Good motivational skills
- Good technical background
- Receptiveness for suggestions
- Excellent communication skills

4.1.2   Knowledge Characteristics

The characteristics of knowledge to be acquired depend on both the nature of the problem to be solved as well as the type and level of expertise of the domain expert. Figure 4.1 presents a model of knowledge transfer.

SOURCES OF KNOWLEDGE   The characteristics of knowledge are often dictated by the source of the knowledge to be acquired. Typical sources of knowledge are:

- Direct consultation with human experts.
- Printed materials such as books.
- Direct task observation.
- Direct task performance.
- Third-party account of expert procedures.

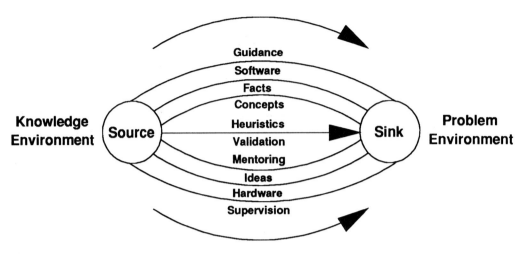

Figure 4.1. Knowledge transfer formats

Of all the available sources of knowledge, direct consultation with human experts poses the greatest difficulty but offers the highest level of reliability. By contrast, third-party accounts offer the least reliable method of acquiring knowledge. Books and other printed materials are particularly suitable as stable sources of knowledge. Handbooks, magazines, journals, and printed guides can form the basis for an initial knowledge base. The initial knowledge base may then be expanded with the aid of one or more experts. To acquire knowledge from an expert, one must first choose the expert and secure the expert's cooperation.

4.1.3 Choosing the Expert

Experts can serve as knowledge engineers and knowledge engineers can serve as experts. In some cases, expert systems are best designed, developed, and implemented by experts themselves. That is, the domain expert can also be the knowledge engineer in certain cases. This is true for problems where the transfer of knowledge is extremely complex. The domain expert can also serve as the knowledge engineer in cases where the expert wishes to learn and experiment with expert systems to capture his own expertise. If an expert becomes proficient in the creation of knowledge bases, he or she may find that it offers the most productive way of documenting new problem solving techniques. The experience may also increase the expert's awareness of his own techniques. The process of knowledge extraction from oneself may reveal prevailing inefficiencies in the expert's problem-solving approaches and help identify potential avenues for improvement.

In other cases, the consolidation of the roles of domain expert and knowledge engineer is not recommended because bias may be introduced into the expert system development process. For example, the choice of a development tool, knowledge representation scheme, and specific contents of the knowledge base may be biased by the characteristics and background of the person making the choice. A domain expert acting also as a knowledge engineer may have preferences that a trained knowledge engineer might not even consider.

Several criteria may be used in identifying the best expert for a given problem scenario. Some of the most common criteria are presented below:

(1). The expert must be able and willing to communicate personal knowledge and experience.

(2). The expert must be outwardly cooperative.

(3). The expert must be able to coordinate multiple functional responsibilities.

(4). The expert must have developed his or her domain expertise by actual practice over a reasonable length of time.

(5). The expert must be able to explicitly explain the methods used to apply his or her expertise to the problem under consideration.

(6). The expert must be easy to work with.

(7). The expert must be willing to commit a substantial amount of time to the development process.

One of the most significant criteria that can be used is the expert's wide acceptance as a true expert by his peers. If he is recognized by others in his field as an expert, then his judgment is respected and reliable. Domain experts should not be directly paid for their contribution to the knowledge acquisition process. Direct financial remuneration can be counterproductive because it can lead to knowledge prostitution; in which case the expert furnishes his knowledge to the highest bidder.

THE PARADOX OF THE EXCELLENT EXPERT   One of the difficulties that may arise in the selection of an expert is due to the inability of some experts to describe their own reasoning techniques. The paradox of the effectiveness of an excellent expert is that the expert may be unable to explain his reasoning approach. He may be so proficient in solving the problems in his domain that most of the processes are ingrained. So, the experienced expert solves problems without the use of conscious reasoning. This, of course, makes it difficult for him to explain his solution approaches. A better expert may be the one who is good at solving problems, but is still at the stage where he has to consciously evaluate his actions and reasoning approaches. Such a fledgling expert may be better able to transfer knowledge for expert systems purposes.

Good experts may also ignore their own "simple" knowledge in an effort to extract deep knowledge, due to their familiarity with the domain. In many cases, it is the simple knowledge that solves most of the problems. Unfortunately, a very good expert may trivialize simple knowledge and, thereby, deprive the expert system of an important resource. In general, good domain experts should possess certain characteristics that must be considered when selecting an expert for knowledge acquisition purposes. Characteristics of good experts include:

(1). A well developed sense of perception.

(2). Ability to distinguish between relevant and irrelevant information.

(3). Ability to simplify and organize complicated problem scenarios.

(4). Strong oral and written communication skills.

(5). A strong sense of responsibility and accountability for their decisions.

(6). Ability to adapt to changing problem conditions.

(7). Ability to perform under stress.

(8). Innovativeness.

(9). Respect for professional service.

According to Harmon and King (1985), a world-class expert has 50,000 to 100,000 bits of heuristic information about his particular specialty. Further, it is believed that it takes at least 10 years to accumulate 50,000 bits. Therefore, as a minimum, the candidates being considered as experts should have 10 years of study and practice in their fields. The view of this author is that the length of experience is not as crucial as some authors suggest. In some tasks, particularly in high technology operations, the learning curve may be such that a person can learn much within a short period of time. In other tasks, the learning curve may be relatively flat, thereby, precluding fast learning. Consequently, the traditional view of expertise based on length of service may not be very informative.

4.1.4   Knowledge Extraction versus Knowledge Acquisition

Sometimes, it is essential to make distinctions between knowledge extraction and knowledge acquisition (Vandamme 1986). Knowledge extraction may be viewed as the actual solicitation of knowledge by asking or watching an expert. On the other hand, knowledge acquisition is referred to as the process which provides for the creation of new concept structures or the rules that govern the structures. In other words, knowledge acquisition gives the person acquiring the knowledge the opportunity to independently generate new approaches to solving problems in the domain under consideration. By comparison, knowledge extraction merely uses the person doing the extracting as a medium for getting knowledge from one point (the expert) to another point (the knowledge base).

KNOWLEDGE DISCOVERY   One of the preliminary requirements of a knowledge engineer is to become familiar with the domain in which he or she will be working. This is the knowledge discovery phase. Knowledge discovery is necessary in the process of defining the size and characteristics of the domain. It also allows the knowledge engineer to get a feel for the typical reasoning scenarios, basic rules, and concepts of the domain. The knowledge engineer must also learn the terminology of the domain at this time. Without an understanding of the language, consultation with experts will be difficult.

During the knowledge discovery phase, it is important for the knowledge engineer to keep an open mind. Preliminary consultations with several experts and end users will uncover subtle problems inherent to the domain. For example, the knowledge engineer may want to interview end users to find out whether they prefer a long explanation of the decision by the expert system or just a simple recommendation. An initial prototype of the high level system may be designed by the knowledge engineer before the formal knowledge extraction using this "discovered" knowledge. This prototype can incorporate the basic structure of the task such as the form of input and output to be used by the expert system and the typical solutions or classes of solutions. In acquiring knowledge, the knowledge engineer must evaluate the causative and consequential relationships among the parameters in a problem. Figure 4.2 presents a model of the input/output relationships of problem parameters.

4.2 METHODS OF EXTRACTING KNOWLEDGE FROM EXPERTS

Knowledge acquisition is not a science with predictable results. Expert systems developers must use knowledge acquisition methodologies that fit the problem situation and the needs of those involved in the acquisition process. The domain expert is a key player in the knowledge acquisition process. The knowledge engineer serves as the facilitator for knowledge elicitation, acquisition, and representation. One or more experts may be consulted during the preliminary stages of an expert system effort. This may be needed, for example, to determine the scope of the problem domain. The first in-depth attempt to elicit knowledge usually takes place after the initial knowledge discovery. Hoffman (1987) discusses the problems of extracting knowledge from experts. Following, are some of the techniques for knowledge elicitation from an expert.

Figure 4.2. Causative and consequential relationships

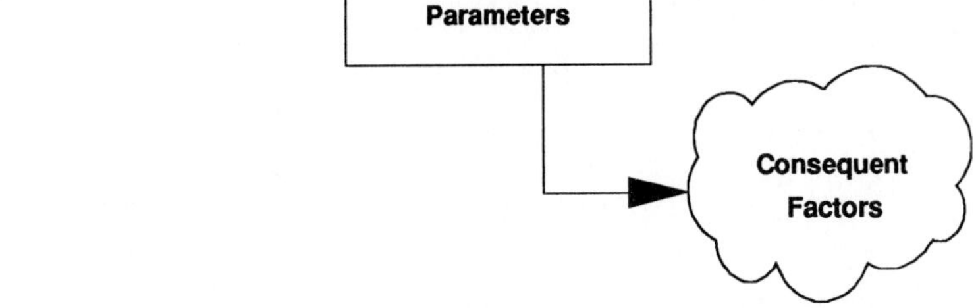

INTERVIEWS   The most popular and widely used form of expert knowledge extraction is the interview. In the unstructured method of interview, the knowledge engineer sits with the expert and goes through the process of solving a problem. The expert may describe the process verbally only or verbally while a task is being performed. The knowledge engineer records the information and asks spontaneous questions in order to obtain more information concerning the expert's problem solving approaches. Some specific methods that are often used during interviews for knowledge extraction include the following:

(1). *Problem discussion:* This explores the kind of data, knowledge, and procedures needed to solve specific problems.

(2). *Problem description:* This requires that the expert describe a prototype problem for each category of answer in the domain.

(3). *Problem analysis:* This presents the expert with a series of realistic problems to solve explicitly while probing the rationale behind the reasoning steps.

(4). *Refinement:* This requires that the expert present a series of problems to solve using the knowledge acquired during previous interviews.

(5). *Examination:* This requires that the expert examine and critique the prototype rules and control structure.

(6). *Validation:* This requires the presentation of the sample problems solved by the expert and the prototype system to other outside experts.

An unstructured interview may be first used in the preliminary stage of the knowledge acquisition to obtain a large amount of general information. Later, a structured interview can be used to gain specific information about one particular aspect of the expert's technique. It is also useful to record the interview on audio or video tape. Recording helps to document the interview and also provides a way for the knowledge engineer to analyze the expert's verbal and facial gestures. However, recording alone is not enough, the knowledge engineer must take good notes during interviews. Privacy is very important and interruptions during interview sessions should be kept to a minimum.

OPEN-ENDED INTERVIEWS   This type of interview requires either a pilot knowledge base (possibly from unstructured interviews) or a knowledge engineer with a significant amount of domain knowledge. When a preliminary knowledge base exists, the expert goes over the contents, making comments on each one. This way additions or deletions may be made very quickly and easily. Tape recording this interview may not be necessary since the expert can write notes directly on a copy of the pilot knowledge base. When the knowledge engineer possesses a large amount of domain knowledge, the same process can take place. The interview consists of specific questions directed at certain aspects of the domain. The expert answers the questions and elaborates where necessary.

ADVANTAGES AND DISADVANTAGES OF INTERVIEWS   In general, unstructured interviews have the advantage of generating a large amount of data. This is especially true in the early stages of expert systems development. It is the job of the knowledge engineer to keep the expert from digressing to other unrelated topics and to control the amount and detail of the expert's comments. The main disadvantage of interviews is the fact that they are very time-consuming. Unstructured interviews may take weeks to conduct and may be very inefficient due to their informal nature.

Structured interviews may also be very time-consuming due to the fact that preliminary knowledge bases, by nature, may be very long and covering the material may take a long time. This method, however, tends to be more efficient than unstructured interviews.

In terms of the validity of the data, the effectiveness of interviews depends mainly upon the skill of the interviewer in asking the right questions and the skill of the expert in conveying his knowledge and techniques. Not all experts have this skill. Some of the shortcomings associated with interviews are:

(1). There is a tendency to focus on the leading items in a sequence of events when reasoning about the entire problem sequence.

(2). Easily available data sets are often utilized without regard to their relevance.

(3). There is a tendency to be conservative in complex decision problems.

(4). The manner in which data is presented may affect the ability to retrieve the inherent information.

(5). Too much unnecessary data complicates the problem scenario and may overwhelm the knowledge engineer.

(6). People believe something because it is thought to be important.

(7). There is a tendency to use past successful strategies whether or not they fit new situations.

(8). There is a tendency to remember the first and last items in a sequence better than the middle ones.

(9). There is a tendency not to explore the subtle aspects of the problem domain.

(10). Dynamic memory is required when handling multiple pieces of information with multiple levels of interactions.

TASK PERFORMANCE AND PROTOCOLS The observation of an expert performing a familiar problem-solving task can be a very productive way to gather detailed knowledge. In the case of early data gathering, the task may be a simple or routine one. This gives the knowledge engineer the framework of the expert's thought process. The expert must be encouraged to "think aloud" as the task is being performed. Care must be taken, however, not to interrupt this thought process except for reminders to keep to the subject matter. The process may be videotaped or audio-taped in order to obtain an accurate record of the expert's words and actions. These can later be analyzed by the knowledge engineer. The knowledge engineer may also ask the expert to repeat the task, adding detailed comments as the process continues. In this method of knowledge acquisition, the study of the expert's actions is sometimes called protocol analysis.

ANALYZING THE EXPERT'S THOUGHT PROCESS   After observing a knowledge acquisition task, the knowledge engineer should conduct a structured interview in order to analyze the sequence of events associated with the task. Questions that should be asked include:

"What led you from this conclusion to the next?"
"What data did you consider?"
"What past experiences came to mind at this point?"

These questions are necessary to elicit further thoughts from the expert. Verbal explanations must be evaluated in an effort to extract any of the expert's factual and heuristic knowledge. Internal dialogue used by the expert may be indicated by phrases such as:

"Something tells me . . ."
"I bet that it is . . ."
"This reminds me of . . ."
"The last time I saw this . . ."

These phrases help to indicate the expert's attempt to relate current problem situations to previous experiences. The knowledge engineer must take care to understand the expert's reasoning process and adequately document it rather than introducing his own methods of reasoning into the knowledge acquisition process. The performance of a simple task and the subsequent analysis of the data gathered can be a very good source of detailed knowledge. The knowledge engineer must be very observant, inquisitive, and skillful in his approach to knowledge acquisition.

CONSTRAINED TASK   A constrained task approach involves asking the expert to perform a task under a certain constraint. The constraint could be a limit on the time allotted to examine a piece of evidence or reach a conclusion based on the facts presented. This method provides information on the strategies and high-level structures of the expert's thought process. The objective of the constrained task approach is to challenge the expert and bring out the intuitive problem-solving approach of the expert.

TOUGH CASE METHOD   The tough case method of knowledge acquisition involves providing the expert with a tough test problem to solve. The test problems are selected from a rare set of problems that occur only occasionally in the expert's normal function. The expert may be requested to use a tape recorder for recording the account of how a tough case is solved whenever it is encountered. The expert is requested to "think aloud" during the solution process.

QUESTIONNAIRES AND SURVEYS   Questionnaires and surveys are other methods of knowledge acquisition. Open-ended questionnaires ask the expert to describe the methods and reasoning used to solve a problem. This may be useful in the knowledge discovery stage to provide broad information. The disadvantage of the approach is that the knowledge engineer is not present to moderate the expert and to make sure the responses are really relevant to the questions.

An alternative is to use a short-answer questionnaire format. This is used to elicit the opinion of multiple experts quickly and easily. The information that can be gathered with this method is usually limited to simple descriptions or techniques. The knowledge engineer should be sufficiently educated in the domain in order to create meaningful questions to be useful for short-answer questionnaires.

Forced-answer questionnaires can be used as a knowledge base validation tool. These questionnaires call for "yes" or "no" answers or multiple choice answers. For example, forced-answer questionnaires may be used to validate a production rule by asking whether the *If* clause really yields the *Then* clause.

DOCUMENTATION AND ANALYSIS OF ACQUIRED KNOWLEDGE   Proper documentation should be accumulated throughout the knowledge acquisition effort. Written documentation, audio, and video records of the knowledge acquisition sessions are essential for clarifying the expert's reasoning process during the actual development of the knowledge base. Data related to the acquired knowledge should be kept in an organized and easily accessible format. The transcription of the interviews and verbal information generates a great deal of additional written information. The documentation and analysis should address the following:

(1). *Transcription:* Verbal exchanges during knowledge acquisition should be documented in writing.

(2). *Phrase indexing:* Key phrases in the problem domain should be indexed with proper notes and references attached.

(3). *Knowledge coding:* Knowledge elements acquired should be grouped into descriptive and procedural categories.

The analysis of the acquired knowledge may be performed concurrently with the knowledge acquisition process. It is not necessary to wait until the acquisition stage is complete before beginning the analysis. Concurrent analysis and validation can help identify areas that should be further explored during the knowledge acquisition process.

4.2.1 Expert's Block

Like writers who can experience the legendary "writer's block," domain experts can also experience expert's block. This is the situation in which the expert cannot generate any additional output for the knowledge acquisition process. A skilled knowledge engineer can help the expert by providing appropriate hints and posing probing questions that can resuscitate the expert's reasoning process. If a complete problem analysis has been performed as presented in Chapter 3, it should not be very difficult to identify subtle elements of the problem domain that will be useful in generating additional links to new problem-solving rules. If the block persists, the knowledge acquisition session should be temporarily terminated and recommenced at a later time. The mutual interaction of the knowledge engineer and the domain expert is presented in Figure 4.3. The knowledge engineer provides the leads necessary for the expert to come up with additional inferences.

4.3 KNOWLEDGE ACQUISITION MEETINGS

Meetings are an important component of the knowledge acquisition process. Effective management of knowledge acquisition meetings is an important skill for the knowledge engineer. If a knowledge acquisition meeting is poorly organized, improperly managed, or called at the wrong time, valuable cooperation may be lost very quickly. Meetings are essential for communication and decision making related to the problem to be solved by the proposed expert system. Some impor-

Figure 4.3. Interaction between domain expert and knowledge engineer

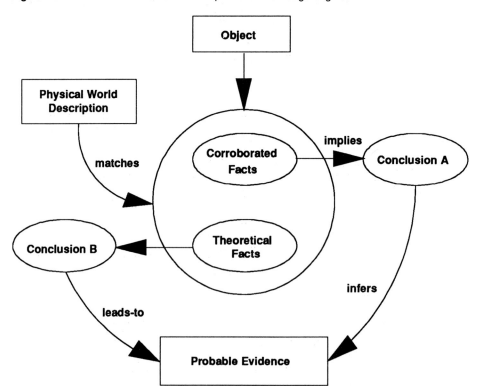

tant points should be kept in mind for knowledge acquisition meetings. These include:

(1). Carefully review the items to be discussed at the meeting and determine which can be more effectively disseminated through brief memoranda. The powers of desktop computers and electronic mail should be fully exploited to complement knowledge acquisition meetings.

(2). Ensure that only those who need to be at the knowledge acquisition meeting are invited to be there. The point of diminishing returns for any meeting is equal to the number of people that are actually needed for the meeting. The larger the number of people at a meeting, the lower the productivity of the meeting. The extra attendees serve to generate unconstructive and conflicting ideas that only impede the success of the meeting.

(3). Those not invited to the knowledge acquisition meeting should, however, be informed of how they may contribute to the process and how the proceedings of the meeting may affect them.

(4). The prospective end users of the proposed expert system should be offered avenues through which they may contribute to the knowledge acquisition process.

(5). Avoid allowing a knowledge acquisition meeting to degenerate into a social gathering.

Some guidelines for conducting knowledge acquisition meetings more effectively are presented below:

(1). Do pre-meeting homework:
- Clarify the problem area.
- Identify the topics to be discussed.
- Establish the desired outcome for each topic.
- Determine how the outcome will be verified.
- Determine who really needs to be there.
- Evaluate the suitability of meeting time and venue.
- Allow enough time duration to address each topic.
- Identify complementary communication media (telephone, mail, etc).

(2). Circulate written agenda of the knowledge acquisition process prior to the meeting.

(3). Emphasize the importance of the problem domain and the criticality of the knowledge acquisition process in solving the problem.

(4). Start the meeting on time.

(5). Review the knowledge acquisition agenda at the beginning.

(6). Get everyone present at the meeting involved in the knowledge elicitation process by posing direct questions to each participant.

(7). Keep to the agenda; do not add new items unless absolutely essential.

(8). Quickly resolve conflicts that may develop from diverging views of domain experts.

(9). Keep digression from the knowledge acquisition mission to a minimum.

(10). Recap the accomplishments of each topic before going to the next.

(11). Let those who have made commitments know what is expected of them.

(12). Evaluate meeting success relative to specified goals.

(13). Adjourn the meeting on time.

(14). Prepare and distribute the minutes or proceedings of the meeting.

(15). Highlight the knowledge acquired through the knowledge acquisition meeting.

4.4 GROUP KNOWLEDGE ACQUISITION

Many problem situations are complex and poorly understood. No one person has all the information to make all decisions accurately. As a result, crucial decisions are better made by a group of people. Some organizations use outside consultants with appropriate expertise to make recommendations for important problem decisions. Other organizations set up their own internal consulting groups that attend to decision problems without having to go outside the organization. Many companies now have internal expert systems consulting groups geared towards providing technical assistance for expert systems development throughout the company. Decisions can be made through linear responsibility, in which case one person makes the final decision based on input from other people. Alternately, decisions can be made through shared responsibility, in which case a group of people share the responsibility for making joint decisions. The major advantages of group decision making are:

(1). Ability to share experience, knowledge, and resources: Many heads are better than one. A group will possess greater collective ability to solve a given decision problem.

(2). Increased credibility: Decisions made by a group of people often carry more weight in an organization.

(3). Improved morale: Personnel morale can be positively influenced because many people have the opportunity to participate in the decision making and knowledge acquisition processes.

(4). Better rationalization: The opportunity to observe other people's views can lead to an improvement in an individual's reasoning process.

Knowledge acquisition through group decision making can be achieved by using several approaches. Some of the approaches are discussed below.

BRAINSTORMING   Brainstorming is a way of generating many new ideas. In brainstorming, the decision group comes together to discuss alternate ways of solving a decision problem. The members of the brainstorming group may be from different departments, may have different backgrounds and training, and may not even know one another. The diversity of the constituents helps to create a stimulating environment for generating many different ideas. The technique encourages free outward expression of new ideas no matter how remote the ideas might appear. No criticism of any new idea is permitted during the brainstorming session. A major concern in brainstorming is that extroverts may take control of the discussions. For this reason, an experienced and respected leader is needed to manage the brainstorming discussions. The group leader establishes the procedure for proposing ideas, keeps the discussions in line with the group's mission, discourages disruptive statements, and encourages the participation of all members.

After the group runs out of ideas, open discussions are held to weed out the unsuitable ones. It is expected that even the rejected ideas may stimulate the generation of other ideas which may eventually lead to other favored ideas. Some guidelines for improving the brainstorming session for knowledge acquisition are:

- Focus on a specific problem to be solved.
- Keep ideas relevant to the intended knowledge acquisition mission.
- Be receptive to all new ideas.
- Evaluate the ideas on a relative basis after exhausting new ideas.
- Maintain an atmosphere conducive to cooperative discussions.
- Maintain a documentation of the ideas generated and how they impact the knowledge acquisition process.

DELPHI METHOD   The traditional approach to group decision making is to obtain the opinion of experienced experts through open discussions. An attempt is then made to reach a consensus among the experts. However, open group discussions are often biased because of the influence or even subtle intimidation of dominant individuals. Even when the threat of a dominant individual is not present, opinions may still be swayed by group pressure. This is often called the "bandwagon effect" of group decision making.

The Delphi method attempts to overcome these difficulties by requiring individuals to present their opinions anonymously through an intermediary. The method differs from the other interactive group methods because it eliminates face-to-face confrontations. It was originally developed for forecasting applications. But it has been modified in various ways for application to different types of decision making. The method can be quite useful for knowledge acquisition purposes. It is particularly effective when decisions must be based on a broad set of factors. The Delphi method is normally implemented as follows:

(1). Problem definition: A decision problem that is considered significant to the organization is identified and clearly described.

(2). Group selection: An appropriate group of experts or experienced individuals is formed to address the particular decision problem. Both internal and external experts may be involved in the Delphi process. A leading individual is appointed to serve as the administrator of the decision process. The group may operate through the mail or gather together in a room. In either case, all opinions are expressed anonymously on paper. If the group meets in the same room, care should be taken to provide enough room so that each member does not have the feeling that someone may accidentally or deliberately spot his responses.

(3). Initial opinion poll: The technique is initiated by describing the problem to be addressed in unambiguous terms. The group members are requested to submit a list of major areas of concern in their specialty areas as they relate to the decision problem.

(4). Questionnaire design and distribution: Questionnaires are prepared to address the areas of concern related to the decision problem. The written responses to the questionnaires are collected and organized by the administrator. The administrator aggregates the responses in a statistical format. For example, the average, mode, and median of the responses may be computed. This analysis is distributed to the decision group. Each member can then see how his or her responses compare with the anonymous views of the other members.

(5). Iterative balloting: Additional questionnaires based on the previous responses are passed to the members. The members submit their responses again. They may choose to alter or not alter their previous responses.

(6). Silent discussions and consensus: The iterative balloting may involve anonymous written discussions of why some responses are correct or incorrect. The process is continued until a consensus is reached. A consensus may be declared after five or six iterations of the balloting or when a specified percentage (e.g., 80 percent) of the group agrees on the questionnaires. If a consensus cannot be declared on a particular point, it may be displayed to the whole group with a note that it does not represent a consensus.

In addition to its use in technological forecasting, the Delphi method has been widely used in other general decision making. Its major characteristics of anonymity of responses, statistical summary of responses, and controlled procedure make it a reliable mechanism for obtaining numeric data from subjective opinion. The major limitations of the Delphi method are:

(1). Its effectiveness may be limited in cultures where strict hierarchy, seniority, age, or devout reverence for expertise influence decision-making processes.

(2). Some experts may not readily accept the contribution of nonexperts to the group decision-making process.

(3). Since opinions are expressed anonymously, some members may take advantage of the situation to make ludicrous statements. However, if the group composition is carefully reviewed, this problem could be avoided.

NOMINAL GROUP TECHNIQUE   Nominal group technique is a silent version of brainstorming. Rather than asking people to state their ideas aloud, the team leader asks each member to jot down a minimum number of ideas, for example, five or six. A single list of ideas is then composed on a chalkboard for the whole group to see. The group then discusses the ideas and weeds out some iteratively until a final decision is reached. The nominal group technique is easier to control. Unlike brainstorming where members may get into shouting matches, it permits members to silently present their views. In addition, it allows introversive members to contribute to the decision without the pressure of having to speak out too often.

In all of the group decision-making techniques, an important aspect that can enhance and expedite the decision-making process is to require that members review all pertinent data before coming to the group meeting. This will ensure that the knowledge acquisition process is not impeded by trivial preliminary discussions. Some disadvantages of group decision making are:

(1). Peer pressure in a group situation may influence a participant's opinion and contributions.

(2). In a large group, some members may not get to participate effectively in the discussions.

(3). A member's relative reputation in the group may influence how well his or her opinion is received.

(4). A member with a dominant personality may overwhelm the other members in the discussions.

(5). The limited time available to the group may create a time pressure that forces some members to present their opinions without fully evaluating the ramifications of the available data.

(6). It is often difficult to get all members of a decision group together at the same time.

Despite the noted disadvantages, group decision making definitely has many advantages that may alleviate the shortcomings. The advantages as presented earlier will have varying levels of effect from one problem situation to another. Team knowledge acquisition can be enhanced by following the guidelines below:

(1). Get a willing group of experts together.

(2). Set an achievable goal for the group.

(3). Determine the limitations of the group.

(4). Develop a set of guiding rules for the group.

(5). Create an atmosphere conducive to group synergism.

(6). For major expert systems projects and extended knowledge acquisition activities, arrange for team training, which allows the group to learn the decision rules and responsibilities involved in the problem.

4.5 KNOWLEDGE ACQUISITION SOFTWARE

To aid in the difficult process of knowledge acquisition, knowledge engineers and programmers have been developing software tools which are designed to gather knowledge by interacting directly with the expert. Knowledge acquistion software offers distinct advantages over the traditional pencil and paper approach. One of the advantages of knowledge acquisition software is that the expert may contribute to the knowledge base at his or her pace and convenience. The tools can be classified into two categories:

(1). Knowledge elicitation tools.
(2). Induction by example tools.

KNOWLEDGE ELICITATION TOOLS   These consist of computer programs which interact directly with the expert. The expert enters information about the domain directly into a computer. The program guides the expert through the classification and clarification processes of knowledge acquisition. Knowledge acquisition software can interactively manipulate the data collected from the expert by using various statistical, clustering, and multidimensional data organization techniques. Figure 4.4 shows a model of the interaction of knowledge elements in a multidimensional format. Knowledge base rules are generated from the organized data. Knowledge acquisition software tools have been shown to be successful alternatives to the traditional interactions between the knowledge engineer and the expert (Silverman 1990; Di Piazza and Helsabeck 1990).

Newquist (1988) describes a knowledge acquisition tool known as the Knowledge Acquisition Module (KAM). This PC-based program can scan text and create rules, relationships, if-then statements, and heuristics based on constraints set by the expert. The program can scan the text of an interview with an expert and generate relevant rules. Prerau (1987) discusses the techniques used for acquiring knowledge for a multiparadigm expert system named COMPASS (Central Office Maintenance Printout Analysis and Suggestion System). COMPASS was developed by GTE laboratories for telephone switching system maintenance. OPAL (Oncology Protocol Acquisition Laboratory) is a computer-based knowledge acquisition tool developed at Stanford University for the Oncocin project. Domain experts (physicians) interact directly with the software to encode their knowledge. This removes the potential for knowledge acquisition bottleneck. OPAL has the advantage of giving the domain expert some experience as a knowledge engineer.

One of the first commercial interactive knowledge acquisition products was AutoIntelligence developed by IntelligenceWare, Inc. AutoIntelligence is an auto-

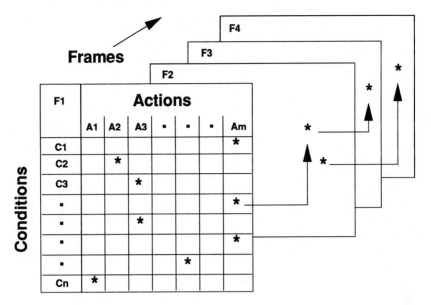

Figure 4.4. Multidimensional factor relationships in knowledge acquisition

matic knowledge acquisition system which captures the knowledge of an expert through interactive interviews, condenses the knowledge and then automatically generates an expert system. By using AutoIntelligence, the time and money spent in the interview process with the knowledge engineer is saved and it is not necessary to know how to type in rules, since rules are generated automatically. The system helps experts without a knowledge engineer to capture their own expertise.

INDUCTION BY EXAMPLE TOOLS   In this method, a program will infer rules based on examples generated by the expert. The program models the decision-making process of the expert based on the conclusions reached in the examples. Because there is a limit to the number of unique examples the expert may generate, induction by example programs are most effective for small expert systems. However, new software techniques are being used to enhance the capability of induction-based knowledge acquisition programs so that they can handle large problem domains.

Di Piazza and Helsabeck (1990) discuss a knowledge acquisition program named Laps. Laps is a software package designed for interviewing experts. The software combines the functions of gathering, organizing, and testing knowledge related to specified problems. Laps begins with a case in the form of a sample solution path elicited from the domain expert. This sample solution path is refined by a process called dechunking, which facilitates finding a model of the expert's reasoning process. The model guides the determination of the structure of alternatives by using an effective level of abstraction. The information gathered is organized into tables which the expert uses to generate additional rows of knowledge elements. The process is continued until a complete knowledge base is developed. Knowledge acquisition software should not be developed to replace the role of the knowledge engineer. Rather, the software should be developed to aid both the expert and knowledge engineer to produce more effective knowledge bases quickly.

4.6 EXERCISES

4.1 Discuss the advantages and disadvantages of each of the five knowledge sources presented in this chapter.

4.2 Discuss the personal characteristics that should be common to both the domain expert and the knowledge engineer.

4.3 Develop a strategy for selecting a pool of experts for knowledge acquisition in a problem involving engineering design diagnostics.

4.4 Discuss the pros and cons of having one domain expert serve as a knowledge engineer to interview another domain expert for knowledge acquisition purposes.

4.5 Discuss the differences between knowledge elicitation, knowledge extraction, and knowledge acquisition.

4.6 List 10 potential causes of knowledge acquisition bottleneck in expert system development. Recommend a solution for each of the causes you listed.

4.7 Discuss the differences between declarative knowledge and procedural knowledge.

4.8 Outline how a knowledge engineer might acquire declarative knowledge.

4.9 Outline how a knowledge engineer might acquire procedural knowledge.

4.10 Discuss the potential contents of each of the elements shown in the knowledge transfer format in Figure 4.1.

4.11 Discuss the relative reliability of each of the sources of knowledge presented in this chapter.

4.12 How would you deal with an uncooperative expert?

4.13 Present a detailed discussion of the *paradox of the excellent expert.*

4.14 Is "knowledge discovery" the same thing as "problem identification"? Explain.

4.15 Discuss the pros and cons of using interviews to acquire knowledge.

4.16 Would a psychologist be a better knowledge engineer? Discuss.

4.17 Compare face-to-face interviews with anonymous questionnaires and surveys in terms of knowledge acquisition.

4.18 Discuss some of the potential causes of "expert's block."

4.19 Discuss the advantages of group knowledge acquisition over conventional one-on-one knowledge acquisition.

4.20 Discuss how problem reduction and partition can enhance the knowledge acquisition process.

5

Knowledge Representation

This chapter presents the major knowledge representation techniques and the relevant reasoning models. Methods for handling uncertainty in expert systems are presented in the next chapter.

5.1 CHARACTERISTICS OF KNOWLEDGE

The purpose of knowledge representation is to organize the required knowledge into a form such that the expert system can readily access it for decision-making purposes. Knowledge does not always come compiled and ready for use. The term knowledge is used to describe a variety of bits of understanding that enable people and machines to perform their intended functions.

5.1.1 Types of Knowledge

Knowledge can be broadly classified into two types: *surface knowledge* and *deep knowledge*. The classification is based on the prevailing information circumstances and the intended (conscious or subconscious) uses of knowledge. Surface knowledge is based on heuristics and experience acquired from having successfully solved many similar problems. Deep knowledge involves reasoning from basic principles involving laws of nature and complex behavioral models. Some of the characteristics of the two types are:

Surface knowledge:

- It is composed of situation and action pairs.
- It is capable of solving simple domain problems.
- It is often used in cursory situations.
- It is faster to implement.

Deep knowledge:

- It is composed of cause and effect relationships.
- It is based on hierarchical cognition of events.
- It involves goals and plans to achieve the goals.
- It is capable of solving difficult problems.

Knowledge, whether surface or deep, must be extracted and encoded into usable forms for solving problems. When deep knowledge is organized, indexed, and stored in such a way that it is easily retrieved for solving problems, we obtain what is known as *compiled knowledge*. Sometimes, the source of knowledge may be so dormant that a great deal of effort must be made to extract it. Once extracted, an element of knowledge must undergo other transformations before it can achieve an operational form. Extraction involves eliciting the basic concepts of the problem domain from a reliable knowledge source. The two major sources of knowledge are:

(1). Active human expertise.
(2). Latent expertise.

Active human expertise relates to the expertise available from an expert who is currently active in solving problems in the problem domain. Latent expertise refers to the type of knowledge available in the form of printed material. This type of expertise is dormant until someone derives some use from it by converting the printed material into a usable form. Knowledge extraction from the source of expertise is performed to obtain enough problem solving knowledge to develop an expert system knowledge base. Heuristics constitute the key product of knowledge extraction from the source of expertise. Once enough knowledge is available, the knowledge engineer selects an appropriate scheme or technique for representing the knowledge. The encoding of the knowledge base begins after the knowledge engineer has selected the framework and knowledge representation techniques. Before encoding, knowledge may be subdivided into two categories: *declarative knowledge* or *procedural knowledge*.

Declarative knowledge refers to facts and assertions while procedural knowledge refers to sequence of actions and consequences. Declarative knowledge is associated with *knowing what* is involved in solving a problem. Procedural knowledge is associated with *knowing how* to apply appropriate problem-solving strategies to solve a given problem. Declarative knowledge representation uses logic-based and relational approaches. Logical representation involves the use of propositional and predicate logic. Relational models are implemented by using decision trees, graphs, or semantic networks. Procedural knowledge representation involves the use of rule-based approaches to store the knowledge of *how to* solve problems. The example below illustrates the difference between declarative and procedural knowledge.

The complete table of the standard normal random variable widely used in probability and statistics analysis represents declarative knowledge encompassing a large body of knowledge of the relationship between a value of the random variable and the probability of observing a value less than or equal to that particular value. By comparison, procedural knowledge refers to the compiled sequence of the procedures and actions showing how to compute probabilities using the normal table.

Declarative knowledge representation is usually more comprehensive and difficult to implement while procedural knowledge representation is more compact and easy to implement. Many practical problems will require the use of both declarative and procedural representations. The choice of a representation model will be dictated by the nature of the problem to be solved and the type of knowledge available.

5.2 KNOWLEDGE REPRESENTATION MODELS

A knowledge-based expert system performs the tasks that would normally be performed by experts. For the expert system to be effective, the knowledge acquired from the expert must be properly represented to prevent ambiguities in the problem solving procedures. Different knowledge representation techniques are available. Some techniques are suitable for a majority of problems typically encountered by expert systems. There are, however, some problems that require unique knowledge representation approaches. The major knowledge representation models are:

(1). Semantic networks
(2). Frames
(3). Production rules
(4). Predicate logic
(5). O-A-V (Object-Atribute-Value) triplets
(6). Hybrids
(7). Scripts

5.2.1 Semantic Networks

Semantic networks are the most general and, perhaps, the oldest representational structure for expert system knowledge base. It serves as the basis for other knowledge representations. It is a scheme for representing abstract relations among objects in a problem domain, such as membership in a class. Since most reasoning processes associate objects based on classes and relationships of known objects, the semantic network structure provides a general framework from which other representation methods can be derived.

Semantic networks consist of a collection of nodes that are linked to form object relationships. Arcs linking nodes carry notations that indicate the type of relationships. The nodes in a semantic network typically represent objects or facts. Examples of object relationships are:

Gear is-a part-of a *Rotor Assembly.*

Gear can-be produced by *Machining.*

Machining is-done-in *The-Shop.*

Rotor Assembly needs *Inspection.*

Such relationships may be represented graphically by a network of nodes and links where nodes represent objects and links represent the relationships among the objects. In this case the nodes would represent the objects *Gear, Rotor Assembly, Machining, The-Shop, and Inspection.* The links would represent the relations IS-A, PART-OF, CAN-BE, IS-DONE-IN, and NEEDS. The network as a whole forms a taxonomy of the available knowledge. An example of a semantic network for manufacture and inspection of a gear is presented in Figure 5.1.

The IS-A relation establishes a property of inheritance in object hierarchy in the network. Items lower in the network can inherit properties from items higher up in the network. This permits concise representation since information about similar nodes does not have to be repeated at each node. Semantic networks have been used successfully to represent knowledge in domains that use well-established taxonomies to simplify problem solving. Some of the advantages of semantic networks are:

(1). Flexibility in adding, modifying, or deleting new nodes and arcs.

(2). Ability to inherit relationships from other nodes.

(3). Ease of drawing inferences about inheritance hierarchy.

The major disadvantage of semantic networks is the lack of a formal definitive structure which makes it difficult to implement in an operational setting. However, simple representation forms such as frames and rules can be derived from the network.

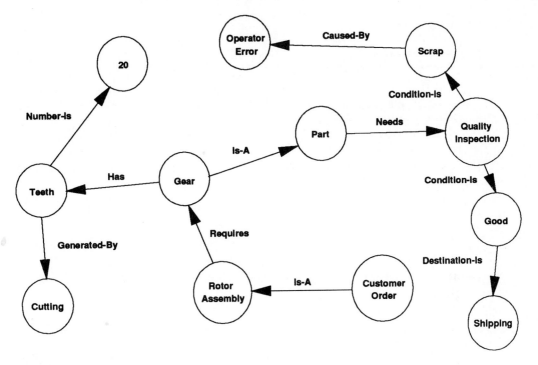

Figure 5.1. Example of semantic network

5.2.2   Frames

A frame consists of a collection of slots that contain attributes to describe an object, a class of objects, a situation, an action, or an event. Frames differ from semantic networks in the sense that frames contain a subset of the items that may be represented in a semantic network. In a semantic network, information about an object can be randomly placed throughout the knowledge base. By contrast, in a frame, the information is grouped together into a single unit called a frame. Frames are used for representing declarative knowledge. As discussed earlier, declarative knowledge is knowledge that cannot be immediately executed but can be stored and retrieved as needed to provide information for solving a problem.

Frames provide a description of an object by using a tabulation of information associated with the object. This organization of useful relationships helps to mimic the way an expert typically organizes the information about an object into chunks of data. Psychologists believe that when experts recall the information about a particular object, all the typical attributes of the objects are recalled at the same time as a group. This grouping of object attributes is what is known as a frame. Frame-based reasoning is based on seeking items that fill the slots of information required to solve a problem. If a frame is not relevant to a given problem situation, control will move to another frame. Advantages of frames are on page 82.

Gear	
Teeth Number	20
Assembly	Rotor
Production Method	Cutting
Delivery Date	9/2/91

Figure 5.2. Frame representation for gear production

(1). Frames are arranged in a hierarchical manner such that they can inherit relationships from other frames.

(2). Frames facilitate faster searches of the knowledge base through the concise and compact representation of information.

(3). Frames permit the representation of inheritance relationships among objects.

Using the earlier gear example, a frame representation might be constructed as shown in Figure 5.2. The knowledge base presented in Table 5.1 is a sample knowledge base in the PC PLUS expert systems development tool from Texas In-

Table 5.1. Root frame and subframe organization

ROOT FRAME	SUBFRAME

Frame Name: ASSET
PARMS:
    LESSEE-CASH
    CASH-RESERVE-NEEDED
    PRESERVES-CASH
    CANNOT-BORROW
    ACQUIRE-BY
RULES:
1. IF LESSEE-CREDIT = POOR
    THEN CANNOT-BORROW
    AND ACQUIRE = LEASE
2. IF CANNOT-BORROW OR PRESERVES-CASH
    THEN HOW-TO-ACQUIRE = LEASE
    AND ACQUIRE-BY = LEASE
3. IF LESSEE-CREDIT = FAIR
    AND LESSEE-CASH = FAIR
    AND CASH-RESERVE-NEEDED
    THEN PRESERVES-CASH
4. IF HOW-TO-ACQUIRE IS NOTKNOWN
    THEN HOW-TO-ACQUIRE =
    BUY-THE-ASSET
    AND ACQUIRE-BY = PURCHASE
 	
GOALS:
HOW-TO-ACQUIRE, PAYMENT
	Frame Name: FINANCE
	PARMS:
	    FINANCE-INTEREST
	    FINANCE-PERIOD
	    DOWN-PAYMENT
	    ASSET-COST
	
	RULES:
	1. IF ACQUIRE-BY = PURCHASE
	    THEN FINANCE-IT (calculation)
	2. IF ACQUIRE-BY = LEASE
	    THEN FINANCE-IT =
	    (external calculation)
	3. IF FINANCE-IT IS KNOWN
	    THEN PAYMENT =
	    (external calculation)
	
	GOAL:
	FINANCE-IT

struments, Inc. The knowledge base analyzes the problem of buying or leasing an asset. Once a buy or lease conclusion has been reached, the knowledge base determines the best financing method for the acquisition of the asset. The consultation process involves three goal parameters ordered as follows:

$$\text{HOW-TO-ACQUIRE} \implies \text{PAYMENT} \implies \text{FINANCE-IT}$$

"HOW-TO-ACQUIRE" represents the "buy or lease" decision option, "PAYMENT" represents the installment payment needed to acquire the asset, and "FINANCE-IT" represents the finance method appropriate for the particular scenario of the client. It seems logical to organize the knowledge base rules into frames according to their relationships with the goal parameters. As shown in the table, rules relevant to "HOW-TO-ACQUIRE" and "PAYMENT" are located in the root frame while rules relevant to "FINANCE-IT" are in the subframe. When dealing with large knowledge bases, it is helpful to have an analytical tool for investigating the relationships and logical groupings of the knowledge elements. Frames facilitate such an efficient organization.

5.2.3 Scripts

Script is a knowledge representation technique suggested by Schank (Schank and Childers 1984). Scripts are a special form of frames. A script describes a stereotyped sequence of events in a particular context. It presents the expected sequence of events and their associated information in a linked time-based series of frames. For example, the frame discussed previously for gear production may be linked to other frames which contain detailed information on the cutting operation in the time sequence of events in the production schedule. Details of script representation are presented by Schank and Abelson (1977), Minsky (1975), Kuipers (1975), and Hayes (1979). The components of a script include the following:

(1). *Entry conditions:* Conditions for entering the script.

(2). *Results:* Outcomes that are expected after the events described in the script have occurred.

(3). *Props:* Slots representing objects in the script. Recall that a script is a collection of frames where each frame is associated with a certain object.

(4). *Roles:* Slots representing entities (e.g. people) that perform the actions specified in the script.

(5). *Track:* Specific case of a general pattern that is represented by a specific script. For example, at a professional conference, several "tracks" of technical presentations are conducted simultaneously under the general theme of the conference.

(6). *Scenes:* Actual sequences of events that occur. Typical scenes at a professional conference might be registration, selection of sessions to attend, attendance at the sessions, and adjournment.

5.2.4   Rules

Rules are the most popular and versatile of all the representation schemes. Rules provide a formal way of representing recommendations, directives, or strategies. *If-Then* rules link antecedents to their associated consequents. Rules are appropriate for a variety of expert systems problem domains. The if-then structure of rules link pairs of objects or attributes as shown below:

> IF *premise*, THEN *conclusion*.
> IF *input*, THEN *output*.
> IF *condition*, THEN *action*.
> IF *antecedent*, THEN *consequent*.
> IF *data*, THEN *outcome*.
> IF *action*, THEN *goal*.

Premise refers to the fact that must be true before a certain conclusion can be drawn. Input refers to the data that must be available before a certain output can be obtained. Condition refers to circumstances that must prevail before a certain action can be taken. Antecedent refers to the situation that must occur before a certain consequence can be observed. Action refers to the activities that must be undertaken before a certain outcome can be expected. Note that the "action" which is an antecedent in this particular case was generated as a consequent from a condition/action pair. Data refers to the information that must be available before a certain goal can be realized. In subsequent discussions, the terms premise, condition, and antecedent are used interchangeably.

The antecedent typically contains several clauses linked by the logical connectives AND and OR. The consequent consists of one or more phrases that specify the action to be taken. Advantages of rules are:

(1). They are flexible in that individual rules can be easily added, removed, or updated.
(2). They provide a straight-forward representation of knowledge that is easy to interpret.
(3). They are structured in a way similar to the way people rationalize to solve problems.
(4). They are useful for representing the interaction between declarative and procedural knowledge.

The major disadvantage of rules is the requirement for a very efficient search mechanism for finding appropriate rules during an expert system consultation. An example of a rule that might be used in the gear production example is:

Antecedent

IF thickness for any tooth is large and circular pitch is small and face width is medium

Consequent

THEN production method is cutting

Rules can be classified into two categories: first-order rules and meta rules (higher-order). A first-order rule is a simple rule consisting of antecedents and consequents. A meta rule is a rule whose antecedents and consequents contain information about other rules. Examples are given below:

First-order rule:

IF node *j* is inactive and arc *i* has a reliability < 0.9
THEN set (1,n) connectedness $= 0$

Meta rule:

IF arc *k* has a failure rate similar to arc *m*
AND arc *k* uses rule *R1*
THEN activate rule *R1*

A familiar example of a meta rule is the popular office sign which reads:

Rule Number One

The boss is always right

Rule Number Two

IF the boss is wrong
THEN refer to rule Number One

Rules are versatile and widely applicable for representing knowledge in a variety of problem domains. However, there are certain unique problem domains where rules may not be readily applicable. Pattern recognition or machine vision are two problem domains where rules might be difficult to apply. Machine vision problems lend themselves to solutions using frames and scripts or other related techniques. Rules might be used during a postprocessing part after enough features have been extracted from a particular vision scenario.

5.2.5 Predicate Logic

Propositional calculus is an elementary system of formal logic that is used to determine whether a given proposition is true or false. Predicate calculus adds the capability of specifying relationships and making generalizations about propositions. Logical expressions use predicate calculus to generate inferences by asserting the truthfulness or otherwise of propositional statements. Adding functions and other analytical features to predicate calculus creates first-order predicate calculus. A function is a logical construct that yields a value. For example, when a function defined as "*is-made-by*" is applied to the object gear, the result might be "*machining.*" That is,

(IS-MADE-BY (GEAR MACHINING)).

The statement, "Gear is-a machined part" is a statement that is either true or not-true in the context of the problem being addressed. Many forms of logic have been developed for use within AI. Propositional calculus, predicate calculus, first-order logic, modal logic, temporal logic, and fuzzy logic are just a few of the prevailing logic forms. First-order logic, an extension of predicate logic is, perhaps, the most commonly used. A predicate symbol expresses a statement about individual elements, either singly or in relation to other elements. A function symbol expresses a mapping from one element or a group of elements to another element. For example, in the formula below, the predicate (noun) PRODUCT denotes a relationship between three arguments: a particular class of item, material, and shape.

Product (Shaft, Metal, Cylindrical)

The predicate will return a value of "true" if a given item matches the description of a cylindrical metal shaft. Similarly, the function symbol "use" in the formula below maps metal shafts to a particular usage category.

Product (Shaft, Metal, Use (Crankshaft))

If "crankshaft" is used as the argument in the function "use," the function will, most probably, return the value "cylindrical" since most crankshafts are cylindrical in shape. The value "cylindrical" is then used by the predicate "Product" to identify a specific type of product. Subsets of product types can be formed, for example, by further classifying cylindrical metal shafts into diameter size categories. Thus, product inheritance relationships can be represented by considering the predicate "part-of" as shown in the formula below:

$$\{\textbf{PART-OF } (x,y)\} \cap \{\textbf{PART-OF } (y,z)\} = \textbf{PART-OF } (x,z)$$

Predicate logic relies on the truth and rules of inferences to represent symbols and their relationships to each other. It can be used to determine the truthfulness or falsity of a statement and can also be used to represent statements about specific objects or individuals. The advantages of predicate logic include:

(1). Simplicity of notation allows descriptions to be readily understandable.
(2). Modularity allows statements to be added, deleted, or modified without affecting other statements in the knowledge base.
(3). Conciseness is an advantage because each fact has to be represented only once.
(4). Theorem-proving techniques can be used to derive new facts from old ones.

Predicate logic is best used in domains of concise and unified theories such as physics, chemistry, and other mathematical or theoretical fields. The disadvantages of predicate logic are:

(1). Difficulty in representing procedural and heuristic knowledge.

(2). Difficulty in managing large knowledge bases due to restricted organizational structure.

(3). Limited data manipulation procedures.

5.2.6   O-A-V Triplets

An O-A-V Triplet is a common type of semantic network commonly used within the framework of other representation models. It is divided into three parts: *Object*, *Attribute*, and *Value*. The representation presents a serial list of an object and an attribute of interest. Objects are viewed as physical or conceptual entities. Attributes are general properties defining the Object, while the Values indicate the specific descriptions of the Attribute. Using a segment of the semantic network presented earlier in Figure 5.1, an example of O-A-V triplet for the gear production problem is:

Object	Attribute	Value
Gear	Number of Teeth	20

O-A-V representation is used within the framework of other representation techniques. For example, in semantic network, each object may have an attribute of interest identified and the associated value of the attribute may be used in determining further links within the network structure.

5.2.7   Hybrids

Each knowledge representation technique has its advantages and disadvantages. For example, rules are especially useful for representing procedural knowledge (methods for accomplishing goals). Semantic networks are good for representing relations among objects. Frame-based semantic networks can concisely store a large amount of knowledge about object properties and relations. Predicate logic provides a means for explicitly expressing different types of knowledge. Early expert systems tended to use one technique or another exclusively. More recently the tendency has been to combine different representation techniques, so as to take advantage of the capabilities of each technique within the context of the prevailing problem. A system might use rules to define procedures for discovering attributes of objects, semantic networks to define the relationships among the objects referenced in the rules, and frames to describe the objects' typical attributes. The frame example presented earlier in Table 5.1 is a good example of combining rule and frame representations.

5.2.8 Specialized Representation Techniques

Specialized representation techniques are sometimes needed to address the unique characteristics of certain problem domains. The specialized approaches may be needed to take advantage of specific search strategies. For example, Badiru (1987a) presents a Cantor set representational technique described below:

5.2.8.1 Cantor Set Model for Knowledge Representation: The Cantor set (Sagan 1974) is often referred to as the "set of the excluded middle thirds." A unique property of the Cantor set is that it contains an infinite number of elements, but its representative points occupy no space, in the geometric sense, on the real number line. The concept of excluded middle thirds may have relevance in certain problem domains requiring specialized search strategies. These are domains where associative property inheritance relationships exist among the elements of the knowledge base such that the elements can be stored in an ordered fashion using a key property. Examples of such domains are:

(1). Computer-Aided Design (CAD): Knowledge bases where design elements are stored by some design characteristic. For example, drive shaft designs that are stored in order of shaft diameters and bending stresses.
(2). Group Technology: Group technology and process planning applications where items are grouped into product families in a predetermined sequence.
(3). Chemical Analysis: Knowledge bases where materials are stored in order of some key property, say atomic weight or electrical conductivity. Experimental searches for materials properties is a suitable application for Cantor set search approach.

Mathematically, the Cantor set is denoted as:

$$C = \left\{ x \in \Omega \mid x \in \bigcup_{k=0}^{\infty} \delta_k \right\}$$

where $\Omega = [0,1]$. The interval, δ_k, is as explained below:
Consider the closed interval $\Omega = [0,1]$ and the open intervals generated by successive removal of the middle thirds of intervals left after previous removals. The interval deletions are shown geometrically in Figure 5.3. Note that:

$$\bigcup_{k=0}^{\infty} \delta_k = [0,1]$$

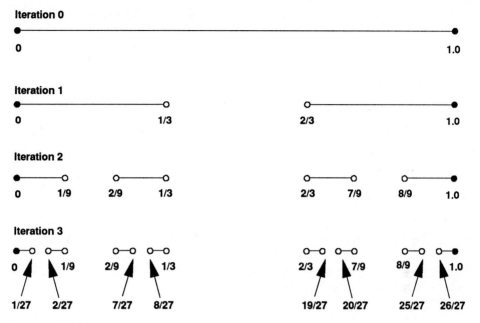

Figure 5.3. Cantor set representation

The interval δ_k is the union of the intervals deleted from Ω after the kth search iteration. The deleted intervals are represented mathematically below:

$$\delta_0 = \phi \; (\textit{null set})$$

$$\delta_1 = \left[\frac{1}{3}, \frac{2}{3} \right] \longrightarrow \text{deleted interval range}$$

$$\delta_2 = \left[\frac{1}{9}, \frac{2}{9} \right] \cup \left[\frac{1}{3}, \frac{2}{3} \right] \cup \left[\frac{7}{9}, \frac{8}{9} \right]$$

- i.e, the more intelligent the search is, what you
- add to the Union becomes smaller & smaller.
-

If Ω is considered as the universal set, then we may also express the Cantor set as the complement of the original set C. That is, alternately,

$$C = \left(\bigcup_{k=0}^{\infty} \delta_k \right)^c,$$

which, by DeMorgan's Law, implies

$$C = \bigcap_{k=0}^{\infty} (\delta_k)^c.$$

If we use the following simplifying notation for the complement,

$\lambda_k =$ Remaining Search Space $(\delta_k)^c = \lambda_k,$

we would obtain the following alternate representation:

$$C = \bigcap_{k=0}^{\infty} \lambda_k,$$

where

$$\lambda_0 = [\ 0, \ 1\ ]$$

$$\lambda_1 = \left[\ 0, \ \frac{1}{3}\ \right) \cup \left(\ \frac{2}{3}, \ 1\ \right]$$

$$\lambda_2 = \left[\ 0, \ \frac{1}{9}\ \right) \cup \left(\ \frac{2}{9}, \ \frac{1}{3}\ \right) \cup \left(\ \frac{2}{3}, \ \frac{7}{9}\ \right) \cup \left(\ \frac{8}{9}, \ 1\ \right]$$

.

.

.

It should be noted that λ_k is the remaining search space available for the kth search iteration. Also note that λ_k consists of 2^k closed and nonoverlapping intervals each of real length $(1/3^k)$.

5.2.8.2 Application of the Cantor Set Approach: Knowledge bases for expert systems consist of pieces of information on the basis of which inferences are drawn for a particular problem situation. For large domain problems, the knowledge base "lookup" or search can easily lead to a combinatorial explosion of possibilities. For example, if we have 50 pieces of evidence each of which is either true or false, then there are 2^{50} possible combinations. From a practical point of view, we need search procedures that can considerably reduce the dimensionality of the search space.

In a manufacturing context, two physical objects are exactly alike only if they are fully interchangeable. In an actual manufacturing situation, items in a group will not necessarily have characteristics that are fully identical. Recalling the earlier example of shafts, a group of objects may consist of items that are related by their classification as "shafts." Differences within the group may pertain to the items' diameters or any other characteristic of interest. For example, we may be interested in diameters that range from 3 inches to 7 inches. Arranging shaft designs in increasing or decreasing order of shaft diameter can be used to indicate the degree of relationship or the level of property inheritance of the items in the group. Thus, in a knowledge base, inferences can be drawn to relate to certain subsets of a given set of the knowledge elements. Graphically, the shaft example may be represented as shown in Figure 5.4.

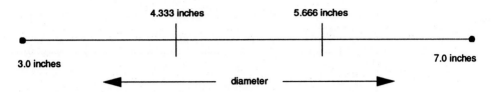

Figure 5.4. Range of shaft diameters as a search space

Suppose we are interested in a shaft that meets a certain quality characteristic. We can conduct an exhaustive search to check if each shaft meets the desired quality characteristic. But exhaustive searches are very costly and time consuming particularly where we have a large number of items to search. An efficient search strategy would be helpful in reducing the time and expense of finding the item that meets the specified characteristic. Suppose we know the distribution of the shaft diameters over the range of 3 inches to 7 inches. If the distribution can be reasonably expected to follow a bell-shaped curve such as the normal distribution shown in Figure 5.5, then the Cantor set strategy may be employed. The search strategy would proceed as shown below:

Step 1: Identify a known property of the items to be searched (e.g., diameter sizes).

Step 2: Determine the range of values of the known property. This establishes the search space.

Step 3: Specify the desired characteristic of the item to be searched (e.g., quality characteristic).

Anquis Thesis. (About Search Space)

Figure 5.5. Bell-shaped curve model for Cantor search strategy (if database organized correctly).

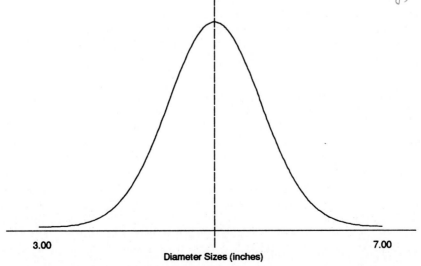

Diameter Sizes (inches)

Step 4: Determine the distribution of the items based on the known property (e.g., bell-shaped).

Step 5: Sort the items in increasing or decreasing order of the known property.

Step 6: Apply the Cantor set search procedure iteratively until an item matching the specified characteristic is found.

Instead of conducting an exhaustive search over the entire search interval, we would check the middle third first. If the item that meets the requirement is not found in that interval, we would delete the interval from further consideration. The middle thirds of the remaining intervals are then searched in successive iterations.

COMMENTS ON THE SEARCH PROCEDURE

(1). If the distribution of the items is bell-shaped, then searching the first middle third before any other interval is logical since that is where the majority of the items are located.

(2). The largest search effort will involve the first middle third. The search process becomes less efficient as more iterations are needed to find the desired item.

(3). In the second and subsequent iterations, a decision must be made concerning which middle third interval to search next. For example, Figure 5.6 shows the search space left after deleting the first middle third. We have the option of first searching the middle third of Interval A and then the middle third of Interval B and vice versa. Since the intervals are equally likely to contain the desired item, one can flip a coin to determine which interval to search first. The decision becomes more difficult in the third iteration since, as shown in Figure 5.7, the remaining four intervals are not equi-probable. Figure 5.8 shows the search intervals for the first three iterations of the Cantor search strategy.

In the Cantor search procedure, the desired item is found only when it is located in the middle third of some interval. If the value of interest is in the interval (4.333, 5.666), then only one interval search would be needed to find it. If it is in

Figure 5.6. Search space for the second iteration of Cantor search

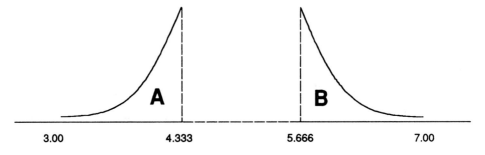

| 3.00 | 4.333 | 5.666 | 7.00 |

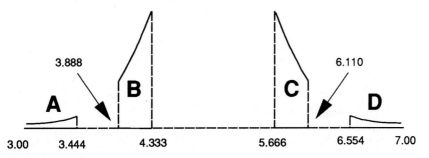

Figure 5.7. Search space for the third iteration of Cantor search

the interval (3.444, 3.888) ∪ (6.110, 6.554), then at most three interval searches would be needed. If the value is in the interval (3.148, 3.296) ∪ (4.036, 4.184) ∪ (5.814, 5.962) ∪ (6.702, 6.85), then at most seven interval searches would be needed. In general, the maximum number of interval searches, N, needed to locate an item in a Cantor set search strategy is one of the following:

$$N_k = 1, 3, 7, 15, 31, \ldots,$$

where k is the iteration number. That is,

$$N_0 = 0$$

No search in the First interval.
at all

$$N_k = N_{k-1} + 2^{k-1}$$

(Kth Interval)

$$= \sum_{j=0}^{k-1} 2^j$$

$$= (2^k) - 1$$

Figure 5.8. Successive search iterations

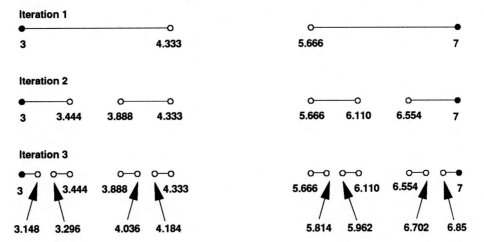

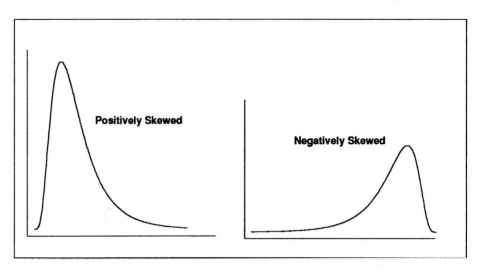

Figure 5.9. Skewed distributions not suitable for Cantor search

It should be noted that if the distribution of the items to be searched is skewed to the right or left (e.g., chi-squared or lognormal distributions), as shown in Figure 5.9, then the basic Cantor set search strategy would not be appropriate.

5.2.8.3   Modified Search Procedure: The deficiency mentioned in the third comment on the Cantor search procedure can be overcome by using the following modification of the procedure. The modification improves the efficiency of the search strategy.

Consider the search intervals to be used for the second iteration (shown earlier in Figure 5.6). Instead of considering the intervals [3.00, 4.333] and [5.666, 7.00] as separate search intervals, we can merge the intervals as shown in Figure 5.10. Then, the next middle third to be searched during the second iteration would be [3.89, 6.11]. Recall that the items in the interval [4.333, 5.666] have already been deleted in the first iteration and are not contained within the modified middle third interval of [3.89, 6.11]. This process is repeated consecutively until the desired item is found. Figure 5.11 shows the search interval for the third iteration using the merged interval modification.

5.2.8.4   Alternate Search Preference: The conventional Cantor set search strategy gives first preference to the middle third of the ordered set of items to be searched. As mentioned previously, this is suitable if the distribution of the property of interest is bell-shaped. If, by contrast, the distribution is bimodal "end-heavy," then an alternate ordering of the items may be required. An example of a bimodal end-heavy distribution is shown in Figure 5.12, which is representative of typical hazard functions in product reliability analysis. The bathtub shaped distribution is a special form of the beta distribution with shape parameters of $\alpha = 0.001$ and $\beta = 0.001$.

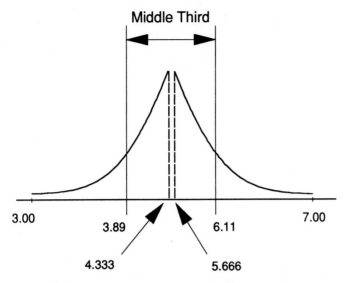

Figure 5.10. Merged search intervals for the second iteration

It is noted that most of the items to be searched are located in the regions close to the minimum and maximum points. An alternate arrangement of the items is achieved by bisecting the ordered set through the median and flipping over the half-sets generated. This is shown graphically in Figure 5.13. This alternate arrangement gives first preference to the end points of the original set of the items to be searched.

Figure 5.11. Merged search intervals for the third iteration

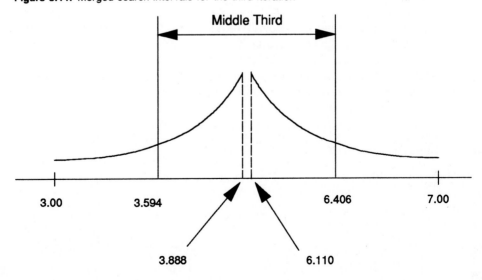

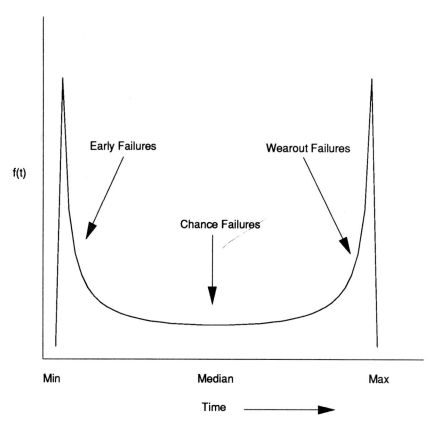

Figure 5.12. Bathtub shaped distribution

5.3 CONCEPT OF KNOWLEDGE SETS

Experts differ in personal cognitive reasoning skills and will follow different patterns of reasoning. The peculiar features of a problem domain are important in determining how the knowledge acquired in the domain should be represented. The organization of medical knowledge, for example, would have certain unique characteristics and requirements compared to the representation of financial management knowledge. Medical information concerning specific patient data may be more dynamic than the information in other problem domains. These differences must be taken into account in organizing knowledge into an efficient form for problem solving.

5.3.1   Properties of Knowledge Sets

Badiru (1987b) presents a collection of concepts based on set theory for organizing elements in expert systems knowledge bases. A knowledge set may be defined as a collection of heuristics or facts that constitute a problem-solving technique. Specific distinguishable contents of the knowledge set are the knowledge ele-

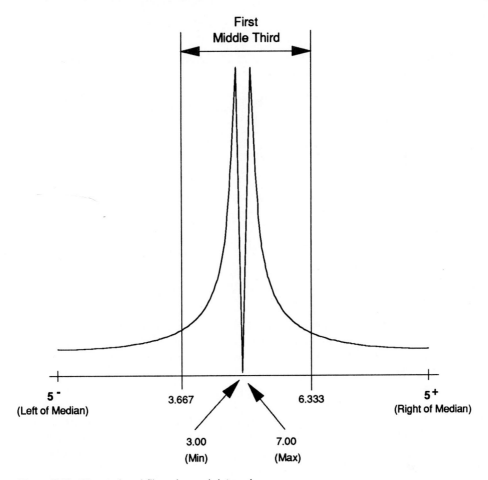

Figure 5.13. Bisected and flipped search interval

ments. When the knowledge set is applied to a specific problem domain, then we have what is referred to as a knowledge base. Presented below are some set properties defined in the context of knowledge base organization.

EQUIVALENT KNOWLEDGE BASES   Two knowledge bases A and B are equivalent if and only if they both yield the same consultation result for the same problem scenario. That is:

$$A \equiv B$$

As shown in Figure 5.14, the two knowledge bases, KB1 and KB2, are equivalent if they both yield the same conclusion, X, for the same given set of data. An evaluation of the equivalence of knowledge bases may be useful in a comparative analysis of competing products that are designed to solve the same problem with comparable performance.

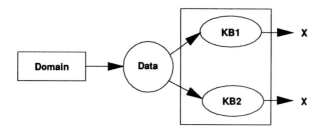

Figure 5.14. Equivalent knowledge bases

EQUALITY OF KNOWLEDGE BASES   Knowledge bases A and B are equal if and only if they contain identical knowledge elements. That is:

$$A = B \ni \forall x \in A, x \in B$$

and

$$B = A \ni \forall x \in B, x \in A$$

Figure 5.15 shows the equality of two knowledge base sets. If A is equal to B, then an element x belonging to A implies that B also contains x. Knowledge bases that are equal are not necessarily equivalent since different organizations of the knowledge elements can lead to different reasoning paths and, thus, yield different results.

SUBJUGATION OF KNOWLEDGE SETS   Let A and B be knowledge bases. If every rule element of A is a rule element of B, then A is a subset of B and B is a superset of A as presented mathematically below and graphically in Figure 5.16.

$$A \subseteq B \ni \forall x \in A \Rightarrow x \in B$$
$$A \subseteq B \ni \forall x \in A, x \in B$$

Figure 5.15. Equality of knowledge bases

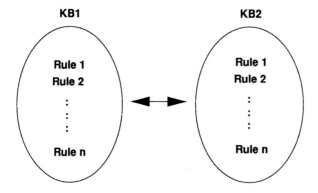

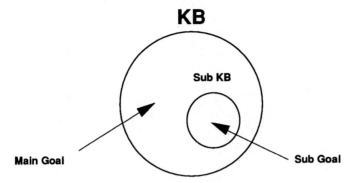

Figure 5.16. Formation of a subset of a knowledge base

A true subset of a knowledge base should solve a subproblem of the main problem that the knowledge base is designed to solve. In terms of expert systems consultation, a subset of a knowledge base is that portion of the knowledge that would yield a subgoal of the main goal. This concept is useful for problem partition purposes. The partitions (or subsets) of a given knowledge base may be used to construct subframes associated with specific subgoals as shown in Figure 5.17. The union of the root frame and subframes make up the entire knowledge base.

Figure 5.17. Partition of problem into subframes

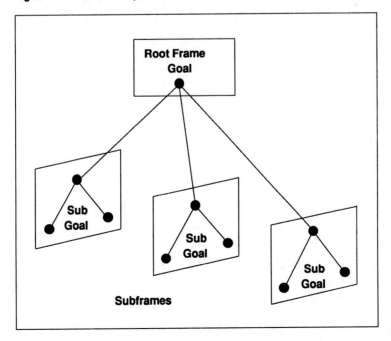

ORDERED PAIRS OF KNOWLEDGE ELEMENTS   Given any two objects a and b, we may form a new object (a,b), called the "ordered pair a,b" with the property that:

$$(a,b) \neq (b,a)$$

Two ordered pairs (a,b) and (c,d) are equal if and only if a=c and b=d. The concept of ordered pairs is useful in the symbolic representation technique of artificial intelligence. For example, the words "down" and "town" can form two distinct ordered pairs of "down town" and "town down". The first pair represents a central location of a geographic area while the second may be viewed as describing the "down" or depressed condition of the geographic region. Obviously,

down-town ≠ town-down.

To further elaborate the concept of ordered knowledge elements in symbolic representation, we may consider the following words: "bills" and "foot". They may symbolically be ordered to yield ordered pairs with two distinct interpretations:

(1). (bills-foot) referring to a part of the body of a person named Bill.

(2). (foot-bills) referring to an action state (i.e., to incur consequential expenses).

Similarly, the TV commercial that says "no salt is sodium free" may be used to illustrate an ordered pair. For example, "(No-Salt) is sodium-free" implies that the product named "no-salt" contains no sodium. By comparison, "No-(Salt) is sodium-free" implies that there is no salt that is sodium-free (i.e. all salts contain sodium). In an analogous manner, the phrase "No news is good news" indicates that there is no news that is good news. Whereas, the phrase "No-news is good news" declares the object "no-news" as being "good news."

CARTESIAN PRODUCTS OF KNOWLEDGE SETS   Let A and B be two knowledge sets. The set of all ordered pairs (a,b), where a and b are specific parameters of objects, with "*a*" belonging to **A** and "*b*" belonging to **B**, is the Cartesian product of **A** and **B** denoted by **AXB**.

$$\mathbf{AXB} = \{(a,b) \,|\, a \in \mathbf{A}, b \in \mathbf{B}\}$$

For example,

Let **A** = {hammer, foot, kick}

and

B = {head, bill, bucket}.

Then,

AXB = {(hammer, head), (hammer, bill), (hammer, bucket), (foot, head), (foot, bill), (foot, bucket), (kick, head), (kick, bill), (kick, bucket)}.

Some of the elements of **AXB** may be combined to obtain symbolic representations that convey different inferences. For example, as discussed in Chapter 2,

$$(\text{hammer-head})\text{-}(\text{kick-bucket})$$

could be the symbolic representation for the statement: "If the victim's head is hammered, then the victim may kick the bucket." Likewise,

$$(\text{kick-head})\text{-}(\text{foot-bill})$$

could symbolically represent the statement: "If victim's head is kicked, the assailant will foot the bill incurred as a result of the injury." We note that the words "head" and "kick" are common to the two representations above. However, the way they are ordered in combination with two other words creates two different meanings.

KNOWLEDGE SET RELATIONS   Given knowledge sets **A** and **B**, not necessarily distinct, a relation **R** from **A** to **B** is a subset of the Cartesian product **AXB**. Thus, an element "a" of **A** is related to another element "b" of **B** by the relation **R**. This relation is written as:

$$a\mathbf{R}b \text{ to indicate that } (a,b) \in \mathbf{R}.$$

The symbol $a\mathbf{R}b$ is read as "a is R-related to b." Several distinct relations can be defined within a given knowledge base. For example, relations may be of "equality", "opposite", "synonym", and so on. If the sets **A** and **B** are the same set, say K, then R is defined as a relation in K instead of a relation from K to K. In a community of people denoted by C, the symbol "(Paul)H(Joan)" may define a relation **H** (of being the husband of . . .) and imply that Paul is the husband of Joan. Thus, we are considering an ordered pair (Paul, Joan) in the relation **H**. The order can be reversed to define a different relation. For example, (Joan)**W**(Paul) defines a relation **W** (of being the wife of . . .) in C. As another illustration of relations, we can define a relation, S, for synonyms with the example of:

$$(\text{Large})\mathbf{S}(\text{Big}).$$

The synonym relation can have useful applications in knowledge base searches since it would permit consultations to proceed successfully on the basis of the instantiation of synonym parameters rather than the specific parameters requested. A relation **R** is said to be *symmetric* if and only if $x\mathbf{R}y$ implies $y\mathbf{R}x$. For example, a brother-to-brother relation. The relations **H** and **W** discussed above are not symmetric. But the **S** relation is symmetric since large is a synonym for big and big is a synonym for large. Here, "big" and "large" represent specific values of an attribute of a given object. The relation **R** is said to be *transitive* if and only if $x\mathbf{R}y$ and $y\mathbf{R}z$ imply that $x\mathbf{R}z$. For example, brother-to-brother-to-brother relations.

    INVERSE RELATIONS Each knowledge base relation, **R**, may have an inverse that is defined as:

$$\mathbf{R}^{-1} = \{(b,a) \mid (a,b) \in \mathbf{R}\}.$$

The inverse relation may be used to obtain parameter negation instead of explicitly reversing parameter values. In a knowledge base, particularly one dealing with natural language applications, it may be necessary to define a relation of synonym as well as an inverse relation of antonym. In quantitative analysis, a relation of "greater-than" and the relation of "less-than" may be of interest. Using the earlier synonym relation as an example, a parameter, P, can be instantiated by any synonym of the word "known" as shown below:

$$P = x \in \{a \mid a\mathbf{S}\text{known}\}.$$

So, any word "x" that is a synonym for "known" can be a suitable value for the instantiation of P. Thus, we have

$$(\text{KNOWN})synonym(\mathrm{x}),$$

where x may be any element in the set of words given by:

A = {available, accessible, handy, ready, within-reach, identified, recognized, specified, understood, asserted, justified, stated, inferred, given, observed, realized}

Instead of defining another parameter value of "unknown" to achieve parameter negation for "known," a generic inverse relation can be used. This is shown mathematically as:

$$P = x \in \{a \mid a\mathbf{S}^{-1}\text{known}\}.$$

Thus, the inverse relation facilitates a compact representation of a large body of knowledge. The major advantage of the inverse relation is that a single relation can be applied generally across various parameters within a given knowledge base.

DOMAIN OF KNOWLEDGE SET RELATIONS   If **R** is a relation from set **A** to set **B**, then the domain of **R** is the set of all parameter "a" belonging to A such that aRb for some parameter b belonging to **B**. That is,

$$\text{Dom}(\mathbf{R}) = \{a \in \mathbf{A} \mid (a,b) \in \mathbf{R} \text{ for some } b \in \mathbf{B}\}.$$

As an example, consider the two frames in Figure 5.18. Let Frame **A** contain the subgoals $a1$, $a2$, $a3$, $a4$, $a5$ while Frame **B** contains the subgoals $b1$, $b2$, $b3$, $b4$, $b5$, $b6$, $b7$, $b8$. Define a relation **Z** from **A** to **B** such that an element a belonging to **A** is related to an element b belonging to **B** if and only if there is a rule in **B** that has a as a premise and b as a conclusion.

Now suppose only the following rules exist in frame **B**:

If $a1$ Then $b2$

If $a2$ Then $b5$

If $a3$ Then $b6$.

The domain of **Z** is then given by the set:

$$\text{Dom}(\mathbf{Z}) = \{a1, a2, a3\},$$

since the elements $a1$, $a2$, and $a3$ are the only elements of **A** that can successfully trigger rules in **B**. The image of the relation, **R**, is defined as:

$$\text{Im}(\mathbf{R}) = \{b \in \mathbf{B} \mid (a,b) \in \mathbf{R} \text{ for some } a \in \mathbf{A}\}.$$

Thus, the image of the relation **Z** is:

$$\text{Im}(\mathbf{Z}) = \{b2, b5, b6\}$$

Figure 5.18. Relations on knowledge base sets

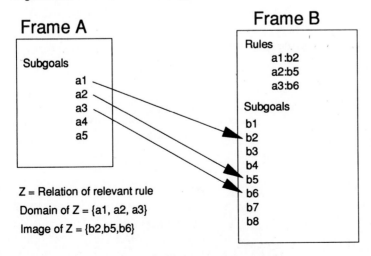

which corresponds to the set of rules that are triggered in Frame **B**. A special kind of relation on knowledge sets is parameter mapping in which there is one-to-one correspondence between parameters in knowledge subsets. An example of parameter mapping is shown in Figure 5.19. An identification of the specific correspondence between parameters in the subsets of a knowledge can lead to a better control of the inference process. For example, in Figure 5.19, parameter j is known to be capable of producing only subgoal i.

IDENTITY RELATIONS ON PARAMETERS An identity relation in a knowledge base is a relation that relates every knowledge element with itself such that:

$$\mathbf{R} = \{(a,a) \mid a \in \mathbf{A}\}.$$

This is referred to as the *reflexive* property of the relation **R**. For example, a relation defined as **DIVISION-BY-ONE** will preserve the characteristics of any given element to which it is applied. For example,

$$\mathbf{DIVISION\text{-}BY\text{-}ONE}(argument) = argument.$$

By contrast, a relation defined as **SQUARE** is not a reflexive relation since it does not preserve the characteristics of all the arguments to which it is applied.

BINARY OPERATIONS ON KNOWLEDGE SETS A binary operation on a knowledge set, S, is a function from the Cartesian square SXS to S. That is, an operation that uses an ordered pair from SXS to produce another element of S. For example, let S be the set of groups of words in a knowledge base dictionary. An operation may be defined for the process of forming natural language statements (or new groups of words) in the set. The new groups of words belong to the original set of words.

MAPPING OF KNOWLEDGE SETS If the set **C** is a subset of the Cartesian product, **AXB**, of the knowledge sets **A** and **B**, then **C** is a mapping from **A** to **B** such

Figure 5.19. Parameter mapping in knowledge base frames

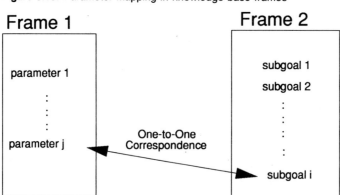

that for each *a* belonging to **A** there is exactly one *b* belonging to **B** for which (*a,b*) belong to **C**. In other words, the mapping, **C**, is the collection of the elements of **AXB** that have one-to-one correspondence with the elements of **A** and **B**. The elements of the sets **A**, **B**, and **C** are specific parameters of objects contained in the knowledge base of interest.

In the example presented earlier, **C** = **AXB** since each element *a* of **A**, in combination with each element *b* of **B**, yields a unique (distinct) ordered pair of words. In the experiment of tossing two fair dice and observing the sum of the faces that show, only two of the 36 elements of the sample space can form a mapping. The element "sum=2" can be obtained in only one way (1+1) while the element "sum=12" can be obtained also in only one way (6+6). The other number combinations produce sums that are not unique. For example, 1+2=3 and 2+1=3. An understanding of the mapping of parameters is quite useful in the organization of parameter data for knowledge base construction. The knowledge engineer can analyze and identify what combination of parameters produce which instantiations. Thus, redundancy can be identified and eliminated.

INTERSECTION OF KNOWLEDGE SETS Successful parameter instantiation can occur only in the intersection of the domain, knowledge, and data sets. This intersection is not the same as in the physical sense of conventional sets. It is a conceptual intersection which relates to which data fits which problem situation and the contents of the knowledge base. This is shown graphically in Figure 5.20. Set **A** is the set of all available parameters in the knowledge base rules, set **B** is the set of problem domain parameters, and set **C** is the set of all parameters in the available data.

Figure 5.20. Intersection of domain, knowledge, and data sets

Entire Set of Rules   **Entire Problem Domain**

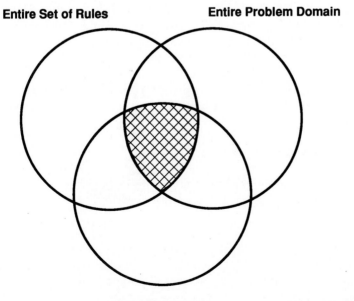

Entire Set of Data

It is obvious that not all available rules will match the problem domain and the available data simultaneously. To reduce the processing time for expert systems consultation, the minimum most applicable set of knowledge base should be used. This minimum set can be identified by finding the conceptual "intersection" of the three sets **A**, **B**, and **C**. There is a tendency to measure the robustness of an expert system by the number of rules it contains. But a close and careful review may reveal that a large percentage of the rules included in a knowledge base are irrelevant for the type or amount of data available.

INTEGRATION OF SET CONCEPTS   As expert systems and artificial intelligence products find their ways into various areas of applications, the need to make those products more compact and efficient will become a major concern. Many researchers are now beginning to address the problems associated with the shortcomings of the present systems. An integration of the set concepts presented in the preceding sections should be applicable to the solution of the prevailing problems in knowledge base organization.

5.4 REASONING MODELS

Once problem solving knowledge has been identified, the way it is encoded for drawing inferences depends on the reasoning approach desired for the chosen problem domain. The search strategy, inference process, and control structure are all important for knowledge representation purposes. The structure of the problems in some domains will dictate which reasoning approach would be most applicable or effective. *Reasoning* is the process of drawing inferences from known or assumed facts. An *inference* is the logical conclusion or implication based on available information. Sometimes, it is possible to draw an inference based on *intuition*. In such a case, one reaches a conclusion without a conscious use of reasoning. Presented below are some important concepts and models for drawing inferences during expert systems consultation.

DEDUCTIVE REASONING   This is the process of reasoning from general information about a class of objects or events to specific information about a given member of the class.

INDUCTIVE REASONING   In inductive reasoning, one draws a general conclusion based on specific facts. For example, the specific information about individual members of a class of objects or events may lead to a general conjecture about the whole class.

MONOTONIC REASONING   This involves a unidirectional parameter instantiation. Parameter instantiation refers to the assignment of a specific value to a parameter. In monotonic reasoning, parameter instantiation is irrevocable regardless of whatever new information may become available. For example, the statement,

Once a thief, always a thief

conveys the notion of monotonic reasoning. The observer's view of a thief never changes regardless of any new information that may indicate the rehabilitation of the thief.

NONMONOTONIC REASONING   In nonmonotonic reasoning, parameters can be reinstantiated if new information warrants the assignment of a new value to the parameter.

FORWARD CHAINING   Forward chaining is the process of reasoning forward from a given set of data to some possibly remote goal state or conclusion. It is also commonly known as *forward reasoning* or *data-driven search*. Forward chaining is generally of the heuristic form:

IF (data condition),
THEN (conclusion).

If we can assume that people normally like those that they trust, then a forward chaining rule to convey that assumption is:

IF *person x* trusts *person y*,
THEN *person x* likes *person y*.

The conclusion part of a rule may become the condition part of another rule. Thus, we can extend the above example to the one below:

IF *person x* likes *person y*,
THEN *person x* enjoys-the-company-of *person y*.

BACKWARD CHAINING   In backward chaining, the reasoning process starts from a goal state and backtracks to the paths that might have led to the goal. It is also called *backward reasoning* or *goal-driven search*. Backward chaining is generally of the form:

Goal State,
IF (data condition).

A backward chaining rule based on the previous example is:

person x likes *person y*,
IF *person x* trusts *person y*.

This example asserts that liking someone requires a precondition of trust. As discussed below, such an assertion may not be precise. If, for example, only eighty percent of the population falls in the category of the rule assertion, then we could assign some level of certainty or confidence to the rule. Then the rule might be stated as:

person x likes *person y,*

IF *person x* trusts *person y* (Certainty Factor = 0.80).

Backward chaining is often implemented in expert systems in the coding format of a forward chaining rule. In that case, the goal is specified in the antecedent of the rule and the condition leading to the goal is specified in the conclusion part of the rule. For the example of interpersonal relationship, the backward chaining rule can be written as:

IF *person x* is-to-like *person y,*

THEN *person x* must-trust *person y.*

BREADTH-FIRST SEARCH The process of drawing inferences using an expert system knowledge base involves searching for parameters and values that match certain conditions. In breadth-first search, all the available premises at a decision node are evaluated before going into the deeper details of each premise. Figure 5.21 shows an example of a breadth-first search. All the branches at each decision node are evaluated before selecting the branch to follow for the next search. The breadth-first search generates all nodes in the search tree at level k before investigating the nodes at level $k+1$. The complexity of the search process is, thus, a function of the number of nodes investigated.

Since the procedure exhaustively investigates the branches at each level before proceeding to the next lower level, breadth-first search will always find the search path of shortest length. Thus, if search path length is the basis for evaluating the efficiency of the search, then breadth-first search is optimal. However, it is time-consuming and sometimes impractical particularly if the goal state is located deep in the search tree and there are many branches at each node. If the search tree has X branches at each node and there are Y levels in the tree, then there are X^Y alternate paths to be investigated. However, not all searches will go to the same depth and not all nodes will have the same number of branches. So, it is necessary to develop some aggregate measure of branches and levels to determine the number of alternate paths to be investigated. This is left as an exercise for the reader (see Questions at the end of this chapter).

DEPTH-FIRST SEARCH Depth-first search involves the evaluation of all the ramifications of each premise before going to the next one. This is shown in Figure 5.22. An important aspect of depth-first search is that it only requires keeping track of the current path. Consequently, storage and memory requirements to perform a depth-first search are less than for a breadth-first search. For this reason, depth-first search is often preferred to breadth-first search. An advantage of breadth-first search is that if a solution path exists and there are a finite number of branches in the search tree, then there is a guarantee that the solution would be found.

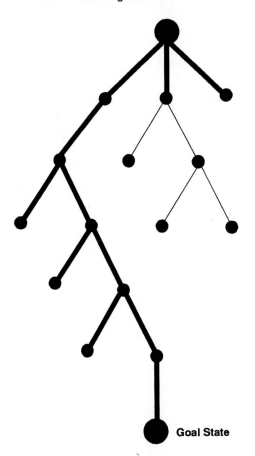

→ Can go three
Ways to Start with

Figure 5.21. Breadth-first search

An example of the comparison of depth-first search to breadth-first search may be drawn from the screening of job applicants. Under breadth-first search, all the applicants are broadly reviewed before deciding whom to invite for interview. Whereas, under depth-first search, the first applicant is reviewed, interviewed, and evaluated before considering other applicants.

MODUS PONENS   Modus ponens is one of the most common inference strategies in knowledge-based systems. This is a logical reasoning that states that when the premise of a rule is known to be true, then it is valid to believe that the conclusion is true. For example, modus ponens allows us to reach the conclusion about B as shown below:

Given Rule: If A is true then B is true.

Known Fact: A is true.

Valid conclusion: B is true.

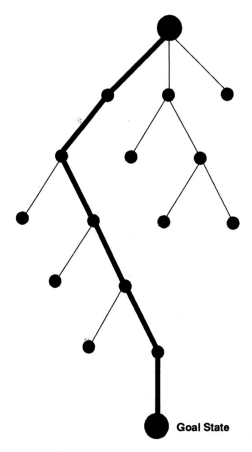

Goal State

Figure 5.22. Depth-first search

Test Quest

MODUS TOLLENS Modus tollens is the converse of modus ponens. Modus tollens reasoning states that if the premise of a rule must be true for the rule's conclusion to be true, then the falsity of the conclusion implies the falsity of the premise. As an example, consider the rule below:

Given Rule: If SAT-SCORE is-greater-than 1200, then ADMISSION = yes.

Known Fact: ADMISSION = no.

Modus tollens conclusion: SAT-SCORE is-not-greater-than 1200.

As can be seen in the above example, modus tollens reasoning may not necessarily hold in many practical problem scenarios. The fact that ADMISSION=no does not necessarily imply that the applicant did not have an SAT score greater than 1200. Admission might have been denied for other reasons besides SAT score. When it can be shown to be applicable, modus tollens reasoning can be a powerful inference strategy.

BLACKBOARD ARCHITECTURE Blackboard architecture is a special type of knowledge-based system which uses a form of opportunistic reasoning whereby several knowledge sources contribute to the reasoning strategy (see Engelmore and Morgan 1988, Hallam 1990, Nii 1986). The basic characteristics of blackboard architecture are:

(1). There are multiple sources of knowledge willing to contribute to the problem-solving process. Each knowledge source is considered to be an expert in some limited aspect of the problem to be solved. That is, each knowledge source can solve a subset of the overall problem.

(2). The knowledge sources may contain knowledge in the form of procedures, rules, or other knowledge representation schema.

(3). The knowledge sources work collectively to achieve synergism needed to solve the overall problem.

(4). A globally accessible data base structure, the *blackboard*, is available. The blackboard contains information about the current state of the problem being solved. Each knowledge source checks the blackboard to find out what information is required for the next stage of the solution and determines how it may contribute to that next solution step. The knowledge sources make changes to the blackboard data incrementally until the desired solution is reached.

(5). The knowledge sources cannot communicate with each other directly. Communication and interactions between the knowledge sources are accomplished solely through the blackboard.

(6). Control information for the blackboard architecture may be contained within the knowledge sources, on the blackboard itself, or in a separate data base module. The controller monitors the changes to the blackboard and determines the next immediate requirement in the solution process. Figure 5.23 presents the components of the blackboard architecture.

5.5 EXERCISES

5.1 Develop a realistic example problem that can be represented by a Script. For the example, identify the following: Entry Conditions, Results, Props, Roles, Track, and Scenes.

5.2 Develop a semantic network diagram for an engineering design problem indicating the various stages of the design process.

5.3 Refer to the Cantor set representation. Show by induction that C_k consists of 2^k open intervals each of length $(1/3^k)$ where C_k is defined as $\bigcup_{i=1}^{k} \delta_i$.

5.4 Give two examples of reflexive relations that preserve the characteristics of the arguments to which they are applied.

5.5 List five knowledge representation techniques and give an example of each.

5.6 Which search strategy (forward reasoning or backward reasoning) would you recommend for a medical research to find a cure for cancer?

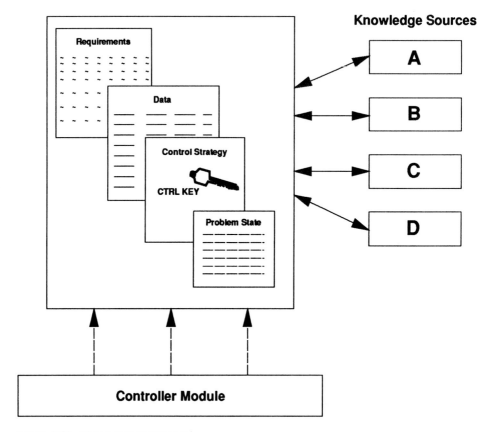

Figure 5.23. Blackboard architecture

5.7 Give an example of a problem domain where knowledge cannot be represented using rules.

5.8 Write three practical examples of rules using modus tollens and explain the implication of the falsity of the conclusions of the rules.

5.9 Give a practical example each for breadth-first search and depth-first search.

5.10 Develop a quantitative measure of the complexity of breadth-first search using the number of branches to be investigated at each node and the number of levels (depth) of nodes in the search tree as the complexity parameters.

5.11 Give examples of problem domains where blackboard architecture would be appropriate.

5.12 Given an initial Cantor search interval of [10, 25] for a bell-shaped distribution, write the sequence for δ_k and λ_k for $k = 0,1,2,3,4$.

5.13 Repeat Question 12, but use the modified Cantor search procedure.

5.14 Describe and use examples to illustrate the differences between flowcharts in conventional programs and semantic networks in expert systems.

5.15 Use examples to distinguish between monotonic reasoning and nonmonotonic reasoning.

5.16 Develop a sensible and logical example that integrates the use of frames and rules in a knowledge base. The example should be such that the parameter values in the condition(s) part of a rule are obtained from an appropriate frame.

5.17 Construct a knowledge base example for the case where rules are embedded in frames.

5.18 Give a practical example of the use of each of the following: metarule, blackboard architecture, and inductive reasoning.

5.19 Discuss why the Cantor set is referred to as the set of "excluded middle thirds."

5.20 Consider the *Flight Attendant Logic Problem* presented below.

Each Friday evening, five flight attendants reunite in Chicago, where each has a short stopover on her east-to-west flight. The following clues are available about the flight attendants.

1. The five attendants are Andrea, Eva, Ms. Norris, the one whose flight originates in Boston, and the attendant whose destination is San Francisco.

2. Betty, Ms. Layton, and the attendant on the flight to Houston all have two-hour stopovers in Chicago.

3. The one on the Cleveland-to-Los Angeles flight is not Eva.

4. Andrea is the attendant on the flight to Seattle.

5. Diane and the attendant on the flight from New York have one-hour stopovers in Chicago.

6. Ms. Kelly is on the flight from Baltimore, which does not end in Houston.

7. Carol is not Ms. Mill.

8. Ms. Jones is not on either the flight originating in Boston or the one from Philadelphia.

9. Betty is not the attendant on the San Francisco flight.

10. One attendant is flying to Denver.

From the clues given, determine each attendant's full name, the city in which her flight originates, and its destination city. Use any appropriate graphical representation technique in the solution procedure. For example, a table similar to the one below may be used.

	Lastnames	Originations	Destinations
First Names			
Destinations			
Originations		*Use X to eliminate infeasible cells*	

5.21 Can you use expert system knowledge representation techniques to solve problem 5.20? If so, do it.

6

Reasoning Under Uncertainty

This chapter presents common techniques for handling uncertainty in expert systems. Expert systems consultations for practical problems often require that some simplifying assumptions be made. The assumptions may involve the elimination of certain parameters, the truncation of certain data sets, or the inclusion of facts that have little bearing on the problem domain. Unfortunately, these simplifying assumptions, coupled with other inherent limitations in the inference process, create uncertainties that complicate our reasoning processes.

6.1 HUMAN REASONING AND PROBABILITY

How human reasoning differs from machine reasoning has been a subject of much research for many years. Humans possess definite advantages over computers when it comes to structural reasoning. Humans have intuitive insight that has, thus far, been difficult to implement in computer-based systems. Uncertainty is a reality in human reasoning and decision making. In many practical situations, it is difficult to have problem conditions that involve certain, complete, and consistent facts. Uncertainty can arise from several sources. For example, the information available may be incomplete, the information may be very volatile, the facts of the decision problem may be unstable, important data may be missing, the problem scenario may be too dynamic, key facts may be imprecise, the problem statement may be too vague, and so on. All of these situations compound the decision-making environment.

Several techniques have been developed to handle uncertainty in decision making. Many of these techniques are now being incorporated into expert systems. Probability analysis appears to be the most natural way to handle uncertainty in expert systems. However, it has certain limitations that make it difficult to implement. Simplified techniques that do not resort to rigorous theoretical basis have been developed as alternatives to probability in handling uncertainty in expert systems.

6.2 THE BAYESIAN APPROACH TO HANDLING UNCERTAINTY

By using probability theory, we can generalize observations about events to arrive at statements about a population of objects or, conversely, from the population to specific events. The Bayesian approach uses Bayes' Theorem for handling uncertainty in the process of drawing inference about objects or events. Bayes' Theorem states:

Let $\{B_1, B_2,..., B_n\}$ be a set of events forming a partition of the sample space S, where $P(B_i) \neq 0$, for i = 1, 2, ..., n. Let A be any event of S such that $P(A) \neq 0$. Then, for k = 1, 2, ..., n, we have

$$P(B_k \mid A) = \frac{P(B_k \cap A)}{\sum_{i=1}^{n} P(B_i \cap A)}$$

$$= \frac{P(B_k)P(A \mid B_k)}{\sum_{i=1}^{n} P(B_i)P(A \mid B_i)}.$$

In Figure 6.1 the shaded area is the event A that we are given and the events labeled B_i are the events about which inferences are to be drawn. Bayes' Theorem allows us to calculate the probability of having an event B_i given that the event A has occurred. Bayes' Rule can be restated in terms of objects and parameters in a knowledge base as discussed earlier under the concepts of knowledge sets.

For example (Liebowitz 1988), if it is known that 2 percent of a population has tuberculosis (T), then we can define the following:

Given *Fact:* $P(T) = 0.02$
Defined Variables: $P(X|T)$, $P(X|Not\text{-}T)$, $P(T|X)$
    $P(X|T)$ = probability that an X-ray of a tubercular person is positive
$P(X|Not\text{-}T)$ = probability that an X-ray of a healthy person is positive
    $P(T|X)$ = probability that a person with a positive X-ray has tuberculosis

Given *Data:* $P(X|T) = 0.90$
        $P(X|Not\text{-}T) = 0.01$

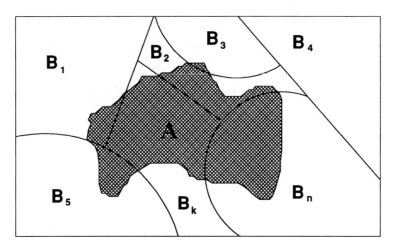

Figure 6.1. Events in a sample space

Required: $P(T|X)$

Using Bayes' Theorem, we can calculate $P(T|X)$ as follows:

$$P(T|X) = \frac{P(T)P(X|T)}{P(T)P(X|T) + P(Not-T)P(X|Not-T)}$$

$$= \frac{(.02)(.90)}{(.02)(.90) + (.98)(.01)}$$

$$= .648$$

While the techniques for applying the probability approach are well developed, there are many reasons why conventional probabilistic analysis has not been very popular in expert systems. Some of these reasons are:

(1). The events that partition the sample space (knowledge base) must be disjoint. This, of course, is not necessarily the case in the reasoning approach that humans use in solving practical problems.

(2). The prior probabilities, $P(A|B_i)$, must be known. Since most heuristic problem-solving methods rely on expert judgment rather than mathematical facts, these prior probabilities are usually not available. Even when they are available, they are often unreliable.

(3). Bayesian reasoning could lead to a combinatorial explosion of the analysis. Since the boundaries of the events leading to a problem solution are usually indeterminate or ambiguous, there is the tendency to over-partition the sample space. This, subsequently, leads to large data requirements and analysis.

(4). Users not familiar with probabilistic statements are likely to misinterpret the results of a probability analysis.

(5). New users are likely to find probability analysis intimidating.

Statistical approaches to reasoning can be optimal from a theoretical perspective. However, practicality often precludes their implementation in expert systems. The probability approach has been used only in a few expert systems. In many cases, simplifying assumptions are made in an attempt to achieve practicality. Unfortunately, such assumptions reduce the power of the probability approach. Presented below are some important relations defined for parameters and assertions in handling uncertainty in expert systems.

LOGICAL RELATIONS   With logical relations (like predicate calculus), the truthfulness of a hypothesis is completely determined by the truthfulness of the assertions defining it. The relations include primitive logical operations of conjunction (AND), disjunction (OR), and negation (NOT). The logical AND is the minimum of the probability values of the component assertions, and the logical OR is the maximum of the probability values of the component assertions.

PLAUSIBLE RELATIONS   Each assertion contributes "weights" for or against the truthfulness of an hypothesis. Each rule has a rule strength associated with it which defines the degree to which a change in the probability of the evidence changes the probability of the hypothesis. The change can be positive or negative and favor or disfavor the hypothesis.

CONTEXTUAL RELATIONS   This relation expresses a condition which must be established before an assertion can be brought into the reasoning process. This is an example of the data-driven approach of forward chaining.

6.3 DECISION TABLES AND TREES

Decision tree analysis is used to evaluate sequential decision problems. In engineering analysis, a decision tree may be useful in evaluating sequential events. A decision problem under certainty has two elements: *action* and *consequence*. The decision maker's choices are the actions while the results of those actions are the consequences. For example, in an activity network planning (Badiru 1991), the choice of one task among three potential tasks in a given time slot represents a potential action. The consequences of choosing one task over another may be characterized in terms of the slack time created in the network, the cost of performing the selected task, the resulting effect on the project completion time, or the degree to which a specified performance criterion is satisfied.

If the decision is made under uncertainty, as in stochastic network analysis, a third element is introduced into the decision problem. This third element is defined as an *event*. If we extend the deterministic task selection process to a stochastic process, the actions may be defined as Select Task 1, Select Task 2, and Select Task 3. The durations associated with the three possible actions can be categorized as "long task duration," "medium task duration," and "short task duration." The actual duration of each task is uncertain. Thus, each task has some probability of exhibiting long, medium, or short durations. The events can be identified as weather incidents: rain or no rain. The incidents of rain or no rain are uncertain. The consequences may be defined as "increased project completion time," "decreased project completion time," and "unchanged project completion time." However, these consequences are uncertain due to the probabilistic durations of the tasks and the variable choices of the decision maker. That is, the consequences are determined partly by choice and partly by chance.

To simplify the decision analysis, the decision elements may be summarized by using a decision table. A decision table indicates the relationship between pairs of decision elements. The decision table for the preceding example is presented in Table 6.1. In the table, each row corresponds to an event and each column corresponds to an action. The consequences appear as entries in the body of the table. The consequences have been coded as I (Increased), D (Decreased), U (Unchanged). Each event-action combination has a specific consequence associated with it. In some decision problems, the consequences may not be unique. Thus, a consequence that is associated with a particular event-action pair may also be associated with another event-action pair. The actions included in the decision table are the only ones that the decision maker wishes to consider. For example, subcontracting or task elimination could be other possible choices for the decision maker. The actions included in the decision problem are mutually exclusive and collectively exhaustive, so that exactly one will be selected. The events are also mutually exclusive and collectively exhaustive.

The decision problem can also be conveniently represented as a decision tree as shown in Figure 6.2. The tree representation is particularly convenient for decision problems with choices that must be made at different times over an extended period. For example, resource allocation decisions must be made several times during the life cycle of an engineering project. The choice of actions is shown as a fork with a separate branch for each action. The events are also represented by branches in separate forks. To avoid confusion, the nodes for action forks are represented by squares while the nodes for event forks are represented by circles. The basic guideline for constructing a tree diagram is that the flow of

Table 6.1. Decision table for task selection

	Actions								
	Task 1			Task 2			Task 3		
Event	Long	Medium	Short	Long	Medium	Short	Long	Medium	Short
Rain	I	I	U	I	U	D	I	I	U
No Rain	I	D	D	U	D	D	U	U	U

I = Increased duration; D = Decreased duration; U = Unchanged duration

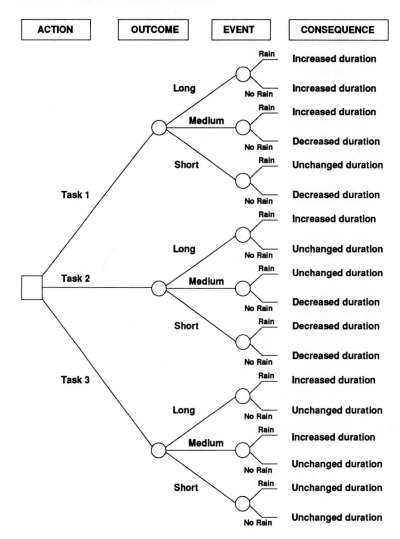

ACTION	OUTCOME	EVENT	CONSEQUENCE

Figure 6.2. Decision tree for task selection

events should be chronological from left to right. The actions are shown on the initial fork because the decision must be made before the actual event is known. The events are, thus, shown as branches in the third-stage forks. The consequence resulting from an event-action combination is shown as the endpoint of the corresponding path from the root of the tree.

Figure 6.2 reveals that there are six paths leading to an increase in the project duration, five paths leading to a decrease in project duration, and seven paths leading to an unchanged project duration. The total number of paths is given by:

$$P = \prod_{i=1}^{N} n_i$$

where
P = total number of paths in the decision tree
N = number of decision stages in the tree
n_i = number of branches emanating from each node in stage i

Thus, for the example in Figure 6.2, the number of paths is $P = (3)(3)(2) = 18$ paths. As mentioned previously, some of the paths, even though they are distinct, lead to identical consequences. Probability values can be incorporated into the decision structure as shown in Figure 6.3. Note that the selection of a task at the decision node is based on choice rather than probability. In this example, it is assumed that the probability of having a particular task duration is independent of whether or not it rains. In some cases, the weather sensitivity of a task may influence the duration of the task. Also, the probability of rain or no rain is independent of any other element in the decision structure.

If the items in the probability tree are interdependent, then the appropriate conditional probabilities would need to be computed. This will be the case if the

Figure 6.3. Decision tree with probability values

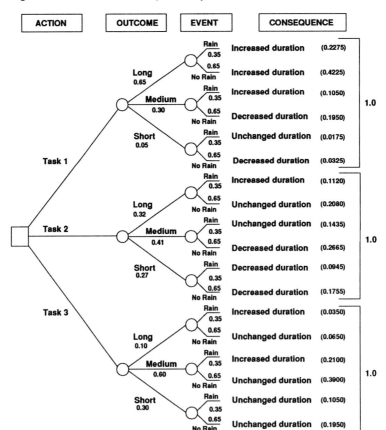

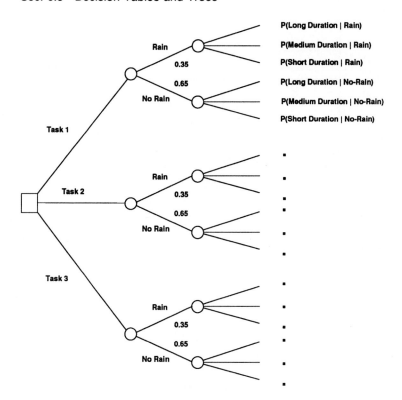

Figure 6.4. Decision tree with conditional probability

duration of a task is influenced by the events "rain" and "no-rain." In such a case, the probability tree should be redrawn as shown in Figure 6.4, which indicates that the weather event will need to be observed first before the task duration event can be determined. For Figure 6.4, the conditional probability of each type of duration, given that it rains or it does not rain, will need to be calculated.

The respective probabilities of the three possible consequences are shown in Figure 6.3. The probability at the end of each path is computed by multiplying the individual probabilities along the path. For example, in Figure 6.3, the probability of having an increased project completion time along the first path (Task 1, Long Duration, and Rain) is calculated as:

$$(0.65)(0.35) = 0.2275.$$

Similarly, the probability for the second path (Task 1, Long duration, and No Rain) is calculated as:

$$(0.65)(0.65) = 0.4225.$$

The sum of the probabilities at the end of the paths associated with each action (choice) is equal to one as expected. Table 6.2 presents a summary of the re-

Consequence	Selected Task		
	Task 1	Task 2	Task 3
Increased Duration	.2275 + .4225 + .105 = 0.755	.112 = 0.112	.035 + .21 = 0.245
Decreased Duration	.195 + .0325 = 0.2275	.2665 + .0945+ .1755 = 0.5365	.0 = 0.0
Unchanged Duration	.0175 = 0.0175	.208 + .1435 = 0.3515	.065 + .39 + .105 + .195 = 0.755
Column Sum	1.0	1.0	1.0

Table 6.2. Probability summary for project completion time

spective probabilities of the three consequences based on the selection of each task. For example, the probability of having an increased project duration when Task 1 is selected is calculated as:

$$Probability = 0.2275 + 0.4225 + 0.105 = 0.755.$$

Likewise, the probability of having an increased project duration when Task 3 is selected is calculated as:

$$Probability = 0.035 + 0.21 = 0.245.$$

If the selection of tasks at the first node is probabilistic in nature, then the respective probabilities would be included in the calculation procedure. For example, Figure 6.5 shows a case where Task 1 is selected 25 percent of the time, Task 2 is selected 45 percent of the time, and Task 3 is selected 30 percent of the time. The resulting end probabilities for the three possible consequences have been revised accordingly. Note that all the probabilities at the end of all the paths add up to one in this case. Table 6.3 presents the summary of the probabilities of the three consequences for the scenario in Figure 6.5. The examples presented above can be extended to other decision problems in engineering and manufacturing that can be represented in terms of decision tables and trees.

6.4 DEMPSTER-SHAFER THEORY

Dempster-Shafer theory is another technique of handling uncertainty in expert systems. The theory attempts to distinguish between ignorance and uncertainty. Ignorance is definitely different from uncertainty and should be treated differ-

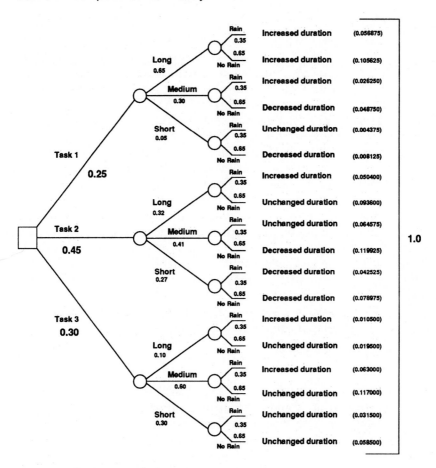

Figure 6.5. Probability distribution for task selection

Table 6.3. Probability summary for Figure 6.5

Consequence	Path Probabilities	Row Total
Increased Duration	0.056875 + 0.105625 + 0.02625 + 0.0504 + 0.0105 + 0.063	0.312650
Decreased Duration	0.04875 + 0.119925 + 0.042525 + 0.078975	0.290175
Unchanged Duration	0.004375 + 0.008125 + 0.0936 + 0.064575 + 0.0195 + 0.117 + 0.0315 + 0.0585	0.397175
	Column Total	1.0

ently. Not knowing the specific value of a variable does not necessarily imply that the variable is subject to uncertainty. With classical probability theory, we are required to consider belief and disbelief as functional opposites. That is, if A, B, and C are the only three events in a sample space (S) and we know that $P(A) = 0.3$ and $P(B) = 0.6$, then classical probability theory would calculate 0.1 as the probability for the event C since $P(S) = 1.0$ and $P(A) + P(B) + P(C) = P(S)$. Unfortunately, this may not be accurate in representing human reasoning because it is possible for a person to believe or disbelieve three different items by the same level of assurance (or probability). The "probability" of C may actually have nothing to do with uncertainty or probability. The fact may be that we are ignorant of the assurance level of C. Thus, knowing the probabilities of A and B does not necessarily imply that we can infer the probability of C.

In an attempt to overcome the shortcomings of classical probability in representing human reasoning, Dempster (1968) proposed a generalized theory of uncertainty versus ignorance. The theory, which was later extended by Shafer (1976), has come to be known as the Dempster-Shafer (D-S) theory of evidence. The theory is based on the notion that separate probability masses may be assigned to all subsets of a universe of discourse rather than just to indivisible single members as required in traditional probability theory. As a result, D-S theory permits the following inequality:

$$P(A) + P(B) \leq 1.0$$

To illustrate the application of D-S theory, let us assume a universe of discourse representation **X** and a set corresponding to n propositions. We will assume that one and only one of the propositions is true. The propositions are assumed to be exhaustive and mutually exclusive. Define all the subsets of **X** as follows:

$$\mathbf{H} = \{A\} \ni A \subseteq X.$$

The set **H** contains 2^n elements including the null set and **X** itself. Let the set function f, called the basic probability assignment, defined on **H** be a mapping to the interval [0, 1]. That is,

$$f:\mathbf{H} \rightarrow [0,1] \ni \forall A \subseteq X, f(\phi) = 0 \text{ and } \sum_{A \subseteq X} f(A) = 1$$

The function f defines a probability distribution on **H** as well as **X**. This is in contrast to classical probability theory where probability distribution is defined only on the individual elements of the sample space **X**. The function f represents the measure of belief committed exactly to A. A belief function, *Bel*, corresponding to a specific f for the set A, is defined as the sum of beliefs committed to every subset of A by f. In order words, *Bel*(A) is a measure of the total support or belief committed to the set A and establishes a minimum value for its likelihood. The belief function is defined in terms of all belief assigned to A as well as to all proper subsets of A. That is,

$$Bel(A) = \sum_{B \subseteq A} f(B)$$

For example, if **X** contains the mutually exclusive subsets P, Q, U, V, and W and we are interested in the particular subset A = {P, Q, W}, then we would have:

$$Bel(\{P,\ Q,\ W\}) = f(\{P,Q,W\}) + f(\{P,Q\}) + f(\{Q,W\}) + f(\{P,W\})$$
$$+ f(\{P\}) + f(\{Q\}) + f(\{W\})$$

Some important definitions related to D-S theory are presented below:

SUPPORT FUNCTION   The support function of the subset A is defined as *Bel*(A).

PLAUSIBILITY   The plausibility of A is defined as:

$$PL(A) = 1 - Bel(A^c)$$

UNCERTAINTY OF A   The uncertainty of a subset A of **X** is defined as

$$U(A) = PL(A) - Bel(A)$$

BELIEF INTERVAL   The belief interval for a subset A (i.e. the *confidence* in A) is defined as the subinterval

$$[Bel(A),\ PL(A)] \text{ of the interval } [0,\ 1]$$

FOCAL ELEMENTS   The subsets A of **X** are called *focal elements* of the support function *Bel* when f(A) > 0. We further define the following:

$$Bel(\phi) = 0$$

This indicates that no belief should be assigned to the null set.

$$Bel(X) = 1$$

This indicates that the "truth" is contained within **X**.

DOUBT FUNCTION   The doubt of A is defined as:

$$D(A) = Bel(A^c)$$

This is a measure of the extent to which one believes in the complement of A. That is, the level of doubt associated with A.

Some of the most common operational properties of belief and plausibility functions are presented below:

$$PL(\phi) = 0$$

$$PL(X) = 1$$

$$PL(A) \geq Bel(A), \ \forall \ A$$

$$Bel(A) + Bel(A^c) \leq 1, \ \forall \ A$$

$$Bel(A) \leq Bel(B), \ \forall \ A \subseteq B$$

$$PL(A) \leq PL(B), \ \forall \ A \subseteq B$$

Some examples of belief intervals and their explanations are presented below:

$[Bel(A), PL(A)] = [0, 0]$ Denotes belief that the proposition is false.

$[Bel(A), PL(A)] = [1, 1]$ Denotes belief that the proposition is true.

$[Bel(A), PL(A)] = [0, 1]$ Denotes no belief that supports the proposition.

$[Bel(A), PL(A)] = [.5, 1]$ Denotes belief that supports the proposition.

$[Bel(A), PL(A)] = [0, .9]$ Denotes partial disbelief in the proposition.

$[Bel(A), PL(A)] = [.4, 1]$ Denotes partial belief in the proposition.

$[Bel(A), PL(A)] = [.4, .8]$ Partial belief and disbelief in the proposition.

A consolidation function is used in D-S theory to combine evidence available from multiple knowledge sources to reduce uncertainty. The combining function is defined as $Bel_1 \odot Bel_2$. Given two probability assignment functions, f_1 and f_2 corresponding to the belief functions Bel_1 and Bel_2, let $A_1, \ldots, A_k$ be the focal elements for Bel_1 and let $B_1, \ldots, B_p$ be the focal elements for Bel_2. Then $f_1(A_i)$ and $f_2(B_j)$ each assign probability masses on the unit interval $[0, 1]$. The probability masses are combined orthogonally as shown in Figure 6.6.

The unit square in the figure represents the total probability mass assigned by both f_1 and f_2 for all their common subsets. A particular cell within the square, shown shaded in the figure, has an assigned value depicted as $f_1(A_i)f_2(B_j)$. Any subset C of X may have one or more of the cells committed to it. Consequently, the total probability mass committed to C is defined as:

$$f(C) = \sum_{ij} f_1(A_i)f_2(B_j), \ \forall \ i,j \ni A_i \cap B_j = C$$

The sum in the above equation must be normalized to account for the null intersections that have positive probabilities. These null intersections $A_i \cap B_j = \phi$ must be disregarded in the combination of the belief functions. Thus, the general form of Dempster's rule of combination is given by:

$$f_1 \odot f_2 = \frac{\displaystyle\sum_{A_i \cap B_j} f_1(A_i)f_2(B_j)}{\displaystyle\sum_{A_i \cap B_j \neq \phi} f_1(A_i)f_2(B_j)}, \ \forall \ i,j$$

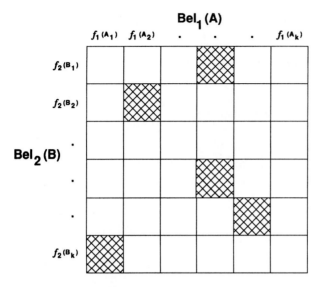

Figure 6.6. Combination of belief functions

6.5 CERTAINTY FACTORS

Most heuristic methods use some sort of pseudo-probabilistic techniques to handle uncertainty. Two of these techniques are *certainty factors* and *fuzzy logic*. The most common representation of heuristic weights is the use of *certainty factors* (or confidence factors). In this approach, numbers greater than 0 are used for positive evidence and numbers less than 0 are used for negative evidence (e.g., -1 to 1, -100 to 100). These numbers are used merely as heuristics, and no criterion of theoretical correctness is associated with them.

The popular MYCIN expert system uses certainty factors in handling uncertainties. MYCIN was developed to diagnose and recommend therapies for bacterial infections in blood. It associates a certainty factor (CF) with each of its production rules. The certainty factor indicates the degree of certainty with which each fact or rule is believed to hold and is a number between -1 and 1. In MYCIN consultation, a frequently fatal cause of a disease would be assigned a higher certainty than another one that is more likely, but rarely fatal. To evaluate MYCIN's production rules, the following steps are followed (Buchanan and Shortliffe 1984):

(1). The CF of a conjunction of several facts is taken to be the minimum of the CF's of the individual facts. This is analogous to the view that "the weakest link in a chain determines the strength of the chain."

(2). The CF of a disjunction of several facts is taken to be the maximum of the CF's of the individual facts.

(3). The CF for the conclusion produced by a rule is the CF of its premise multiplied by the CF of the rule.

(4). The CF for a fact produced as the conclusion of one or more rules is the maximum of the CF's produced by the rules yielding that conclusion.

Most of the procedures for manipulating certainty factors follow what is known as *ad hoc* techniques. These techniques typically have intuitive appeal but with no rigorous theoretical backing. They are used in place of the more formal methods as a practical approach to dealing with uncertainty. The formal theoretical approaches often pose difficulties in implementation. Several ad hoc procedures have been used with acceptable results in expert systems. The example below illustrates one ad hoc technique for combining certainty factors. Suppose we want to establish fact D, and the only rules available are the following:

Rule 1: IF A and B and C, THEN CONCLUDE D (CF = .8).

Rule 2: IF H and I and J, THEN CONCLUDE D (CF = .7).

If facts A, B, C, H, I, and J are known with the respective CF's of .7, .3, .5, .8, .7, and .9, then the following computations would produce a CF of .49 for D.
From Rule 1:

Min {CF(A), CF(B), CF(C)} $\quad$ = Min {.7, .3, .5}
$\qquad\qquad\qquad\qquad\qquad$ = .3

CF(D) based on Rule 1 $\qquad\quad$ = Min {CF(A), CF(B), CF(C)} (Rule 1 CF)
$\qquad\qquad\qquad\qquad\qquad$ = .3(.8)
$\qquad\qquad\qquad\qquad\qquad$ = .24

From Rule 2:

Min {CF(H), CF(I), CF(J)} $\quad$ = Min {.8, .7, .9}
$\qquad\qquad\qquad\qquad\qquad$ = .7

CF(D) based on Rule 2 $\qquad\quad$ = Min {CF(H), CF(I), CF(J)} (Rule 2 CF)
$\qquad\qquad\qquad\qquad\qquad$ = .7(.7)
$\qquad\qquad\qquad\qquad\qquad$ = .49

Rule combination:

CF(D) $\qquad\qquad\qquad\qquad\quad$ = Max {$CF(D)_1$, $CF(D)_2$}
$\qquad\qquad\qquad\qquad\qquad$ = Max {.24, .49}
$\qquad\qquad\qquad\qquad\qquad$ = .49

This method of handling uncertainty has been used quite extensively in many expert systems. However, it does have some flaws. For example, it is not suitable for situations involving high levels of interactions between goals. Several variations of the mathematical approach to combining certainty factors have been proposed and used in many systems.

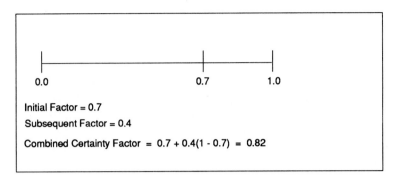

Figure 6.7. Combination of certainty factors

Figure 6.7 shows an example of combining a series of certainty factors for one parameter. The method illustrated in the figure uses certainty levels between 0 and 1 (or between 0% and 100%). This method may be suitable for systems using nonmonotonic reasoning in which case parameter instantiations may vary based on subsequent levels of certainty. The combined certainty factor is calculated by the formula below:

$$CCF = (\text{Initial CF}) + (\text{Subsequent CF})(1 - \text{Initial CF}).$$

The formula is applied repeatedly in case of more than two certainty factors in series. The flaw in this method, though, is that if the very first certainty factor encountered for the parameter is 1, then all subsequent certainty values for the parameter would not have any effect on the prior instantiation. The method then regresses to monotonic logic.

Figure 6.8 shows how the certainty level of a premise induces a certainty level on the conclusion of a rule. Figure 6.9 shows the effect of combining an uncertain premise and an uncertain rule. Researchers and developers of expert systems continue to investigate mechanisms that could more accurately reflect the reasoning process of humans when dealing with uncertain information. Despite their deficiencies, ad hoc methods for combining certainty factors have been used

Figure 6.8. Premise certainty factor induced on conclusion

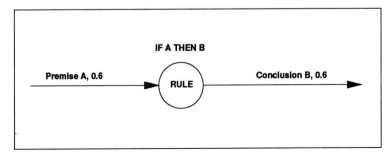

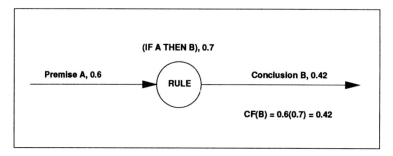

Figure 6.9. Conclusion certainty factor

more extensively than the more formal approaches. This is because the formal approaches are difficult to implement particularly if certain assumptions must be met for them to be valid. Sensitivity analysis conducted by Buchanan et al (1984) shows that the ad hoc approaches, while not optimal, satisfy the basic needs in most problem scenarios. However, much more research is needed before a standard approach can be developed.

6.6 FUZZY LOGIC

Another approach to managing uncertainty is the concept of fuzzy sets. Zadeh (1965) first introduced fuzzy sets. The objective of fuzzy sets is to generalize the notions of a set and propositions to accommodate the type of fuzziness or vagueness in many decision problems. Since they were introduced in 1965, fuzzy sets have attracted much attention. The emergence of practical applications of artificial intelligence has intensified the interest and research in fuzzy sets. Recently, fuzzy logic has found a wide variety of applications ranging from industrial process control and consumer electronics to medical diagnosis and investment management (Zadeh 1991). In contrast to classical logic, fuzzy logic is aimed at providing a body of concepts and techniques for dealing with modes of reasoning which are approximate rather than exact. Extensions of fuzzy sets now include concepts such as *fuzzy arithmetic, possibility distributions, fuzzy statistics, fuzzy random variables,* and *fuzzy set functions.* Among the derived concepts is the concept of fuzzification, which permits the incorporation of fuzzy reasoning into any normal set.

In formal truth logic, it is required that every proposition be either true (1) or false (0). While "0" or "1" treatment fits conventional computer processing perfectly, it can impose serious restrictions on machine reasoning intended to duplicate the imprecise aspects of human reasoning. Fuzzy logic is a technique for dealing with sources of imprecision and uncertainty that are nonstatistical in nature.

Fuzzy logic uses a multivalued membership function to denote membership of an object in a class rather than the classical binary True or False values used to denote membership. In fuzzy logic, the source of imprecision is the absence of sharply defined criteria for class membership rather than the presence of random variables. Each class contains a continuum of grades of membership. Thus, a product will not be considered to be either good or bad. Depending on the product's actual quality level, it will have a certain degree of being good or being bad. A question of interest is to determine when a product makes the transition from being a bad product to being a good product.

In many practical real world problems, the transition point is not clearly defined. It is fuzzy! The degree of membership in one category or another will depend on the membership functions that users or producers define to convey the varying levels of quality of the product. A fuzzy set is described by a membership function that maps a set of objects onto the interval of real numbers between 0 and 1. In standard set theory, an object is either a member of a set or not a member of the set. In fuzzy set, the transition from membership to nonmembership is gradual rather than abrupt because there are no distinguishable boundaries.

To illustrate the concept of fuzzy sets, we define set **A** to be the class of "high" academic grade point averages. Because the definition of high is subjective, we assign a range of average points and corresponding possibility values to the set **A** as shown in Table 6.4.

The term high can be modified with terms such as "quite," "very," and "somewhat." Figure 6.10 shows a distribution of grade points based on linguistic qualifiers. Given a particular specification of grade point level, the distribution can be used to determine an appropriate classification of the grade point level. For example, a grade point of 3.6 may have a classification of "very high" with fuzzy confidence of 0.7, a classification of "high" with confidence of 0.9, or a classification of "somewhat high" with a fuzzy confidence of 0.99.

With the use of fuzzy sets, the imprecise aspects of human reasoning can be captured into machine reasoning. Even though the theory of fuzzy logic has been

Table 6.4. Degree of membership for fuzzy set: high academic grade

Average Points	Grade of Membership (Possibility Value)
2.00	0.00
2.25	0.12
2.50	0.25
. . .	. . .
3.50	0.82
3.60	0.90
4.00	1.00

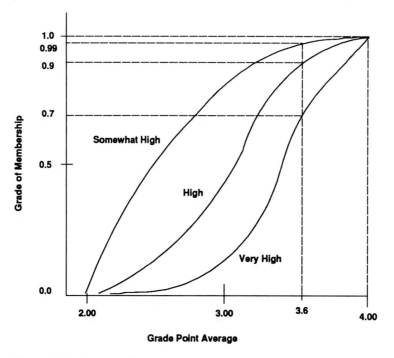

Figure 6.10. Example of fuzzy set distribution with modifiers

around for quite a while, it is just becoming popular for knowledge-based systems applications.

MATHEMATICAL DEFINITION OF FUZZY SET   Let **A** be a set of objects defined over a sample space **X**. For a finite set defined as

$$\mathbf{X} = x_1, x_2, \ldots, x_n,$$

we can represent **A** as a fuzzy set with the linear combination below:

$$\mathbf{A} = u_1(x_1), u_2(x_2), \ldots, u_n(x_n),$$

where u_i is the grade of membership of x_i in **A**. In general, for a sample space of objects defined as $\mathbf{X} = \{x\}$, the fuzzy set **A** in **X** is a set of ordered pairs defined as:

$$\mathbf{A} = \{x, u_a(x)\}, \; x \in \mathbf{X}.$$

A value of $u_a(x) = 0$ indicates that x is not a member of **A**, while $u_a(x) = 1$ implies that x is completely contained in **A**. Values of $u_a(x)$ between 0 and 1 indicate that x is a partial member of **A**. Characteristic membership functions for fuzzy sets are different from probabilities and should not be confused with probabilities. Probability is a measure of the degree of uncertainty based on the frequency or proportion of occurrence of an event. By contrast, a fuzzy characteristic function relates to the degree of vagueness which measures the ease with which an event can be attained.

With the definition of fuzzy set, we have a means of expressing a function GOOD(x) to convey the information about the quality level of a manufactured product. The fuzzy set **A** can be defined as:

$$\mathbf{A} = \{good\}.$$

That is, A is the set containing those items that can be classified as *good*. Obviously, some items will be stronger members of the set than other items. There will be some items at the low end of good and some items at the high end of good.

For this example, we can define x as a quantitative measure of a particular quality characteristic of the product. An example is the measure of the surface finish or surface roughness of the product. If the measures of surface roughness range from, say, 1 to 50, then we might assign the membership values shown in Table 6.5. A surface roughness of 1 is the most desirable while a surface roughness of 50 is the least desirable in this particular example. Note that Table 6.5 indicates that the highest degree of membership is 0.95 (less than one). This is logical since it may be impossible to obtain a perfect surface finish without any roughness at all. A fuzzy set is said to be *normal* if its highest degree of membership is one.

Figure 6.11 presents what the author calls a fuzzy set grid. The grid shows the gradual change in the degree of membership from one level to another. Even though discrete lines are used to depict the grid in the figure, the changes in membership grade are, in fact, so gradual that the changes do not follow a discrete pat-

Table 6.5. Product quality classification using fuzzy set

Surface Roughness (x)	Degree of Membership in the GOOD Set $u_a(x)$
1.00	0.95
5.20	0.88
10.50	0.70
. . .	. . .
35.00	0.10
45.00	0.05
50.00	0.00

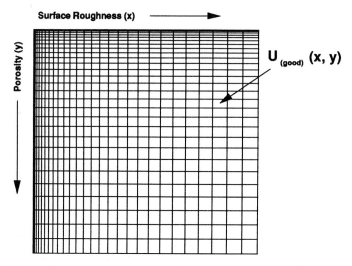

Figure 6.11. Fuzzy set membership grid

tern. The figure represents a bivariate set whereby an item is classified as "good" based on two quality characteristics: surface roughness and porosity. Items with low values of surface roughness (i.e., high surface finish) and low values of porosity have the strongest degree of membership in the fuzzy set A, which is defined as A = {good}. That is, A is the set of good products. The degree of membership in set A slowly decreases as surface roughness and porosity increase.

An item located in the upper left-hand corner of the grid has the highest degree of membership in A. That is, it is the best of the good items. An item located in the lower right-hand corner of the grid has the lowest degree of membership in A. That is, it is the worst of the good items. The bivariate fuzzy set grid may be extended to a trivariate (three factors) case. In that case, the grid would be represented as a solid *box* with nonhomogeneous density. The density of the box would change gradually in different directions to indicate varying degrees of membership in the trivariate fuzzy set.

Operations on fuzzy sets are similar, in some respects, to the operations on conventional sets. The standard operations and characteristics of fuzzy sets are presented below. Let **A, B, C, D**, . . . be fuzzy sets defined on the universal set **X**. Then we have the following:

Equality:

$$\mathbf{A} = \mathbf{B} \text{ if and only if } u_A(x) = u_B(x), \ \forall \ x \in X$$

Containment:

$$\mathbf{A} \subseteq \mathbf{B} \text{ if and only if } u_A(x) \leq u_B(x), \ \forall \ x \in X$$

Intersection:

$$u_{A \cap B}(x) = \min_x \{u_A(x), u_B(x)\}$$

Union:

$$u_{A \cup B}(x) = \max_x \{u_A(x), u_B(x)\}$$

Complement:

$$u_{A'}(x) = 1 - u_A(x)$$

The intersection of two fuzzy sets **A** and **B** is the largest fuzzy subset that is a subset of both. Similarly, the union of two fuzzy sets **A** and **B** is the smallest fuzzy subset having both **A** and **B** as subsets. Note that in the properties defined above, the min and max operators are applied to the membership values $u_A(x)$ and $u_B(x)$ and not the fuzzy sets themselves. Thus, the min and max operators should not be confused with the largest and smallest fuzzy subsets explained above. Operational properties which hold for fuzzy sets are presented below:

Distributive property:

$$A \cup (B \cap C) = (A \cup B) \cap (A \cup C)$$
$$A \cap (B \cup C) = (A \cap B (\cup (A \cap C)$$

Associative property:

$$(A \cup B) \cup C = A \cup (B \cup C)$$
$$(A \cap B) \cap C = A \cap (B \cap C)$$

Commutative property:

$$A \cap B = B \cap A$$
$$A \cup B = B \cup A$$

Idempotence property:

$$A \cap A = A$$
$$A \cup A = A$$

DeMorgan's law:

$$u_{(A \cap B)'}(x) = u_{A' \cup B'}(x)$$
$$u_{(A \cup B)'}(x) = u_{A' \cap B'}(x)$$

The following relationships should also be noted:

$$A \cap A' = \phi$$
$$A \cup A' = X$$
$$A \cap \phi = \phi$$
$$A \cup \phi = A$$
$$A \cap X = A$$
$$A \cup X = X$$

The first two expressions above hold because for $u_A(x) = a$, where $0 < a < 1$, we have:

$$u_{A \cup A'}(x) = \max\{a, \quad 1-a\}$$
$$\neq 1$$

$$u_{A \cap A'}(x) = \min\{a, \quad 1-a\}$$
$$\neq 0$$

Referring to our earlier example, Table 6.5 gives the membership values for the set GOOD based on the observed surface finish of the product. Such membership values may be obtained through empirical studies or subjective experimentations. In some cases, it is possible to define a function that generates the membership values directly. Such a function might be of the form presented below. Figure 6.12 presents a plot of the function $u_A(x)$.

$$u_A(x) = \begin{cases} \sqrt{x-1}, & \text{if } 1 \leq x \leq 2 \\ 0, & \text{otherwise} \end{cases}$$

Figure 6.12. Plot of degree of membership function

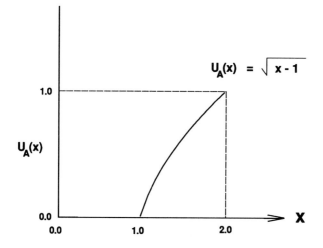

The functional form of the membership function may be based on characteristics relating to the utility of the item with respect to its various quality levels or some other criterion of interest.

Certain operations that are unique to fuzzy sets are presented below:

Dilation:

The dilation of A is defined as:

$$DIL(A) = \sqrt{u_A(x)}, \ \forall \ x \in X$$

Concentration:

The concentration of A is defined as:

$$CON(A) = [u_A(x)]^2, \ \forall \ x \in X$$

Normalization:

The normalization of A is defined as:

$$NORM(A) = \frac{u_a(x)}{\max_x\{u_A(x)\}}, \ \forall \ x \in X$$

For the function presented in Figure 6.12, DIL(A), CON(A), and NORM(A) are shown in Figure 6.13. Dilation tends to increase the degree of membership of all partial members. Concentration is the opposite of dilation. It tends to decrease the degree of membership of all partial members. Normalization performs the function of normalizing the membership function.

Fuzzy membership functions can be used to generate confidence factors in modus ponens reasoning as an alternative to probability and certainty factors. For example, referring to the product quality example presented earlier, we may have the following rule:

IF surface-roughness is-less-than 10,
THEN product-quality is good.

Now, suppose we are given the following premise:
Surface-roughness is 10.5.

Our conclusion would be that the product is good but with a certain level of fuzzy membership level (FML). That is,

Product-quality is *good* (FML = 0.70).
where FML = $U_A(10.5)$ = 0.70 as presented in Table 6.5.

Figure 6.14 presents two unidirectional membership functions. Curve A is defined for the set of *good* products based on the surface roughness. Note that as surface roughness increases, the degree of membership in the GOOD set decreases. Curve B is defined for the set of *bad* products. As the surface roughness increases the degree of membership in the BAD set increases. Under fuzzy set

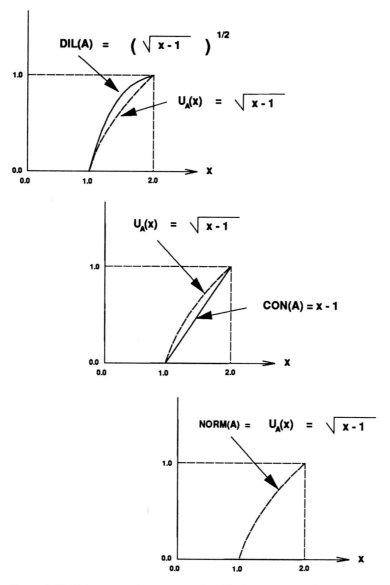

Figure 6.13. Unique operations on membership functions

reasoning, a product can be classified as being both *good* and *bad*. It is the degree of membership in the specific fuzzy set that makes a difference. An item that is a strong member of the GOOD set will be a weak member of the BAD set and vice versa. Note that an item with a surface roughness located at the intersection of curves A and B has equivalent degrees of membership in either of the two sets GOOD and BAD. At this point, we would be indifferent to classifying the item as either good or bad.

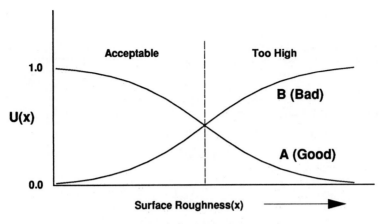

Figure 6.14. Unidirectional membership functions

Figure 6.15 presents two bidirectional membership functions. A bidirectional function is defined as one that starts at one end, reaches a peak or valley, and then changes direction. Curve B may be suitable for applications dealing with parameters, such as temperature, where both the low end and high end of the function are not desirable. As shown in Figure 6.15, temperatures at the low end and at the high end have lower degrees of membership in the set of ACCEPTABLE-TEMPERATURE, while temperature values in the middle range have higher degrees of membership. This, for example, may be the case when one monitors the ambient temperature of a work station. Temperatures that are too low are not desirable. Similarly, temperatures that are too high are not desirable. Curve A in Figure 6.15 presents a situation that is opposite to the temperature example. Curve A indicates that both the values at the low and high ends are more desirable than those in the middle range. Examples for this case are left as an exercise for the reader (see Exercise 6.10).

Figure 6.15. Bidirectional membership functions

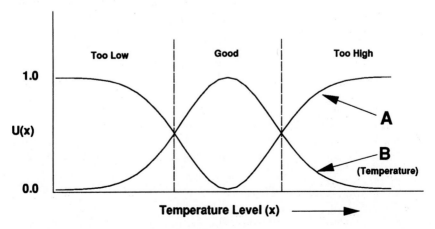

6.7 EXERCISES

6.1 In a manufacturing operation, parts are classified into one of two possible categories after inspection. The categories are GOOD and BAD. The quality inspector is known not to be 100% accurate. Previous studies indicate the following facts:

1. 2.5% of the parts produced are BAD.

2. The probability that a BAD part will be classified as GOOD is 0.05.

3. The probability that a GOOD part will be classified as BAD is 0.87.

Required: Use Bayesian reasoning procedure to find the certainty factor (probability) for the following statement:

"Part-is GOOD"

That is, we want the probability that a part is indeed good when the inspector says that it is good.

6.2 Find the composite certainty factor for a hypothesis that has the following four certainty factors in series: 0.4, 0.5, 0.8, and 0.5.

6.3 *Given: Rule 1:*

{If A is true, then B is true} (CF = 0.63)

User input: A is true (CF = 0.98)

Find the CF (certainty factor) for the conclusion on B

6.4 Assume the following rules with the respective certainty factors (CFs) are available for establishing fact D:

Rule 1: {If A and B and C then D} (CF = 0.60)

Rule 2: {If (E or F) and G then D} (CF = 0.90)

Given:

CF(A) = 0.75

CF(B) = 0.49

CF(C) = 0.50

CF(E) = 0.25

CF(F) = 0.40

CF(G) = 0.35

Required: Find the CF for the conclusion on D.

6.5 Show that the dilation of the fuzzy set A = CON(B) is the fuzzy set B.

6.6 Give five examples of using fuzzy membership functions to obtain the level of confidence on modus ponens rules.

6.7 Define a reasonable, real-valued fuzzy membership function for the variable TASK-COMPLEXITY.

6.8   Given $P(B|A) = 0.70$, $P(A) = 0.25$, and $P(B) = 0.41$, find the probability of the event A given that event B has occurred.

6.9   Give five examples of practical problems (other than the temperature example) whereby Curve A in Figure 6.15 is applicable.

6.10 List and discuss five engineering problems suitable for fuzzy logic application.

6.11 List and discuss five manufacturing problems suitable for fuzzy logic application.

6.12 Draw a sketch of a trivariate fuzzy set *box*.

6.13 Discuss how humans typically use reasoning under uncertainty in their day-to-day decision making.

6.14 Discuss the rationale for the application of Dempster-Shafer Theory in expert systems.

6.15 Discuss the potential sources of uncertainty in expert system consultations and the influence of the sources on the selection of methods for handling the uncertainty.

6.16 Define a real valued fuzzy function for the linguistic variable HIGH-QUALITY: $u_{\text{HIGH-QUALITY}}(x)$.

6.17 Given two pieces of evidence (A and B) and the following probabilities, $P(A) = 1/3$, $P(B) = 1/4$, and $P(A \cap B) = 1/6$, find the following probabilities: $P(A^c)$, $P(A^c \text{ union } B)$, $P(A \text{ union } B^c)$, $P(A \cap B^c)$, $P(A^c \text{ union } B^c)$.

6.18 Define an engineering problem scenario that fits the evidence and probability statements in Exercise 6.17. Discuss the implications of the probabilities calculated with respect to the problem scenario.

6.19 *The Birthday Problem.* Given that there are N students in a class, find the following (assume 365 days per year):

  a) The probability that at least two students have the same birthday.

  b) The minimum value of N which yields a probability of 1/2 that at least two students have the same birthday.

  c) Define an expert system decision problem in which the probability calculated in part (a) would be of interest.

  d) Define an expert system decision problem in which the value calculated in part (b) would be of interest.

6.20 A knowledge engineer goes to work following one of three routes A, B, or C. His choice of route is independent of the weather. If it rains, the probabilities of arriving late through routes A, B, and C are 0.06, 0.15, 0.12, respectively. The corresponding probabilities if it does not rain are: 0.05, 0.10, 0.15. On the average, one out of every four days is rainy.

  a) Given that on a sunny day he arrives late, what is the probability that he took route C?

  b) If he arrives late on a given day, what is the probability that it is a rainy day?

  c) How would the knowledge of the probabilities above aid the knowledge engineer in making decisions about which route to take?

6.21 Show that $PL(\phi) = 0$.

7

Selecting a
Development Tool

This chapter presents a discussion of the selection of a development tool. A development tool should be selected on the basis of the nature of the problem to be solved. A tool should be selected to fit the unique requirements of the problem rather than the other way around. A careful problem analysis as discussed in Chapter 3 will help identify those unique requirements. A tool may be as simple as a high-level programming language or as comprehensive as a high-end commercial development shell.

7.1 THE APPLICATIONS ENVIRONMENT

The expert systems applications environment in engineering and manufacturing is very complex. The environment requires interaction between several functional areas. The specific tasks involved in each functional area often require specialized tools. The specialized tools may be in terms of custom programs developed in one of the major programming languages or commercial applications programs such as spreadsheet and data base programs. An expert system serves as the unification point for the various tools. Figure 7.1 presents a representation of an expert systems applications environment in engineering and manufacturing. Hybrid expert systems make use of a combination of programming languages and turnkey development shells. Not all programming languages are suitable for expert systems work. And not all turnkey development shells are suitable for all expert systems applications. A careful analysis must be performed to select the right expert systems development tools.

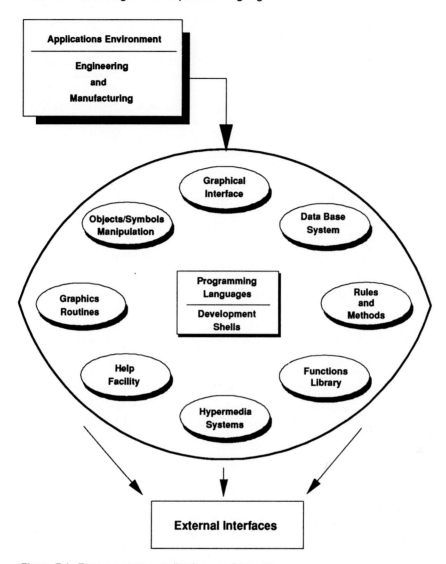

Figure 7.1. Expert systems applications environment

7.2 SELECTING A DEVELOPMENT LANGUAGE

The development of high-level programming languages is one of the many by-products of AI research. AI programming languages offer various advantages over other conventional programming languages like FORTRAN and BASIC. Another important by-product of AI work is the evolution of innovative software products or development shells. A crucial aspect of developing expert systems is the selection of the development tool to be used. For certain kinds of applications, it may be necessary to develop a custom inference structure from scratch by using an AI programming language directly. For most expert systems applications, a generic commercial development tool would suffice. The selection of a development language is as important as the selection of a commercial development tool.

THE NEED FOR SPECIAL PROGRAMMING LANGUAGES Special programming languages are needed for artificial intelligence and expert systems work because of the unique features of their applications. AI programs are different from conventional programs in many ways including those listed below:

(1). AI programming is usually done through experimental or exploratory programming in a very interactive environment.

(2). AI programming uses sophisticated programming procedures such as object-oriented analysis and symbolic processing.

(3). AI programming languages offer recursive processing that is not easily implemented in conventional languages.

(4). AI programming languages make use of dynamic memory allocation to adapt to various problem sizes.

Although it may be possible to write programs in any programming language, certain languages are better at executing certain types of programs than others. Generally, the languages developed for other purposes have not proven to be especially efficient for developing AI programs. For example, the techniques used for numeric programming are not very useful in simulating human intelligence. Special languages are needed to achieve efficient manipulation of conceptual symbols in expert systems.

LANGUAGE OPTIONS LISP and PROLOG programming languages are specifically designed to solve problems in knowledge representation and natural language processing. They reduce programming time and effort for many AI applications and provide efficient support for knowledge representation. PASCAL has been successfully used to program many expert system shells and tools. The major appeal of PASCAL is its structured coding format. Its orientation towards computational analysis has made it very popular for engineering and scientific applications.

The preferred language used for AI work in the early to mid-1980s was LISP. Basically, the language manipulates lists of rules and is designed for standalone use. LISP contains its own operating system, which hinders its acceptance among developers writing for more general operating environments. However, it is quite suitable for the narrow domains of AI research studies. PROLOG, by comparison, does symbolic processing and is especially suited to doing high-level data structures. It has been used effectively as a productivity tool to be integrated with other programming languages such as C. For this reason, PROLOG presently seems to be enjoying more commercial appeal.

FORTRAN is a very popular language that is useful for mathematical and scientific computations in engineering problems. Attempts to use FORTRAN for

AI programming have not achieved very satisfactory results. However, with the advent of procedures for interfacing expert systems to external programs and functions, FORTRAN is beginning to get more attention in AI work; not as a primary programming tool, but as a tool for corequisite computations. In applications requiring auxiliary computations, FORTRAN can serve as the external program that generates the desired numeric variables that are exported to the expert systems environment. The major advantage of FORTRAN is that a large percentage of the science and engineering community is familiar with it.

The C programming language is a strong alternative to LISP and PROLOG. Its portability and good data handling capability are its strongest features. The C language permits applications developed on one machine to run without much problem on other machines. This portability feature is exactly what is needed for the expertise transfer objective of expert systems. The difficulty of learning C for the novice user is a shortcoming of the language. The efficient data structures employed by C constitute the reason it has been utilized for many commercial data base management software packages. The commercial rise of expert systems has been credited to the general use of C-based languages in development tools.

ADA is a programming language that has been mandated for military applications by the U.S. Department of Defense (DOD). This language still remains relatively unknown to much of the programming community. Military spending on artificial intelligence has intensified considerably in recent years. As a result, there is a prevailing haste to develop new artificial intelligence and expert system tools in ADA. There is even now a special interest group on the use of ADA in military applications of artificial intelligence.

OPERATING ENVIRONMENTS   The operating environment for expert systems development is a major factor in the success of the technology. Many MS-DOS-based systems are available. But they generally suffer from the limited power offered by the PC environment. Unix is emerging as a major platform for implementing expert systems. Unix is helping to move artificial intelligence and expert systems technology into successful real-world applications. For certain applications, Unix systems provide a powerful, cost-effective platform that delivers the added benefit of widespread portability. The introduction of Microsoft Windows 3.0 has also added a significant boost to expert systems implementations. Many software developers have introduced Windows-based development tools for expert systems. KnowledgePro Windows from Knowledge Garden, Inc. was one of the first Windows-based inference engines available on the market. The graphical user interface offered by Windows 3.0 is especially suited to the highly interactive environment needed by expert systems consultations.

7.2.1   Hierarchy of AI Programming Languages

A program is a list of coded instructions that a computer follows in a specified order so as to perform a specific task. A program is written in a programming language. A programming language is a collection of symbols designed to represent specific operations to be performed by the computer. There are three levels of programming languages.

MACHINE LANGUAGE   Machine language programming is accomplished by giving instructions to the computer in terms of the binary codes of 0's and 1's (e.g., 101001101). This is called machine language because the binary representation of information is the only language the computer understands directly.

ASSEMBLY LANGUAGE   An assembly language simplifies the task of programming by using short mnemonic words and numbers (e.g., ADD, R6) to represent collections of binary codes. The words and numbers are translated into the 0's and 1's of machine language by a special program called an assembler. The assembly language is called a low-level language because each individual assembly instruction is "assembled" into one machine language instruction.

HIGH-LEVEL LANGUAGES   A high-level language gives instructions to the computer by using a coding procedure that resembles English language statements. This makes it easier for the programmer to specify what the computer should do. High-level languages are essentially designed for programmer convenience. The program instructions are translated into machine-level codes before processing by the computer. Some of the most common high-level languages are FORTRAN (FORmula TRANslator), BASIC (Beginner's All-purpose Symbolic Instruction Code), COBOL (COmmon Business Oriented Language), C, PASCAL, LISP (List Processing), and PROLOG (Programming in Logic).

There are two types of special programs that are used to translate programs written in high-level languages into machine language.

(1). A *compiler* generates a complete copy of the high-level program in the machine language format. The compiled program is then executed directly by the computer without any interruptions.

(2). An *interpreter* translates each instruction into machine language one at a time when that instruction is ready to be executed by the computer. The program execution can be interrupted at any point during the computer processing.

There are advantages and disadvantages of each method of program translation. The program development process is slower with a compiler. This is because the entire program must be compiled and run in order to debug the program. The program must be recompiled each time the programmer makes any change in the program. However, a compiled program runs faster than an interpreted program. An interpreter simplifies the debugging process because each instruction is translated at run time. This makes it easy for the programmer to identify and correct errors. Program execution can be resumed at the point of interruption. However, the process of translating program lines one at a time considerably slows down program execution.

There are generally three domains of programming languages: functional, relational, and procedural. There are fundamental differences in the ways programs are written with each type of language.

FUNCTIONAL LANGUAGE   A functional programming language, also referred to as an applicative programming language, is one which achieves its effect by applying functions recursively or by composition. The principles of frequency of reference is an important aspect of developing expressions in a functional programming language.

In a functional language, the programmer defines the relevant values. The basic unit from which functional programs are built is the expression. In the functional program, the expressions are evaluated until the final value of the function is determined. LISP is an example of a functional programming language.

RELATIONAL LANGUAGE   A relational language, also referred to as a logic programming language, specifies a relationship among values. Logic programming eliminates a direct dependence on program sequencing. In a relational programming language, only the facts on which an operation would be based need be specified. The specific sequence of steps to be performed does not necessarily have to be specified. In logic programming, the logic and control components of a program can be specified separately. The logic programming is viewed as a definition of a relationship. Each clause of the definition specifies that the relationship holds under certain conditions. PROLOG is an example of relational language.

PROCEDURAL LANGUAGE   In a procedural programming language, the sequence of steps is important. The order in which the steps are executed is specified and that order eventually produces a desired effect. Procedural programming languages were developed as a technique for describing operations that can be performed by a machine. The atomic unit of a procedural program is a statement. The procedural program is understood by tracing through an execution of the statements making up the program.

7.2.2   LISP as a Functional Programming Language

LISP, an acronym for List Processing, was designed and implemented at the Massachusetts Institute of Technology by John McCarthy in the late 1950s. It is used as one of the major applicative programming languages for implementing artificial intelligence systems. As a symbolic programming language, it facilitates the representation of complex data and the relationships among different data for a variety of artificial intelligence applications. LISP was first implemented on the IBM704. It is second only to FORTRAN in being the oldest programming language still in widespread use. A prototype interactive LISP system was demonstrated in 1960 and was one of the earliest examples of interactive computing. LISP systems then rapidly spread to other computers and now exist on many machines, including microcomputers.

The method of data structuring provided by LISP is called the list. Processing such lists approximates associative memory in human beings and, therefore, makes it possible to simulate human thought. These capabilities make LISP a good programming language for expert systems and other advanced program-development environments. The fact that LISP represents both programs and data by lists is of utmost importance. In order to allow computation with symbolic data, these lists of data are manipulated. LISP manipulates lists just like other languages manipulate numbers; they can be compared, passed to functions, added, or subtracted. Syntactically, a list is represented when its elements are written in sequence with the whole list enclosed in parentheses. An example of this is the statement:

(set 'text' (expert special studies))

The second argument to "set" is the list: (expert special studies).

LISP provides operations for pulling atoms together to make a list and for extracting atoms out of a list. LISP also allows lists to be constructed from other lists. For example, the list:

((expert systems special studies) summer ninety one))

has two sublists:

(expert systems special studies)

(summer ninety one)

The above example refers to an "expert systems special studies for Summer of 1991. Simple algebraic expressions can be represented by lists of atoms such as

(PLUS x y)

(TIMES a z)

In this case a "prefix" notation is used that places operators ahead of their operands. A more complicated algebraic expression such as

$$X^2 + 2XY + Y^2$$

can be represented by the list structure below:

(PLUS (EXP X 2) (PLUS (TIMES 2 (TIMES X Y) (EXP Y 2))).

THE LISP INTERPRETER   FORTRAN and other high level languages are generally implemented as compiled languages. A program in one of such languages is read by a compiler, which translates it into the machine language (low level instructions) of the machine being used. This machine language program is then executed in order to produce the desired results. Unlike these compiler based languages, LISP is usually implemented as an interpreter language. A flow-chart for basic LISP interpretation is shown in Figure 7.2. A LISP program consists of a sequence of commands that are to be evaluated. Typically, a command is a procedure call of a procedure definition. The interpreter is a program that receives a

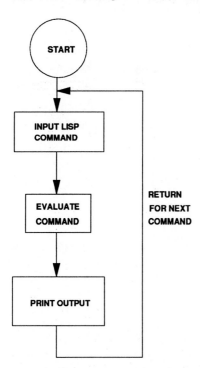

Figure 7.2. Operation of the LISP interpreter

command, evaluates the command, generates outputs, and then repeats the steps until it runs out of command inputs. The LISP interpreter operates as an interactive language. The user may present a command to the interpreter and receive its output. The next command is then presented. The interpreter does not translate the entire program into machine language before execution begins. Instead each command is read and evaluated before the next command is evaluated.

LIST REPRESENTATION   Lists are normally represented by records, each of which contains two pointers to other records. One pointer is the CAR and another is the CDR. A list (A (B C) D) can be represented by the diagram in Figure 7.3. Atoms are represented as records of other types. The last cell points to "nil," representing the end of the list. The two parts of the cell are called the left part and the right part. The final null pointer is often drawn as a slash through the right half of the last cell. Each pointer is associated with a type field describing the nature of the record pointed to. The other part of the pointer is the address part. The list shown above, with type fields added, is shown in Figure 7.4.

STORAGE MANAGEMENT   In order to understand basic LISP functions, it is helpful to examine the way LISP data sets are stored in typical LISP programs. LISP data are called S-expressions (symbolic expressions) and are represented by atoms and parentheses. An atom can be numeric or symbolic. Symbolic atoms are

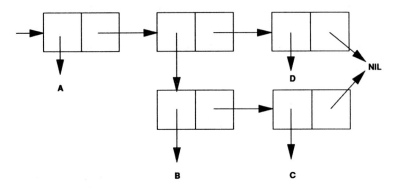

Figure 7.3. LISP list

indivisible. Therefore, the only operations that can be performed on them are equality testing and concatenation. A numeric atom is a sequence of digits preceded by a sign. The S-expression for a list of one element is that element dotted with the atom Nil. The atom Nil plays a special role as a "list terminator" in the list. Thus, the S-expression for the list (A) is (A, NIL).

The empty list containing no elements, written as ( ), corresponds to the S-Expression Nil. Memory assignment in LISP begins with the "free" list or HEAP, which can be referred to as the list of unused memory elements. Heap memory is built from conventional memory. Each element of the heap memory consists of a data word and a link pointer, called a pointer pair. The link pointer points to the next element in the list or to a terminator element "Nil." Creating a new list is done by taking elements from the free list. When a portion of the list is discarded, its elements are returned to the free list. The use of lists (or linked lists) as the basic data structure together with operations for general list modification is the basis of most LISP algorithms. The important storage management technique of Garbage collection was first introduced in LISP. Garbage refers to memory locations that were allocated but are no longer referenced within the program. Garbage Collection retrieves all the memory elements in discarded lists and pieces of lists and returns them to the free list.

Figure 7.4. LISP list with specification of types

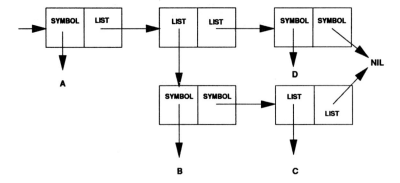

BASIC LISP FUNCTIONS AND EXPRESSIONS   A complete set of operations for a composite data type, such as lists, requires operations for building the structures and operations for taking the structures apart. Operations for building a structure are called constructors, and those that extract their parts are called selectors. LISP has one constructor called CONS and two selectors called CAR and CDR. These primitive functions are needed in order to manipulate S-expressions.

CONS   The first primitive function on S-expressions, called CONS, is an operator that allows a programmer to construct arbitrarily complex lists. If X and Y are variables, then CONS(X,Y) constructs a dotted pair whose left part is the value of X and whose right part is the value of Y. For example, if the value of X is the atom A and the value of Y is the atom B, then CONS(X,Y)=(A,B). Hence, CONS(X,Y) means the construct of the values of the variables X and Y. Also, CONS[A (B C)]=(A B C).

CAR   The second function is called CAR (Contents of the Address Register). This function allows one to select the first element of a list. For example, the CAR of "[((Expert Systems) (Special Studies))]" is the list "(Expert Systems)," whose CAR is "Expert," whose CAR is nil.

CDR   The third function is called CDR (Contents of the Decrement Register). The CDR of a list is the list one gets by deleting the first member of the list. For example:

$$CDR[(A\ B)] = (B)$$

$$CDR[(B)] = NIL$$

Hence, using CAR and CDR we can select out any element of a list.

LENGTH   The function LENGTH is defined for all lists where the length of the empty list is zero and the length of $(X_1, X_2,.....,X_n)$ is N. For example,

$$LENGTH[(A)] = 1$$

$$LENGTH[(A)(B)] = 2$$

$$LENGTH[(A\ B)] = 2$$

$$LENGTH[(A(B)(C\ D))] = 3$$

There are many special purpose functions available in LISP. The ones presented above are shown just to give the reader a feel for some selected capabilities of LISP. Readers interested in learning the LISP programming language may consult any of the numerous books available on the subject. Fortunately, with the availability of many development tools, a user does not need to know any of the programming languages in order to benefit from the expert system technology.

LISP IMPLEMENTATIONS The following is an overview of some dialects of LISP that are currently used in various AI applications. Due to the numerous dialects of LISP available, programmer proficiency is sometimes hampered by the inability to fully transfer programming knowledge from one dialect to another.

COMMON LISP Common LISP is a derivation of MacLISP. Its structure is similar to that of ZetaLISP. It has good capabilities for development tools. It provides a variety of types of data objects.

FRANZ LISP This dialect of LISP was written at the University of California at Berkeley. It was originally intended to be a LISP dialect suitable for running a version of MACSYMA on VAX. It evolved into one of the most commonly available LISP dialects on UNIX Machines.

GOLDEN COMMON LISP (GCLISP) A product of Gold Hill computer, GCLISP is the most advanced version of LISP to be offered for micro environments. It is more efficient than any other PC dialect of LISP. The GCLISP interpreter has over 100 of the most frequently used LISP functions in compiled form.

IQLISP This was one of the first versions of LISP available for the PC. Some very useful applications have been written in it, including the Expert System KES (Knowledge Engineering System). IQLISP was written specially for the PC and makes a special use of various features of the PC environment. The most important of these is its ability to address the full memory space of the PC.

LISP AND FORTRAN An interesting fact about LISP and FORTRAN is that both of these languages were created at approximately the same time in the early days of computing during the late 1950s. FORTRAN was created to make writing computer programs easier for people, whereas LISP was created for advanced problems in mathematical logic. LISP can be understood as a functional language whereas FORTRAN is an example of a procedural language. Some of the features that make LISP different from FORTRAN are described in this section. LISP deals with symbolic structures as its primary variables whereas FORTRAN deals with numbers. In LISP, the bottom elements are "atoms" instead of files (as in FORTRAN) and users deal with lists of atom names in the same way they deal with directories of files. LISP represents list structures by list pointers, in the same sense that FORTRAN represents numbers as patterns of bits in a word.

MACLISP This was one of the first dialects of LISP written on the PDP-10. It enjoys a large routine system, which includes an interpreter written in assembly language. It was derived from the PDP-6 LISP, which was written during the middle 1960s.

NIL NIL (New Implementation of LISP) was developed at MIT for VAX computers. It was originally designed as the first modern LISP dialect after the introduction of LISP Machine. LISP machines are computers that are developed specifically to run the LISP programming language. They efficiently take advantage of the most useful properties of LISP. One of the most popular LISP machines is the Texas Instruments Explorer computer.

PC SCHEME   This is a microcomputer implementation of LISP by Texas Instruments Corporation. This dialect was developed specifically to provide a PC environment for the TI Personal Consultant series of expert system tools.

PORTABLE STANDARD LISP (PSL)   PSL is an attempt to write a quality LISP program in LISP itself as much as possible, with only minor amounts of code written by hand in assembly language or other system languages. Its development started at the University of Utah in 1980.

S-1 LISP   This is an implementation of CommonLISP and runs on the S-1 Mark IIA computer. This implementation has a compiler that produces code for numerical computations. It is competitive in execution speed with that produced by a FORTRAN compiler. The S-1 LISP compiler extends the work done in MacLISP to produce very efficient numerical code. LISP is frequently criticized for its inefficient handling of numerical computations. However, some special-purpose dialects of LISP have evolved over the years to meet the number-crunching challenge (at least partially).

SPICELISP   This is an implementation of Common LISP written mostly in Common LISP and partly in microcode. The initial implementation was done at Carnegie Mellon University on the Perq computer. Perq is a computer that was built by Perq Systems Corporation. It is user microcodable.

TOP-LEVEL COMMON LISP   Top Level, Inc. developed a language and programming environment for multiprocessing software development. The language, named TopCL, is a full standard Common LISP for Unix System V and X-Window-based multiprocessing systems. TopCL includes a foreign function interface, allowing easy access to existing C and FORTRAN software.

VAX COMMON LISP   The basic strategy behind this implementation was to bring up a Common LISP on the VAX rapidly by the help of the SpiceLISP System. It runs on all of the DEC VAX models under the VMS operating system.

WALTZ LISP   WALTZ LISP (WLISP) is available in over 75 CP/M formats. One of the major attractions of WLISP is its speed. It is much faster than many other dialects.

ZETALISP   This dialect of LISP is a direct outgrowth of the MIT LISP Machine's LISP. It was developed for the MIT LISP Machine "CADR" and also runs on the symbolics LM-2.

Programming in LISP is done by defining functions that build up a language in terms of previously defined functions or machine code rather than by writing a list of instructions in a fixed language. One of LISP's most useful features is its interactive programming capability. In FORTRAN, programmers generally write an entire program or module before they begin testing. LISP's entire program does not need to be written before testing. It is written and interpreted function by function. In this way, recompilation and relinking are done quickly and automatically.

A LISP program and data are stored as linked lists, nonsequential structures whose components are linked with pointers. FORTRAN, by comparison, stores data and instructions in sequential locations. Adding one line to a FORTRAN program or even one element to an array requires recompiling and relinking of the code to accommodate the address change. In FORTRAN, when a reference to an array is removed, the array memory remains but cannot be accessed or relocated, whereas in LISP location can be quickly reclaimed by garbage collection. LISP uses a heap memory based on dynamic allocation as opposed to the linear array memory that is used by FORTRAN. In heap memory, words in memory are not part of a large, contiguous block of memory but are individually assignable and may be linked together to form lists. This feature completely solves the memory allocation problem that is associated with conventional systems used in FORTRAN.

Another useful feature of LISP is recursion. A recursive language permits an implicit definition of a function as a parameter for itself. This capability is not easily achieved with conventional programming languages.

FORTRAN LISP   Though FORTRAN is not very well suited for pure AI applications, it is still far more capable of performing pure numerical processing than LISP. A hybrid language called FORTRAN LISP, developed by Systems Research Laboratories, combines features found in both LISP and FORTRAN. FORTRAN LISP is a powerful language which can be used to implement an artificial intelligence system that requires both numerical and symbolic data processing.

There are four major implementations of FORTRAN LISP: an intelligent data base, an English-language interpreter, a robotic control, and a neuron network. The first two systems operate in the symbolic domain and are typical of a pure LISP environment. The latter systems combine the true attributes of FORTRAN LISP through numeric and symbolic processing. FORTRAN LISP can serve as a valuable tool in environments that dictate the need for traditional programming coupled with artificial intelligence techniques.

LISP AND C LANGUAGE   C is a general-purpose programming language. It has been closely associated with the UNIX system because it was developed on that system and because UNIX and its software packages are written in C. C language has been called a "system programming language" because it is useful for writing operating systems. It has been used equally well to write major numerical, text processing, and data base programs. C helps to overcome the drawbacks of using only assembly or high level languages. C integrates the best features from both types of languages, having many of the high productivity features of high level languages, combined with the bit-handling features of assembly languages.

In order to take advantage of such features offered by C language and to make it compatible with high level languages for various artificial intelligence applications, an experimental language called XLISP has been designed. XLISP is regarded as a variation of common LISP written in C. It is suitable for studying object-oriented programming concepts. Since the XLISP syntax is quite standard, this dialect will also run applications written for other LISP environments with few modifications. XLISP has over 100 predefined functions, some of which are related to an object-oriented class system. These include EVAL, symbol, list, property list functions, as well as many control functions. It is in the public domain and is currently available on many CP/M-oriented bulletin board systems.

7.2.3 PROLOG as a Relational Programming Language

PROLOG, an acronym for PROgramming in LOGic, is a language developed in 1973 by Alain Colmerauer and his colleagues in the Artificial Intelligence Group (GIA - Groupe d'Intellegence Artificielle) in Marseilles, France. It was originally created to integrate a development in mathematical logic into a programming logic (Colmerauer 1985). It is called logic programming language because its statements are interpreted as sentences of a logic. The principles governing PROLOG's original design were based both on language theory and on traditional mathematical logic. This facilitated the design of a programming language that would enable a programmer to develop programs to simulate human thinking process by making deductions from information given in a logical fashion.

PROLOG is a simple but powerful programming language. Clear, readable, concise programs can be written quickly with few errors. PROLOG programs can be written in conjunction with LISP, where LISP provides functions and actions complementary to PROLOG. This is because conventional PROLOG deals only with logical statements and does not perform numeric operations. LISP machines therefore served as the first PROLOG machines. PROLOG, a language based on Horn Clauses, can be described as an implication in which the conjunction of zero or more conditions implies at most one conclusion. The syntax and semantics of a PROLOG program are affected by the deterministic order of execution imposed by the language.

Having its foundations in logic, PROLOG encourages the programmer to describe problems in a logical manner that facilitates checking for correctness and consequently reduces the debugging effort. The conciseness of PROLOG programs, with the resulting decrease in development time, makes it an ideal language for prototyping. In PROLOG, procedures may contain parameters that are both input and output.

THE PROLOG INTERPRETER   The first experimental interpreter for PROLOG was written in ALGOL-W by Philippe Roussel in 1972. In 1973, a better technique was incorporated by using the Merseille interpreter. A PROLOG interpreter written in PASCAL has also been implemented. Other PROLOG interpreters have also been implemented for many mainframe and minicomputer systems. Backward chaining is a feature used by the PROLOG interpreter. The interpreter checks each element of the statement to see if it is true. To process the statement or rule, the interpreter goes to each fact in the rule in turn. When it encounters a fact, it scans all the other rules in the list, looking for rules that generate that fact.

Rules can be a statement of the form "this fact is true." If the interpreter finds one of these, it records the fact in the rule it is evaluating as true, and moves to the next one. If all the facts stated in the rule are true, its result is true. If, during the processing of the statement, the interpreter finds a rule that states that its resultant fact is true only if another set of facts is true, the interpreter then evaluates this new rule in an attempt to prove its result and so to prove the original rule. This new rule is evaluated in the same manner as the original one (i.e., by attempting to find out whether its required facts are true). The process continues until it terminates on a known true fact or until no rule can be found to prove the fact.

THE HORN CLAUSES   A PROLOG program is constructed from a number of clauses. These clauses are of three types: hypotheses, goals, and conditions.

Clauses	Examples
Hypotheses:	Mother (Mary, Cindy)
Goals:	Ancestor (John, X)
Conditions:	Grandparent (X,Z), Parent (X,Y), Parent (Y,Z)

The order of these clauses is irrelevant to the logic of the program. The general body of a clause is: <head><body>. If the <head> is omitted, it is considered a goal; if the <body> is omitted, it is considered an hypothesis. Both the <head> and the <body> are composed of "predications," which are applications of a "predicate" (such as "father") to one or more terms (such as "John" and "X"): Father(John,X) indicates the query "Is there an X whose father is John?" Most of the logic programming systems allow at most one predication in the <head> but any number in the <body>. This restriction is called the Horn Clause Form. Predications are intended to represent relationships among the individuals of the problem domain. In Horn Clauses, the conjunction of zero or more conditions implies at most one conclusion.

Being represented as a pair of descriptor and internal lists, a PROLOG program doesn't have any specifically defined terms for functions, atoms, integers, and variables, etc. The internal lists are represented by

$$[. \ldots . . .]$$

A list $[t_1, \ldots, t_n]$ is represented internally by the pair

$$(D)[(t_1), \ldots, (t_n)]),$$

Where $(t_1), \ldots, (t_n)$ are internal representations of $t_1, \ldots, t_n$.

D is the descriptor that contains the type of the object. That is, the type of the function, atom, integer, list, or variable and the relative position of the end of the object value. For instance, in the case of the object "variable," the relative position of the variable is indicated in its associated context.

A function $f(t_1, \ldots, t_n)$ is represented internally as the pair $(Df,[(f), (t_1), \ldots, (t_n)])$ where $(t_1), \ldots, (t_n)$ are internal representations of $t_1, \ldots, t_n$ and (f) the internal representation of the atom "f".

Similarly an "atom" is represented as the pair $(Da,[atom])$ and an "integer" as the pair $(Di,[integer])$.

The terms defined in the PROLOG program are called "static terms" and are represented as indicated above. The terms generated during execution are called "dynamic terms" and are represented by a pointer to a static term and a pointer to a context which defines an instance of its variables. A dynamic term can point to a part of the internal list; this is referred to as a dynamic sublist.

A "module" is a PROLOG program consisting of a pair such as (literal, defining module), which means that the definition of the literal is supposed to be in the "defining module." An "instance of the module" is the state of the execution of the module. It is composed of a "static part" and a "dynamic part." The static part is the portion that remains after the end of its execution and the dynamic part is the portion that lasts as long as the execution and is lost after the end of the execution.

There are four "stacks" in a PROLOG implementation: the clause stack, the execution stack, the variable stack, and the backtracking stack. The clause stack contains clauses, dictionaries, and access to clauses. The execution stack is a list of nodes containing information related to the backtracking. The clause stack refers to the static part of the program whereas other stacks are related to the dynamic part of the PROLOG program.

PROLOG IMPLEMENTATIONS   PROLOG uses predicate logic to perform symbolic and logical computations. It has several built-in features that limit its flexibility. But the fixed features greatly simplify programming particularly for AI applications. The language now exists in many forms on many different machines. The current implementations of PROLOG vary in syntax and features. Some of the well known variations are listed below.

DEC 10 PROLOG   Developed at the University of Edinburgh, DEC 10 PROLOG takes advantage of the high level statement specification of Horn Clauses.

LM PROLOG   LM PROLOG is integrated with, and runs under, ZetaLISP, using an advanced computing environment.

M PROLOG (I-PROLOG)   This dialect is developed for Apollo, Digital Equipment VAX, IBM, SUN, and Tektronix 4404. It is written in portable CDL-Z, an intermediate computer compiler development language.

MICRO-PROLOG   Developed by Logic Programming Associates Limited of London for Z-80 systems running CP/M. Augmented-PROLOG for Expert Systems (APES) is based on this dialect.

PROLOG-1   This is developed by Expert Systems International (ESI). The products that have been implemented in it include two popular expert systems: M-1 and ES/P advisor.

PROLOG-86   PROLOG-86 is intended primarily for those who are interested in learning the language. It is noted for its fast execution.

PROLOG/VM (Waterloo PROLOG)   This runs on IBM system 370 and interfaces directly with LISP/VM as well as other IBM programs.

TURBO PROLOG   Turbo PROLOG was developed by Borland. It is one of the most popular PC-based implementations of PROLOG.

PROLOG IN LISP   It is known that both PROLOG and LISP have advantages and disadvantages. The ideal is to have a combined implementation of both so as to exploit the advantages they offer individually. There are two ways to do this. One way is to use a function that can call and run external functions. Complex architectures can be designed using this method for applications that use PROLOG for some parts and LISP for others and call one another as needed. The second way is to use both in an integrated form. There are now many PROLOG-in-LISP (PiL) systems available. Some of these contain very comprehensive features. The most important one is that the whole LISP system, with all of its features, can often be made available from within the PROLOG function.

In PROLOG-in-LISP systems, PROLOG acts as a function in LISP. The biggest drawback with such systems, however, is that they are often very slow. The development of the current implementation of PROLOG-in-LISP was preceded by the development of two similar systems called LOGLISP and QLOG. PROLOG-in-LISP systems are far better than QLOG and LOGLISP systems because they have simpler and more LISP-like syntax and they rely on a depth-first control structure. Other advantages of the combined programming environment are listed below:

(1). It provides LISP users with the benefits of PROLOG while not giving up those of LISP.

(2). Its syntax resembles the list syntax of LISP, enabling a more flexible logic language.

(3). It allows a PROLOG programmer to define predicates and functions easily in LISP.

7.3 DATA BASE CAPABILITIES

Data base systems have become an important component of expert system models. Many data base features are now available to facilitate effective expert system consultation interface. Presented below are some of the important capabilities needed for expert system data base interface:

Speed: Heuristic query optimization techniques enable some data base programs to choose the fastest method of executing a command, on the basis of such considerations as how much RAM is available, how much data needs to be processed, and the destination of the data. This permits operations like sorting, view processing, and CROSSTAB to execute much faster than the older generations of data base programs.

Powerful programming: Newer data base programs offer programming environments that emulate conventional programming languages. Mathematical, statistical, financial, string manipulation, logic, trigonometric, and data type functions are available in some programs. This provides comprehensive computational capability for rapid and complex data analysis that may be needed during expert system consultation.

User interface: Friendly menu-driven interfaces are available to aid both beginning and experienced users. For example, PromptByExample (PBE) used by R:BASE is a menu-driven, interactive user interface that provides capabilities to structure, enter, update, query, and retrieve data without programming. Users are guided though data base command creation without having to remember commands or syntax.

Embedded query language: Many of the commands of the popular structured query language (SQL) are now embedded in the newest of the data base management systems. See further discussions on SQL in the next section.

Connectivity: Data exchange is becoming more and more important in these days of limited resources. Decision makers are finding out that data need not be regenerated in its original form at each application site. Each information system does not need to individually maintain a copy of a file if that file can be accessed in a central repository. Data file import and export capabilities have become a major objective of many data management programs. Connectivity in the form of PC-to-PC or PC-to-mainframe is essential for expert system implementations. For example, an expert system may access corporate data bases for cost estimation purposes.

Multiple-user configuration: Many data base systems now have capabilities for simultaneous data entry and edit with concurrent control. Multiple users can safely edit or update information in the same database. Protection procedures are incorporated into the programs so that databases and application files are not accidentally destroyed in the multiple-user environment. An example is the "automatic time lock release" used by R:BASE to provide protection against the lockup of a data base when two users attempt to lock the same set of tables at the same time.

Data security: Passwords can be assigned to data bases, tables, and views. Individual users can be given selective access privileges through special commands. For example, in dBASE IV, memo fields in a data base can be encrypted for confidentiality, either explicitly, through use of the PROTECT command, or automatically, when the associated data base is encrypted.

7.3.1 Structured Query Language

In small data bases, one can locate a record by browsing through the contents of the data base. However, in large data bases, browsing through the records could be slow and inefficient. A more efficient way would be to retrieve only the specific files or records that are needed rather than to browse through all of them.

The Structured Query Language (SQL) is a way for a user to easily retrieve pertinent records from a file. With simple English-like words, the user queries the data base about the desired data. The query is composed of clauses such as FROM, SELECT, WHERE, and ORDER. The clauses are used to specify search parameters. For example,

FROM identifies from which file(s) to retrieve the records.

SELECT identifies the field(s) to be retrieved.

WHERE sets specific conditions that the field(s) data must meet.

ORDER sorts the records by a key field alphabetically or numerically.

The FROM clause is mandatory since it specifies the name of the file to be searched. The other clauses are optional; their use depends on the data being requested. All the clauses do not have to be used at once, but if they are, they must follow the order FROM, SELECT, WHERE, and ORDER. Both relational operators and logical operators can be used in the query. Some of the permissible operators are presented below:

Relational operators:

Greater than ($>$)

Less than ($<$)

Greater than or equal to ($>=$)

Less than or equal to ($<=$)

Equal to ($=$)

Not equal to ($<>$)

Logical operators:

    AND

    OR

    NOT

The AND operator requires that all the stated conditions must be met before a record can be retrieved. The OR operator requires that any one of the conditions may be satisfied in order to retrieve the record. The NOT operator requires that the record be retrieved only if the stated condition(s) are not satisfied. The use of SQL to retrieve a record is illustrated with the example below:

```
FROM       PROJECT
SELECT     TASK, DURATION, DUE_DATE
WHERE      DURATION > 5 AND DUE_DATE < 10
ORDER      DUE_DATE
```

The above query retrieves records from the PROJECT file. The data fields of interest are TASK, DURATION, and DUE_DATE. The selected records must have durations greater than 5 time units and due dates less than 10 time units. Once the records are selected, they are arranged in numeric order by due dates. This example may be a case where we need a list of project tasks that have imminent due dates but are likely to exceed the due dates because of their long durations.

SQL had been the standard for accessing mainframe data base systems. It had just recently begun to make its appearance on microcomputers, which makes the powerful data management system more accessible to decision makers. Many data base professionals now view SQL as the data base interface of the future. The move to SQL is driven by the growing prevalence of microcomputers as a data base management tool. Thousands of small businesses now employ microcomputers to track and manage their important data. The growing awareness that standalone data bases would, in the future, need to share information with other systems, has prompted the move towards SQL as the standard for such data base interactions.

Ashton-Tate, the developer of the dBASE series, is moving in the SQL direction. The latest addition to the dBASE series, dBASE IV has an SQL facility. Informix Software, Inc. of Menlo Park, California, now has its own version of SQL called Informix-SQL. Informix also has a fourth-generation language called Informix-4GL and a product called ESQL/C, which allows C programmers to incorporate SQL into user-written programs. SQL can also be embedded in mainframe languages such as COBOL and PL/1. SQL has the major advantage of bringing the distributed computing and data integrity of mainframes to the PC level.

An alternative to the SQL facility in OS/2 Extended Edition is the SQL Server jointly marketed by Ashton-Tate and Microsoft. The SQL Server is an operating-system software package that is designed to allow multiple-user SQL data base programs to run on OS/2-based networks. For users of data base programs that do not offer SQL, add-on packages could be the answer. An example is dQuery from QuadBase Systems, Inc. The add-on package is a low-cost enhancement tool that allows dBASE and Lotus 1-2-3 users to access their local data files with SQL commands. Since SQL is implemented across a wide variety of hardware and software units, SQL-based data base software running on one type of system can often exchange data with SQL data bases on another.

Despite its advantages and unavoidable emergence as a standard, SQL does have some drawbacks. One drawback is the difficulty of learning the language. However, enhancements to the language that can improve its user-friendliness. For expert systems, SQL, even with its present PC-level limitations, can be beneficial. Expert system implementations often require evaluation of data sets that are based on heuristics. SQL already has the rudiments for implementing such heuristics for prompt decisions.

7.4 SELECTING A COMMERCIAL SHELL

The market for commercial expert systems development tools is growing rapidly. Many options are now available both at the high-end and low-end levels. New tools are being introduced while older versions are being updated. The expert systems software market is very competitive. Many packages that were originally developed for specific and narrow applications, such as data analysis and conventional decision support, now offer expert systems capabilities. Prospective buyers are often overwhelmed by the range of products available.

The frequency of new offerings and updates make it impossible to have an up-to-date compilation of the products available. The survey of commercial tools presented in Appendix B at the end of this book is intended to be only a general guide for the status of the market. Readers interested in an up-to-date guide to available packages should consult some of the frequently published computer-oriented magazines such as *Software* and *PC Week*. Harmon et al (1988) present a comprehensive overview of expert systems tools. Unfortunately, many of the commercial tools they covered are already outdated because new products have emerged since the book was published. However, the book is still a good general guide to expert systems tools.

This section presents general criteria for evaluating and selecting commercial development tools. Development tools, also known as *inference engines* or *shells*, offer a generic environment for developing expert systems. The early expert systems development tools were designed for the mainframe environment. Recently, more tools are being introduced for the personal computer environment. The emerging proliferation of powerful work station level computers has also contributed to the segmentation of the market. Commercial tools are now available in three distinct categories outlined as follows:

Low-end tools: These are designed for single user applications at the PC level.

Medium-level tools: These are designed to run on powerful work stations, such as LISP machines.

High-end tools: These are designed for mainframes. Some of the high-end tools also run on high-end work stations.

As commercial expert systems tools move into the 1990s, users and developers can look forward to significant improvements in ease of use and accessibility. The nucleus of the improvements will be the emergence of graphical user interface (GUI). The GUI technology was first pioneered in the microcomputer industry by Apple Computer, Inc. The release of Microsoft Windows and OS/2 Presentation Manager operating systems have made the GUI a reality for most PC users. Many expert systems software companies are now incorporating GUI capabilities into their products. For example, KnowledgePro Windows is one of the first PC-based shells to be ported to the Windows environment. Important questions to ask when evaluating expert systems GUI include the following:

- Does the graphical interface improve system performance?

- Does the interface offer more convenient organization and representation of the data needed by the expert system?

- Does the interface contain better analytic tools for data analysis?

- Can graphical outputs be customized for different levels of report?

- Does the graphical interface offer more flexibility than conventional user interfaces?

- Does the graphical interface require previous graphics experience?

- Is a utility program provided for capturing the screen display for hardcopy printing?

- What type of hardware configuration is required by the graphical interface?

Although most of the low-end expert systems development tools can run on the basic PC compatible systems, users of programs with graphical user interfaces often require more powerful systems. A good knowledge engineer would use his or her knowledge, training, expertise, experience and the tools available to develop effective expert systems. Computer hardware and software constitute one group of tools that is available to the knowledge engineer. A major task for the expert systems developer is to evaluate available development tools. The decision is usually not that of whether or not software is needed, but which software should be used and how.

7.4.1   Factors Influencing Shell Selection

Currently, there is very little standardization or compatibility in expert system shells. Unlike conventional application packages such as spreadsheet programs, expert systems shells often look, behave, and respond quite differently. Thus, a very careful evaluation of prospective shells must be conducted. Presented below are some of the several factors and questions that are important for evaluating expert systems shells. Figure 7.5 presents some of the factors or driving forces influencing the evaluation and selection of expert systems shells.

(1). *Cost*:
   - Can the software be procured for a reasonable amount relative to the organization's budget and intended use?

(2). *Justification*:
   - Has the justification for the software been fully documented?
   - Is there or will there be a knowledgeable person who can run the software?

(3). *Knowledge representation*:
   - What knowledge representation models are provided?
   - Can rules be prioritized in the knowledge base?
   - Does the shell search for rules in a predefined order?

(4). *External interface*:
   - Can the shell interface properly with external programs and data bases?

(5). Report capability:
   - What kinds of reports can be produced by the shell?

Figure 7.5. Factors influencing shell selection

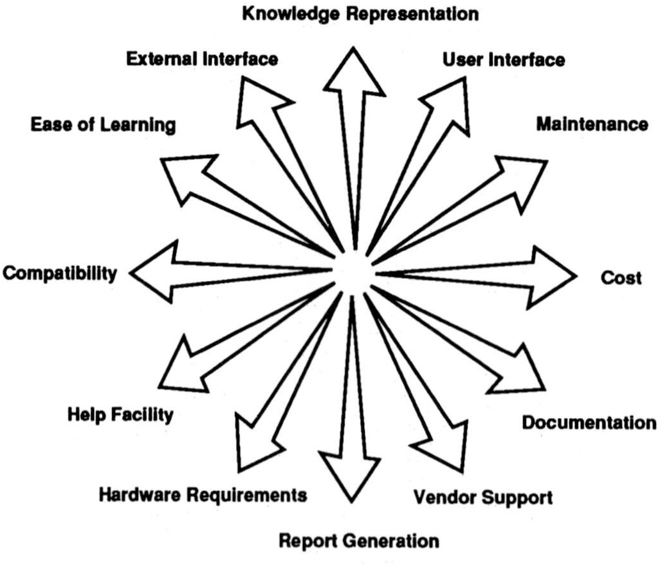

(6). *Quality of documentation*:
- Conciseness
- Clarity
- Length
- Binding and ruggedness

(7). *Ease of learning*:
- On line tutorial
- Familiarity of screen layout
- Data entry formats

(8). *Ease of use*:
- On-line training and help
- Input format
- Output format and contents
- Facilities for maintaining knowledge bases

(9). *General characteristics*:
- Software version
Later versions of a program, for example *version 3.2*, tend to have fewer bugs and more enhanced features. However, the existence of excessively high version numbers, for example *Version 8.1*, within a very short time span, could indicate that numerous bugs exist in the product.
- Compactness and interface structure for the program routines
- File import/export capability
- Availability of demo package
- Copy protection and backup procedures
- Does the program permit limited or unlimited hard disk installations?
- Speed of execution
- Compatibility with the computer hardware and other software used in the organization

(10). *Hardware requirements*:
- Disk drive requirement (floppy, fixed, high density, size, etc.)
- RAM requirement
- Math coprocessor or special hardware requirements
- Input devices (mouse, joystick, keyboard, etc.)
- Output devices (types of printers supported)
- Monitor requirements (CGA, EGA, VGA, Super VGA, etc.)

(11). *Vendor*:
- Reputation
- How long in business
- Sales volume
- Replacement support
- Product support
- Customer service (toll-free telephone line, technical support)
- Cost of program updates
- Other supporting products

The knowledge representation model used by a shell is an important consideration in shell selection. There are many different ways to store expert systems knowledge. But most commercial shells use one or both of two common approaches: rules and frames. The more common approach is to use rules. The discrete *If-Then* structure of rules works best in applications that have many assertions and rules that have some structural linking. Despite their popularity, however, rule-oriented structures have several shortcomings. A major drawback is the search time required. The shell must scan the knowledge base looking for candidate rules to evaluate. As the number of rules and input assertions grows, the search time can quickly increase beyond control.

The other major method is to store knowledge in frames. In contrast to the individual statements of rules and assertions, frames are basically structures that contain a set of data attributes, or slots, and usually some rules related to those slots. Each of the slots can contain a piece of information (or a rule) about whatever the frame describes, so a single frame can hold a great deal of information. The biggest advantage of frames is that they can represent knowledge about real-world events simply and easily. The inheritance capabilities of frames make them the best choice for applications in which the domain knowledge is hierarchical or context-dependent, such as simulation or natural-language translation. A disadvantage, however, is that expert systems shells that use frames generally require more powerful inference engines than those that use rules. This is the reason that most PC-based shells use rules for their knowledge representation.

While expert system shells use different problem-solving algorithms, the two most prevalent strategies are backward chaining and forward chaining. The more common method is backward chaining. Backward chaining starts with an answer and tries to work backward to reach the input assertions. It chooses the rules to try on the basis of their conclusions. The shell repeats this process until either the starting goal leads to the input assertions or until it cannot find any more rules to fire. In that case, it moves on to the next possible goal. Forward chaining uses a procedural approach opposite to that of backward chaining. Forward chaining starts with input assertions and fires every rule that those assertions require. The shell then checks to see if any of those rules led to a goal. If not, it repeats the process by firing every rule that the results of the previous assertions made possible. This iterative and recursive process is maintained until a goal is reached.

Forward chaining is best for those applications in which the user knows initially everything that the shell will need to reach a conclusion as well as those in which input assertions are more than the possible answers. Applications that commonly produce Yes/No answers are good candidates for forward chaining. Backward chaining is best for applications in which the user can supply a good starting guess. It is often better than forward chaining for applications in which there are many possible answers and fewer input assertions. The more powerful expert systems shells often offer both types of search strategies. Execution speed is another aspect of interest in selecting shells. But speed can be influenced by several factors including match between shell capability and problem requirements and the accuracy of input data. Some of the above factors may be more important than others in specific expert systems projects. As a result, a careful overall analysis should be done by the developer.

Computer hardware is another essential aspect of the selection of a shell for expert systems development. Even if the best software is selected, the best performance may not be obtained if the available hardware is not fully compatible with the needs of the software. Software developers are now cramming their products with features that call for heavier duty hardware configurations. An important aspect of buying and using expert systems tools is the matching of hardware, software, and the required applications. Figure 7.6 shows a graphical representation of the ways software and hardware must be matched to satisfy the required applications. The objective of the developer is to increase, as much as possible, the area in which software, hardware, and expert systems applications overlap. In this effort, the following points should be kept in mind:

- Not all of the required expert systems applications will fit the available hardware and software.

- Not all of the capabilities of the available software will fit the available hardware and the required applications.

- Not all of the available hardware capability will fit the required applications and the available software.

Figure 7.6. Intersection of hardware, software, and applications

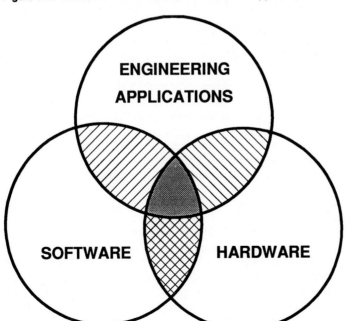

The ideal case is to have all the three circles in Figure 7.6 overlap perfectly. But ideal is one thing, feasibility is another. The recommended procedure is to clearly define the required expert systems applications and then match software and hardware to those applications as closely as possible. Once a feasible match has been achieved, expert systems development can commence.

7.5 EXERCISES

7.1 Give examples of two procedure-oriented programming languages in the following areas of applications: business, engineering, and manufacturing.

7.2 What is the general name given to the programs that translate source programs to machine language?

7.3 What is the difference between applications programs and systems programs?

7.4 Discuss the difference between a program and a programming language.

7.5 List other factors that may be of interest in selecting a commercial expert system development shell.

7.6 If you have access to any development shell, evaluate the shell on the basis of the suggestions presented in this chapter. Would you recommend the shell to someone else? Why or why not?

7.7 Compare and contrast the selection of an expert system development tool and the selection of a general software tool.

7.8 Describe the various characteristics of an applications environment that can influence the selection of an expert system development tool.

7.9 Discuss the need for evaluating the applications environment before selecting a development tool.

7.10 How is the selection of a development language different from the selection of a development shell?

7.11 Does access to a comprehensive development shell eliminate the need for a programming language during an expert system development process? Discuss.

7.12 Discuss the major language options for AI work with respect to comparative advantages and disadvantages.

7.13 Discuss the advantages and limitations of each of the elements in the hierarchy of programming languages.

7.14 Compare and contrast relational, procedural, and functional languages with respect to inference engine design.

7.15 Which AI programming languages are most suitable for expert systems applications in engineering and manufacturing? Discuss why.

7.16 Why is the list manipulation capability of LISP an important factor in expert system construction?

7.17 Why is the logic programming capability of PROLOG an important factor in expert system construction?

7.18 Discuss the potential advantages and disadvantages of integrating LISP and PROLOG for inference engine development.

7.19 Develop a set of guidelines for selecting an expert system development shell for engineering and manufacturing applications.

7.20 Write ten command words or statements in LISP and explain what each does.

7.21 Write ten command words or statements in PROLOG and explain what each does.

8

Constructing
the Knowledge Base

This chapter presents a general guideline for the expert system development process. The chapter covers the development cycle and presents illustrative examples of knowledge base construction.

8.1 EXPERT SYSTEMS DEVELOPMENT LIFE CYCLE

The generic life cycle of an expert system project consists of the following:

(1). Problem identification and analysis
(2). Design specifications
(3). Knowledge acquisition and representation
(4). Prototyping
(5). Verification, validation, and testing
(6). Implementation and integration
(7). Maintenance

The first three items in the life cycle above are covered in the preceding chapters. This chapter focuses on the prototyping process. Subsequent chapters cover verification, validation, and implementation. Many variations of this generic life cycle are used in practice. The specific contents of the life cycle will be dictated by the nature of the particular expert system being developed and organi-

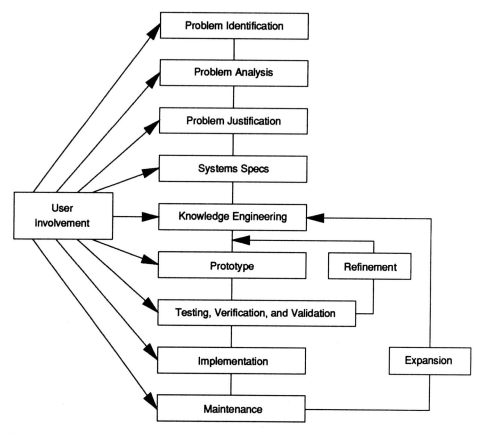

Figure 8.1. Expert system development process

zational preferences. Other specific steps that may be contained in the develop-ment process are *initial consultation with management*, *hardware/software selection*, *organization of the project team*, and *feasibility study*. Some of these other issues are discussed in this chapter and the chapters that follow. Figure 8.1 presents an overview of the development process for an expert system.

8.1.1 Organizational Support

Before embarking on the expert system development process, it is important to secure the full support of both management and users. The first expert system de-veloped by an organization should be viewed as an exploratory investment in the technology. The full benefits of expert systems would probably come from subse-quent efforts. After a successful introduction of the technology, subsequent expert systems can be expected to yield acceptable returns on the investment.

The developers or analysts must be unpretentious about what is expected from the system. An expert system developer should not promise more than can be delivered. It is prudent to deliver good quality, accurate, and useful versions of the system early in the development effort, even if the versions deal only with a very small subset of the eventual scope of the project. This will gain credibility for the development team and win support for the technology. Good early impressions of the effort will help secure the confidence of users and sponsors. It is also critical to get the users involved right from the early stages of the project. The concept of participative design should be adopted. This will make the users feel that they have an important role in the development effort and there will be fewer grounds for user criticisms later. Those who are familiar with the problem to be addressed by an expert system should be involved in the development process.

8.1.2   Systems Approach to Expert Systems Development

The emergence of systems development has had an extensive effect on technical operations in recent years. A system is defined as a collection of interrelated elements brought together to achieve a specified objective. In an expert system context, the purpose of the system is to create opportunities for productivity improvement and to facilitate effective decision making. An expert system cannot achieve this goal all alone. It would need the help and support of other subsystems within the same organization. An expert system should not be developed as an island of functionality. It must be viewed as a subsystem. As a subsystem it would have its own subsystems. For example, the knowledge base, data base, functions library, and the working memory act as subsystems of an expert system. Some of the common characteristics of a system include:

(1). Interaction with the environment

(2). Objective

(3). Self-regulation

(4). Self-adjustment

The various elements (or subsystems) of the organization act simultaneously in a separate but interrelated fashion to achieve a common goal. This synergism helps to expedite the decision process and to enhance the effectiveness of decisions. The supporting contributions from other subsystems of the organization serve to counterbalance the weaknesses of a given subsystem. Thus, the overall effectiveness of the system is greater than the sum of the individual results from the subsystems. Figure 8.2 shows an example of the role of an expert system in a manufacturing system. Inputs from the environment are capital, labor, raw material, knowledge, hardware, software, and technical information. The synergistic components of the overall system include the expert system, engineering functions, production operations, personnel functions, manufacturing management, and facilities planning. These components interact under an expert system guidance to produce better products, better services, and increased profit. An expert system should be developed simply as a component of a larger system. This will give consideration to all the interfaces necessary to make the expert system successful. Some of the important considerations in developing an expert system include the following:

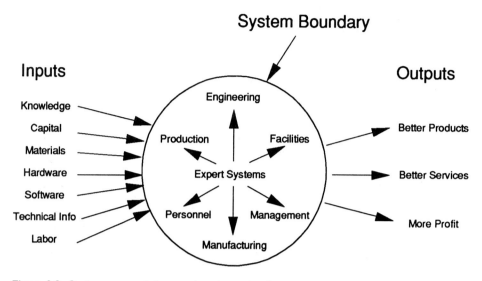

Figure 8.2. System approach to expert systems development

(1). Identifying how the expert system affects other functions in the overall system.

(2). Identifying how the other components of the overall system may affect the operations of the expert system.

(3). Identifying the personnel interfaces required to develop, implement, and maintain the expert system.

(4). Identifying the input-output relationships between the expert system and other subsystems operating in the same environment.

(5). Determining the criteria for verifying and validating the expert system.

(6). Establishing the performance evaluation criteria for the expert system in the context of the overall system.

(7). Establishing the guidelines for documenting the usage of the expert system.

8.2 CODING THE KNOWLEDGE BASE

Once all the groundwork has been completed for the project, the next major step is the actual construction of the expert system. The compilation of the knowledge base forms the nucleus of the development effort. Unfortunately, it is usually the component that creates the bottleneck between expert systems concepts and practical implementation. Once the desired knowledge has been acquired and a representational model has been selected as presented in the preceding chapters, the next step is the actual coding of the knowledge base.

The following section presents an example of the use of a decision tree to formulate the rule structure for a knowledge base. A decision tree is a technique used to define the various logical paths that a knowledge base must follow to reach conclusions. Several examples are used to illustrate the procedure.

8.2.1   Using a Decision Tree to Develop the Knowledge Structure

The example presented here is based on an example used by Thompson and Thompson (1985) to illustrate the MicroExpert inference engine. The example involves the identification of the botanical family for a plant. The objective is to identify the *family* type that a particular plant belongs to. We need to determine the *type* and *class* of the plant before being able to identify its *family*. The possible types of plant are: tree, shrub, vine, and herb. The two classes of plant involved are: angiosperm and gymnosperm. The possible families into which the plant can fall are: pine, cypress, and bald cypress. Using O-A-V representation, we have the following:

OBJECT	Plant
ATTRIBUTE	Family
VALUE	Pine, cypress, or bald cypress

When consulting with the plant classification expert system, some of the queries needed by the system include the following:

"Is the stem of the plant woody or green?"

"Is the position of the stem upright or creeping?"

"Does the plant have one main trunk?"

The user will respond to the queries on the basis of the observed characteristics of the plant being examined. The question to ask at each stage of the consultation will depend on the current status of the consultation. Figure 8.3 shows the beginning point of the knowledge representation. First, we look at a single path in the decision tree. This single path leads to the subgoal of plant type. The other possible paths to that subgoal are then evaluated as shown in Figure 8.4.

Figure 8.3. Decision path to a subgoal

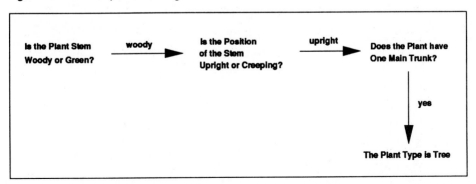

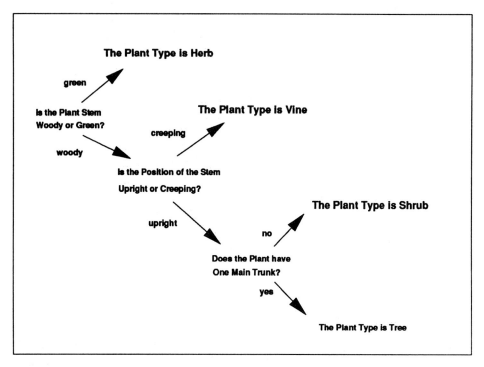

Figure 8.4. Expansion of a decision path

Once we have the plant type, we would explore the possible directions in the tree that could lead to the plant class. This is shown in Figure 8.5. From the node indicating the class of plant, we would progress through the appropriate paths that may lead to the plant family as shown in Figure 8.6. We would now begin to write our If-Then rules on the basis of the detailed decision tree. All the paths emanating from each node must be evaluated and their terminal points must be determined before starting to write the rules. The separate segments of the decision tree may be combined into one integrated tree. However, that may be too cumbersome and cluttered for large problems. A wise approach is to have a subgoal of the

Figure 8.5. Decision paths emanating from a subgoal

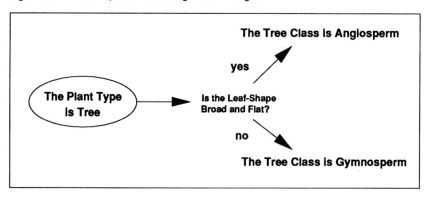

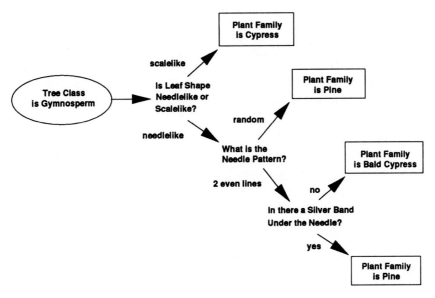

Figure 8.6. Decision path to consultation goal

overall goal as the initial node for each segment of the decision tree. All the segments of the decision tree are linked appropriately when the knowledge base is coded.

8.2.2 Constructing the Knowledge Base

While writing the rules from the decision trees, we may spot duplications or redundant relationships. These are eliminated by pruning the tree into a more compact form. This may necessitate combining or eliminating some rules. Once we have written all the rules relevant to each node in the decision tree, we have our initial knowledge base. The knowledge base can then be coded into the specific format required by our inference engine being used. At this stage, the nature of the knowledge to be represented may dictate the type of development tool or inference engine suitable for the expert system. Examples of the rules generated from the decision trees in Figure 8.6 are shown below:

Rule 1:

> If stem is *woody*
> and position is *upright*
> and one-main-trunk is *yes*,
> Then plant-type is *tree*

Rule 2:

> If plant-type is *tree*
> and leaves-broad-and-flat is *no*,
> Then plant-class is *gymnosperm*

Rule 3:

> If plant-class is gymnosperm
> and leaf-shape is *needlelike*
> and needle-pattern is *2-even-lines*
> and silver-bands is *no,*
> Then plant-family is *bald cypress*

Each node in the decision trees can be expanded to explore other paths in the problem domain. It should be noted that some paths in the example presented here terminate prematurely. The example has been abbreviated for illustration purposes. But in an actual expert system development, a decision path may terminate prematurely for several reasons. Some of these reasons are:

- Lack of additional information for the decision path.
- Link to external programs or other knowledge bases.
- Deliberate limitation of the scope of the problem.
- Design requirement for future expansion of the system.

The complete knowledge base for our plant identification problem consists of the ten rules presented below.

Rule 1:

> If class is gymnosperm
>   and leaf-shape is scalelike,
> Then family is cypress.

Rule 2:

> If class is gymnosperm
>   and leaf-shape is needlelike
>   and needle-pattern is random,
> Then family is pine.

Rule 3:

> If class is gymnosperm
>   and leaf-shape is needlelike
>   and needle-pattern is two-even-lines
>   and silver-bands is yes,
> Then family is pine.

Rule 4:

    If class is gymnosperm
        and leaf-shape is needlelike
        and needle-pattern is two-even-lines
        and silver-bands is no,
    Then family is bald cypress.

Rule 5:

    If type-of-plant is tree
        and broad-and-flat is yes,
    Then class is angiosperm.

Rule 6:

    If type-of-plant is tree
        and broad-and-flat is no,
    Then class is gymnosperm.

Rule 7:

    If stem is green,
    Then type-of-plant is herb.

Rule 8:

    If stem is woody
        and position is creeping,
    Then type-of-plant is vine.

Rule 9:

    If stem is woody
        and position is upright
        and one-main-trunk is yes,
    Then type-of-plant is tree.

Rule 10:

    If stem is woody
        and position is upright
        and one-main-trunk is no,
    Then type-of-plant is shrub.

   To further illustrate the construction of a knowledge base, another small system was developed using the *VP Expert* inference engine. The problem involves home medical diagnosis of spots that may appear on children. The example is based on the "Spots Advisor" example presented by Sell (1985). The initial system covers simple medical ailments such as Measles, Impetigo, Chicken Pox, Shingles, Rubella, Heat Rash, Athlete's Foot, and Acne. It consists of 31 rules. The parameters (symptoms) used in arriving at the diagnosis are Temperature (feverish, normal), State (severe pain, mild, no pain), Location (feet, face) and Appearance (weeping-pus, blotchy-spots, pink-spots, blistery-spots). The subgoal and goal of the consultation are Ailment and Recommendation, respectively.

   If the user requests just a diagnosis of the ailment, the system prints one of the ailments listed above or it will inform the user that the ailment for the specific

Figure 8.7. Initial decision paths for Spots Advisor

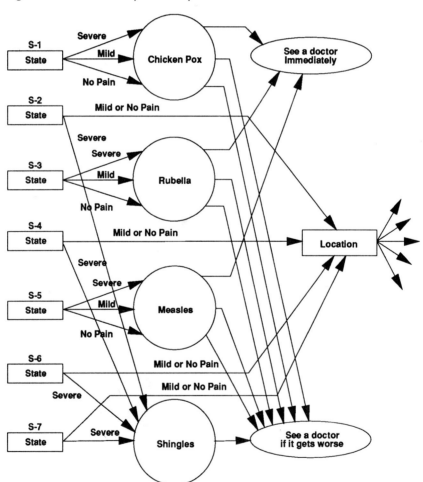

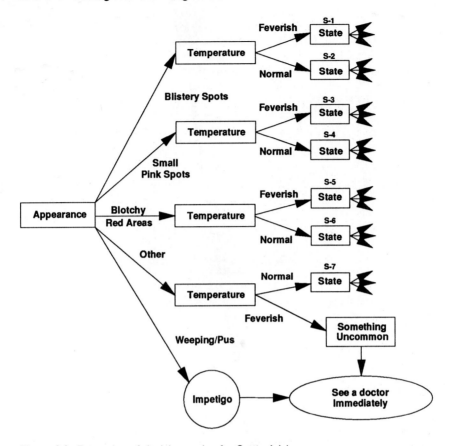

Figure 8.8. Expansion of decision nodes for Spots Advisor

symptoms presented is something uncommon to its knowledge base. If the user specifies Recommendation as the desired final goal of the consultation, the system will print a recommendation such as "See a doctor immediately" or "See a doctor if it gets worse." It may be a while before parents have complete confidence in the recommendations by Spots Advisor. However, the example does demonstrate the viability and good prospects of using expert systems even for routine decisions in the home.

Figure 8.7 shows a graphical illustration of the initial decision paths for Spots Advisor. The consultation parameters are shown in rectangles. The diagnoses based on specific parameter values are shown in circles. The final recommendations based on the diagnoses are shown in ellipses. The parameter "State" can be reached through seven different paths. These are identified as S-1, S-2, . . . , and S-7. Each state node is then expanded as shown in Figure 8.8 to further explore the consultation paths.

Figure 8.9 shows the goal nodes that emanate from the node for the parameter "Location." Based on the prevailing set of symptoms, some consultations will

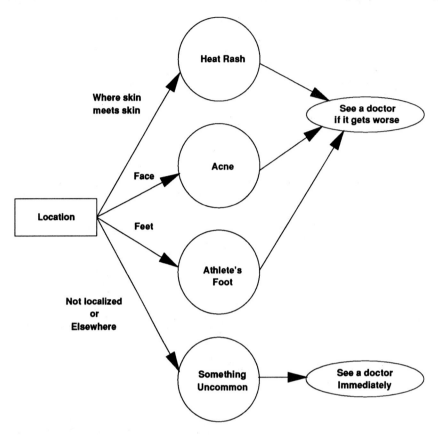

Figure 8.9. Goal nodes for Spots Advisor

take fairly short paths and reach the final goal quickly. In such cases, it will not be necessary to instantiate all the parameters in the decision tree. The reader may want to study the decision paths represented in Figures 8.7, 8.8, and 8.9 to determine how the consultation routes can be enhanced by pruning or expanding the decision tree at appropriate points. It may also be useful to integrate the three figures sequentially to see the overall structure of the decision tree.

Even though the illustration above uses a small and simple problem domain, the process of organizing any acquired knowledge into a formal knowledge base follows the same general methodology. However, for complex problem domains, care must be taken to analyze the maze of interrelationships in the decision trees. The individual elements (or rules) in the knowledge base must be carefully organized to follow a logical inference structure germane to the problem domain.

Expert systems developers acquire confidence and practical skill by first developing small expert systems with manageable complexity comparable to the example problem presented in this section. Once the generic rule construction methodology is understood, it is just a matter of becoming familiar with the specific knowledge base format of the development tool being used. Even if a different knowledge representation model is to be used (e.g., frames, semantic networks, predicate calculus), rules can still form the basis for implementing the alternate representation model. For example, the Personal Consultant Plus inference engine uses a combination of rules and frames. Once the developer is familiar with the rule structure, the frame organization can be easily mastered. Hence, the emphasis here is to show the reader how expert systems rules are formulated. The same concepts, rationale, and procedures that are used in handling the minor problems are what should be extended to handle the more complex expert systems problems in engineering and manufacturing.

The knowledge base for the Spots Advisor, as implemented with VP Expert inference engine, is printed below. The knowledge base structure may be modified to fit the specific structure required by another development tool other than VP-EXPERT.

KNOWLEDGE BASE FOR SPOTS ADVISOR

```
BKCOLOR=5;
RUNTIME;
ACTIONS
        COLOR=0
        DISPLAY "


                        How do you feel?

    If you think there is something medically wrong with you, but you are not sure if
    you should go to the doctor or not, then this consultation is for you.

    Please answer the questions by using the arrow keys to move the lightbar to the cor-
    rect answer, press RETURN, then press END. To cancel a selection before pressing
    END, press the DEL key while the lightbar is over the item you wish to change.

Please press any key to begin.~"
CLS
        FIND RECOMMENDATION
        COLOR=20
DISPLAY "

    Using the answers to the questions I have asked you, I have determined that you have
    {AILMENT} and that you should {RECOMMENDATION}.

                        I hope you get well soon.~";


RULE 1
IF        APPEARANCE=WEEPING-PUS
THEN      AILMENT=IMPETIGO;
```

RULE 2
IF   APPEARANCE=BLISTERY-SPOTS
          AND TEMPERATURE=FEVERISH
THEN   AILMENT=CHICKENPOX;

RULE 3
IF   APPEARANCE=SMALL-PINK-SPOTS
          AND TEMPERATURE=FEVERISH
THEN   AILMENT=RUBELLA-GERMAN-MEASLES;

RULE 4
IF   APPEARANCE=BLOTCHY-RED
          AND TEMPERATURE=FEVERISH
THEN   AILMENT=MEASLES;

RULE 5
IF   APPEARANCE=OTHER
          AND TEMPERATURE=FEVERISH
THEN   AILMENT=SOMETHING-UNCOMMON;

RULE 6
IF   TEMPERATURE=NORMAL
          AND STATE=IN-MILD-PAIN
          AND LOCATION=FEET
THEN   AILMENT=ATHLETES-FOOT-TINEA;

RULE 7
IF   TEMPERATURE=NORMAL
          AND STATE=IN-SEVERE-PAIN
THEN   AILMENT=SHINGLES;

RULE 8
IF   TEMPERATURE=NORMAL
          AND STATE=IN-MILD-PAIN
          AND LOCATION=FACE
THEN   AILMENT=ACNE;

RULE 9
IF   TEMPERATURE=NORMAL
          AND STATE=IN-MILD-PAIN
          AND LOCATION=WHERE-SKIN-MEETS-SKIN
THEN   AILMENT=HEAT-RASH;

RULE 10
IF   TEMPERATURE=NORMAL
          AND STATE=IN-MILD-PAIN
          AND LOCATION=ELSEWHERE
THEN   AILMENT=SOMETHING-UNCOMMON;

```
RULE 11
IF        AILMENT=IMPETIGO
THEN      RECOMMENDATION=SEE_A_DOCTOR_IMMEDIATELY;


RULE 12
IF        AILMENT=CHICKENPOX
          AND STATE=IN-SEVERE-PAIN
THEN      RECOMMENDATION=SEE_A_DOCTOR_IMMEDIATELY;


RULE 13
IF        AILMENT=RUBELLA-GERMAN-MEASLES
          AND STATE=IN-SEVERE-PAIN
THEN      RECOMMENDATION=SEE_A_DOCTOR_IMMEDIATELY;


RULE 14
IF        AILMENT=MEASLES
          AND STATE=IN-SEVERE-PAIN
THEN      RECOMMENDATION=SEE_A_DOCTOR_IMMEDIATELY;


RULE 15
IF        AILMENT=SOMETHING-UNCOMMON
THEN      RECOMMENDATION=SEE_A_DOCTOR_IMMEDIATELY;


RULE 16
IF        AILMENT=SHINGLES
THEN      RECOMMENDATION=SEE_A_DOCTOR_IF_IT_GETS_WORSE;


RULE 17
IF        AILMENT=ATHLETES-FOOT-TINEA
THEN      RECOMMENDATION=SEE_A_DOCTOR_IF_IT_GETS_WORSE;


RULE 18
IF        AILMENT=ACNE
THEN      RECOMMENDATION=SEE_A_DOCTOR_IF_IT_GETS_WORSE;


RULE 19
IF        AILMENT=HEAT-RASH
THEN      RECOMMENDATION=SEE_A_DOCTOR_IF_IT_GETS_WORSE;


RULE 20
IF        AILMENT=CHICKENPOX
          AND STATE=IN-MILD=PAIN
THEN      RECOMMENDATION=SEE_A_DOCTOR_IF_IT_GETS_WORSE;


RULE 21
IF        AILMENT=RUBELLA-GERMAN-MEASLES
          AND STATE=IN-MILD=PAIN
THEN      RECOMMENDATION=SEE_A_DOCTOR_IF_IT_GETS_WORSE;
```

```
RULE 22
IF      AILMENT=MEASLES
        AND STATE=IN-MILD=PAIN
THEN    RECOMMENDATION=SEE_A_DOCTOR_IF_IT_GETS_WORSE;


RULE 23
IF      TEMPERATURE=NORMAL
        AND STATE=NO-PAIN
        AND LOCATION=FEET
THEN    AILMENT=ATHLETES-FOOT-TINEA;


RULE 24
IF      TEMPERATURE=NORMAL
        AND STATE=NO-PAIN
        AND LOCATION=FACE
THEN    AILMENT=ACNE;


RULE 25
IF      TEMPERATURE=NORMAL
        AND STATE=NO-PAIN
        AND LOCATION=WHERE-SKIN-MEETS-SKIN
THEN    AILMENT=HEAT-RASH;


RULE 26
IF      TEMPERATURE=NORMAL
        AND STATE=NO-PAIN
        AND LOCATION=ELSEWHERE
THEN    AILMENT=SOMETHING-UNCOMMON;


RULE 27
IF      TEMPERATURE=NORMAL
        AND STATE=IN-MILD-PAIN
        AND LOCATION=NOT-LOCALIZED
THEN    AILMENT=SOMETHING-UNCOMMON;


RULE 28
IF      TEMPERATURE=NORMAL
        AND STATE=NO-PAIN
        AND LOCATION=NOT-LOCALIZED
THEN    AILMENT=SOMETHING-UNCOMMON;


RULE 29
IF      AILMENT=CHICKENPOX
        AND STATE=NO-PAIN
THEN    RECOMMENDATION=SEE_A_DOCTOR_IF_IT_GETS_WORSE;


RULE 30
IF      AILMENT=RUBELLA-GERMAN-MEASLES
        AND STATE=NO-PAIN
THEN    RECOMMENDATION=SEE_A_DOCTOR_IF_IT_GETS_WORSE;
```

```
RULE 31
IF      AILMENT=MEASLES
        AND STATE=NO-PAIN
THEN    RECOMMENDATION=SEE_A_DOCTOR_IF_IT_GETS_WORSE;
```

ASK APPEARANCE: "What are the symptoms of your ailment?";
CHOICES APPEARANCE: WEEPING-OR-PUS-SPOTS, BLISTERY-SPOTS, SMALL-PINK-SPOTS, BLOTCHY-RED-AREAS, OTHER;

ASK TEMPERATURE: "What is your temperature?";
CHOICES TEMPERATURE: NORMAL, FEVERISH;

ASK STATE: "How serious is the pain you are feeling?";
CHOICES STATE: SEVERE, MILD, NO-PAIN;

ASK LOCATION: "What part of the body are the symptoms located?";
CHOICES LOCATION: FEET, FACE, WHERE-SKIN-MEETS-SKIN, ELSEWHERE, NOT-LOCALIZED;

8.2.3   Extending the Knowledge Base

After a successful implementation of the original Spots Advisor knowledge base, it was decided to extend the knowledge base to include other common ailments. Mumps and Flu were added to the knowledge base. Because the number of consultation parameters increased, the number of decision paths also increased, and the number of rules increased from 31 to 57. The rules in the extended knowledge base are presented below:

```
RULE 1
IF   DISEASE=NON_SKIN AND
     APPEARANCE=DULL AND
     STATE=SEVERE_PAIN OR
     STATE=MILD_PAIN OR
     STATE=NO_PAIN AND
     LOCATION=FEET OR
     LOCATION=FACE OR
     LOCATION=SKIN_MEETS_SKIN OR
     LOCATION=NOT_LOCALIZED OR
     LOCATION=ELSEWHERE AND
     TEMPERATURE=FEVERISH OR
     TEMPERATURE=NORMAL AND
     COLD=YES OR
     COLD=NO
THEN   AILMENT=SOMETHING_UNCOMMON;

RULE 2
IF   DISEASE=SKIN AND
     APPEARANCE=DULL AND
     STATE=SEVERE_PAIN OR
     STATE=MILD_PAIN OR
```

```
        STATE=NO_PAIN AND
        LOCATION=FEET OR
        LOCATION=FACE OR
        LOCATION=NOT_LOCALIZED OR
        LOCATION=THROAT OR
        LOCATION=ELSEWHERE OR
        LOCATION=SKIN_MEETS_SKIN AND
        TEMPERATURE=FEVERISH OR
        TEMPERATURE=NORMAL
THEN  AILMENT=SOMETHING_UNCOMMON;

RULE 3
IF    DISEASE=NON_SKIN AND
      APPEARANCE=WEEPING_PUS OR
      APPEARANCE=BLISTERY_SPOTS OR
      APPEARANCE=OTHER OR
      APPEARANCE=SMALL_PINK_SPOTS OR
      APPEARANCE=BLOTCHY_RED AND
      STATE=SEVERE_PAIN OR
      STATE=MILD_PAIN OR
      STATE=NO_PAIN AND
      LOCATION=FEET OR
      LOCATION=FACE OR
      LOCATION=SKIN_MEETS_SKIN OR
      LOCATION=NOT_LOCALIZED OR
      LOCATION=ELSEWHERE OR
      LOCATION=THROAT AND
      TEMPERATURE=FEVERISH OR
      TEMPERATURE=NORMAL AND
      COLD=YES OR
      COLD=NO
THEN  AILMENT=SOMETHING_UNCOMMON;

RULE 4
IF    DISEASE=SKIN AND
      APPEARANCE=WEEPING_PUS
THEN  AILMENT=IMPETIGO;

RULE 5
IF    DISEASE=SKIN AND
      APPEARANCE=BLISTERY_SPOTS AND
      STATE=SEVERE_PAIN AND
      TEMPERATURE=FEVERISH
THEN  AILMENT=CHICKENPOX;

RULE 6
IF    DISEASE=SKIN AND
      APPEARANCE=BLISTERY_SPOTS AND
      STATE=MILD_PAIN AND
      TEMPERATURE=FEVERISH
THEN  AILMENT=CHICKENPOX;
```

```
RULE 7
IF   DISEASE=SKIN AND
     APPEARANCE=BLISTERY_SPOTS AND
     STATE=NO_PAIN AND
     TEMPERATURE=FEVERISH
THEN  AILMENT=CHICKENPOX;


RULE 8
IF   DISEASE=SKIN AND
     APPEARANCE=SMALL_PINK_SPOTS AND
     STATE=SEVERE_PAIN AND
     TEMPERATURE=FEVERISH
THEN  AILMENT=RUBELLA_MEASLES;


RULE 9
IF   DISEASE=SKIN AND
     APPEARANCE=SMALL_PINK_SPOTS AND
     STATE=MILD_PAIN AND
     TEMPERATURE=FEVERISH
THEN  AILMENT=RUBELLA_MEASLES;


RULE 10
IF   DISEASE=SKIN AND
     APPEARANCE=SMALL_PINK_SPOTS AND
     STATE=NO_PAIN AND
     TEMPERATURE=FEVERISH
THEN  AILMENT=RUBELLA_MEASLES;


RULE 11
IF   DISEASE=SKIN AND
     APPEARANCE=BLOTCHY_RED AND
     STATE=SEVERE_PAIN AND
     TEMPERATURE=FEVERISH
THEN  AILMENT=MEASLES;


RULE 12
IF   DISEASE=SKIN AND
     APPEARANCE=BLOTCHY_RED AND
     STATE=MILD_PAIN AND
     TEMPERATURE=FEVERISH
THEN  AILMENT=MEASLES;


RULE 13
IF   DISEASE=SKIN AND
     APPEARANCE=BLOTCHY_RED AND
     STATE=NO_PAIN AND
     TEMPERATURE=FEVERISH
THEN  AILMENT=MEASLES;
```

```
RULE 14
IF   DISEASE=SKIN AND
     STATE=MILD_PAIN AND
     LOCATION=FEET AND
     TEMPERATURE=NORMAL
THEN  AILMENT=ATHLETE_TINEA;


RULE 15
IF   DISEASE=SKIN AND
     STATE=NO_PAIN AND
     LOCATION=FEET AND
     TEMPERATURE=NORMAL
THEN  AILMENT=ATHLETE_TINEA;


RULE 16
IF   DISEASE=SKIN AND
     STATE=SEVERE_PAIN AND
     TEMPERATURE=NORMAL
THEN  AILMENT=SHINGLES;


RULE 17
IF   DISEASE=SKIN AND
     STATE=MILD_PAIN AND
     LOCATION=FACE AND
     TEMPERATURE=NORMAL
THEN  AILMENT=ACNE;


RULE 18
IF   DISEASE=SKIN AND
     STATE=NO_PAIN AND
     LOCATION=FACE AND
     TEMPERATURE=NORMAL
THEN  AILMENT=ACNE;


RULE 19
IF   DISEASE=SKIN AND
     STATE=MILD_PAIN AND
     LOCATION=SKIN_MEETS_SKIN AND
     TEMPERATURE=NORMAL
THEN  AILMENT=HEAT_RASH;


RULE 20
IF   DISEASE=SKIN AND
     STATE=NO_PAIN AND
     LOCATION=SKIN_MEETS_SKIN AND
     TEMPERATURE=NORMAL
THEN  AILMENT=HEAT_RASH;
```

RULE 21
IF   DISEASE=SKIN AND
     APPEARANCE=OTHER AND
     TEMPERATURE=FEVERISH
THEN AILMENT=SOMETHING_UNCOMMON;

RULE 22
IF   DISEASE=SKIN AND
     STATE=MILD_PAIN AND
     LOCATION=ELSEWHERE AND
     TEMPERATURE=NORMAL
THEN AILMENT=SOMETHING_UNCOMMON;

RULE 23
IF   DISEASE=SKIN AND
     STATE=NO_PAIN AND
     LOCATION=ELSEWHERE AND
     TEMPERATURE=NORMAL
THEN AILMENT=SOMETHING_UNCOMMON;

RULE 24
IF   DISEASE=SKIN AND
     STATE=MILD_PAIN AND
     LOCATION=NOT_LOCALIZED AND
     TEMPERATURE=NORMAL
THEN AILMENT=SOMETHING_UNCOMMON;

RULE 25
IF   DISEASE=SKIN AND
     STATE=NO_PAIN AND
     LOCATION=NOT_LOCALIZED AND
     TEMPERATURE=NORMAL
THEN AILMENT=SOMETHING_UNCOMMON;

RULE 26
IF   DISEASE=NON_SKIN AND
     APPEARANCE=DULL AND
     STATE=SEVERE_PAIN OR
     STATE=MILD_PAIN AND
     LOCATION=NOT_LOCALIZED AND
     TEMPERATURE=FEVERISH AND
     COLD=YES
THEN   AILMENT=FLU;

RULE 27
IF   DISEASE=NON_SKIN AND
     APPEARANCE=DULL AND
     STATE=SEVERE_PAIN OR
     STATE=NO_PAIN AND
     LOCATION=NOT_LOCALIZED AND

```
        TEMPERATURE=FEVERISH AND
        COLD=NO
THEN  AILMENT=FLU;


RULE 28
IF   DISEASE=NON_SKIN AND
     APPEARANCE=DULL AND
     STATE=SEVERE_PAIN OR
     STATE=MILD_PAIN AND
     LOCATION=NOT_LOCALIZED AND
     TEMPERATURE=NORMAL AND
     COLD=YES
THEN  AILMENT=SOMETHING_UNCOMMON;


RULE 29
IF   DISEASE=NON_SKIN AND
     APPEARANCE=DULL AND
     STATE=SEVERE_PAIN OR
     STATE=NO_PAIN AND
     LOCATION=NOT_LOCALIZED AND
     TEMPERATURE=NORMAL AND
     COLD=NO
THEN  AILMENT=SOMETHING_UNCOMMON;


RULE 30
IF   DISEASE=NON_SKIN AND
     APPEARANCE=DULL AND
     STATE=SEVERE_PAIN OR
     STATE=MILD_PAIN AND
     LOCATION=THROAT AND
     TEMPERATURE=FEVERISH
THEN  AILMENT=MUMPS;


RULE 31
IF   DISEASE=NON_SKIN AND
     APPEARANCE=DULL AND
     STATE=SEVERE_PAIN OR
     STATE=NO_PAIN AND
     LOCATION=THROAT AND
     TEMPERATURE=FEVERISH
THEN  AILMENT=MUMPS;


RULE 32
IF   DISEASE=NON_SKIN AND
     APPEARANCE=DULL AND
     STATE=SEVERE_PAIN OR
     STATE=MILD_PAIN AND
     LOCATION=THROAT AND
     TEMPERATURE=NORMAL
THEN  AILMENT=SOMETHING_UNCOMMON;
```

RULE 33
IF   DISEASE=NON_SKIN AND
     APPEARANCE=DULL AND
     STATE=SEVERE_PAIN OR
     STATE=NO_PAIN AND
     LOCATION=THROAT AND
     TEMPERATURE=NORMAL
THEN   AILMENT=SOMETHING_UNCOMMON;

RULE 34
IF   AILMENT=IMPETIGO
THEN   RECOMMENDATION=SEE_A_DOCTOR_IMMEDIATELY;

RULE 35
IF   AILMENT=CHICKENPOX AND
     STATE=SEVERE_PAIN AND
     TEMPERATURE=FEVERISH
THEN   RECOMMENDATION=SEE_A_DOCTOR_IMMEDIATELY;

RULE 36
IF   AILMENT=CHICKENPOX AND
     STATE=MILD_PAIN AND
     TEMPERATURE=FEVERISH
THEN   RECOMMENDATION=SEE_A_DOCTOR_IF_IT_GETS_WORSE;

RULE 37
IF   AILMENT=CHICKENPOX AND
     STATE=NO_PAIN AND
     TEMPERATURE=FEVERISH
THEN   RECOMMENDATION=SEE_A_DOCTOR_IF_IT_GETS_WORSE;

RULE 38
IF   AILMENT=RUBELLA_MEASLES AND
     STATE=SEVERE_PAIN AND
     TEMPERATURE=FEVERISH
THEN   RECOMMENDATION=SEE_A_DOCTOR_IMMEDIATELY;

RULE 39
IF   AILMENT=RUBELLA_MEASLES AND
     STATE=MILD_PAIN AND
     TEMPERATURE=FEVERISH
THEN   RECOMMENDATION=SEE_A_DOCTOR_IF_IT_GETS_WORSE;

RULE 40
IF   AILMENT=RUBELLA_MEASLES AND
     STATE=NO_PAIN AND
     TEMPERATURE=FEVERISH
THEN   RECOMMENDATION=SEE_A_DOCTOR_IF_IT_GETS_WORSE;

```
RULE 41
IF   AILMENT=MEASLES AND
     STATE=SEVERE_PAIN AND
     TEMPERATURE=FEVERISH
THEN  RECOMMENDATION=SEE_A_DOCTOR_IMMEDIATELY;


RULE 42
IF   AILMENT=MEASLES AND
     STATE=MILD_PAIN AND
     TEMPERATURE=FEVERISH
THEN  RECOMMENDATION=SEE_A_DOCTOR_IF_IT_GETS_WORSE;


RULE 43
IF   AILMENT=MEASLES AND
     STATE=NO_PAIN AND
     TEMPERATURE=FEVERISH
THEN  RECOMMENDATION=SEE_A_DOCTOR_IF_IT_GETS_WORSE;


RULE 44
IF   AILMENT=ATHLETE_TINEA AND
     STATE=MILD_PAIN AND
     TEMPERATURE=NORMAL
THEN  RECOMMENDATION=SEE_A_DOCTOR_IF_IT_GETS_WORSE;


RULE 45
IF   AILMENT=ATHLETE_TINEA AND
     STATE=NO_PAIN AND
     TEMPERATURE=NORMAL
THEN  RECOMMENDATION=SEE_A_DOCTOR_IF_IT_GETS_WORSE;


RULE 46
IF   AILMENT=SHINGLES AND
     STATE=SEVERE_PAIN AND
     TEMPERATURE=NORMAL
THEN  RECOMMENDATION=SEE_A_DOCTOR_IF_IT_GETS_WORSE;


RULE 47
IF   AILMENT=ACNE AND
     STATE=MILD_PAIN AND
     TEMPERATURE=NORMAL
THEN  RECOMMENDATION=SEE_A_DOCTOR_IF_IT_GETS_WORSE;


RULE 48
IF   AILMENT=ACNE AND
     STATE=NO_PAIN AND
     TEMPERATURE=NORMAL
THEN  RECOMMENDATION=SEE_A_DOCTOR_IF_IT_GETS_WORSE;
```

RULE 49
IF   AILMENT=HEAT_RASH AND
     STATE=MILD_PAIN AND
     TEMPERATURE=NORMAL
THEN RECOMMENDATION=SEE_A_DOCTOR_IF_IT_GETS_WORSE;

RULE 50
IF   AILMENT=HEAT_RASH AND
     STATE=NO_PAIN AND
     TEMPERATURE=NORMAL
THEN RECOMMENDATION=SEE_A_DOCTOR_IF_IT_GETS_WORSE;

RULE 51
IF   AILMENT=SOMETHING_UNCOMMON AND
     TEMPERATURE=FEVERISH
THEN RECOMMENDATION=SEE_A_DOCTOR_IMMEDIATELY;

RULE 52
IF   AILMENT=SOMETHING_UNCOMMON AND
     STATE=MILD_PAIN AND
     TEMPERATURE=NORMAL
THEN RECOMMENDATION=SEE_A_DOCTOR_IMMEDIATELY;

RULE 53
IF   AILMENT=SOMETHING_UNCOMMON AND
     STATE=NO_PAIN AND
     TEMPERATURE=NORMAL
THEN RECOMMENDATION=SEE_A_DOCTOR_IMMEDIATELY;

RULE 54
IF   AILMENT=FLU AND
     STATE=MILD_PAIN AND
     TEMPERATURE=FEVERISH
THEN RECOMMENDATION=SEE_A_DOCTOR_IMMEDIATELY;

RULE 55
IF   AILMENT=FLU AND
     STATE=NO_PAIN AND
     TEMPERATURE=FEVERISH
THEN RECOMMENDATION=SEE_A_DOCTOR_IF_IT_GETS_WORSE;

RULE 56
IF   AILMENT=MUMPS AND
     STATE=SEVERE_PAIN OR
     STATE=MILD_PAIN AND
     TEMPERATURE=FEVERISH
THEN RECOMMENDATION=SEE_A_DOCTOR_IMMEDIATELY;

```
RULE 57
IF   AILMENT=MUMPS AND
     STATE=NO_PAIN AND
     TEMPERATURE=FEVERISH
THEN  RECOMMENDATION=SEE_A_DOCTOR_IF_IT_GETS_WORSE;
```

The two examples presented above show a generic procedure for constructing expert systems knowledge bases. The sample problems used are of a general nature. However, the procedure can be extended for the construction of a knowledge base in any problem domain. Questions at the end of this chapter require that the reader develop sample knowledge bases for applications in engineering and manufacturing.

8.2.4 Modular Knowledge Base Design

For many applications, it is prudent to do the coding of the knowledge base in a modular architecture. This is particularly important for large problems having many distinct but closely related components. Figure 8.10 presents the organization of a modular knowledge base. Modularity provides the following advantages:

(1). Modularity enhances the operation of the expert system.

(2). Each knowledge base module can be independently updated as new information affecting the module becomes available.

(3). The knowledge base is easy to debug.

(4). The modules can be reorganized and linked easily to take advantage of new problem structures.

(5). Certain modules can be used interchangeably in other knowledge bases with little or no modification.

(6). Consultation control is possible through the operation of the master knowledge base.

Figure 8.10. Modular knowledge base design

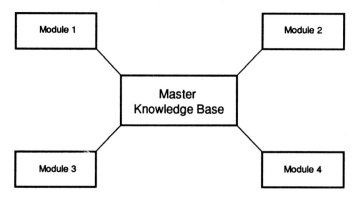

(7). Modularity facilitates the extension of data management concepts to "knowledge management."

In a modular knowledge base architecture, the master knowledge base performs the function of determining which module is applicable for the current state of the problem being solved. Modular knowledge base design is similar but different from the blackboard architecture discussed in the preceding chapter. In a blackboard architecture, multiple knowledge sources are used. Each knowledge source is a specialist in a given aspect of the problem to be solved. In a modular knowledge base design, all the knowledge base modules may very well come from the same expert. Modular design is a technique for organizing the knowledge base efficiently. Blackboard architecture is a technique for sharing the knowledge of multiple experts in solving a problem.

8.2.5   External Interface Structure

A major challenge facing the current and future generations of expert systems is the need for better integration with external programs. These external programs may include data base systems, spreadsheet models, and custom applications programs. A spreadsheet model may be responsible for performing a numeric analysis, the result of which may be needed during an expert system consultation. An external data base model may be needed to store passive data sets that may be recalled as needed to instantiate appropriate parameters during an expert system consultation. External custom programs may be needed to perform unique analyses such as optimization, complex computations, and graphics manipulation. For example, the emerging concept of object-oriented programming requires a good interface structure for the object components of a problem. Figure 8.11 shows a model for the integration of external programs into an expert systems environment. The example presented in the next section illustrates the design of an expert system that takes advantage of program integration.

8.2.6   Example: Comparison of Manufacturing Alternatives

The comparison of alternatives is a major focus in decision analysis. Alternatives may need to be compared on the basis of cost, efficiency, productivity, quality, or any other criterion of interest. The example presented here involves the selection of an alternative for the production of a part in a manufacturing operation. Two competing alternatives are used for the illustration here. A question at the end of the chapter requires that the reader extend the expert system model to the case of more than two competing alternatives. First we present the problem statement, then we present some concepts on the use of breakeven point for the comparison of alternatives on the basis of cost or profit. Finally, we present an expert system model to solve the problem presented.

PROBLEM STATEMENT   In a production operation, it is desired to determine the point(s) of equivalence (breakeven points) for two competing alternatives, I

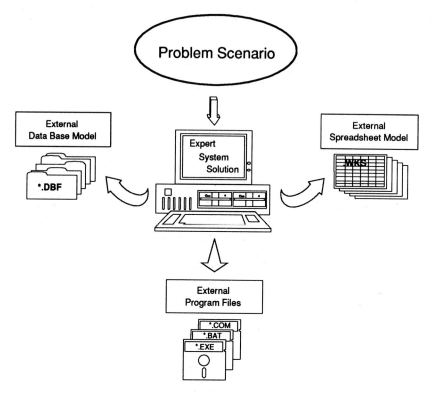

Figure 8.11. External interface structure

and II. The net cost or net profit from each alternative is expressed in terms of quadratic functions of the form shown below:

$$F_i = a + bX + cX^2,$$

where
i = alternative number
X = number of units to be produced

Rules are to be developed to determine at what values of X each alternative should be selected depending on the given cost or profit functions. The specifications for the expert system design are presented below:

(1). Create a spreadsheet file (using Lotus 1-2-3 or any other package) to store the coefficients of the two cost or profit functions as shown in the layout below:

Alternative	a	b	c	Type
1	2.10	1.00	4.00	Cost
2	3.75	2.60	−3.00	Cost

The example in the spreadsheet layout above is for the case where the functions given are *cost functions* expressed as:

$$C_1 = 2.1 + X + 4X^2$$
$$C_2 = 3.75 + 2.6X - 3X^2$$

(2). Write a computer program (using BASIC, PASCAL, C, FORTRAN, or any other language) to solve a quadratic function given the appropriate coefficients. The quadratic function to be solved will be the one needed to obtain the breakeven point(s) of the competing alternatives.

(3). Develop a data base file that contains the description and other details about the two alternatives being compared. An example of a data base layout is presented below:

Alter. #	Description	Resources Required	Cost	Date Available
1	Fine Operation	Three operators	$5,000	10/31/90
2	Rough Operation	One operator	$2,175	10/15/90

(4). Create a VP-Expert knowledge base that will contain the rules for recommending which alternative to select when a value of X is input by the user.

OPERATIONAL REQUIREMENTS   The expert system will read the function coefficients from the spreadsheet file and determine whether they are cost or profit functions. It will then call the computer program to solve for the breakeven points. The breakeven solution is reported back to the expert system. On the basis of the breakeven solution, the expert system will use the knowledge base rules to determine which alternative to select. Before presenting the recommendation to the user, the expert system will read all the information about the recommended alternative from the data base file. The recommendation and the associated information are then printed on the screen for the user. At this point, the user will be given the option of storing the consultation result in an external text file. If the equation to solve for the breakeven points does not have real roots, the expert system would notify the user to modify the coefficients in the spreadsheet file.

PROCEDURE FOR BREAKEVEN ANALYSIS   Once all the cost aspects of alternatives are documented and properly organized, several types of economic analysis can be performed. An example of the procedure for breakeven analysis is presented here. The procedure is modeled later as a component of an expert system solution to the problem stated above.

The total cost of an operation may be expressed as the sum of the fixed and variable costs with respect to output quantity. That is,

$$TC(x) = FC + VC(x),$$

where x is the number of units produced, $TC(x)$ is the total cost of producing x units, FC is the total fixed cost, and $VC(x)$ is the total variable costs associated with producing x units. The total revenue resulting from the sale of x units is defined as:

$$TR(x) = px,$$

where p is the price per unit. The profit due to the production and sale of x units of the product is calculated as:

$$P(x) = TR(x) - TC(x).$$

The breakeven point of an operation is defined as the value of a given parameter that will result in neither a profit nor a loss. The parameter of interest may be the number of units produced, the number of hours of operation, the number of units of a resource type allocated, or any other measure of interest. At the breakeven point, we have the following relationship:

$$TR(x) = TC(x)$$

or

$$P(x) = 0.$$

In some cases, the relationship between cost and a parameter of interest can be expressed in a mathematical formula. For example, there may be a linear cost relationship between the total cost of a manufacturing alternative and the number of units produced. The cost expressions facilitate straightforward analysis for decision-making purposes. Figure 8.12 shows an example of a breakeven point for a single alternative. Figure 8.13 shows examples of multiple breakeven points when multiple alternatives are compared. When two alternatives are compared, the breakeven point refers to the point of indifference between the two alternatives. In Figure 8.13, $x1^*$ represents the point where both alternatives A and B are equally desirable, $x2^*$ represents where A and C are equally desirable, and $x3^*$ represents where B and C are equally desirable. The figure shows that if we are operating below a production level of $x2$ units, then alternative C is the preferred alternative out of the three. If we are operating at a level more than $x2$ units, then alternative A is the best choice.

BREAKEVEN EXAMPLE   Three alternatives are being considered for producing a new product. The required analysis involves determining which alternative should be selected on the basis of how many units of the product are produced per year. On the basis of past records, there is a known relationship between the number of units produced per year, x, and the net annual profit, $P(x)$, from each alternative. The level of production is expected to be between zero and 250 units per year. The net annual profits (in thousands of dollars) are given below for each alternative:

Alternative A: $P(x) = 3x - 200$

Alternative B: $P(x) = x$

Alternative C: $P(x) = (1/50)x^2 - 300$

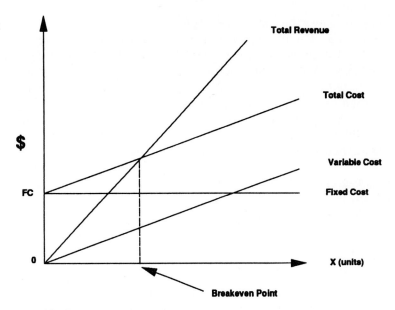

Figure 8.12. Example of breakeven point

Figure 8.13. Breakeven points for multiple alternatives

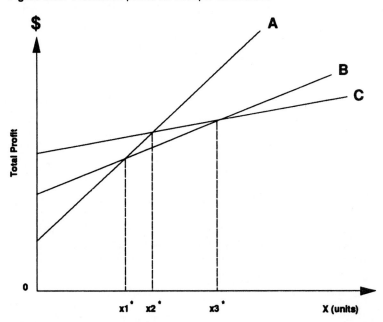

This problem can be solved analytically by finding the intersection points of the profit functions and evaluating the respective profits over the given range of product units. The analytic solution is the approach used in the expert system solution discussed later. Figure 8.14 presents a breakeven chart for a graphical solution of the problem.

The figure shows the simultaneous plot of the profit functions for the competing alternatives. The plot shows that Alternative B should be selected if between zero and 100 units are to be produced. Alternative A should be selected if between 100 and 178.1 units (178 actual units) are to be produced. Alternative C should be selected if more than 178 units are to be produced. It should be noted that if less than 66.7 units (66 actual units) are produced, Alternative A would generate a net loss rather than net profit. Similarly, Alternative C would generate losses if less than 122.5 units (122 actual units) are produced. The graphical results are presented in terms of the rules shown below:

If *units* is-greater-than-or-equal-to 0
And *units* is-less-than 100,
Then *selection* is Alternative-B.

If *units* is-greater-than 100
And *units* is-less-than 178.1,
Then *selection* is Alternative-A.

Figure 8.14. Plot of profit functions for competing alternatives

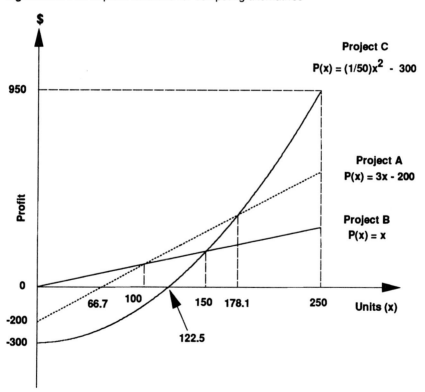

If *units* is-greater-than 178.1
AND *units* is-less-than-or-equal-to 250,
Then *selection* is Alternative-C.

If *units* is-equal-to 100,
Then *selection* is Alternative-A or Alternative-B.

If *units* is-equal-to 178.1,
Then *selection* is Alternative-A or Alternative-C.

EXPERT SYSTEM SOLUTION   We now return to the original problem presented at the beginning of this section. We recall that the problem involves the selection of a manufacturing alternative based on breakeven analysis. Figure 8.15 presents the expert system structure for comparing the two manufacturing alternatives. VP-Expert is the inference engine used to develop the expert system. Detailed information about the alternatives to be compared is stored in the external data base file. The external spreadsheet file stores the data on the cost or profit functions associated with each alternative. The external program (written in FORTRAN, C, PASCAL, or BASIC) performs the computational analysis needed to obtain the breakeven points.

If the quadratic equation used to compute the breakeven points does not have real roots, VP-Expert informs the user to select new function coefficients. The spreadsheet file is then updated with the new function coefficients and the

Figure 8.15. Expert system structure for breakeven analysis

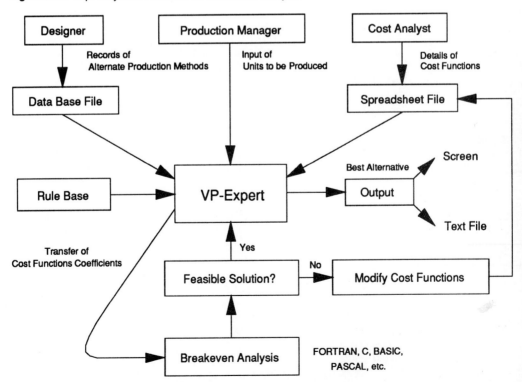

consultation is repeated. The user inputs the number of units to be produced. The number of units is used to instantiate parameters in the rule base, where a conclusion is reached on which alternative to select. The consultation result is presented to the user on the screen. The user has the option of requesting that the result be saved to a text file to be printed out later. Figure 8.16 presents the decision tree for the breakeven procedure. A PASCAL program for calculating the breakeven points is presented below:

PASCAL PROGRAM

```
(* This program is used to calculate breakeven points *)
(* The program is called by VP-Expert during consultation*)
program calculate;
var
      fpin,fpout:text;
      a1,b1,c1,a2,b2,c2,a3,b3,c3,p1,p2,x,rt,root1,root2:real;
begin
      assign(fpin,'coeff');
      assign(fpout,'result');
      reset(fpin);
      rewrite(fpout);
      readln(fpin,c1);     (* Reading the coefficients of function *)
readln(fpin,b1);
      readln(fpin,a1);
      readln(fpin,c2);
      readln(fpin,b2);
      readln(fpin,a2);
      readln(fpin,x);      (* Reading the specified x *)
      a3:=a1-a2;           (* Computing the breakeven points *)
      b3:=b1-b2;
      c3:=c1-c2;
      rt:=(b3*b3-4*a3*c3);
      if (rt>=0)
      then begin
                  root1:=(( (-b3)+sqrt(rt) )/(2*a3));
                  root2:=(( (-b3)-sqrt(rt) )/(2*a3));
                  end
      else begin
                  writeln(fpout,'No_value');
                  close(fpout);
                  exit;
                  end;
      writeln(fpout,root1);
      writeln(fpout,root2);
      p1:=a1*(x*x)+b1*x+c1;
      p2:=a2*(x*x)+b2*x+c2;
      writeln(fpout,p1);
      writeln(fpout,p2);
      close(fpout);
end.
```

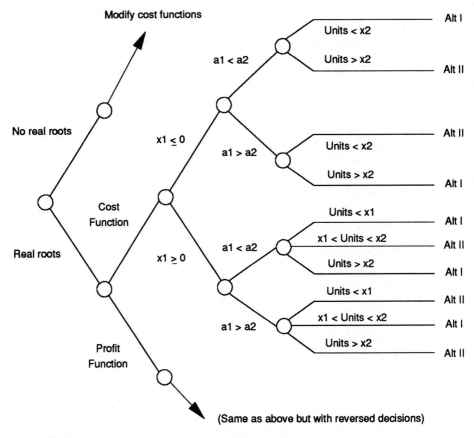

Figure 8.16. Decision tree for breakeven analysis

The knowledge base that calls the above PASCAL program is presented below:

KNOWLEDGE BASE

```
!This program demonstrates the external interface capabilities of VPX
RUNTIME;
ACTIONS
    BCALL clear        !Delete the unused file by last execution
    i=1
    CLS
    FIND lot_file
    l_file=(lot_file)
    DISPLAY ""
    DISPLAY "Please wait ..."
    DISPLAY ""
    DISPLAY "Getting the coeffients of two functions from spreadsheet file...."
    WKS poly_coeff,B1..D2,@lot_file !Get the coeffients from spreadsheet file
    WHILETRUE i<7 THEN
        SHIP coeff,poly_coeff[i]
        i=(i+1)
    END
```

```
        CLS
        FIND x
        DISPLAY "Please wait..."
        SHIP coeff,x
        WKS fun_type,E1..E2,@lot_file
        DISPLAY "The function is {fun_type[1]} function"
        CLROFF
        DISPLAY ""
        DISPLAY "Computing the breakeven points, please wait..."
        CALL calc,""   !Compute the breakeven points
        RECEIVE result,breakeven1
        RECEIVE result,breakeven2
        RECEIVE result,poly1
        RECEIVE result,poly2

FIND Value_or_not !Check the breakeven point exist or not
WHILETRUE Value_or_not=Yes then
        DISPLAY ""
        DISPLAY "The type of the functions is {fun_type[1]} functions."
        DISPLAY "The breakeven points are {breakeven1} and {breakeven2}"
        DISPLAY ""
        FIND answer
        FIND the_altern
        FIND db_file
        DISPLAY "Getting the detail description of selected function..."
        GET the_altern=altern,@db_file,ALL !Get the description from dbase
        DISPLAY ""
        DISPLAY "What we suggest to choose is alternative #{the_altern}"
        DISPLAY ""
        DISPLAY " ALTER.#  Description  Resource Required  Cost  Date Avail "
        DISPLAY " {altern}  {descript}  {resource}  ${cost}  {date_avail}"
        string=ALTER_#
        DISPLAY ""
        FIND formula
        FIND store_or_not
        FIND storing
        Value_or_not=No
END;

RULE 1
   IF l_file=lot1
   THEN db_file=db1;

RULE 2
   IF l_file=lot2
   THEN db_file=db2;

RULE 3
   IF l_file=lot3
   THEN db_file=db3;

RULE 4
   IF breakeven1=No_value
```

```
    THEN Value_or_not=No
       DISPLAY " "
       DISPLAY "The breakeven points do not have real roots!"
       DISPLAY " "
       DISPLAY "Please modify the coeffients in the spreadsheet file!!"
    ELSE Value_or_not=Yes;

RULE 5
   IF fun_type[1]=cost
   THEN answer=lower
   ELSE answer=higher;

RULE 6
   IF answer=lower AND poly1>(poly2)
   THEN the_altern=2;

RULE 7
   IF answer=lower AND poly1<=(poly2)
   THEN the_altern=1;

RULE 8
   IF answer=higher AND poly1>=(poly2)
   THEN the_altern=1;

RULE 9
   IF answer=higher AND poly1<(poly2)
   THEN the_altern=2;

RULE 10
   IF store_or_not=Yes
   THEN storing=yes
       DISPLAY " "
       DISPLAY "Storing your consultation..."
       SHIP consult,string
       SHIP consult,the_altern
       DISPLAY " "
       DISPLAY "Your consultation is stored in the file -- consult "
   ELSE storing=no;

RULE 11
   IF the_altern=1
   THEN formula=1
       DISPLAY "The alternation function that you choose is --"
       DISPLAY " {poly_coeff[1]} + {poly_coeff[2]}*X + {poly_coeff[3]}*X*X";

RULE 12
   IF the_altern=2
   THEN formula=2
       DISPLAY "The alternation function that you choose is --"
       DISPLAY " {poly_coeff[4]} + {poly_coeff[5]}*X + {poly_coeff[6]}*X*X";
ASK lot_file: "Which spreadsheet file do you want to choose?";
CHOICES lot_file: lot1,lot2,lot3;
ASK x: "Please specify the number of units?";
ASK store_or_not: "Do you want to store the consultation?";
CHOICES store_or_not: Yes,No;
```

The user interface is an important component of the expert system. An attractive design of the user interface can be pleasing and appealing to users. A well-designed interface encourages the user to explore the capabilities of the expert system. The expert system above, named INVESTMENT COUNSELLOR, makes a good use of the multiple window capabilities of VP-Expert to enhance the user interface. Samples of the screen displays for an example run are presented in Figures 8.17 through 8.21. The example involves the following cost functions for two competing manufacturing alternatives.

Alternative	a	b	c	Type
1	5	−7	2	Cost
2	2	−3	1	Cost

$$C_1 = 5 - 7X + 2X^2$$
$$C_2 = 2 - 3X + X^2$$

where
i = alternative number
X = number of units to be produced per hour

Figure 8.17. VP-Expert startup screen

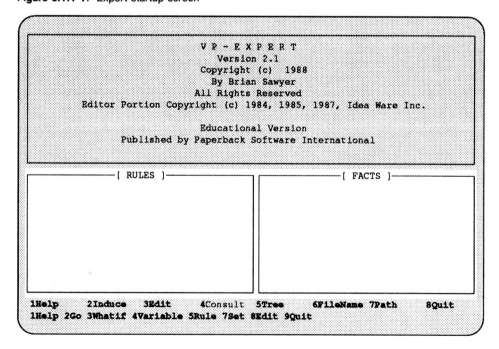

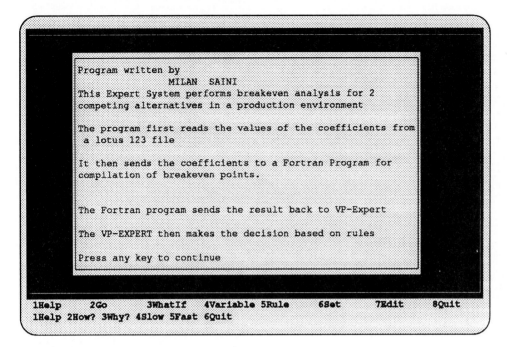

Figure 8.18. Consultation introduction screen

Figure 8.19. Multiple window layout screen in VP-Expert

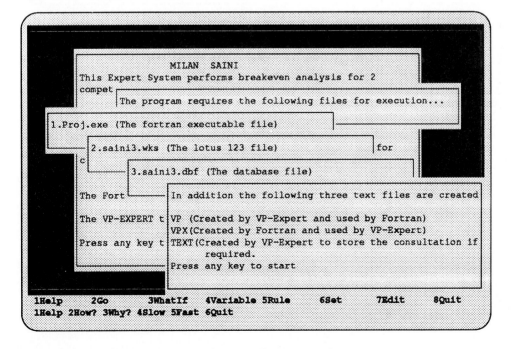

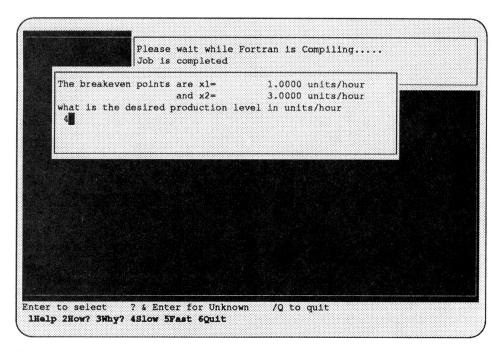

Figure 8.20. Result of breakeven analysis

Figure 8.21. Final conclusion screen

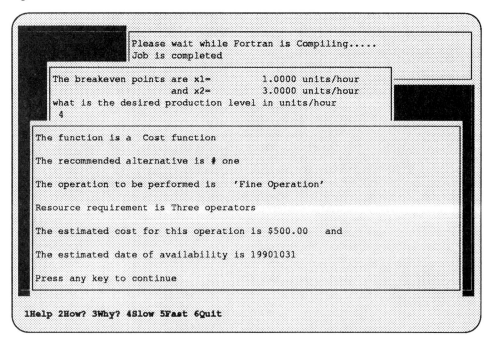

The expert system consultation result (see Figure 8.21) indicates that Alternative I should be selected if the desired production rate is four units per hour. From the data base record of the alternative the following information was retrieved:

Type of operation: *Fine operation*

Resources required: *Three operators*

Estimated cost: *$500*

Availability date: *October 31, 1990*

The breakeven program could be written in any other callable language instead of PASCAL. VP-Expert can call .BAT, .COM, and .EXE files. The listings of alternate programs written in FORTRAN, C, and BASIC are presented below. The programs are compiled to .EXE files before being interfaced with VP-Expert.

FORTRAN PROGRAM

```
      Real a1,b1,c1,a2,b2,c2,d,x1,x2,lowcost,qty,
     + DP,bep1,bep2,highpt,x,COST,PROFIT
      Integer cflag,pflag
      Open (Unit=10,File='alt1para',status='OLD')
      Open (Unit=20,File='alt2para',status='OLD')
      Open (Unit=30,File='quantity',Status='OLD')
      Read (10,*) a1,b1,c1
      Read (20,*) a2,b2,c2
      Read (30,*) qty
10    FORMAT (F10.2,F10.2,F10.2)

      Open (Unit=4,File='Result',Status='NEW')

        d=(b2-b1)**2.0 - 4.0*(a2-a1)*(c2-c1)
        If (d.GE.0) Then
          x1=(-(b2-b1)+Sqrt(d))/(2.0*(a2-a1))
          x2=(-(b2-b1)-Sqrt(d))/(2.0*(a2-a1))
          bep1=Min(x1,x2)
          bep2=Max(x1,x2)
          Write (4,*) bep1
          Write (4,*) bep2
40    FORMAT (F10.3,1X,F10.3)
        DP= (a2-a1)*x**2.0+(b2-b1)*x +(c2-c1)
        x=bep1 - 1.0
        If (DP.GT.0) Then
        If (qty.LT.bep1) Then
        Write (4,*) DP
50    Format ('DP for X < bep1 is',1X,F10.2)
        x=qty
        highpt=c2+b2*x+a2*x**2.0
        lowcost=c1+b1*x+a1*x**2.0
        cflag=1
        pflag=2
```

```
        Endif
       Else If(qty.LT.bep1) Then
         Write (4,*) DP
55  Format ('DP for X < bep1 is',1X,F10.2)
           x=qty
         highpt=c1+b1*x+a1*x**2.0
         lowcost=c2+b2*x+a2*x**2.0
         cflag=2
         pflag=1
       Endif
       x=bep2 + 1.0
       If ( DP.GT.0) Then
        If ( qty.GT.bep2) Then
          Write (4,*) DP
60  FORMAT ('DP for x > bep2 is',1X,F10.2)
         x=qty
         highpt=c2+b2*x+a2*x**2.0
         lowcost=c1+b1*x+a1*x**2.0
         cflag=1
         pflag=2
         Endif
      Else If ( qty.GT.bep2) Then
         Write (4,*) DP
65  Format ('DP for x > bep2 is',1X,F10.2)
         x=qty
         highpt=c1+b1*x+c1*x**2.0
         lowcost=c2+b2*x+c2*x**2.0
         cflag=2
         plag=1

      Endif

     x=abs(bep2 -bep1)/2.0
     If (DP.GT.0) Then
      If (qty.LE.bep2. And. qty.GE.bep1) Then
        Write (4,*) DP
70  FORMAT ('DP for x in between beps is',1x,F10.2)
         x=qty
         highpt=c1+b1*x+a1*x**2.0
         lowcost=c2+b2*x+a2*x**2.0
         cflag=2
         plag=1
         Endif
      Else If (qty.LE.bep2. And. qty.GE.bep1) Then
         Write (4,*) DP
75  Format ('DP for x in between beps is',1X,F10.2)

         x=qty
         highpt=c2+b2*x+a2*x**2.0
         lowcost=c1+b1*x+a1*x**2.0
         cflag=1
         pflag=2
```

```
      Endif
      Write (4,*) lowcost
      Write (4,*) highpt
      Write (4,*) cflag
      Write (4,*) pflag
80  Format (I10.2,1X,I10.2)
      Else
      cflag=0
      pflag=0
      Write (4,*) cflag
      Write (4,*) pflag
90  Format (2I10.2)

      Endif
      Stop
      End
```

C PROGRAM

```c
#include<stdio.h>
#include<math.h>
main()
{
float a1,b1,c1,a2,b2,c2,x1,x2,x,y1,y2,y3,f1y1,f1y2,f1y3,f2y1,f2y2,f2y3,f,temp,f2;
int s,t,alt;
FILE *fp;
FILE *fg;
fp=fopen("a:SHARM","r");
fg=fopen("a:OUTPUT","w");
fscanf(fp,"%f %f %f %f %f %f %f %d",&a1,&b1,&c1,&a2,&b2,&c2,&x,&t);
if((pow((b1-b2),2)-4*(a1-a2)*(c1-c2))<0)
{
s=0;
goto abc;
}
s=1;
x1=-((b1-b2)+sqrt((b1-b2)*(b1-b2)-4*(a1-a2)*(c1-c2)))/(2*(a1-a2));
x2=-((b1-b2)-sqrt((b1-b2)*(b1-b2)-4*(a1-a2)*(c1-c2)))/(2*(a1-a2));
if(x1>x2)
{
temp=x1;
x1=x2;
x2=temp;
}
y1=x1-1;
y2=(x1+x2)/2;
y3=x2+1;
f1y1=a1*pow(y1,2)+b1*y1+c1;
f2y1=a2*pow(y1,2)+b2*y1+c2;
f1y2=a1*pow(y2,2)+b1*y2+c1;
f2y2=a2*pow(y2,2)+b2*y2+c2;
```

```
f1y3=a1*pow(y3,2)+b1*y3+c1;
f2y3=a2*pow(y3,2)+b2*y3+c2;
if(x<=x1)
{
if(f1y1<f2y1)
if(t==0)
{ f=a1*pow(x,2)+b1*x+c1;
f2=a2*pow(x,2)+b2*x+c2;
alt=1;
}
else
{f=a2*pow(x,2)+b2*x+c2;
f2=a1*pow(x,2)+b1*x+c1;
alt=2;
}
else
if(t==0)
{f=a2*pow(x,2)+b2*x+c2;
f2=a1*pow(x,2)+b1*x+c1;
alt=1;
}
else
{f=a1*pow(x,2)+b1*x+c1;
f2=a2*pow(x,2)+b2*x+c2;
alt=2;
}
}
if(x>x1 && x<x2)
{
if(f1y2<f2y2)
if(t==0)
{f=a1*pow(x,2)+b1*x+c1;
f2=a2*pow(x,2)+b2*x+c2;
alt=1;
}
else
{ f=a2*pow(x,2)+b2*x+c2;
f2=a1*pow(x,2)+b1*x+c1;
alt=2;
}
else
if(t==0)
{f=a2*pow(x,2)+b2*x+c2;
f2=a1*pow(x,2)+b1*x+c1;
alt=1;
}
else
{f=a1*pow(x,2)+b1*x+c1;
f2=a2*pow(x,2)+b2*x+c2;
alt=2;
```

```
}
}
if(x>=x2)
{
if(f1y3<f2y3)
if(t==0)
{f=a1*pow(x,2)+b1*x+c1;
f2=a2*pow(x,2)+b2*x+c2;
alt=1;
}
else
{ f=a2*pow(x,2)+b2*x+c2;
f2=a1*pow(x,2)+b1*x+c1;
alt=2;
}
else
if(t==0)
{f=a2*pow(x,2)+b2*x+c2;
f2=a1*pow(x,2)+b1*x+c1;
alt=2;
}
else
{f=a1*pow(x,2)+b1*x+c1;
f2=a2*pow(x,2)+b2*x+c2;
alt=1;
}
}
abc:
fprintf(fg,"%f \n %f \n %d \n %f \n %f \n %d \n",x1,x2,s,f,f2,alt);
}
```

BASIC PROGRAM

```
10 REM TO CALCULATE THE BREAKEVEN POINTS
20 OPEN "COEF" FOR INPUT AS #1
30 INPUT #1,a1,b1,c1,a2,b2,c2
40 A = a1-a2
50 B = b1-b2
60 C = c1-c2
70 Z = B*B-4.0*A*C
90 X1 = (-B+SQR(Z))/2.0*C
100 X2 = (-B-SQR(Z))/2.0*C
110 IF (X1<X2) THEN 150
120 temp=X1
130 X1=X2
140 X2=temp
150 COST1=a1+b1*(X1-1)+c1*(X1-1)*(X1-1)
160 COST2=a2+b2*(X1-1)+c2*(X1-1)*(X1-1)
165 OPEN "BRKEVEN" FOR OUTPUT AS #2
170 PRINT #2,X1
180 PRINT #2,X2
```

```
190 PRINT #2,COST1
200 PRINT #2,COST2
205 GOTO 230
210 PRINT "THE BREAKEVEN POINTS ARE IMAGINARY. PLEASE ENTER A NEW"
225 PRINT "SET OF COEFFICIENTS."
230 CLOSE
240 STOP
250 END
```

8.3 EXPERT SYSTEMS PROTOTYPE CLASSIFICATIONS

Expert systems should be continually updated with new knowledge base information as the information becomes available. For this reason some developers prefer to refer to an expert system as being in the prototype stage. The system, in effect, is never closed since it is always ready to "learn" more about the problem domain. The author has classified the different prototype stages of an expert system as follows:

Conceptual prototype: This is when the expert system is in the concept stage and no actual development effort has been carried out.

Developmental prototype: This is the stage when actual development activities (problem formulation, knowledge acquisition, coding, etc.) are being undertaken.

Operational prototype: This is the stage where the expert system actually operates. It can accept inputs and it can produce results. This prototype may be useful in evaluating user interface requirements and performance. Noncritical or hypothetical problems may be used to test the operations of the system. This is the stage that most developers refer to simply as the *prototype* or *pilot* system. The operational details of this level of prototype must be verified.

Functional prototype: This is the stage when the expert system is actually deployed to a specific functional area and is capable of solving actual problems. The results produced by the expert system at this stage must be validated.

Commercial prototype: This is the stage where the expert system is of commercial quality and can be offered to the market if desired. It should be noted that even commercial expert systems must continue to be updated.

8.4 EXERCISES

8.1   Refer to the plant example presented in this chapter. Use the procedure presented to develop an example dealing with the classification of part groups in a manufacturing operation.

8.2   Refer to the spots advisor example. Use the example as a model for developing a sample knowledge base dealing with a diagnostic problem in an engineering discipline that you are familiar with.

8.3   This is a restatement of the example problem presented earlier in this chapter. The problem has been extended to more than two competing alternatives. Develop an expert system to solve the problem using the specifications presented below.

Problem Statement
In a production operation, it is desired to determine the point(s) of equivalence (breakeven points) for multiple competing alternatives. The alternatives are numbered as $1, 2, \ldots, n$. The net cost or net profit from each alternative is expressed in terms of quadratic functions of the form shown below:

$$F_i = a + bX + cX^2,$$

where
i = alternative number
X = number of units to be produced

Rules are to be developed to determine at what values of X each alternative is the preferred alternative depending on the results of a breakeven analysis involving the given cost or profit functions.

Required
a) Create a spreadsheet file (using Lotus 1-2-3 or any other package) to store the coefficients of the cost or profit functions as shown in the layout below:

Alternative	a	b	c	Type
1	a_1	b_1	c_1	Cost or Profit
2	a_2	b_2	c_2	Cost or Profit
.	.	.	.	.
.	.	.	.	.
n	a_n	b_n	c_n	Cost or Profit

b) Write a computer program (using BASIC, PASCAL, C, FORTRAN, or any other language) to solve a quadratic function given the appropriate coefficients. The quadratic function to be solved will be the one needed to obtain the breakeven point(s) of the competing alternatives.

c) Develop a data base file that contains the description and other details about the two alternatives being compared. An example is presented below:

Alter. #	Description	Resources Required	Cost	Date Available
1	Fine Operation	Three operators	$5,000	10/31/90
2	Rough Operation	One operator	$2,175	10/15/90

d) Create a knowledge base that will contain the rules for recommending which alternative to select when a value of X is specified. Use any development tool available to you.

Operational Requirements: The expert system will read the function coefficients from the spreadsheet file and determine whether they are cost or profit functions. It will then call the computer program to solve for the breakeven points. The breakeven solution is reported back to the expert system. On the basis of the breakeven solution, the expert system will use the knowledge base rules to determine which alternative to select. Before presenting the recommendation to the user, the expert system will read all the information about the recommended alternative from the data base file. The recommendation and the associated information are then printed on the screen for the user. At this point, the user will be given the option of storing the consultation result in an external text file. If the equation to solve for the breakeven points does not have real roots, the expert system should notify the user to modify the coefficients in the spreadsheet file.

8.4 In a product quality inspection problem, the operator is expected to inspect three important characteristics of the product:
Color
Surface finish
Physical dimensions

After inspection, the product is classified into one of the following three categories:
Good
Rework
Scrap

To be classified as "good," the product must satisfy the specs for all three quality characteristics. If it fails all three, it is scrapped. If it fails any one or two of the three quality characteristics, it is sent back for rework.
Operators sometimes forget to check all three product characteristics. That is, an operator may check only one, any two, or all three characteristics. In each case, the operator still may classify the product into any of the three categories.

Required
a) Draw a tree diagram showing all the possible paths for inspecting the product and the resulting decisions.
b) Develop a knowledge base for the diagram in part (a) using any development tool available to you. You may make the knowledge base as brief or detailed as you prefer.

8.5 Inventory control is a potential area for the application of expert systems. Inventory policies are often based on quantitative analysis coupled with expert heuristics.

Required:
Develop an expert system to implement an inventory control decision aid. The expert system structure should contain at least the following:
a) Knowledge Base containing heuristic rules for inventory management.
b) Database file containing records of items maintained in inventory.
c) Spreadsheet file containing cost and other numeric data for the inventoried items.

Prepare a detailed documentation of the development process and the knowledge source. You should also prepare a user's guide for the expert system.

8.7 Discuss the development cycle for an expert system for engineering or manufacturing application.

8.8 Refer to a good home medical reference book. Develop an expert system to diagnose chest pains.

8.9 Refer to a good automobile repair manual. Develop an expert system to diagnose mechanical faults if an automobile will not start.

8.10 Discuss the differences between the design of the expert system in Exercise 8.8 and Exercise 8.9.

8.11 Following the tree classification example, develop a decision tree to classify part types in a manufacturing operation.

8.12 Construct a simple knowledge base that uses meta rules.

8.13 *The Farmer's Problem.* A farmer and his wolf, goat, and cabbage come to the edge of a river they wish to cross. There is a boat at the river's edge. Only the farmer can row the boat. The boat can carry only two items at a time. If the wolf is left alone with the goat, the wolf will eat the goat. If the goat is left alone with the cabbage, the goat will eat the cabbage.

a) Develop a sequence of crossings of the river so that all four items (farmer, goat, cabbage, and wolf) arrive safely on the other side of the river.

b) Develop a graphical representation or flowchart for the solution in part (a).

c) Construct a set of knowledge base rules to implement the solution in part (a).

8.14 *The Two-Pail Problem.* We are given two empty water pails, one with a capacity of 6 gallons and the other with a capacity of 8 gallons. There are no measuring marks on the pails.

a) Given that we can fill either pail at will (i.e., unlimited supply of water), how can we get the 8-gallon pail exactly half full?

b) Construct a set of knowledge base rules to implement the solution in part (a).

8.15 Develop an expert system application that interfaces a knowledge base with external spreadsheet and data base files.

8.16 Write a conventional program that performs simple matrix multiplication: $\mathbf{C} = \mathbf{AB}$. Interface the program with an expert system such that the coefficients of matrix A and matrix B are entered through the expert system's user interface but the matrix multiplication is done in the external program.

8.17 Write the following questions as knowledge base rules:
Is the stem of the plant woody or green?
Is the position of the stem upright or creeping?
Does the plant have one main trunk?

8.18 Incorporate levels of certainty factors into the rules constructed in Exercise 8.17.

8.19 Refer to the Spots Advisor knowledge base presented in this chapter. Extend the knowledge base to include other ailments that can be easily diagnosed in the home.

8.20 Develop an expert system that will advise a knowledge engineer on the procedure for developing an expert system for engineering problems.

9

Verification, Validation, and Integration

Expert systems must be verified and validated before being deployed. Without proper verification and validation, disappointing results can occur. Because of their attempt to mimic human intelligence, expert systems have a greater need for verification and validation than conventional computer programs. Conventional programs are based on much stronger ground because they implement proven algorithms and scientific facts. By contrast, expert systems are less assertive, depending mainly on flexible and reliable heuristics that may not have ever been subjected to rigorous scrutiny. An important reason for performing careful verification is that when expert systems malfunction the source of the problem may not be as obvious as in the case of conventional programs. Thus, the problem may go undetected until serious harm has been done.

9.1 WHAT IS VERIFICATION?

Verification involves the determination of whether or not the system is functioning as intended. This may involve program debugging, error analysis, input acceptance, output generation, reasonableness of operation, run time control, and scope of problem.

9.2 WHAT IS VALIDATION?

Validation concerns a diagnosis of how closely the expert system's solution matches a human expert's solution. If the expert system is valid, then the decisions, conclusions, or recommendations it offers can essentially substitute for those of a human expert. The validation should be done through the use of different problem scenarios to simulate consultation sessions. Those who served as the domain experts during the system development should play an active role in the validation effort.

Sometimes, it may be impossible to validate an expert system for all the anticipated problems because the data for such problems may not yet be available. In such a case, the closest possible representation of the expected scenario should be utilized for the validation.

The successful validation of MYCIN was one of the first indicators of how beneficial expert systems could be. After the system was developed at Stanford University, the performance of MYCIN was evaluated against the performances of physicians in the selection of antimicrobials for cases of acute meningitis. The evaluation was done before the causative agent was identified. Ten cases of infectious meningitis were selected and summarized. This summary data was given both to MYCIN and to nine clinicians not associated with the MYCIN project. The humans were asked to review the summaries and prescribe an antimicrobial therapy for each case. After the diagnoses and prescriptions were completed, eight specialists in infectious diseases from institutions other than Stanford University were asked to evaluate the "prescriptions" recommended by MYCIN and the clinicians. The identities of the "prescribers" were not revealed to the external reviewers. Two criteria were used in the evaluation process:

(1). Prescriptions were evaluated to see whether the recommended drugs would be effective against the actual causative agent. MYCIN and three of the human prescribers consistently prescribed therapy that would have been effective in all ten cases.

(2). The prescribed drugs were checked to see whether they adequately covered for other plausible pathogens but were not over-prescribed. In this analysis, MYCIN received a higher rating than any of the humans. The external reviewers rated MYCIN's prescriptions correct in 65 percent of the cases while the success rate of the humans ranged from 42.5 to 62.5 percent.

9.2.1 What to Validate

The knowledge base component of an expert system is the area that requires the most thorough evaluation since it contains the problem-solving strategies of the expert system. This will be the area of focus of this chapter. It is assumed that a properly debugged and functioning inference engine has been purchased or developed and that the user interface has already been efficiently designed.

9.2.2 How Much to Validate

The methodology that one uses to determine how much validation to perform on a knowledge base is largely dependent on the number of representative cases which are available for evaluation. For example, evaluating a knowledge base that diagnoses rare diseases will be much more cumbersome and difficult than evaluating a knowledge base that addresses a common problem. On the basis of the availability of representative cases, special tools may have to be used to perform validation (i.e., sensitivity analysis, what-if analysis).

The degree of validation to be performed on a system is dependent on the degree of significance placed on the system. This is based on the context in which the system will be used. In some cases, an expert system may be viewed as a complete replacement for an actual expert. This results in total dependence on the system and a need for greater validation. In other cases, an expert system may be developed as a complementary tool in problem solving. This type of use does not require highly rigorous validation.

9.2.3 When to Validate

When to perform validation is a key decision in the expert system development process. Since errors can occur anywhere in the development process from compiling the knowledge of a domain expert to distributing the knowledge base for operational use, validating an expert system in stages is very important. Validating a system in stages facilitates catching errors before they become compounded. For very small systems, validation can be performed in one single stage at the completion of the system.

9.3 VERIFICATION AND VALIDATION PROCESS

One mistake commonly made is that only one evaluation of a system is performed in the intermediate stages of development when only a small number of test cases are available. Based on the success of this initial validation, the effectiveness of the knowledge base is never verified after new test cases become available.

Buchanan and Shortliffe (1987) propose a validation process that takes place at nine different stages in the development process. In a very large system, validation should occur at each of these intervals. Smaller and intermediate systems may be able to consolidate some of these intervals. The nine recommended levels are listed below:

(1). Top level design with long range goal definition. State what the measures of the programs success will be and how failure or success will be evaluated.

(2). First version prototype showing feasibility. Demonstrate the feasibility of the system and perform an informal evaluation of a few special test cases.

(3). System refinement. Evaluate with informal test cases and get feedback from experts and possible end users.

(4). Structured evaluation of performance. Perform formalized evaluation using random cases. This phase will usually result in modifications to the knowledge base.

(5). Structured evaluation of acceptability to users. Evaluate the system in its intended users' surroundings. Verify that the system has good human factor concepts (i.e., input/output devices and ease of use). A good example of this is the Oncocin project at Stanford University, in which industrial engineers helped in designing custom keyboard user interfaces for the physicians who would be using the expert system.

(6). Evaluate the functions of the system for an extended period in the prototype environment. Field test and verify the system. Observe the performance of the system and reactions of the users.

(7). Followup studies to show large scale usefulness. Measure large scale usefulness of the system on the basis of key indices before and after the system's introduction.

(8). Incorporate the necessary changes to allow wide distribution of the system. Perform any changes required from step 7 (i.e., condensing the system to run quicker on personal computers, data consolidation, etc.).

(9). Perform a general release and distribution with plans for updating and maintaining the system. A master copy of the system should be retained and updates should be verified.

9.3.1   Factors Involved in Validation

Several major factors should be examined carefully in the verification and validation stages of an expert system. The objective is to verify and validate that for any correct input to the system, a correct output can be obtained. Factors of interest in expert system validation include the following:

(1). *Completeness*: This refers to the thoroughness of the system and includes checks to determine if the system can address all desired problems within its problem domain.

(2). *Efficiency*: This checks how well the system makes use of the available knowledge, data, hardware, software, and time in solving problems within its specified domain. For example, an efficient knowledge-based system should be able to reach a useful conclusion on the basis of limited data.

(3). *Validity*: This involves the correctness of the system outputs. Validity may be viewed as the ability of the expert system to provide accurate results for relevant data inputs.

(4). *Maintainability*: This involves how well the integrity of the system can be preserved even when operating conditions change.

(5). *Consistency*: Consistency requires that the system provide similar results for similar problem scenarios.

(6). *Precision*: This refers to the level of certainty or reliability associated with the consultations provided by the system. Precision is often application dependent. For example, precision in a medical diagnosis may have more importance than precision in many other domains of diagnosis. Compliance with any prevailing rules and regulations is an important component of the precision of an expert system.

(7). *Soundness*: Soundness refers to the solid foundation of the reasoning basis for the expert system. Soundness is typically dependent on the quality of the source of knowledge used in developing the expert system.

(8). *Usability*: This involves an evaluation of how the system might meet users' needs. Questions to be asked include: Is the system usable by the end user? Are questions worded in an easily understood format? Is help available? Is the system able to explain its reasoning process to the user? Is the system compatible with the delivery environment?

(9). *Justification*: A key factor of validation involves justification. An expert system should be justified in terms of cost requirements, operating characteristics, and user requests.

(10). *Reliability*: Under reliability evaluation, the system is expected to perform satisfactorily whenever it is consulted. It should not be subject to erratic performance and results. Several test runs are typically needed to get a good feel for the reliability of an expert system.

(11). *Accommodating*: To be accommodating, the system has to be very forgiving for minor data entry errors by the user. Appropriate prompts should be incorporated into the user interface to inform users of incorrect data inputs and allow corrections of inputs.

(12). *Clarity*: Clarity refers to how well the system presents its prompts to avoid ambiguities in the input/output processes. If the system possesses a high level of clarity, there will be assurance that it will be used as intended by the users.

(13). *Quality*: The quality of an expert system is a function of the level of expertise encoded into the knowledge base. Both the domain expert and the knowledge engineer are responsible for ensuring the quality of the system. The expert is expected to provide effective problem-solving strategies. The knowledge engineer is expected to encode the problem-solving strategies accurately.

9.3.2 How to Evaluate the System

For an expert system based on empirical analysis to be correctly validated, the correct results for test cases must be known and accessible. With known results, an absolute measure of the effectiveness of the system may be computed as the ratio of correct to incorrect results produced by the system. If standard results are not available, then a relative evaluation of the system may be performed on the basis of the performance of other expert systems designed to perform similar functions. Provided below are some guidelines on how to perform the evaluation process:

- Set realistic standards for the performance of the system.
- Define the minimum acceptable standard required for the system to be considered successful.
- Use performance standards that are comparable to those used in evaluating human performance.
- Use controlled experiments whereby the evaluators are not biased by the sources of the results being evaluated.
- Distinguish between "false positive" and "true positive" results produced by the expert system. In a false positive result, the system would diagnose as "true" what is not really "true." In true positive results, the system would diagnose as "true" what is really "true."
- In cases of incorrect results, identify which correct conclusions are closest to being reached. This will be very valuable in performing a refinement of the system later on.

Potential sources of validation problems in a rule base include the following:

(1). *Conflicting rules*: These yield conflicting results for the same premise. In the case of a single domain expert, conflicting rules may be resolved by asking the expert to carefully examine the rules and come up with a unique reasoning path for the given data. In the case of multiple domain experts, a resolution may be achieved by urging the experts to come up with a consensus.

(2). *Redundant rules*: Redundant rules are two rules that yield the same results for the same problem data. Redundant rules can be easily pruned by identifying them and eliminating the ones that are likely to be least used during consultations. In some cases, certain rules are redundant only for a specific problem scenario. The same rules, in other cases, may turn out not to be redundant. So, care must be taken when eliminating portions of redundant rules.

(3). *Closed loop rules*: Closed loop rules are those that lead to a loop in the reasoning process of an expert system. These must be identified and corrected.

(4). *Missing rules*: Missing rules are essential rules that are needed to achieve the desired results but that are missing in the knowledge base. Without those essential rules, the expected consultation results cannot be obtained.

Rules must be verified to ensure that they are represented as intended during the knowledge acquisition process. If rules appear to be coded properly but the desired results are not being achieved, potential actions needed to modify the rules may include the following:

(1). Modifying the applicable certainty factor associated with the conclusion of a rule. An increase in the certainty factor would make the rule more general whereas a decrease would make it more specific and, thus, more prone to errors.

(2). Decomposing any multiple antecedents associated with the troublesome rules. Rules based on single antecedents are easier to satisfy and are also easier to identify in case of problems. Multiple antecedents can lead to combinatorial interactions of parameters that may make it difficult to debug rules.

9.4 SENSITIVITY ANALYSIS

To improve the precision of a knowledge base, the knowledge engineer can perform sensitivity analysis. Sensitivity analysis establishes the variability in the conclusions of the system as a function of the variability of the data. That is, we would identify the differences in consultation results that are caused by different levels of changes in the input to the consultation. If minor changes in the consultation inputs lead to large differences in the conclusion then the system is said to be very sensitive to changes in inputs. One effective method of using sensitivity analysis to improve precision is to display as a histogram output values against possible answers for one given input. Sensitive points will be displayed as drastic changes in the histogram. These visual identifications help identify potential trouble spots in the expert system.

Verification and validation are multi-party functions that should involve many of the people that will be affected by the finished product. Figure 9.1 shows the interaction needed between the development team and users during an expert system development process. To maximize the chances of success, users must be involved in all the stages of the development effort. Management should not dictate to users that they must use the system after it is finished. Rather, there should be a two-way communication channel through which management knows what the users need and the users know what management wants. That way, users will be of great value in the verification and validation processes throughout the project.

9.5 EXPERT SYSTEMS QUALITY MANAGEMENT

Expert systems quality objectives must be prioritized, integrated, and applied uniformly throughout the expert system project life cycle. The quality of an expert system should be evaluated on the basis of its performance relative to the following factors:

- Effective solution of organizational problems.
- The feasibility of the solutions offered by the expert system.
- Data input requirements for using the expert system.

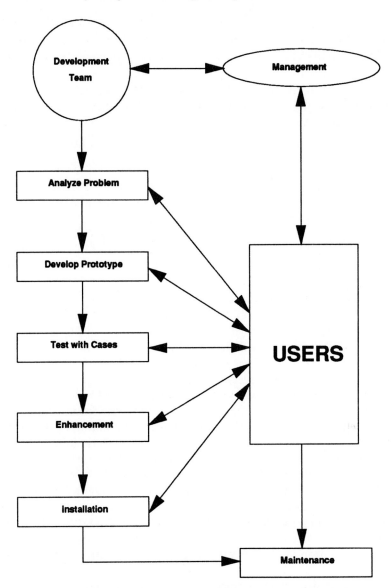

Figure 9.1. User involvement in system development and validation

- Interaction with existing systems in the organization.
- The frequency of use of the expert system.
- The level of promptness in using the expert system to solve problems.
- Redundancy in the operations of the expert system.
- Compatibility with organizational objectives.

The initial quality of an expert system must be preserved through periodic review of its performance and the making of the necessary updates to the system. Expert system quality can be managed by following the guidelines below:

(1). Evaluate user acceptance of the expert system.

(2). Raise the level of awareness about the implications of low versus high quality of the system.

(3). Adopt a supportive philosophy for expert system quality management.

(4). Provide necessary resources to implement the quality objectives.

(5). Evaluate the pre- and post-expert system productivity levels.

(6). Establish quality liaisons with the users of the system.

(7). Institute periodic quality reporting requirements.

(8). Recognize the limitations of expert system technology.

(9). Make arrangements for the resources needed to keep the system operating satisfactorily.

(10). Develop reliable performance measurement criteria.

9.6 INHERENT LIMITATIONS OF EXPERT SYSTEMS

There are several barriers that presently hinder the widespread adoption of expert systems. Some of the barriers are a result of the prevailing low level of confidence in the technology, while others follow from the inherent resistance that people have towards change. It will take several years of supercomputer processing time to simulate what takes place in the human brain many times every second. The real-time performance of the human brain poses a considerable challenge to the field of AI in terms of mimicking human intelligence.

Even the expert systems that do not have to work in real-time environments have inherent limitations. While research and development work is continuing, the developers and the users need to be aware of these limitations before undertaking major expert systems projects. The limitations make the functions of verification and validation very difficult. Some of the limitations are:

(1). Inability to represent large temporal or spatial knowledge.

(2). Limitations in the scope of the problem domain addressed by an expert system.

(3). Difficulty in performing knowledge acquisition in cases where knowledge is limited or inaccessible.

(4). Lack of standardization of development tools.

(5). Inconsistencies in sources of knowledge to be acquired for expert systems.

(6). Limited or nonexistent learning capabilities in the current generation of expert systems. Learning must be an essential component of expert systems if they are to truly mimic human experts.

9.7 EXPERT SYSTEMS INTEGRATION

No technical system can succeed as an individual entity. With the increasing shortages of resources, more emphasis will be placed on the sharing of resources. Resource sharing will involve physical equipment, conceptual items, information, ideas, and so on. The integration of systems facilitates the sharing of resources. Systems integration should be a major concern in expert systems development. System integration may involve physical integration of technical components, objective integration of operations, conceptual integration of management processes, or a combination of any of these.

Probably the single most important effort in the implementation of expert systems involves integrating the system into the workplace as a regular part of operations. A concerted effort must be made to integrate expert systems into the workplace. An important aspect of expert systems implementation and integration is finding an "owner" for the expert system. This owner would have the responsibility to ensure that the system is used as intended. The owner should periodically review how the expert system has been used to solve problems in the organization.

A definition of what is required in the integration effort should be developed and presented to the prospective users. For example, systems integration involves the linking of components to form subsystems and the linking of subsystems to form composite systems within a single department and/or across departments. It facilitates the coordination of diverse technical and managerial efforts to enhance organizational functions, reduce cost, save energy, improve productivity, and increase the utilization of resources. Systems integration emphasizes the identification and coordination of the interface requirements between the components in an integrated system. The components and subsystems operate synergistically to optimize the performance of the total system. Systems integration ensures that all performance goals are satisfied with a minimum of expenditure of time and resources. Systems integration is based upon integrating compatible functions to achieve the following benefits:

(1). *Dual-use integration:* This involves the use of a single component by separate subsystems to reduce both the initial cost and the operating cost during the project life cycle.

(2). *Dynamic resource integration:* This involves integrating the resource flows of two normally separate subsystems so that the resource flow from one subsystem to another minimizes the total resource requirements in a project.

(3). *Restructuring of functions:* This involves the restructuring of functions and re-integration of subsystems to optimize costs when a new subsystem is introduced into the organization.

Systems integration is particularly important when a new technology, such as an expert system is introduced, into an existing system. It involves coordinating new operations to coexist with existing operations. It may require the adjustment of functions to permit sharing of resources, development of new policies to accommodate product integration, or realignment of managerial responsibilities. It can affect both hardware and software components of an organization. Presented below are guidelines and important questions relevant for expert systems integration:

- What are the unique characteristics of each component in the integrated system?
- How do the characteristics complement one another?
- What physical interfaces exist between the components?
- What data/information interfaces exist between the components?
- What ideological differences exist between the components?
- What are the data flow requirements for the components?
- Are there similar integrated systems operating elsewhere?
- What are the reporting requirements in the integrated system?
- Are there any hierarchical restrictions on the operations of the components of the integrated system?
- What are the internal and external factors expected to influence the integrated system?
- How can the performance of the integrated system be measured?
- What benefit/cost documentations are required for the integrated system?
- What is the cost of designing and implementing the integrated system?
- What are the relative priorities assigned to each component of the integrated system?
- What are the strengths of the integrated system?
- What are the weaknesses of the integrated system?
- What resources are needed to keep the integrated system operating satisfactorily?
- Which section of the organization will have primary responsibility for the operation of the integrated system?
- What are the quality specifications and requirements for the integrated systems?

9.8 INTEGRATION WITH OTHER DECISION SUPPORT TOOLS

Expert systems can be integrated with other decision support tools to provide a more effective mechanism for making decisions in engineering and manufacturing applications. For example, basic linear programming (LP) solutions may be combined with conventional subjective decision analysis of the analytic hierarchy process (AHP) and expert systems. In this section, we show the output of a zero-one mathematical formulation of an investment decision that may be incorporated into the input for AHP analysis. The results of AHP analysis may be used to develop expert system rules for investment decisions. For example, EXSYS, a popular expert systems development tool now offers a direct interface with linear programming. Thus, the analytical capability of an expert system is directly interfaced to the optimization capability of linear programming. Figure 9.2 shows a model of the EXSYS interface.

The EXSYS Professional expert system development shell and LINDO linear programming package combine to incorporate non-numeric constraints and heuristics with LP optimization. Expert system data can be automatically merged into an LP model. External programs, custom screens, graphics, hypertext, and speech systems can be employed to prompt users for data needed in the decision process. Data can be verified by the expert system before being used in an LP model. Conversely, the results of an LP model can be analyzed by the expert system before being presented to the user for final decisions. The symbiotic interface of LP and expert system facilitates a more dynamic and responsive system for making decisions.

Linear programming is one of the most important and effective tools in use today for decision analysis. It is the most widely-used operations research technique. Several software packages are available for solving linear programming (LP) problems. These include LINDO, PC-PROG, STATGRAPHICS, SAS System, XPRESS-MP, XA'llence, GAMS/386, CPlex, TURBO-SIMPLEX, and so on.

The objective of a general linear programming problem is to optimize a dependent variable (objective function) by finding values for a set of independent variables (decision variables), given that there is a variety of restrictions (constraints) on the values of the independent variables. We can define all the relationships and constraints mathematically as shown on the next page:

Figure 9.2. Interface of expert system inference engine with LP

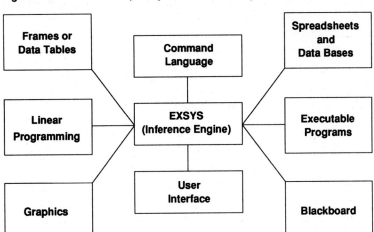

Optimize: $y = f(x_1, x_2, ..., x_n)$

subject to:

$$g_1(x_1, x_2, ..., x_n) \left\{\leq = \geq\right\} 0$$
$$g_2(x_1, x_2, ..., x_n) \left\{\leq = \geq\right\} 0$$
$$.$$
$$.$$
$$.$$
$$g_m(x_1, x_2, ..., x_n) \left\{\leq = \geq\right\} 0$$

where
$x_1, x_2, ..., x_n$ are the decision variables, $y = f(x_1, x_2, ..., x_n)$ is the objective function, and $g_1(.), g_2(.), ... g_m(.)$ represent the constraints.

A *linear program* is one in which the functions f and $g_1, g_2, ... , g_m$ are all linear.

     An important aspect of using LP models is the interpretation of the results to make decisions. An LP solution that is optimal on paper may not necessarily be optimal in a real world environment. However, if the LP model adequately reflects the real system, it can be expected that its solution will be a reasonably good real-world solution. The decision maker must always call on his own subjective judgment when implementing the results of mathematical analyses. Final decisions are often based on a combination of both quantitative and qualitative factors. This is where an interface with an expert system can be of great help. The confidence factors used in expert systems can be used to incorporate risk and uncertainty into the decision process

     The illustrative formulation presented here (Pulat and Badiru 1990) involves the determination of the optimal combination of project investments so as to maximize total return on investment. Suppose a project analyst is given N projects, $X_1, X_2, X_3, ..., X_N$, with the requirement to determine the respective level of investment in each project so that total investment return is maximized subject to a specified limit on available budget. The projects are not mutually exclusive.

     The investment in each project starts at a base level b_i ($i = 1, 2, ..., N$) and increases a variable increments k_{ij} ($j = 1, 2, 3, ..., K_i$), where K_i is the number of increments used for project i. Consequently, the level of investment in project X_i is defined as:

$$x_i = b_i + \sum_{j=1}^{K_i} k_{ij},$$

where

$$x_i \geq 0 \ \forall \ i.$$

For most cases, the base investment will be zero. In those cases, we would have $b_i = 0$. In the modeling procedure used for this problem,

$$X_i = \begin{cases} 1 & \text{if the investment in project } i \text{ is greater than zero} \\ 0 & \text{otherwise} \end{cases}$$

and

$$Y_{ij} = \begin{cases} 1 & \text{if } j\text{'th increment of alternative } i \text{ is used} \\ 0 & \text{otherwise} \end{cases}$$

The variable x_i is the actual level of investment in project i while X_i is an indicator variable indicating whether or not project i is one of the projects selected for investment. Similarly, k_{ij} is the actual magnitude of the j'th increment while Y_{ij} is an indicator variable that indicates whether or not the j'th increment is used for project i. The maximum possible investment in each project is defined as M_i such that:

$$b_i \le x_i \le M_i.$$

There is a specified limit, B, on the total budget available to invest such that:

$$\sum_i x_i \le B.$$

There is a known relationship between the level of investment, x_i, in each project and the expected return, $R(x_i)$. This relationship will be referred to as the *utility function*, $f(x)$, for the project. The utility function may be developed through historical data, regression analysis, and forecasting models. For a given project, the utility function is used to determine the expected return, $R(x_i)$, for a specified level of investment in that project. That is,

$$R(x_i) = f(x_i)$$

$$= \sum_{j=1}^{K_i} r_{ij} Y_{ij}.$$

where r_{ij} is the incremental return obtained when the investment in project i is increased by k_{ij}. If the incremental return decreases as the level of investment increases, the utility function will be *concave*. In that case, we will have the following relationship:

$$r_{ij} \ge r_{i,j+1}$$

or

$$r_{ij} - r_{i,j+1} \ge 0.$$

Thus,

$$Y_{ij} \ge Y_{i,j+1}$$

or

$$Y_{if} - Y_{i,j+1} \ge 0,$$

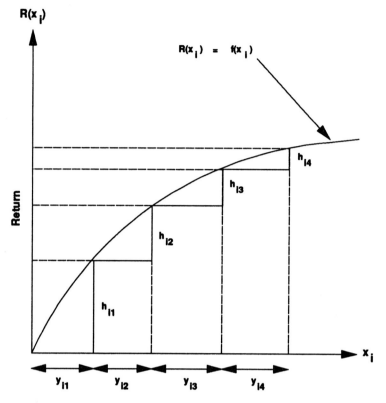

Figure 9.3. Example of concave investment utility function

so that only the first n increments ($j = 1, 2, \ldots, n$) that produce the highest returns are used for project i. Figure 9-3 shows an example of a concave investment
utility function. If the incremental returns do not define a concave function, $f(x_i)$,
then one has to introduce the inequality constraints presented above into the
optimization model. Otherwise, the inequality constraints may be left out of the
model since the first inequality, $Y_{ij} \geq Y_{i,j+1}$, is always implicitly satisfied for concave functions. Our objective is to maximize the total return. That is,

$$\text{Max } Z = \sum_i \sum_j r_{ij} Y_{ij}$$

Subject to the following constraints:

$$x_i = b_i + \sum_j k_{ij} Y_{ij}$$

$$b_i \leq x_i \leq M_i$$

$$Y_{ij} \geq Y_{i,j+1}$$

$$\sum_i x_i \leq B.$$

$$x_i \leq 0$$

$$Y_{ij} = 0 \text{ or } 1$$

ILLUSTRATIVE EXAMPLE   Given four projects (i.e., $N = 4$) and a budget limit of $10 million. The respective investments and returns are shown in Table 9.1, Table 9.2, Table 9.3, and Table 9.4. All values are in millions of dollars. The planning horizon is one year. It is assumed that investments are made at the beginning of the year. The returns are assumed to be realizable at the end of the year. Investment decisions are to be made on a year-to-year basis. For example, in Table 9.1, if an incremental investment of $0.20 million from stage 2 to stage 3 is made in project one, the expected incremental return per year from the project would be $0.30 million. Thus, a total investment of $1.20 million in project one at the beginning of the year would yield a total return of $1.90 million at the end of the year.

The question addressed by the optimization model is to determine how many investment increments should be used for each project. That is, at what level should we stop increasing the investments in a project? Obviously, for a single project, we would continue to invest as long as the incremental returns are larger than the incremental investments. However, for multiple projects, investment interactions complicate the decision so that one cannot determine the optimal investment in one project independent of the other projects. This is where the usefulness of an LP model is manifested.

The above example was formulated as an LP model and solved with LINDO software. The LINDO formulation is as follows:

MAX $1.4Y11 + .2Y12 + .3Y13 + .1Y14 + .1Y15$

$\quad + 6Y21 + .3Y22 + .3Y23 + .2Y24 + .1Y25 + .05Y26 + .05Y27$

$\quad + 4.9Y31 + .3Y32 + .4Y33 + .3Y34 + .2Y35 + .1Y36 + .1Y37 + .1Y38$

$\quad + 3Y41 + .5Y42 + .2Y43 + .1Y44 + .05Y45 + .15Y46$

Table 9.1. Investment data for project 1

Stage (j)	y_{1j} Incremental Investment	x_1 Level of Investment	r_{1j} Incremental Return	$R(x_1)$ Total Return
0	-	0	-	0
1	0.80	0.80	1.40	1.40
2	0.20	1.00	0.20	1.60
3	0.20	1.20	0.30	1.90
4	0.20	1.40	0.10	2.00
5	0.20	1.60	0.10	2.10

Stage (j)	y_{2j} Incremental Investment	x_2 Level of Investment	r_{2j} Incremental Return	$R(x_2)$ Total Return
0	-	0	-	0
1	3.20	3.20	6.00	6.00
2	0.20	3.40	0.30	6.30
3	0.20	3.60	0.30	6.60
4	0.20	3.80	0.20	6.80
5	0.20	4.00	0.10	6.90
6	0.20	4.20	0.05	6.95
7	0.20	4.40	0.05	7.00

Table 9.2. Investment data for project 2

Table 9.3. Investment data for project 3

Stage (j)	y_{3j} Incremental Investment	x_3 Level of Investment	r_{3j} Incremental Return	$R(x_3)$ Total Return
0	0	-	-	0
1	2.00	2.00	4.90	4.90
2	0.20	2.20	0.30	5.20
3	0.20	2.40	0.40	5.60
4	0.20	2.60	0.30	5.90
5	0.20	2.80	0.20	6.10
6	0.20	3.00	0.10	6.20
7	0.20	3.20	0.10	6.30
8	0.20	3.40	0.10	6.40

Subject to:

$$.8Y11 + .2Y12 + .2Y13 + .2Y14 + .2Y15 - X1 = 0$$

$$3.2Y21 + .2Y22 + .2Y23 + .2Y24 + .2Y25 + .2Y26 + .2Y27 - X2 = 0$$

Stage (j)	y_{4j} Incremental Investment	x_4 Level of Investment	r_{4j} Incremental Return	$R(x_4)$ Total Return
0	-	0	-	0
1	1.95	1.95	3.00	3.00
2	0.20	2.15	0.50	3.50
3	0.20	2.35	0.20	3.70
4	0.20	2.55	0.10	3.80
5	0.20	2.75	0.05	3.85
6	0.20	2.95	0.15	4.00
7	0.20	3.15	0.00	4.00

Table 9.4. Investment data for project 4

$2.0Y31 + .2Y32 + .2Y33 + .2Y34 + .2Y35 + .2Y36 + .2Y37 + .2Y38 - X3 = 0$

$1.95Y41 + .2Y42 + .2Y43 + .2Y44 + .2Y45 + .2Y46 + .2Y47 - X4 = 0$

$X1 + X2 + X3 + X4 <= 10$

$Y12 - Y13 >= 0$

$Y13 - Y14 >= 0$

$Y14 - Y15 >= 0$

$Y22 - Y23 >= 0$

$Y26 - Y27 >= 0$

$Y32 - Y33 >= 0$

$Y33 - Y34 >= 0$

$Y34 - Y35 >= 0$

$Y35 - Y36 >= 0$

$Y36 - Y37 >= 0$

$Y37 - Y38 >= 0$

$Y43 - Y44 >= 0$

$Y44 - Y45 >= 0$

$Y45 - Y46 >= 0$

$X_i >= 0$ for $i = 1, 2, \ldots, 5$

$Y_{ij} = 0,1$ for all i,j

It is recalled that the Y_{ij} values indicate whether or not the jth investment increment is used in the ith project. LINDO yielded the following solution for the optimal levels of investment in the respective projects.

Project 1:

$Y11 = 1$, $Y12 = 1$, $Y13 = 1$

$Y14 = 0$, $Y15 = 0$

Thus, the investment in project 1 is given by:

$X1 = 0.80 + 0.20 + 0.20 = \$1.20$ million

The corresponding return is \$1.90 million

Project 2:

$Y21 = 1$, $Y22 = 1$, $Y23 = 1$

$Y24 = 1$, $Y25 = 0$, $Y26 = 0$

$Y27 = 0$

Thus, the investment in project 2 is given by:

$X2 = 3.2 + 0.20 + 0.20 + 0.20 = \$3.80$ million

The corresponding return is \$6.80 million

Project 3:

$Y31 = 1$, $Y32 = 1$, $Y33 = 1$

$Y34 = 1$, $Y35 = 0$, $Y36 = 0$

$Y37 = 0$

Thus, the investment in project 3 is given by:

$X3 = 2.00 + 0.20 + 0.20 + 0.20 = \$2.60$ million

The corresponding return is \$5.90 million

Project 4:

$Y41 = 1$, $Y42 = 1$, $Y43 = 1$

Thus, the investment in project 4 is given by:

$X4 = 1.95 + 0.20 + 0.20 = \$2.35$ million

The corresponding return is \$3.70 million

The total investment in all four projects is $9,950,000. Thus, the optimal solution indicates that not all of the $10,000,000 available should be invested. The expected return from the total investment is $18,300,000. This translates into 83.92 percent return on investment for one year. Figure 9.4 presents a bar chart of the relative investments and the respective returns for the four projects. The respective individual returns on investment from the projects are shown graphically in Figure 9.5. This solution represents the investment decision just for year one. Similar formulations and solutions would need to be developed for subsequent years.

In the above example, the return on total investment appears to be unusually large. But that is exactly the type of level of yield that optimization models are expected to generate. It should be noted that the typical rates of return ranging from 8 to 15 percent used in practice are derived from methods that do not take advantage of the available optimization techniques. If optimization models are incorporated into the normal decision processes, higher rates of return are quite possible. However, the decision maker must take care to ensure that the underlying assumptions of the optimization model do fit the realities of the problem being addressed.

Possible extensions to the LP model above include the incorporation of risk and time value of money into the solution procedure. Risk analysis would be relevant particularly for cases where the levels of returns for the various levels of investment are not known with certainty. Risk can be incorporated explicitly by use of conventional statistical methods. However, the confidence factors approach used in expert systems offers a simple alternative that permits the decision maker to interactively indicate his or her own subjective perception of the level of risk

Figure 9.4. Bar chart of investment levels

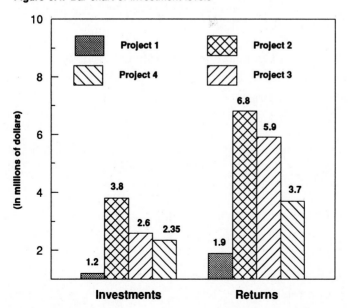

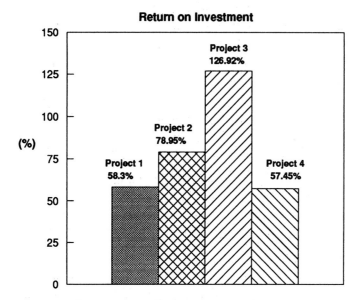

Figure 9.5. Bar chart of relative returns on investment

and uncertainty associated with the decision problem. The incorporation of the time value of money would be appropriate if the investment analysis is to be performed over a planning horizon spanning several years. For example, we might need to make investment decisions to cover the next five years rather than just the next one year.

An example of the incorporation of LP and AHP is presented below. The objective is to "maximize" the net total income from the combination of investment options. Three possible investment projects are available. The investment decision problem is summarized as shown below:

Objective: Select Best Combination of Investment Options

Alternative 1: Bonds

Alternative 2: Mutual Funds

Alternative 3: Oil Stock

The alternatives are to be compared on the basis of factors that the investor considers to be very important. For the purpose of this illustration, the following five factors are used in comparing the alternatives:

Attribute A: Return on Investment (ROI)

Attribute B: Level of Risk

Attribute C: Liquidity

Attribute D: Flexibility

Attribute E: Control

Return on investment refers to the direct rate of return that can be obtained from a prospective project. In the preceding section, the result of the LP model indicates the respective rates of return from alternate projects. Thus, the quantitative results of LP analysis is combined with subjective factors to form the basis for a final investment decision. Level of risk refers to the potential for financial losses associated with each investment alternative. Liquidity refers to how quickly the investor can cash in on his investment. This indicates the short-term cash-in potential for an investment alternative. Flexibility refers to the investor's ability to make short-notice adjustments in the investment once the investment commitment has been made. Control refers to the investor's ability to maneuver his investment strategies with limited external or institutional influence. A complete AHP analysis of the above problem yields the following relative weights of the three investment alternatives:

Alternative 1: 0.208

Alternative 2: 0.244

Alternative 3: 0.548

Thus, Alternative 3 (Oil Stock) is the best option since it has the highest weighted rating of 0.548. An example of the procedure for AHP analysis is presented in Chapter 3.

The scope of decision analysis involving financial investments is complex, unstructured, and does not lend itself easily to algorithmic solutions. The decision maker's experience, policies, values, judgment, and intuition are valuable components of complex decision making. An expert system is a computer tool that can facilitate the integration and consistent usage of all the relevant information in the complex decision process of developing investment strategies. Special interfaces in the expert system structure handle a variety of links that can exist between the expert system and other software systems, such as data base management, spreadsheet analysis, financial analysis, risk management models, and optimization models.

The composite AHP rating obtained for the investment alternatives may be compared on the basis of expert heuristics. On the other hand, individual investment alternatives may be evaluated singularly on the basis of some minimum acceptable rating specified by the decision maker. An example of an expert systems rule for this purpose is the following:

IF *composite-rating* $>= 0.50$,

THEN *project-acceptance* = yes

ELSE *project-acceptance* = no

Similar rules may be developed to compare a set of alternatives. Once the rules have been verified by experts, they may be organized into a comprehensive expert systems knowledge base. This is left as an exercise for the reader (see Exercises at the end of the chapter).

9.9 INTERFACE TO QUANTITATIVE ANALYSIS

Another example of the use of expert systems for conventional quantitative analysis is presented in this section. The VP-Expert inference engine is used for the illustration. Nested loops are very important in many engineering applications. Unfortunately, VP-Expert does not directly support nested loops. But a good VP-Expert user can construct a knowledge base that will perform nested loops. Since VP-Expert does not support nested IF statements, it will be necessary to carefully organize the rules in the knowledge base to perform nested loops without any error.

For this example, it is desired to develop a VP-Expert knowledge base to perform matrix multiplication and print out the result in a nested loop procedure. The computational routine must be written entirely within VP-Expert with no external interface. The user will input the elements of matrices A and B as defined below:

$$
\mathbf{A} = \begin{bmatrix} a_{11} & a_{12} & a_{13} & a_{14} \\ a_{21} & a_{22} & a_{23} & a_{24} \\ a_{31} & a_{32} & a_{33} & a_{34} \end{bmatrix}
$$

$$
\mathbf{B} = \begin{bmatrix} b_{11} & b_{12} & b_{13} \\ b_{21} & b_{22} & b_{23} \\ b_{31} & b_{32} & b_{33} \\ b_{41} & b_{42} & b_{43} \end{bmatrix}
$$

The multiplication result will be stored in matrix C ($C = A \times B$) defined below:

$$
\mathbf{C} = \begin{bmatrix} c_{11} & c_{12} & c_{13} \\ c_{21} & c_{22} & c_{23} \\ c_{31} & c_{32} & c_{33} \end{bmatrix}
$$

The matrix elements a_{ij} and b_{ij} are any real numbers to be input by the user. The pseudocode for the format for the nested loop is presented below:

```
Get inputs
Compute C
Print C to the screen as follows:
      print row i (i=1 to 3)
            print the jth element of row j (j=1 to 3)
            next j
      next i
End
```

The VP-Expert knowledge base for the example is presented below:

```
Runtime;
ACTIONS
   RESET All
   Z = 1
   FIND A[1]
   FIND A[2]
   FIND A[3]
   FIND A[4]
   FIND A[5]
   FIND A[6]
   FIND A[7]
   FIND A[8]
   FIND A[9]
   FIND A[10]
   FIND A[11]
   FIND A[12]
   FIND B[1]
   FIND B[5]
   FIND B[9]
   FIND B[13]
   FIND B[2]
   FIND B[6]
   FIND B[10]
   FIND B[14]
   FIND B[3]
   FIND B[7]
   FIND B[11]
   FIND B[15]
   FIND B[4]
   FIND B[8]
   FIND B[12]
   FIND B[16]
   FIND DISPLAY_A_B     !display the contents of matrix A and B
   DISPLAY " This is going to take a while, please wait !.. "
   FDISPLAY result," This is going to take a while, please wait !.. "
   FOR I=1 TO 4          !the outer loop of the nested loop
   !this handles the column index for the resulting matrix
      RESET INNERLOOP     !to perform the matrix multiplication
      Find INNERLOOP          !see Rule 2 . . .
   END
   Find Display_C        !display the result of the matrix multiplication
   CLOSE All
   RESET All
;
! ***** End of Main Action Block..
```

```
Rule 1
IF Z=1 THEN
  DISPLAY_A_B=display_now
  FORMAT a,7.0
  DISPLAY "     The input matrix A :      "
  DISPLAY " "
  DISPLAY "                    "
  DISPLAY "  {A[1]}  {A[2]}  {A[3]}  {A[4]}   "
  DISPLAY "  {A[5]}  {A[6]}  {A[7]}  {A[8]}   "
  DISPLAY "  {A[9]}  {A[10]}  {A[11]}  {A[12]}   "
  DISPLAY "                    "
  DISPLAY " "
  FORMAT b,7.0
  DISPLAY "     The input matrix B :      "
  DISPLAY "                    "
  DISPLAY "  {B[1]}  {B[5]}  {B[9]}  {B[13]}   "
  DISPLAY "  {B[2]}  {B[6]}  {B[10]}  {B[14]}   "
  DISPLAY "  {B[3]}  {B[7]}  {B[11]}  {B[15]}   "
  DISPLAY "  {B[4]}  {B[8]}  {B[12]}  {B[16]}   "
  DISPLAY "                    "
  FDISPLAY result,"    The input matrix A :      "
  FDISPLAY result," "
  FDISPLAY result,"                    "
  FDISPLAY result,"  {A[1]}  {A[2]}  {A[3]}  {A[4]}   "
  FDISPLAY result,"  {A[5]}  {A[6]}  {A[7]}  {A[8]}   "
  FDISPLAY result,"  {A[9]}  {A[10]}  {A[11]}  {A[12]}   "
  FDISPLAY result,"                    "
  FDISPLAY result,"    The input matrix B :      "
  FDISPLAY result," "
  FDISPLAY result,"                    "
  FDISPLAY result,"  {B[1]}  {B[5]}  {B[9]}  {B[13]}   "
  FDISPLAY result,"  {B[2]}  {B[6]}  {B[10]}  {B[14]}   "
  FDISPLAY result,"  {B[3]}  {B[7]}  {B[11]}  {B[15]}   "
  FDISPLAY result,"  {B[4]}  {B[8]}  {B[12]}  {B[16]}   "
  FDISPLAY result,"                    "
  DISPLAY " ";


Rule 2
IF I<5 THEN
  INNERLOOP=do_inner_loop
  f=((I−1)*3)            !offset element point of matrix C
  g=((I−1)*4)            !offset element pointer of matrix B
  u=(1+(f))
  v=(2+(f))
  w=(3+(f))
  C[u]=0
  C[v]=0
  C[w]=0            !initialize column elements
  FOR J=1 to 4       !The second of the nested loop
  h=(J+g)        !which handles the matrix multiplication.
```

```
a1=(J)     !This handles the row index of the resulting matrix.
a2=(J+4) !pointing the second element of the column
a3=(J+8) !pointing the third element of the column
a4=(J+12) !pointing the fourth element of the column
a5=(J+16) !pointing the fifth element of the column
C[u]=(C[u]+A[a1]*B[h]) !first element of the column
C[v]=(C[v]+A[a2]*B[h]) !second element of the column
C[w]=(C[w]+A[a3]*B[h]) !third element of the column
END
;


Rule 3
IF Z=1 THEN
  DISPLAY_C=display_now
  DISPLAY ""
  DISPLAY "  The matrix C = A * B :"
  DISPLAY ""
  DISPLAY "                        "
  DISPLAY "   {C[1]}   {C[4]}   {C[7]}   {C[10]}   "
  DISPLAY "   {C[2]}   {C[5]}   {C[8]}   {C[11]}   "
  DISPLAY "   {C[3]}   {C[6]}   {C[9]}   {C[12]}   "
  DISPLAY "                        "
  DISPLAY ""
  FDISPLAY result," "
  FDISPLAY result,"  The matrix C = A * B :"
  FDISPLAY result," "
  FDISPLAY result,"                        "
  FDISPLAY result,"   {C[1]}   {C[4]}   {C[7]}   {C[10]}   "
  FDISPLAY result,"   {C[2]}   {C[5]}   {C[8]}   {C[11]}   "
  FDISPLAY result,"   {C[3]}   {C[6]}   {C[9]}   {C[12]}   "
  FDISPLAY result,"                        "
;
ASK A[1]: "What is A[1,1] ?";
ASK A[2]: "What is A[1,2] ?";
ASK A[3]: "What is A[1,3] ?";
ASK A[4]: "What is A[1,4] ?";
ASK A[5]: "What is A[2,1] ?";
ASK A[6]: "What is A[2,2] ?";
ASK A[7]: "What is A[2,3] ?";
ASK A[8]: "What is A[2,4] ?";
ASK A[9]: "What is A[3,1] ?";
ASK A[10]: "What is A[3,2] ?";
ASK A[11]: "What is A[3,3] ?";
ASK A[12]: "What is A[3,4] ?";
ASK B[1]: "What is B[1,1] ?";
ASK B[5]: "What is B[1,2] ?";
ASK B[9]: "What is B[1,3] ?";
ASK B[13]: "What is B[1,4] ?";
ASK B[2]: "What is B[2,1] ?";
ASK B[6]: "What is B[2,2] ?";
```

ASK B[10]: "What is B[2,3] ?";
ASK B[14]: "What is B[2,4] ?";
ASK B[3]: "What is B[3,1] ?";
ASK B[7]: "What is B[3,2] ?";
ASK B[11]: "What is B[3,3] ?";
ASK B[15]: "What is B[3,4] ?";
ASK B[4]: "What is B[4,1] ?";
ASK B[8]: "What is B[4,2] ?";
ASK B[12]: "What is B[4,3] ?";
ASK B[16]: "What is B[4,4] ?";

The output of a sample run of the above knowledge base was verified manually. The output is presented below:

The input matrix A :

```
1  2  1  2
1  2  1  2
1  2  1  2
```

The input matrix B :

```
1  2  1  2
1  2  1  2
1  2  1  2
1  2  1  2
```

The matrix C = A * B :

```
6  12  6  12
6  12  6  12
6  12  6  12
```

An extension of the matrix analysis for expert system decision making is left as an exercise for the reader (see Exercises at the end of the chapter).

9.10 EXERCISES

9.1 Develop a guideline for verifying the performance of an expert system in an engineering operation.

9.2 Develop a guideline for validating the operation of an expert system developed for manufacturing planning.

9.3 Should an expert system be validated before or after integration? Discuss.

9.4 Is it necessary to revalidate an expert system after it has been integrated with other systems? Explain.

9.5 Extend the LP and AHP example presented in this chapter to a full expert system development. Construct several investment rules to make up the knowledge base.

9.6 Construct a decision problem whereby the results of matrix multiplication are used in the decision process. Construct a knowledge base containing decision rules that make use of the outputs of matrix multiplication.

9.7   How can the output of a linear programming model be used in an expert system consultation?

9.8   How can the output of an expert system consultation be used in a linear programming model?

9.9   How would you verify that the decision reached by an expert system based on a linear programming output is effective?

9.10   Develop an expert system that provides an interface between a knowledge base and a linear programming model.

9.11   If a decision problem can be solved by using a mathematical optimization model, is it necessary to investigate the potential of using expert systems to solve such a problem? Discuss.

9.12   How would you verify the integration interface of an expert system with external programs?

9.13   Discuss the differences between verifying and validating an expert system for engineering applications.

9.14   Engineering problems typically permit liberal tolerance (rather than precise results) in solution approaches. Does this make engineering problems very amenable to expert system approaches? Explain.

9.15   Compare and contrast the level of strictness that should be required for validating manufacturing expert systems versus engineering expert systems.

9.16   Critique the rule presented below:

IF *composite-rating* >= 0.50

THEN *project-acceptance* = yes

ELSE *project-acceptance* = no

9.17   Suggest how a knowledge engineer might validate a piece of knowledge acquired from a published reference.

9.18   When is the best time to validate an expert system knowledge base? Justify your response with an hypothetical problem scenario.

9.19   Several items were presented in this chapter as the factors involved in expert system validation. Can you think of other factors that should be considered? Discuss.

9.20   How can sensitivity analysis be used to verify the operation of a knowledge base?

9.21   Discuss the respective responsibilities of the following individuals in expert system testing, verification, and validation: User, Knowledge Engineer, Domain Expert.

9.22   How would revalidation affect the long-term maintenance of an expert system? Discuss.

9.23   Review the concept of Total Quality Management (TQM). How can the concept be applied to expert system development and implementation? Discuss.

10

Implementation and Management Strategies

Successful development and implementation of expert systems call for sound managerial strategies. Expert system development must be carefully planned and executed to avoid conflicts with existing operations within the organization. This chapter presents guidelines for planning, implementing, integrating, and managing expert systems.

10.1 STRATEGIC PLANNING FOR EXPERT SYSTEMS

Planning provides the basis for the initiation, implementation, and termination of an expert system project. It sets guidelines for specific project objectives, project structure, tasks, milestones, personnel, cost, equipment, performance, and problem resolutions. An analysis of what is needed and what is available is conducted in the planning phase of the project. The availability of technical expertise within the organization and outside the organization should be reviewed. If subcontracting is needed, the nature of the contract should undergo a thorough analysis. The question of whether or not the project is needed at all should be addressed. The "make" or "buy," "lease" or "rent," and "do nothing" alternatives should be given unbiased review opportunities. In the initial stage of project planning, the internal and external factors that influence the project should be determined and given priority weights. Examples of internal influences on expert system projects are:

- Organizational goal
- Labor situations
- Computing infrastructure
- Company size
- Market share
- Expected return on investment
- Technical manpower availability
- Resource and capital availability
- Constraints on project time

In addition to internal factors, expert system projects can be influenced by external factors. Such external factors include:

- State of the technology
- Industry direction
- Public relations
- Legal liability aspects of the project
- Government regulations
- Competition

10.1.1 Components of an Expert System Plan

Planning is an ongoing process that is conducted throughout the project life cycle. Initial planning may relate to overall organizational project efforts. This is where specific projects to be undertaken are determined. Subsequent planning will relate to specific objectives of the selected project. Planning should cover the following:

(1). *Summary of project plan*: This is a brief description of what is planned. Project scope and objectives should be enumerated. It should include a statement of how the expert system project complements organizational goals, budget size, and milestones.

(2). *Objectives*: The objectives should be very detailed in outlining what the expert system is expected to achieve and how the expected achievements will contribute to the overall goals of the organization.

(3). *Approach*: The managerial and technical methodologies of implementing the project should be specified. The managerial approach may relate to project organization, communication network, approval hierarchy, responsibility, and accountability. The technical approach may relate to company experience on previous projects and the current state of the technology.

(4). *Contractual requirements*: This portion of an expert system project plan outlines reporting requirements, communication links, customer specifications, user needs, performance specifications, deadlines, review process, project deliverables, delivery schedules, internal and external contacts, data security, policies, and procedures. This section should be as detailed as practically possible. Any item that has the slightest potential of creating problems later should be documented.

(5). *Project schedule*: The project schedule signifies the commitment of resource against time in pursuit of project objectives. The schedule should include reliable time estimates for tasks. The estimates may come from knowledgeable personnel, past records, elemental specificity, or statistical extrapolation. Task milestones should be generated on the basis of objective analysis rather than arbitrary stipulations. The schedule in this planning stage constitutes the master project schedule. Detailed activity schedules should be generated under the project scheduling functions.

(6). *Resources*: Project resources, budget, and costs are to be documented in this section of the expert system plan. Capital requirements should be specified by tasks. Resources may include personnel, equipment, and input data. Special personnel skills, hiring, and training should be explained. Personnel required should be phased with schedule requirements so as to ensure their availability when needed. Budget size and source should be presented. The basis for estimating budget requirements should be justified and the cost allocation and monitoring approach should be shown.

(7). *Performance measures*: Measures of evaluating the progress of the expert system development should be developed. The measures may be based on standard practices or customized needs. The method of monitoring, collecting, and analyzing the measures should also be specified. Corrective actions for specific undesirable events should be outlined.

(8). *Contingency plans*: Courses of actions to be taken in the case of undesirable events should be predetermined. Many projects have failed simply because no plans have been made for emergency situations. In the excitement of getting a project under way, it is often easy to overlook the need for contingency plans. However, in the interest of success, some effort should be directed at plans for adverse developments.

10.1.2 Expert System Feasibility Study

The feasibility of an expert system project can be ascertained in terms of technical factors, economic factors, or both. A feasibility study is documented with a report showing all the ramifications of the system. Elements of project feasibility should normally include:

(1). *Need analysis*: This indicates a recognition of a need for the project. The need may affect the organization itself, another organization, the public, or the government. A preliminary study is then conducted to confirm and evaluate the need. A proposal of how the need may be satisfied is then made. Pertinent questions that should be asked include:

Is the need significant enough to warrant the effort?
Will the need still exist by the time the project is finished?
What are the alternate means of satisfying the need?
What is the economic impact of the need?

(2). *Process work*: This is the preliminary analysis done to determine what will be required to satisfy the need. The work may be performed by a consultant who is an expert in the problem domain.

(3). *Cost estimate*: This involves estimating project cost to an acceptable level of accuracy. Levels of between minus 5 percent to plus 15 percent are customary for budgeting. Both the initial and operating costs are included in the cost estimation.

(4). *Project impacts*: This portion of the feasibility study provides an assessment of the impact of the expert system on the personnel, the environment, the organization, or the public.

(5). *Recommendations*: The feasibility study should end with the overall outcome of the study. This may indicate an endorsement or disapproval of the expert system. Recommendations on what should be done should be included in the feasibility report.

10.1.3   Personnel Motivation

The process of motivating management, personnel, and client about an expert system project should follow the same guidelines used for any conventional project. Motivation may take several forms. The personnel may be motivated to explore and appreciate the merits of a project; the personnel may be motivated to support the project effort; or the personnel may be motivated to contribute directly and significantly to the project. The motivational concepts of Theory X, Theory Y, Hierarchy of Needs, and so on may all be applied successfully in an expert system project management context. For projects that are of a short-term nature, motivation could either be impaired or enhanced. Impairment may occur if the worker views the project as a mere disruption of regular activities. Enhancements may occur if the worker views the project as a temporary disruption that should soon end. Many workers prefer long-term projects that allow them time to adjust to the project environment and, thus, prove their capabilities.

10.2   EXPERT SYSTEMS PROJECT GUIDELINES

In this section, we present ten major items that constitute the life cycle of a typical expert system project.

(1). Definition of the problem area:

 i) Define the problem domain using key words that signify the importance of the problem to the overall organization.

 ii) Emphasize the need for a focused problem domain.

 iii) Locate domain experts willing to contribute expertise to the knowledge base.

 iv) Prepare and announce the development plan.

(2). Personnel assignment:

 i) The project group and the respective tasks should be announced.

 ii) A qualified project manager should be appointed.

 iii) A solid line of command should be established and enforced.

(3). Project initiation:

 i) Arrange an organizational meeting.

 ii) Discuss the general approach to the problem.

 iii) Prepare a specific development plan.

 iv) Arrange for the installation of needed hardware and tools.

(4). System prototype:

 i) Develop a prototype system.

 ii) Test an initial implementation.

 iii) Learn more about the problem area from the test results.

(5). Full system development:

 i) Expand the prototype knowledge base.

 ii) Evaluate the user interface structure.

 iii) Incorporate user training facilities and documentation.

(6). System verification:

 i) Get experts and potential users involved.

 ii) Ensure that the system performs as designed.

 iii) Debug the system as needed.

(7). System validation:

 i) Ensure that the system yields expected outputs.

 ii) Validation can take the form of:

  a) evaluating performance level (e.g., percentage of success in so many trials).

  b) measuring level of deviation from expected outputs.

  c) measuring the effectiveness of the system output in solving the problem under consideration.

(8). System integration:
  i)   Implement the full system as planned.
  ii) Ensure that the system can coexist with systems already in operation.
  iii) Arrange for technology transfer to other projects.

(9). System maintenance:
  i)   Arrange for continuing maintenance of the system.
  ii) Update the knowledge base as new pieces of information become available.
  iii) Retain the responsibility for system performance or delegate it to well-trained and authorized personnel.

(10). Documentation:
  i)   Prepare full documentation of system.
  ii) Prepare a user's guide.
  iii) Appoint a user consultant.

When evaluating a problem area for the application of expert systems, the factors and questions discussed below should be kept in mind. Chapter 3 presents more detailed discussions on problem analysis and selection.

PROBLEM SELECTION   Problems to be selected for expert system implementation should be evaluated on the basis of both their inherent structures and organizational interests. Considerations should, at least, include the following:

(1). *Ease of data collection*: How easy will it be to collect the relevant data for the problem?

(2). *Frequency of problem occurrence*: Does the problem occur frequently enough to warrant the development of an expert system? If not, conventional software may be more appropriate.

(3). *Representation of data*: Can the pertinent knowledge be organized as a knowledge base? Are there clear-cut relationships or heuristics that can be modeled in terms of IF-THEN statement?

(4). *Value of problem domain*: Is the problem significant enough to deserve the necessary commitment?

(5). *Cost justification*: Is the development of an expert system for the problem cost justifiable? Will the expected returns outweigh the investments?

(6). *Availability of human experts*: Is there an access to willing experts to provide inputs that will form the knowledge base?

(7). *Resource availability*: Are the needed resources (computers, programmers, software, etc.) available? What will it cost to upgrade the existing resource to the level required for the project?

SYSTEM DEVELOPMENT PROCEDURE   The basic procedure for a successful expert system development cycle may be summarized as follows:

(1). Start with a modest goal. An overly ambitious project can only lead to unfulfilled expectations. Starting out simply will ensure the success that will be needed as a confidence-booster for subsequent projects. It should be noted that a functionally simple system can easily be upgraded as needed at any time.

(2). Procure the needed resources and make them available to the personnel.

(3). Arrange a training program for both the developing personnel and the intended user personnel. Inform all those that need to know of the project and its merits.

(4). Be prepared for failure on the first expert systems project. Avoid destructive criticism of the project group.

10.3 EXPERT SYSTEMS WORK BREAKDOWN STRUCTURE

A work breakdown structure (WBS) is a flowchart of project operations required to accomplish project objectives. Tasks that are contained in the WBS collectively describe the overall project. The tasks may involve hardware products (e.g., steam generators, O-Rings), software products (e.g., expert systems), services (e.g., testing), and data (e.g., reports, sales data). The WBS serves to describe the link between the end objective and its constituent operations. It shows work elements in the conceptual framework for planning and controlling. The objective of developing a WBS is to study the elemental components of a project in detail. It permits the implementation of the "divide and conquer" concepts. Overall project planning and control are substantially improved through use of WBS. A large project may be broken down into smaller subprojects which may, in turn, be broken down into task groups. Definable subgoals of a problem may be used to determine appropriate points at which to break down an expert system project.

  Individual components in a WBS are referred to as WBS elements and the hierarchy of each is designated by a level identifier. Elements at the same level of subdivision are said to be of the same WBS level. Descending levels provide increasingly detailed definition of project tasks. The complexity of a project and the degree of control desired determine the number of levels in the WBS. An example of a WBS is shown in Figure 10.1 for an expert system project. Each component of the project is successively broken down into smaller details at lower levels. The process may continue until specific project tasks are identified. The basic approach is as follows:

Level 1: Level 1 contains only the final project purpose. This item should be identifiable directly as an organizational budget item.

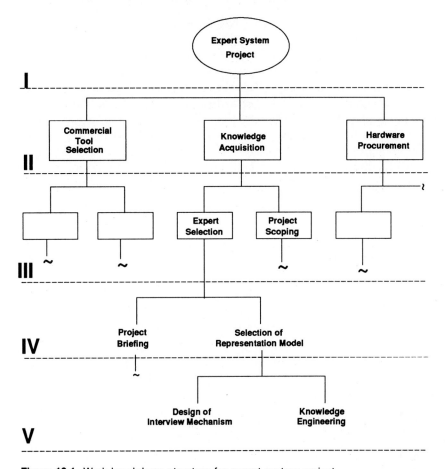

Figure 10.1. Work breakdown structure for expert system project

Level 2: Level 2 contains the major subsections of the project. These subsections are usually identified by their contiguous location or by their related purpose.

Level 3: Level 3 contains definable components of the level 2 subsections.

Subsequent levels are constructed in more specific details depending on the level of control desired. If a complete WBS becomes too crowded, separate WBSs may be drawn for the level 2 components. A specification of work (SOW) or WBS summary should normally accompany the WBS. A statement of work is a narrative of the work to be done. It should include the objectives of the work, its nature, resource requirements, and a tentative schedule. Each WBS element is assigned a code (usually numeric) that is used for the element's identification throughout the project life cycle. Alphanumeric codes may be used to indicate element level as well as component group.

10.4 MANAGING EXPERT SYSTEMS USING TRIPLE C MODEL

The successful implementation of an expert system requires a disciplined approach which should utilize conventional project planning and control techniques. However, many expert system efforts have failed because excited expert system developers ignored the intricate organizational and human factors which come into play in the implementation process.

The success or failure of any project depends on the prevailing levels of communication, cooperation, and coordination. The Triple C principle (Badiru 1988a) facilitates a systematic approach to the implementation of a project by emphasizing the following as distinct managerial functions:

(1). Communication
(2). Cooperation
(3). Coordination

10.4.1   Communication

Instituting an expert system project will, no doubt, arouse the resistance of those who detest change (especially changes involving new technology). Those that will be affected by the project should be informed early as to:

(1). What is being planned?
(2). When will the plan be executed?
(3). How will the project be organized?
(4). Who is in charge?
(5). Why is the project needed?
(6). What are the potential direct and indirect benefits?
(7). What alternatives are available?
(8). What is the expected cost?
(9). What personnel contribution is needed?
(10). What are the possible negative impacts of the project and how can they be alleviated?
(11). What penalty or cost may result from not undertaking the project?
(12). What documented precedents are available for the project?
(13). Who else already knows about the project?
(14). Who will be affected by the failure of the project?

In addition to in-house communication, appropriate external sources should also be consulted. Organizations that have recently implemented expert systems projects can be particularly helpful in providing valuable information.

10.4.2 Cooperation

Not only must people be informed, their cooperation must also be explicitly elicited. Merely signing off on a project is not enough to assure full cooperation. At the present time, it is not unusual for people to be apprehensive about getting involved in expert systems projects. There are simply not enough successful application precedents to supply a motivating force. The personnel must, thus, be convinced of the merits of expert systems and the criticality of their contribution to the project. New domain experts are particularly apt to hold back their cooperation. There may be the fear that expert systems are being designed to replace human experts.

One of the very first tasks involves an evaluation of the resources needed for the expert systems project. Cooperation should be sought from the appropriate quarters with respect to manpower, machinery, and time requirements. The quantity as well as the level of capability for each resource type should be clearly defined with documented justifications.

MANPOWER REQUIREMENT   Manpower needs are usually difficult to quantify because of the variabilities in application objectives, personnel competence, and natural and technological constraints. Requests for manpower resources should be based on the practicality of the project situation. Only then can there be the possibility of effective cooperation. The question of personnel training should also be critically analyzed. Expert systems are still at the stage where there is a limited supply of skilled developers. Thus, organizing a competent project group may be far from trivial.

MACHINE REQUIREMENT   Based on the desired applications, equipment needs for expert systems vary widely. A need is rapidly developing for microcomputer-based expert systems. These are essential for real-time decision applications. A careful identification of the needed tools will facilitate the cooperation needed (from top management) for its procurement. Even if the desired computer is already available in-house, cooperation must be sought for an unobstructed access. Computer systems are now being developed specifically for artificial intelligence applications. Some of these, for example, LISP machines, are still beyond the budget of upstart expert systems projects. Cooperation between two or more departments to jointly share the cost and use of hardware is a realistic alternative in some cases.

TIME REQUIREMENT   Due to the lack of precedents for many expert systems endeavors, it is difficult to reliably estimate the time requirement. When seeking the cooperation of those to be involved in an expert systems project, it will be prudent to propose conservative estimates. The dynamism of a knowledge base makes the estimation even more difficult. Good expert systems should be growth-oriented and adaptable to new knowledge. Consequently, setting a precarious terminal date for the system completion may provide the grounds for criticism

Code:	Individuals Responsible						
R = Responsible							
A = Approve							
C = Consult							
I = Inform							
S = Support	Domain Expert	Knowledge Engineer	Programmer	Project Manager	Documentation Specialist	Plant Manager	Clerical Staff
Actions							
1. Problem Definition						R	
2. Personnel Assignment	C			C		R	
3. Project Initiation				R		A	
4. System Prototype	C	R	R	I		S	
5. Full System	C	R	R	I		S	
6. System Verification	R	R	R	C	I	C	
7. System Validation	R	R	R	R	I	C	
8. System Integration	R	R	R	R	I	A	
9. System Maintenance	R	R	R	C	I	A	
10. Documentation	C	C	C	C	R	A	I

Figure 10.2. Responsibility chart for expert system project

should the deadline not be met. Time allowances should be made for system up-dating. A safe approach is to present time requirements in terms of conservative milestones. This will assure a continuous flow of cooperation (and less criticism) from all quarters over the project life-cycle.

10.4.3 Coordination

Having successfully initiated the communication and cooperation functions, the efforts of the project team must be coordinated. The development of a "responsi-bility chart" can be very helpful at this stage. A responsibility chart is essentially a matrix consisting of columns of individual or functional departments and rows of required actions. Cells within the matrix are filled with relationship codes that in-dicate who is responsible for what. The responsibility chart helps to avoid over-looking critical communication requirements as well as obligations. Questions such as those below are easily resolved by a responsibility chart:

(1). Who is to do what?

(2). Who is responsible for which results?

(3). What personnel interfaces are involved?

Figure 10.2 presents an example of a responsibility chart for an expert system project. Figure 10.3 illustrates the functional interfaces involved in an expert system. People from diverse functional areas and backgrounds are expected to interact to form the basic organizational structure of an expert systems environment. Domain experts work with knowledge engineers to develop the knowledge base in accordance with the design structure of the inference engine, which is constructed by the systems or software engineers. The user interface must provide an unambiguous means for the end user to input problem data in a format that conforms to the requirements of the working memory and the contents of the knowledge base.

There must exist a complete compatibility between the inputs and outputs of the various organizational entities. The achievement of that compatibility rests on effective communication, cooperation, and coordination.

Figure 10.3. Functional interfaces in expert systems implementation

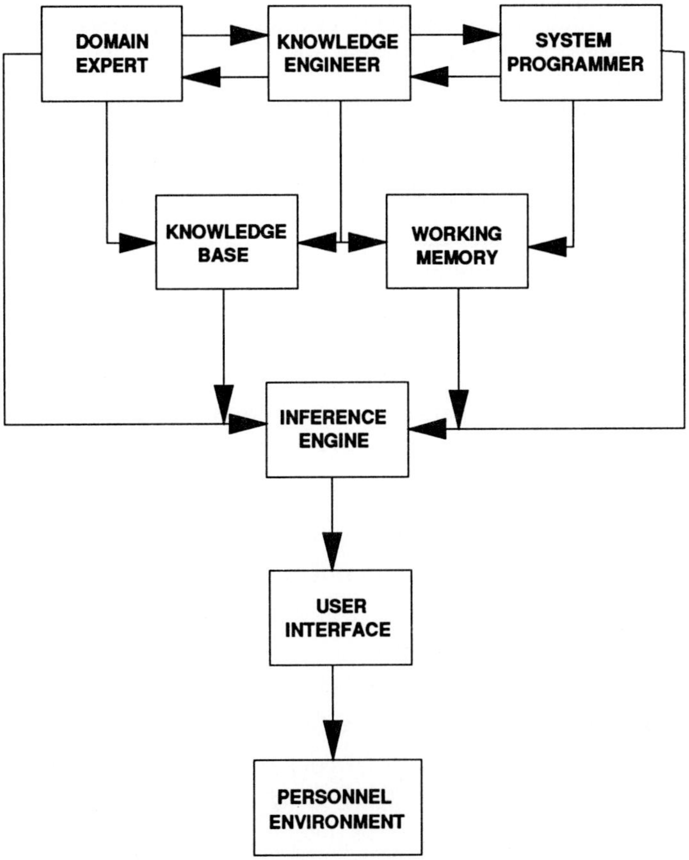

10.5 EXPERT SYSTEMS TECHNOLOGY TRANSFER

The development, transfer, adoption, utilization, and management of expert system technology requires coordinated efforts throughout the project life cycle. Some of the specific problems in expert system technology transfer and management include:

- Formal assessment of current and proposed technologies.
- Controlling technological change.
- Understanding the specific capability of expert systems technology.
- Developing performance measures for expert systems technology.
- Determining the scope of expert system technology transfer.
- Managing the process of entering or exiting expert systems technology.
- Shortening the expert systems technology transfer time.
- Integrating multi-technology objectives.
- Estimating the capital requirements for expert systems technology.
- Identifying a suitable target for expert systems technology transfer.

The managerial functions that will need to be addressed when developing a technology transfer strategy for expert systems are:

(1). Development of a technology transfer plan.
(2). Assessment of technological risk.
(3). Assignment/reassignment of personnel to effect the technology transfer.
(4). Establishment of a transfer manager. In many cases, transfer failures occur because there is no individual whose responsibility is to ensure the success of technology transfer.
(5). Identification and allocation of the resources required for technology transfer.
(6). Setting of guidelines for expert systems technology transfer. For example:
    - specification of phases (development, testing, transfer, etc.).
    - specification of requirements for interphase coordination.
    - identification of training requirements.
    - establishment and implementation of performance measurement.
(7). Identify key factors (both qualitative and quantitative) associated with expert systems technology transfer.
(8). Investigate the way the factors interact.
(9). Develop the hierarchy of importance for the factors.
(10). Formulate a loop system model that considers the forward and backward chains of actions needed to effectively transfer and manage expert systems technology.

(11). Track the outcome of expert systems technology transfer.

To overcome technology transfer problems, an integrated approach must be followed. Technology managers often concentrate on the acquisition of bigger, better, and faster technology. But little attention is given to how to manage and coordinate the operations of the technology once it arrives. When technology fails, it is not necessarily because the technology is deficient. Rather, it is often the communication, cooperation, and coordination functions of technology transfer that are deficient. Technology encompasses factors and attributes beyond mere hardware and software. Consequently, expert system technology transfer involves more than the physical transfer of hardware and software. Several flaws exist in the traditional technology transfer approaches. These flaws include:

- Inadequate assessment of the need of the organization receiving the technology. The target of the transfer may not have the capability to properly absorb the technology.
- Premature transfer of technology. This is particularly acute for emerging technologies that are prone to frequent developmental changes.
- Lack of focus. In the attempt to gain an early lead in the technological race, organizations sometimes force technology in many incompatible directions.
- Intractable implementation problems. Once a new technology is in place, it may be difficult to locate sources of problems that have their roots in the technology transfer phase.
- Lack of transfer precedents. Very few precedents are available on the management of new technology. Managers are, thus, often unprepared for new technology management responsibilities.
- Unwillingness to reorganize priorities. Unworkable technologies sometimes continue to be recycled needlessly in the attempt to find the "right" usage.
- Lack of foresight. Due to the nonexistence of a technology transfer model, managers may not have a basis against which they can evaluate future expectations.
- Insensitivity to external events that may affect the success of technology transfer.
- Suboptimal allocation of resources. There are usually not enough resources available to allocate to technology alternatives.

A FEEDBACK LOOP TECHNOLOGY TRANSFER MODEL   To be effective, a technology transfer process has to operate very much like an input/output/feedback device as shown in Figure 10.4. The figure shows the block diagram representation of input/output relationships of the components in a technology transfer environment.

In Figure 10.4, I(t) represents the input to the transfer environment. The input may be in terms of data, information, raw material, technical skill, or other basic resources. The index t denotes a time reference. A(t) represents the feedback loop actuator. The actuator facilitates the flow of inputs to the various areas of the

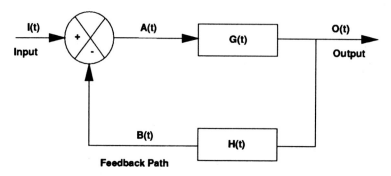

Figure 10.4. Technology transfer feedback loop

technology system. G(t) represents the forward transfer function which coordinates input information and resources to produce the desired output, O(t). H(t) represents the management control process that monitors the transfer status and generates the appropriate feedback information, B(t), which is routed to the input transfer junction. The feedback information is necessary to determine what control actions should be taken at the next technology transfer phase. The primary responsibility of a technology transfer manager should involve ensuring the proper forward and backward flow of information to manage and control the technology transfer efforts. Questions addressed by a feedback loop transfer process include the following:

- What exactly is being transferred?
- What is the cost of acquiring the technology?
- Who will use the technology?
- How is the new technology similar to previous technologies?
- How is the new technology different from previous technologies?
- Are the goals of the existing technology and the new technology similar?
- What is expected from the transferred technology?
- Is there enough technical skill to make use of the transferred technology?
- Is the prevailing management culture receptive to the new technology?
- Is the present infrastructure suitable to support the technology?
- What modifications will be necessary to the technology after it is transferred?
- Where will the new technology be used?
- What is required to maintain the technology?

AN INTEGRATED TRANSFER MODEL   The transfer of expert systems technology can be achieved in various forms. Three basic transfer modes are presented here. A conceptual integrated model of the interaction between the technology source and the technology sink is presented in Figure 10.5. The nature and operational details of the transfer modes are outlined as follows:

(1). *Transfer of complete expert systems products*: In this case, a fully developed product is transferred from a technology source for utilization at a technology sink. Very little product development effort is carried out at the receiving point. However, information about the operations of the product is fed back to the source so that necessary product enhancements can be pursued. The technology recipient generates a "soft" product that serves as an "information resource" for the technology source.

(2). *Transfer of expert systems technology procedures and guidelines*: In this technology transfer mode, technology guidelines and procedures (e.g., design specifications) are transferred from the technology source to the technology sink. The design specifications are implemented locally to generate the desired products. The use of local raw materials and manpower is encouraged for the local production. Under this mode, the implementation of the transferred technology procedures can generate new operating procedures that can be fed back to enhance the original technology. With this symbiotic arrangement, a loop system is created whereby both the transferring and the receiving organizations derive useful benefits.

(3). *Transfer of expert systems technology concepts, theories, and ideas*: This strategy involves the transfer of the basic concepts, theories, and ideas for expert systems technology. The transferred elements can then be enhanced, modified, or customized within local constraints to generate new technological products. The local modifications and enhancements have the potential to generate an identical technology, a new related technology, or a new set of technology concepts, theories, and ideas. These derived products may then

Figure 10.5. Integrated technology transfer model

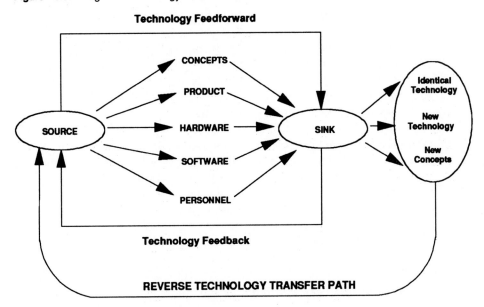

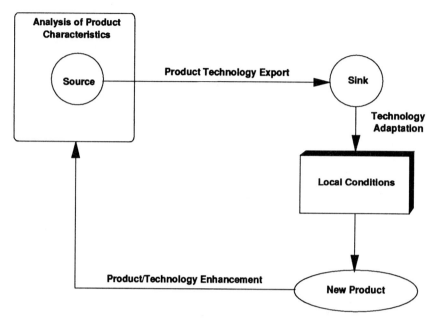

Figure 10.6. Integrated cycle for local adaptation of technology

be transferred back to the original technology source. Figure 10.6 presents a specific integrated cycle for local adaptation and modification of transferred technology.

10.6 EXPERT SYSTEMS IMPLEMENTATION PROCEDURE

Implementation is the last hurdle in an expert system project life cycle. Many excellent systems have failed to have the expected positive impact because of the lack of proper implementation. Expert systems developers often pay enough attention to the development process but very little attention to what is required to implement the system after completion.

Figure 10.7 gives a graphical representation of some of the factors that may affect the implementation of expert systems. Factors such as the cost of implementation, management requirements, compatibility of the system, relevance of the system to organizational goals, implementation personnel, and time requirement should be scrutinized before an attempt is made at implementing the system. If possible, a project implementation team should be set up to oversee the proper implementation of the expert system. Important considerations in planning for the implementation of expert systems include the following:

- What are the unique properties of the system?
- Has the system been verified and validated?

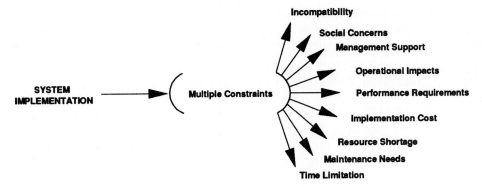

Figure 10.7. Constraints on expert systems implementation

- What will it cost to implement the system?
- Where will the system be implemented?
- Who will be responsible for the implementation?
- How long will it take to implement the system?
- Is the system compatible with other systems in the organization?
- How will the system be integrated with other systems in the organization?
- How is the system relevant to the organizational goal?
- What are the maintenance requirements after implementation?
- What level of management support is available for the implementation?
- What type and level of training are required for the implementation?
- What other factors may influence the implementation?
- Are system documentation and users' guide available?

10.7 SYSTEMS CONVERSION PROCEDURE

Many good systems are unutilized because of system conversion problems. If no adequate plan is made for conversion, a new system might remain unused for a long period of time. By the time the system is finally put to use, it is might be obsolete and there might no longer be replacement or maintenance components available for it. An expert system cannot be considered to be successful until it is put into operation and integrated with existing equipment and people. The system implementation can be effected through any of several conversion methods including the following:

- *Parallel conversion*: The existing system and the new system operate simultaneously until there is confidence that the new system is working properly.
- *Pilot conversion*: The new system is fully implemented on a pilot basis in one segment of the organization.

- *Direct conversion*: The old system is removed totally and the new system takes over. This method is recommended only when there is no existing system or when both systems cannot be kept operational due to incompatibility or cost.

- *Phased conversion*: Modules of the new system are gradually introduced one at a time using either direct or parallel conversion.

The choice of a system conversion method should be made only after several factors have been considered. One of the most important is the criticality of the operations being performed by the system being replaced. Questions of interest include the following:

> What is the impact on the overall operation of the organization when and if the expert system fails to perform the functions being performed by the existing system?

For example, in a system which handles all of the order-processing functions of a company, the criticality of the expert system's being operational at all times is very high. For a system that handles management reports and office automation functions, the criticality of its being constantly operational is not as high since such functions could be performed manually for a short period of time or suspended temporarily.

In a highly critical system which many people and functions depend on in order to perform their jobs, a parallel conversion method would be desirable. During parallel conversion, both the old and the new systems operate concurrently until all parties involved are confident that the new system is operating satisfactorily. Only when confidence in the new system is high is the old system taken out of service. However, parallel conversion requires more resources to maintain both the old and the new systems. If adequate resources are not available, an alternate conversion approach must be considered. The disadvantages of parallel conversion are summarized below:

(1). High level of resource requirement during the conversion.

(2). Loss of operating continuity if the conversion process drags on too long.

(3). Lack of proper operational control because it may be difficult to determine when each of the parallel systems should be used and by whom.

The pilot conversion method is a variation of the parallel conversion method. In this method, the new system is fully implemented in a test department (beta test site). A basic requirement of a test site is that the overall operations of the organization should be relatively insensitive to failures of the new system at the test site. Experience gained from the pilot implementation is then used to determine how to implement (or not implement) the system across the organization.

Direct conversion is the point at which the new system is put into operation and the old system is taken out of service simultaneously. This method is risky if the new system has not been thoroughly tested. If the new system fails to function properly, the old system cannot be immediately put back in place since it has already been decommissioned. A hard lesson on direct conversion was learned by the State of Oklahoma in August 1990. The Oklahoma Department of Finance installed a new payroll system using direct conversion. The new system failed to perform as expected. The entire state payroll system was thrown into disarray for several weeks while many state employees could not be paid. Many people suffered great financial hardships during the conversion process while state officials scampered around to find emergency solutions.

Phased conversion is a process whereby modules of the new system are put into operation one at time and the total conversion process takes place gradually over a period of weeks or months. This method of conversion is generally not applicable for systems that cannot be divided into distinct modules.

CHECKLIST FOR SYSTEM CONVERSION   To ensure the success of the implementation and conversion effort, the expert system should be carefully evaluated by means of the checklist provided below:

(1). Evaluate the user interface:
   Does the user always know what options are available?
   Can the user proceed at his or her own pace?
   Are special functions keys provided for certain operations?
   Are prompts clear and unambiguous?
   Are file printing and saving options clear?
   Is the exiting procedure simple and devoid of data loss risks?
   Is too much information presented on the screen at once?
   Are screen displays well designed and appealing?
   Is important information highlighted or color-coded?
   Are explanations provided for input requests?

(2). Train the user:
   Appoint a training manager.
   Determine the mode of training (hands-on, seminar, observation, etc.).
   Identify who needs to be trained.
   Identify who has already been trained on the system.
   Encourage peer help during training and afterwards.
   Allocate enough time for the training.
   Evaluate the need for retraining.

(3). Update the system:
   Identify who will be responsible for updating the system.
   Allocate needed resources for the updates.
   Survey the users for feedback on system performance.
   Encourage users to maintain records of problems encountered.
   Evaluate the limitations of the system.
   Prioritize suggested improvements.

(4). Follow-up the implementation:
Review the objectives of the system.
Are the promised benefits being realized?
Are users satisfied?
What is needed to further improve the system?
How can the system be ported to other applications?

10.8 BUDGETING FOR EXPERT SYSTEMS PROJECTS

Budgeting is the process of allocating scarce resources to the various endeavors of an organization. It involves the selection of a preferred subset of a set of acceptable projects in view of overall budget constraints. Budget constraints may result from restrictions on capital expenditures, shortage of skilled manpower, shortage of materials, or mutual exclusivity of acceptable projects. Budgeting is frequently the act that determines overall organizational policy. The budget serves many useful purposes including being:

- A plan of how resources are expended.
- A project selection criterion.
- An expression of organizational policy.
- A control mechanism for managers.
- A performance measure.
- A standardization of operations within a given horizon.
- A catalyst for productivity improvement.
- An incentive for efficiency.

Without proper budgeting for an expert system development and implementation, the success of the system will be doubtful. Budgeting for expert systems should not only be in terms of money, but also in terms of technical and manpower resources. The preliminary effort in the preparation of a budget is the collection and proper organization of relevant data. The preparation of a budget for a new technology is more difficult than the preparation of budgets for standard or permanent organization endeavors. Recurring endeavors usually generate historical data which serve as inputs to subsequent estimating functions. New technologies, on the other hand, are often without the benefits of prior data. The input data for the budgeting process typically includes inflationary trends, cost of capital, labor rates, standard cost guides, past records, and quantitative projections. Budget data collection may be accomplished by one of several available methods:

TOP-DOWN BUDGETING This involves collecting data from upper level sources such as top and middle managers. The figures supplied by the managers may come from their judgments, past experiences, or past data on similar project activities. The cost estimates are passed to lower-level managers, who then break the estimates down into specific work components within the project. These estimates may, in turn, be given to line managers, supervisors, and so on to continue the process. Finally, individual activity costs are derived. Figure 10.8 shows the hierarchical structure of the top-down budgeting strategy. The top management issues the global budget while the line worker generates specific activity budget requirements.

One advantage of the top-down budgeting approach is that individual work elements need not be identified prior to approving the overall project budget. Another advantage of the approach is that the aggregate or overall project budget can be reasonably accurate even though specific activity costs may be substantially erroneous. There is usually a keen competition among lower-level managers to get the biggest portion of the overall budget. An example of the distribution of budget is shown in Figure 10.9. Expert systems, at the present time, will belong in the lower 3 percent (Others) of the budget distribution.

BOTTOM-UP BUDGETING   This approach is the reverse of the top-down budgeting. In this method, elemental activities, their schedules, descriptions, and labor skill requirements are used to construct detailed budget requests. The line workers who are actually performing the activities are requested to furnish cost estimates. Estimates are made for each activity in terms of labor time, materials, and machine time. The estimates are then converted to dollar values. The dollar

Figure 10.8. Top-down expert systems budgeting

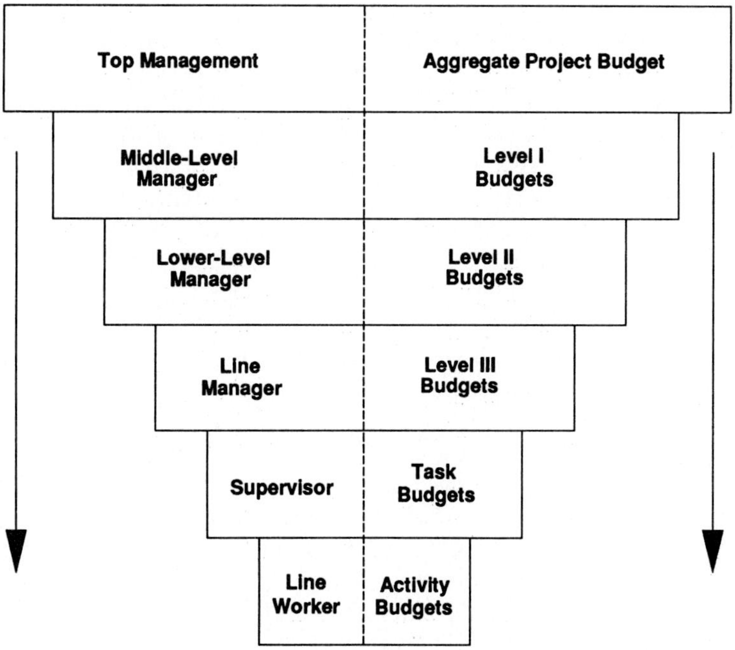

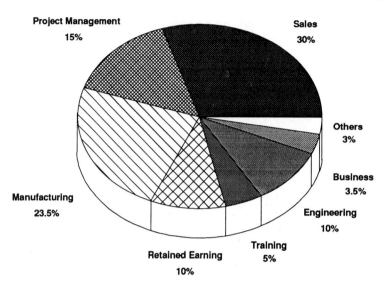

Figure 10.9. Relative distribution of project budgets

estimates are combined into composite budgets at each successive level up the budgeting hierarchy. If estimate discrepancies develop, they can be resolved through the intervention to senior management, junior management, functional managers, project manager, accountants, or standard cost consultants. Analytical tools such as learning curve analysis, work sampling, and statistical estimation may be used in the budgeting process as appropriate to improve the quality of cost estimates.

All component costs and departmental budgets are combined into an overall budget and sent to top management for approval. A common problem with bottom-up budgeting is that individuals tend to overstate their needs with the notion that top management may cut the budget by some percentage. Nobody cares to be the nice and honest guy who finishes last. But the fact is that sending erroneous and misleading estimates, with whatever good intentions, will only lead to a loss of credibility. Top managers, for the most part, are reasonable people. Properly documented and justified budget requests are often spared the budget axe. Honesty and accuracy are invariably the best policies for budgeting.

ZERO-BASE BUDGETING   This is a budgeting approach that bases the level of project funding on previous performance. It is normally applicable to recurring programs especially in the public sector. Accomplishments in past funding cycles are weighed against the level of resource expenditure. Programs that are stagnant in terms of their accomplishments relative to budget size do not receive additional budgets. Programs that have suffered decremental yields are subjected to budget cuts or even elimination. On the other hand, programs that experience incremental accomplishments are rewarded with larger budgets. A major problem with this approach is that it puts participants under tremendous data collection, organization, and program justification pressures. Too much time may be spent documenting program accomplishments to the extent that productivity improvement may be impaired. For this reason, the approach has received only scattered endorsement in practice. However, proponents believe it is an effective means of making managers more conscious of the operations of their programs. In a project management context, the zero-budgeting approach may be used to eliminate specific activities that have not contributed to project goals in the past.

10.9 LEARNING CURVE ANALYSIS IN EXPERT SYSTEMS DEVELOPMENT

Learning refers to the improved efficiency obtained from repetition of a procedure, process, task, or operation. Learning is time dependent and studies have shown that human performance improves with reinforcement or frequent repetitions. Reductions in operation times directly translate to cost savings. As production runs increase, the effects of learning cause a reduction in operation time requirements. However, with the passage of time, the rate of decrease becomes smaller. As Figure 10.10 shows, much of the benefit (productivity increase) of learning is realized early in the production run. For an expert system project, the availability of new tools and enhanced software may boost the learning curve effect.

If the learning effect is not considered, costs may be overestimated and result in waste and inefficiency. We may consider the so-called "80 percent learning effect" as an example. Under this concept, a process is subject to 20 percent unit

Figure 10.10. Typical effect of learning

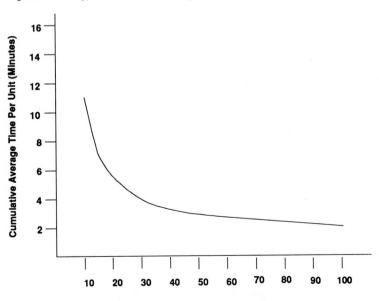

Cumulative Production (x 100 units)

Cumulative Production Units	Cumulative Average Cost Per Unit	Standard Cost Per Unit	Percent Learning	Standard Cost Deviation	Comment
1	$100	$75	-	$-25	Poor
2	80	75	80%	-5	Fair
4	64	75	80%	11	Good
8	51	75	80%	24	Good
16	41	75	80%	34	Good
32	33	75	80%	42	Good
64	26	75	80%	49	Good

Table 10.1. The 80 percent learning effect

cost reduction or 20 percent productivity improvement (i.e., 80 percent learning rate) each time the production quantity doubles. This is shown in Table 10.1. In the Table, the unit cost dropped from $100 to $26 due to the effect of learning. The standard cost deviation of minus $5 in the second batch may be permissible if management is cognizant of the fact that the learning effect is just beginning to work. We realize a 20 percent reduction in unit costs between successive production batches. In actual practice, cost reduction relationships may not be as proportional as suggested by Table 10.1. We may be able to realize even larger reductions in the early iterations than in the later stages when learning levels off.

The point at which the learning curve begins to flatten depends on the degree of similarity of the new operation to previously performed operations. Typical learning rates that have been encountered in practice are: 70 to 80 percent for large or fine assembly work (e.g., aircraft), 80 to 90 percent for welding, and 90 to 95 percent for machining. The percent learning is computed as 100 times the cumulative average cost per unit at a given total production divided by the cumulative average cost per unit at the production level that is half of the given level. When a linear graph paper is used, the learning curve is a hyperbola of the form:

$$C_X = C_1 X^m$$

On a log-log paper, the learning curve is represented by:

$$\log C_X = \log C_1 + m \log X$$

where

C_x = cumulative average cost of X units
C_1 = cost of the first unit
X = number of cumulative units to be produced
m = exponent representing slope of the learning curve on log-log paper

By definition, the learning percent is given by

$$p = 2^m$$

where

$$m = \frac{\log p}{\log 2}$$

Thus, given the slope, m, we can solve for p. Alternately, if p is given, then the slope can be found. For example, assume that 50 units are produced at a cumulative average cost of $20 per unit. We want to compute the learning percentage when 100 units are produced at a cumulative average cost of $15 per unit. That is,

At first production level:

$$\text{units} = \ \ 50; \text{cost} = \$20$$

At second production level:

$$\text{units} = 100; \text{cost} = \$15$$

Using the log relationship, we obtain the following simultaneous equations:

$$\log 20 = \log C_1 + m\log 50$$
$$\log 15 = \log C_1 + m\log 100$$

Subtracting the second equation from the first yields

$$\log 20 - \log 15 = m\log 50 - m\log 100$$

That is,

$$m = \frac{\log 20 - \log 15}{\log 50 - \log 100}$$

$$= \frac{\log(20/15)}{\log(50/100)}$$

$$= -0.415$$

Therefore,

$$p = (2)^{-0.415}$$

$$= 0.75$$

$$= 75 \text{ percent learning}$$

In general,

$$m = \frac{\log C_1 - \log C_2}{\log X_1 - \log X_2}$$

where
C_1 = average cumulative cost per unit at the first production level
X_1 = production volume (units) at the first production level
C_2 = average cumulative cost per unit at the second production level
X_2 = production volume (units) at the second production level.

10.10 EXPERT SYSTEMS FOR PROJECT MANAGEMENT

Just as we can use project management techniques to facilitate a successful implementation of expert systems, we can also use expert systems techniques to enhance the implementation of project management functions. One potential use of
expert systems to project management is the utilization of state space representation for events in the project environment.

10.10.1 State Space Representation

A state is a set of conditions or values that describe a system at a specified point
during processing. The state space is the set of all possible states the system could
be in during the problem-solving process. State space representation solves problems by moving from an initial state in the space to another state, and eventually
to a goal state. The movement from state to state is achieved by the means of operators, typically rules or procedures. A goal is a description of an intended state
that has not yet been achieved. The process of solving a problem involves finding
a sequence of operators that represent a solution path from the initial state to the
goal state.

State space techniques have been used extensively to model continuous system problems in engineering applications (Brooks 1983; Walter 1982; Lozano-
Perez 1981). The techniques have also been applied to management decision
problems (Marshall 1987; Aoki 1981; Szidarovszky 1986; Fox 1987). Pearl (1984)
presents several examples of the application of mathematical models to decision
and management problems. Two typical examples of state space problem solving
are chess-playing and route-finding problems (Shannon 1950). Using an expert

system and state space modeling, the project management decision process can be greatly enhanced. Thus, while project management techniques are used to manage expert systems projects, expert systems themselves could be used to enhance the techniques of project management.

A state space model consists of definition state variables that describe the internal state or prevailing configuration of the system being represented. The state variables are related to the system inputs by an equation. One other equation relates both the state variables and system inputs to the outputs of the system. Examples of potential state variables in a project system include product quality level, budget, due date, resource, skill, and productivity level.

In the case of a model described by a system of differential equations, the state space representation is of the form:

$$\dot{z} = f(z(t), x(t))$$

$$y(t) = g(z(t), x(t))$$

where f and g are vector-valued functions. In the case of linear systems, the representation is of the form:

$$\dot{z} = Az(t) + Bx(t)$$

$$y(t) = Cz(t) + Dx(t)$$

where $z(t)$, $x(t)$, and $y(t)$ are vectors and A, B, C, and D are matrices. The variable y is the output vector while the variable x denotes the inputs. The state vector $z(t)$ is an intermediate vector relating $x(t)$ to $y(t)$.

The state space representation of a discrete-time linear dynamic system, with respect to a suitable time index, is given by:

$$z(t+1) = Az(t) + Bx(t)$$

$$y(t) = Cz(t) + Dx(t).$$

In generic terms, a project system is transformed from one state to another by a driving function that produces a transitional equation given by:

$$\Psi = f(x \mid \theta) + \varepsilon$$

Ψ is the subsequent state, x is the state variable, θ is the initial state, and ε is the error component. The function f is composed of a given action (or a set of actions) applied to the project structure. Each intermediate state may represent a significant milestone in the project system. Thus, a descriptive state space model facilitates an analysis of what actions to apply in order to achieve the next desired state or milestone.

THE PROJECT MODEL   Any human endeavor can be defined as a project. Potential application domains include automated process planning for manufacturing systems, patient monitoring systems in medical applications, military logistics, production scheduling, business movements, economic planning, and R&D planning and control.

A project may be considered as a process of producing a product. The product may be a measurable physical quantity or an intangible conceptual entity. We may consider the product as a single object constructed from a set of subobjects, which are themselves constructed from sub-subobjects. A simple project model is the application of an action to an object which is in a given state or condition.

The application of action constitutes a project activity. The production process involves the planning, coordination, and control of a collection of activities. Project objectives are achieved by state-to-state transformation of successive object abstractions. Figure 10.11 shows the transformation of an object from one state to another through the application of action. The simple representation can be expanded to include other components within the project framework. The hierarchical linking of objects provides a detailed description of the project profile as shown in Figure 10.12.

The project model can further be expanded in accordance with implicit project requirements. These considerations might include grouping of object classes, precedence linking (both technical and procedural), required communication links, and reporting requirements.

The actions to be taken at each state depends on the prevailing conditions. The natures of the subsequent alternate states depend on what actions are actually implemented. Sometimes there are multiple paths that can lead to the desired end result. At other times, there exists only one unique path to the desired objective. In conventional practice, the characteristics of the future states can only be recognized after the fact, thus making it impossible to develop adaptive plans. In terms of control, deviations are often recognized when it is too late to take effective corrective actions. Both the events occurring within and outside the project state boundaries can be taken into account in the planning function. These environmental influences are shown in Figure 10.13.

PROJECT STATE REPRESENTATION We can describe a project system by M state variables s_i. The composite state of the system at any given time can then be represented by an M-component vector $\mathbf{S}$.

$$\mathbf{S} = \{s_1, s_2, ..., s_M\}$$

Figure 10.11. Object transformation

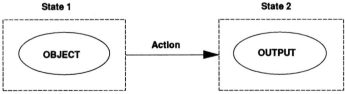

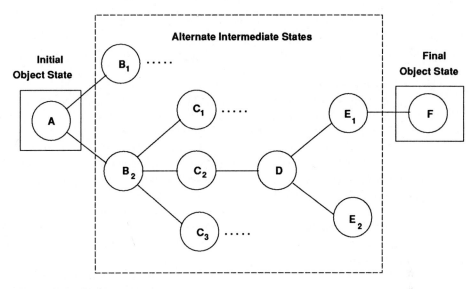

Figure 10.12. Object state paths

The components of the state vector could represent either quantitative or qualitative variables (voltage, investments, energy, color, etc.). We can visualize every state vector as a point in the M-dimensional state space shown in Figure 10.14. The representation is unique since every state vector corresponds to one and only one point in the state space.

PROJECT STATE TRANSFORMATION   Suppose we have a set of actions (transformation agents) that we can apply to a project so as to change it from one state to another within the state space. The transformation will change a state vector into another state vector. A transformation, in practical terms, may be heat treatment,

Figure 10.13. External/internal factors affecting project implementation

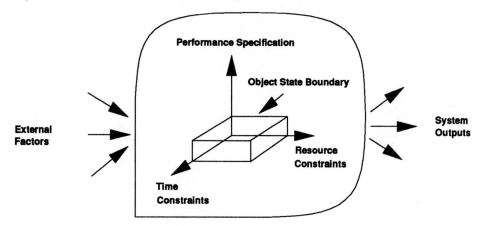

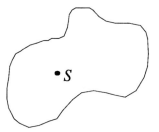

Figure 10.14. Project state space

firing of a rocket, or a change in management policy. We can let T_k be the kth type of transformation. If T_k is applied to the project when it is in state $\mathbf{S}$, the new state vector will be $T_k(\mathbf{S})$, which is another point in the state space. The number of transformations (or actions) available for a project may be finite or countably infinite. We can construct trajectories that describe the potential states of a project as we apply successive transformations. Each transformation may be repeated as many times as needed. For convenience, we can use the notation T_i to indicate the ith transformation in the sequence of transformations applied to the project. Given an initial state $\mathbf{S}$, the sequence of state vectors is then given by:

$$\mathbf{S}_1 = T_1(\mathbf{S})$$
$$\mathbf{S}_2 = T_2(\mathbf{S}_1)$$
$$\mathbf{S}_3 = T_3(\mathbf{S}_2)$$

$$.$$

$$.$$

$$.$$

$$\mathbf{S}_n = T_n(\mathbf{S}_{n-1})$$

The final State $\mathbf{S}_n$ depends on the initial state S and the effects of the transformations applied. The sequence is shown graphically within the state space in Figure 10.15.

STATE PERFORMANCE MEASUREMENT A measure of project performance can be obtained at each state of the transformation trajectories. Thus, we can develop a reward function $r^k(\mathbf{S})$ associated with the kth type transformation (Howard, 1971). The reward specifies the magnitude of gain (time, quality, money, revenue, equipment utilization, etc.) to be achieved by applying a given transformation. The difference between a reward and a performance specification may be used as a criterion for determining project control actions. The performance deviation may be defined as:

$$\delta = r^k(S) - \rho$$

where ρ is the performance specification.

PROJECT POLICY DEVELOPMENT   Given the number of transformations still available and the current state vector, we can develop a policy, P, to be the rule for determining the next transformation to be applied. The total project reward can then be denoted as:

$$r(\mathbf{S} \mid n, P) = r_1(\mathbf{S}) + r_2(\mathbf{S}_1) + \ldots + r_n(\mathbf{S}_{n-1})$$

where n is the number of transformations applied and $r_i(.)$ is the ith reward in the sequence of transformations. We can now visualize a project environment where the starting state vector and the possible actions (transformations) are specified. We have to decide what transformations to use in what order so as to maximize the total reward. That is, we must develop the best project plan.

If we let v represent a quantitative measure of the worth of a project plan based on the reward system described above, then the maximum reward is given by:

$$v(\mathbf{S} \mid n) = \text{Max}\{r(\mathbf{S} \mid n, P)\}$$

The maximization of the reward function is carried out over all possible project policies that can be obtained with n given transformations.

PROBABILISTIC STATES   In many project situations, the results of applying transformations to the system may not be deterministic. Rather, the new state vector, the reward generated, or both may have to be described by random variables. We can define an expected total reward, $Q(\mathbf{S} \mid n)$, as the sum of the individual expected rewards from all possible states. We let $\mathbf{S}^p$ be a possible new state vector generated by the probabilistic process and let $P(\mathbf{S}^p \mid \mathbf{S}, T^k)$ be the probability that

Figure 10.15. Transformation trajectories in state space

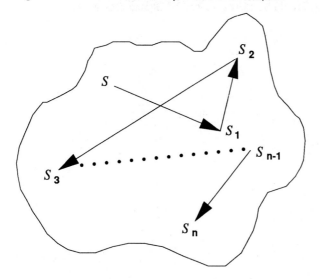

the new state vector will be $\mathbf{S}^p$ if the initial state vector is $\mathbf{S}$ and the transformation T^k is applied. We can now write a recursive relation for the expected total reward:

$$Q(\mathbf{S} \mid n) = \underset{k}{\mathrm{Max}}\left\{\bar{r}^k(\mathbf{S}) + \sum_{\mathbf{S}^p} Q(\mathbf{S}^p \mid n-1)P(\mathbf{S}^p \mid \mathbf{S}, T^k)\right\},$$

$$for \quad n=1,2,3,...$$

The notation $\bar{r}^k(\mathbf{S})$ is used to designate the expected reward received by applying the kth type transformation to the system when it is described by state vector $\mathbf{S}$. The above procedure allows the possibility that the terminal reward itself may be a random variable. Thus, the state space model permits a complete analysis of all the ramifications and uncertainties of the project management system.

10.10.2   State Space and Expert Systems Implementation

The *If-Then* structure of knowledge representation for expert systems provides a mechanism for evaluating the multiplicity of project states under diversified actions. Expert systems have the advantages of consistency, comprehensive evaluation of all available data, accessibility, infinite retention of information, and lack of bias. An integrated project planning and control system using state space and expert systems is shown in Figure 10.16.

A project manager might interact with the state space model and the expert system by doing the following:

Figure 10.16. State space/expert system model

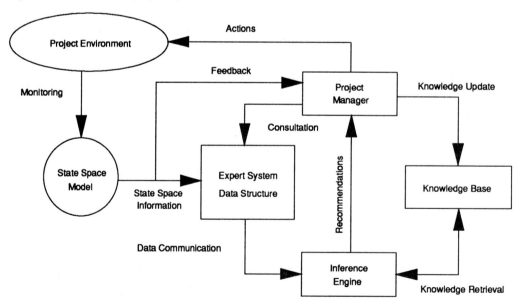

(1). Performing the real-time monitoring of the project and then supplying inputs to the state space model.

(2). Getting feedback from the state model.

(3). Consulting the expert system based on the state space information.

(4). Getting recommendations from the expert system.

(5). Taking project actions that eventually generate further inputs to the state model.

(6). Updating the expert system knowledge base as new project management knowledge is acquired.

The supply of state space information to both the project manager and the expert system in Figure 10.16 will serve as a control measure. In case the manager does not utilize all available information, the expert system can query him or her for justification.

10.10.3 Developing a Project Network Plan

The concept of integrating cost into project network analysis provides management of the tools for effective control of project resources. In today's complex organizational cost structures, there are several factors that influence project implementations. The technology of expert systems offers a considerable potential for real-time integration of project costs. Expert systems can facilitate effective and prompt managerial cost control without the need for extensive run-time data collection.

NETWORK ANALYSIS   A project network is a representation of a project plan such that the relationships between jobs or activities are clarified and can easily be examined. Network analysis reduces the project evaluation to four stages:

- Breaking down the project into a set of individual jobs and events and arranging them into a logical network.
- Estimating the duration and resource requirements of each job.
- Developing a schedule, and finding which job controls the completion of the project.
- Reallocating funds or other resources to improve the schedule.

If done properly, network cost analysis offers the following advantages:

- It forces a thorough preplanning of project tasks.
- It increases coordination.
- It identifies trouble spots in advance and pinpoints responsibility.
- It focuses management's attention on those activities that are cost-critical.

- It indicates cost-effective start and finish times for project activities.
- It enables revisions of project plans without extensive cost changes.
- It suggests where alternative project methods should be sought.
- It makes costs tractable.
- It facilitates fair allocation of resources.
- It minimizes cost overruns.

An expert system can serve as the effective mechanism that aids management in answering questions such as:

a) What are the actual project costs to date?
   single cost estimate
   activity direct costs
   project indirect costs
   three cost estimates
   normal and crash activity costs
b) How do the actual costs to date compare with planned costs to-date?
c) By how much may the project be expected to overrun the total planned cost?
d) How best to allocate limited resources.

The first step in the network cost planning is constructing a network and performing the basic scheduling, which gives the earliest and latest start and finish times for each activity. Then the estimated cost data for each activity may be added to the network and the first cost computation may be made.

As the project progresses, actual expenditures are recorded by activity at specified reporting dates. Any revised estimate of duration or costs of activities are also accounted for at the reporting times. The following computations may be made:

- Summation of all actual costs.
- Summation of budgeted costs at this point in time.
- Summation of budgeted costs for all activities completed and partial costs of activities partially completed.
- Computation of differences in actual costs and planned costs for completed portions of the project.
- Computation of a projection on the expected cost of the total project based on the progress made so far.

Based on the above cost computations and other prevailing cost circumstances, rules can be developed to serve as guides for courses of managerial actions in diverse cost and project scenarios. These rules may then be incorporated into an expert system to facilitate quick real-time managerial decisions.

RULE-BASED COST ANALYSIS   Cost rules compiled as discussed in the previous section may be organized into an expert system knowledge base. For example, the following cost rules may apply to a given project.

Rule 1: If total project budget exceeds 100,000 dollars and expected project duration exceeds 1 year then allocate 10 percent of budget to each 10% of expected duration.

This rule establishes the procedure for spreading the project budget evenly over the duration of the project. This rule may be particularly useful for fixed-budget projects that extend over several years. This provides a safeguard against expending a larger portion of the budget early in the project at the expense of later project needs. The rule, of course, assumes that any initial fixed cost (lump sum) requirements of the project have been accounted for. If not, a subrule such as the following may be utilized:

Rule 1.1: If fixed cost exceeds 10 percent of total budget and 10 percent of expected duration is less than 1 day then compute new budget as total budget minus fixed cost and allocate 10 percent of new budget to each 10% of expected duration.

Rule 2: If number of project activities is greater than 20 then record half of the budget for each activity at the activity's scheduled start time and record the other half of the budget at the activity's scheduled completion time.

This rule is the common 50/50 rule used in reducing cost variance in projects with a large number of elements. One advantage of the 50/50 rule is that it reduces the necessity to continuously determine the percent completion for each activity in the process of allocating cost.

Rule 3: If current costs are more than 5 percent above initial budget, then review the cost of higher-salaried personnel.

This is an example of a rule that may give management an indication of where to start cost troubleshooting.

Rule 4: If the cost of any given project element exceeds 10 percent of total cost then reexamine the work breakdown structure.

Rules similar to the ones presented above can be developed to fit specific organizational needs. Many practical expert systems have been developed using as few as 20 rules. Some systems designed for more robust applications have been known to contain as many as 1000 rules. Specific organizational needs and available expertise, generally, should determine the contents and size of a knowledge base.

RULE STRUCTURE FOR A KNOWLEDGE BASE   An example of a cost decision tree is shown in Figure 10-17. The tree can be used to determine the structure of the knowledge base.

The decision tree can be as complex and detailed as there are relevant leads. Each statement of fact consists of three parts, namely:

Attribute: a keyword or phrase chosen to represent the subject of the fact to be determined (e.g., budget).

Value: a description assigned to the attribute (e.g., large).

Predicate: an item used to relate the value to the attribute (e.g., is)

Referring to Figure 10.17, we can generate the following rules:

(1). If project is subcontracted, then cost information is from subcontractor.

(2). If project elements are large, then 50/50 rule is applicable.

Figure 10.17. Decision tree for project cost analysis

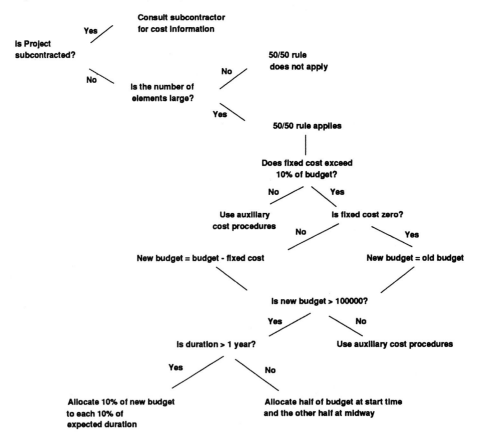

(3). If Fixed cost is-not zero, then new-budget is procedure new-budget.

(4). If 50/50 rule is applicable and new budget is greater-than-100000 and expected duration is greater-than-one-year, then use "10-percent" allocation procedure.

An external procedure is a computational subroutine used to calculate variable values. The computation procedure for new budget may be:

$$(New\ Budget) = (Budget)\ minus\ (Fixed\ cost)$$

The computation procedure for cost allocation may be:

$$Allocation\ for\ 10\%\ of\ duration = 10\%\ (New\ Budget)$$

Prompts are added to the knowledge base to provide facilities for entering project data during the expert system consultation. The prompts are needed for facts that the expert system cannot implicitly infer. Such prompts may be:

(1). Prompt: Fixed cost
             Enter value for fixed cost:?
(2). Prompt: Budget
             Enter value for budget:?
(3). Prompt: Project-type
             Is the project subcontracted?
(4). Prompt: Project size
             Is the number of project elements large?

With an expert system, valuable cost control recommendations can be obtained in a matter of minutes. This will reduce the need to read voluminous cost guides or waste productive time trying to locate an expert to handle routine cost functions. Expert systems can significantly enhance the functions of project analysts. The systems can handle routine cost analysis and rule-based decision analysis, thus freeing the human expert to concentrate his efforts on critical project problems. Project management has always been a fertile area for the utilization of heuristics. The premise of an expert system is the utilization of heuristics to enhance decision processes. Consequently, both areas are inherently suitable for integration.

10.11 EXERCISES

10.1 How would you develop a contingency plan for an expert system project? Discuss the issues that should be addressed in the plan.

10.2 What kinds of information would constitute "feedforward" and "feedback" in an expert system technology transfer process?

10.3 What are some of the organizational problems that can evolve from the rapid introduction of expert system technology?

10.4 Which type of system conversion method is most appropriate for implementing the installation of an expert system in a manufacturing operation?

10.5 Propose a comprehensive measure of performance for an expert system installation.

10.6 List several factors that may impede the implementation of expert systems in a manufacturing environment.

10.7 Develop a work breakdown structure for the installation of an expert system for engineering design.

10.8 Develop a strategic plan for implementing an expert system for manufacturing management.

10.9 What is the most likely item to be transferred in an expert system technology transfer process? Discuss.

10.10 Prepare a complete feasibility study for developing and implementing an expert system for manufacturing quality control.

10.11 For the payroll system case study mentioned in this chapter, recommend which system conversion method would have been appropriate. Discuss.

10.12 Discuss how learning-curve analysis can be used to control expert system development and implementation processes.

10.13 Select a suitable problem for expert system application in the home. Discuss the justification for the problem in terms of frequency of occurrence, development cost, and potential users.

10.14 How would an expert system in the home differ from an expert system in engineering?

10.15 Consider the following formation of an expert system team:

Individual	Role
Domain expert	Source of knowledge
Knowledge engineer	Channel for knowledge transfer
Management	Source of resources
AI sponsor	Source of motivation (champion)
Systems personnel	Integration
Users	Supply of application

Suggest how the roles of the various individuals can be coordinated to facilitate an effective end product.

10.16 Develop a tactical plan for developing an expert system for military applications.

10.17 Describe an application scenario in which an expert system is deployed on a portable PC. What are the potential benefits and drawbacks of such an implementation?

10.18 Describe the differences in a feasibility study for an engineering expert system versus a feasibility study for a financial expert system.

10.19 Describe how an implementation environment may influence problem selection for an expert system application.

10.20 Review the model of the functional interfaces in expert system implementation presented in this chapter. Suggest how the interfaces may be enhanced in the case of a manufacturing expert system.

11

Survey of Engineering and Manufacturing Applications

Expert systems have been developed for solving problems of varying complexities in several problem areas in science, engineering, and manufacturing. The potential applications of expert systems to real problems are limited only by the imagination of users. As manufacturers turn more and more to automation to reduce cost and improve productivity, we should begin to witness more aggressive implementations of artificial intelligence capabilities. To provide a stimulus for the materials in the subsequent chapters of this book, this section presents a survey of past, present, and potential application areas for expert systems.

Many major applications of expert systems can be found in the manufacturing area. Expert systems applications have been developed at many of the stages of the manufacturing process (Badiru 1990a). Expert systems can be utilized in deciding the feasibility of a particular production process given the available resources. It can then be used for assigning resources to specific tasks in the process. The design performance of expert systems in industry has been compared with that obtained from human experts. It has been found that expert systems performance was near optimal as far as comparative human performance is concerned.

11.1 EXPERT SYSTEMS AS INDUSTRIAL CONSULTANTS

An industrial user, who may not be an expert, can consult the computer instead of referring to a human expert on a routine basis. Two scenarios can be visualized: consultation to advise a manager in industry and consultation to advise an engineer in industry.

CONSULTANT TO THE INDUSTRIAL MANAGER   In this scenario the expert system temporarily replaces an engineer who acts as a consultant to a manager. Consultation involves problem solving in several areas such as inventory management, capacity planning, production scheduling, and so on. A typical consultation may involve the following process:

- Discussing the nature of the problem with the manager.
- Identifying and classifying the problem.
- Constructing a model of the problem.
- Analyzing the model to solve the problem.
- Conducting a sensitivity analysis with the model.
- Recommending a solution.
- Implementing the solution.

An analyst can develop an expert system that operates as follows: The computer attempts to diagnose the manager's problem by determining the general nature of the problem (e.g., resource allocation, inventory, production scheduling). Once the general nature of the problem has been determined, the characteristics of the situation are analyzed and a model is jointly constructed by the manager and the computer.

For example, if a resource allocation problem is identified, an attempt is made to construct the objective function and the constraints. A quantitative tool, such as linear programming, may be used for this purpose. The computer then uses the chosen tool to solve the problem. Finally, a "what-if" analysis may be conducted. The expert system may also act as a nonhuman tutor with the ability to explain terminology, concepts, and computational procedures involved in the problem. In addition, the computer can provide supporting reference materials, point out suitable applications, explain general information as requested by the manager, present the underlying assumptions of the decision model, or explain the rationale for selecting a particular model. The implementation of manufacturing expert systems could relieve engineers from routine activities, giving them more time to deal with complex problems and creative activities.

CONSULTANT TO THE ENGINEER IN INDUSTRY   An expert system can serve as a consultant and an assistant to the engineer in industry. The engineer can use the computer as a source of information. He or she can use the expert system as a teaching aid for himself or herself to learn the expertise of specialists in certain industrial problem areas where unique expertise is needed. This implies that an engineer, in addition to (or instead of) referring to a printed manual or a book, or a human expert, can consult the expert system. Finally, expert systems can be used as a personal assistant for providing answers to routine questions that the engineer might have.

11.2 APPLICATIONS IN JOB SHOP SCHEDULING

Expert systems can be of great help in the domain of scheduling activities in a job shop. The essence of the job shop scheduling problem is the computational effort associated with real world problems of practical size. For example, in the case of 5 jobs and 7 machines, there are $(5!)^7$ or approximately 3.5831×10^{14} sequences which would take over eleven years of computer time to process at a rate of one microsecond per sequence. The purpose of using expert systems is to provide a computerized scheduler that has the knowledge and understanding of qualitative measures which the human scheduler might use to schedule jobs. Fox and Smith (1984) described an Intelligent Scheduling and Information System (ISIS) developed at Carnegie Mellon University for job-shop scheduling. This system contains the knowledge necessary to plan and schedule production in a job shop environment. It takes into consideration all relevant constraints in the construction of job schedules.

The system selects a sequence of operations needed to complete an order, determines start and end times, and assigns resources to each operation. It can also act as an intelligent assistant, using its expertise to help schedulers maintain schedule consistency and identify decisions that result in unsatisfied constraints. Knowledge in the system includes organizational goals, such as due dates and costs; physical constraints, such as limitations of particular machines; and causal constraints, such as the order in which operations must be performed. ISIS uses a frame-based knowledge representation scheme together with rules for resolving conflicting constraints.

ISIS also has capabilities of model perusal, reactive plan monitoring, process planning, and resource planning. It can be used successfully for inventory planning, management control, production scheduling, and operations planning.

Engineers at GTE have developed an expert system for thread scheduling. In an environment running over 100 VAX computers, the expert system identifies errors in thread scheduling by interfacing with thousands of lines of ADA code. It determines if an error is caused by software, hardware, or a human.

In addition to scheduling operations on machines, a manager must also schedule personnel. Using an expert system in its tooling division, McDonnell Douglas has been developing a scheduling system to monitor current and future work loads. The system keeps track of personnel and job completion dates and gives an estimation of future overtime needs. It also matches personnel preferences for overtime work slots to produce a feasible schedule of personnel.

At Texas Instruments' automated manufacturing center, expert systems have facilitated the required interfaces between robots, vision systems, machine tools, sensors, computer systems, and humans (Herrod 1988). This has resulted in increased flexibility and efficiency of discrete manufacturing. The automated manufacturing center produces high-precision machined metal parts. The center automatically machines, deburrs, washes, and inspects more than 30 different parts. In order to achieve full flexibility, the system must track and synchronize about 40 pallets and 250 tools while managing resources for eight machines and an automated guided vehicle.

The expert system that was developed to manage the center is composed of a planner, a scheduler, and a dispatcher. The planner interacts with the production control staff members who enter monthly part needs. It formulates the monthly part needs into a daily pallet-release plan. This plan is then passed on to the scheduler, which provides the production control staff with the material requirements for the day and a list of tools needed. The scheduler also establishes the sequence in which the jobs should be completed that day. The job sequence is then sent to the dispatcher, which monitors the state of the equipment through a real-time control system. As machines become available, the dispatcher indicates the next tasks for the machines.

The expert system also determines and updates the action plan based on the information it receives. It is able to replan to meet changing conditions in the automated manufacturing center. These changes are communicated to the real-time control function.

DCLASS, a comprehensive expert system from CAM Software, Inc. of Provo, Utah, is a good example of a successful system. The system was developed by a research center at Brigham Young University to fill a need for more consistent and efficient decision making in the manufacturing environment. DCLASS installation sites in many parts of the world have reported thousands of dollars worth of savings in areas such as process planning, classification and coding, cost estimating, and design retrieval.

11.3 APPLICATIONS IN FLEXIBLE MANUFACTURING SYSTEM DESIGN

The design of a flexible manufacturing system (FMS) is a potential source of challenging expert systems applications in industry. Mellichamp and Wahab (1987) developed an expert system which is capable of analyzing the output from an FMS simulation model. The system can determine whether operational and financial objectives are all met and can identify deficiencies. In addition, it can propose suitable designs for overcoming the deficiencies it had identified earlier. The system uses an analysis-diagnosis-recommendation process and inputs from simulation analysis to analyze the FMS design. Design changes recommended by the system are incorporated into the simulation model and the process repeats until an acceptable design is obtained. When the total capital investment goal of the FMS is not met, the system identifies the replacement for which the cost differential between the specified equipment and the potential substitute is maximum.

Bruno, Elia, and Laface (1986) describe an expert system for production scheduling. The system determines the sequence of part lots to be machined in an FMS and assists in meeting the due dates of lots, while taking into account several related problems such as minimizing machine idle times, machine queues, and work in progress. Blessing and Watford (1987) also report the use of expert systems techniques for shop floor control (loading) in the FMS environment. Kusiak (1987) presents two new approaches to designing expert systems for scheduling in a flexible manufacturing system. The approaches are the goal-based approach and the model-based approach.

In the goal-based approach, the scheduling problem can be formulated as follows: Given the goal schedule, resources (e.g., machines, tools, fixtures, and pallets) are scheduled in such a way that the deviation between the goal schedule and the current schedule is minimized. In the model-based approach, the scheduling problem is tackled on the basis of known solutions to commonly encountered shop setups. Examples of such scheduling models are presented by French (1982). Kusiak uses the following three rules to illustrate the nature of a scheduling knowledge base:

Rule 1:
IF parts p_i and p_j use fixture f_k,
THEN they should be scheduled at least t units of time apart.

Rule 2:
IF part p_i is to be dispatched for machine m_b which is occupied by another part p_j,
THEN check availability of an alternative machine m_a.

Rule 3:
IF a set of tools T is to be loaded into a tool magazine t_m for processing a part p_i on a machine m_b and there is not enough space in t_m,
THEN remove from the tool magazine t_m as many tools as required by the set of tools T to be loaded.

11.4 APPLICATIONS IN OPERATIONS AND PROCESS PLANNING

Process control systems are designed to regulate physical parameters in the process. Real-time expert systems use control system data to provide operators with diagnostic and interpretive information about their processes and equipment. Real-time expert systems advise operators on problems such as:

- Process failures
- Equipment problems
- Operating trends
- Alarm conditions
- Instrument malfunctions
- Production optimization

Expert systems can be used in manufacturing for detail planning of machine operations. Operations planning is defined as the specification of parameters for the individual operations within a part's process plan. For machining operations, this activity includes selection of the cutting tool, cut sequence, cutting conditions, tool replacement strategy, and so on to produce a single feature (e.g., slot, hole, etc.) on a part. The selection of cutting tool, depth of cut, speed, and feed requires machining expertise that is not always available from computerized process planning systems or inexperienced process planners.

An expert system, called CUTTECH, is currently in operation in many shops. The system captures metal cutting technology and data for use in recommending productive and economical tools and cutting parameters for machining. It acts as both a knowledge source and a knowledge collection point in a machining facility and its functions include selection of cutting tools, cut sequence, speed, and feeds for selective user-defined part features to be machined. The rules are stored in decision tables and algorithms and are applied in descending order of importance in sorting the tools. The system makes it possible for an engineer, who may have little machining experience, to obtain good machining recommendations for a given part feature.

Process planning has been mostly an art that is intuitive and subjective. It is learned after considerable experience in the shop. Today, very few potential process engineers are gaining shop experience while the older generation of process planners are retiring. Process planning involves the selection of operations and processes needed to produce multiple features on a part and transform the raw material into a finished part. Process planning in the industrial environment is an area requiring considerable amount of human expertise and has been one of the actively pursued areas of expert systems applications. Expert Computer-Aided Process Planning System (EXCAP) developed by Davies and Darbyshire (1984) is an expert system for generating process plans for machining of rotational components. Freedman and Frail (1987) describe an expert system (OPGEN) developed for Hazeltine Corporation (Greenlawn, NY). OPGEN handles the previously manually-implemented process planning for printed circuit boards.

GARI (Kumara et al 1986) is another popular knowledge-based system for process planning. Its domain is restricted to the metal cutting industry. The knowledge base of GARI is represented by production rules, where each rule consists of conditions about the part to be manufactured, and the rule actions contain pieces of advice representing technological and economical preferences. The system consists of a planner and a "knowledge box" (Mill and Spraggett 1984). The "box" contains the manufacturing rules used to guide the search for a solution to the process planning problem for a given component. Nau and Chang (1985) introduced an expert system named SIPP. The system, programmed in PROLOG, uses a frame-based knowledge representation scheme. The knowledge base consists of machinable surfaces and capabilities of various machining operations, and a control structure that manipulates the knowledge base in order to construct process plans. SIPP uses best-first strategy based on branch and bound and produces least-cost process plans based on cost criteria that the user desires.

Kumara et al (1986) describe another rule-based system, named TOM, which has been implemented at the University of Tokyo. The system does not produce complete machine plans but focuses on producing detailed machining plans for some specified features.

Metcut Research Associates, Inc. of Cincinnati, Ohio has one of the most comprehensive process planning systems on the market. Their product,

MetCAPP, is an integrated planning system consisting of several modules. The first module is CUTDATA, which is equivalent to a library of machining data. CUTDATA's functions are to retrieve machining recommendations and calculate data for planning. This module contains more than 81,000 recommendations for machining several hundred alloys with 40 machining processes.

The second module is CUTTECH. This module provides expert machining operation planning details for part features. The module is built upon the database of CUTDATA, with a generative system that specifies the process to machine part features. CUTTECH provides process planners and/or NC programmers with everything they need except the specific geometry of the tool path.

CUTPLAN, the third component of the process planning system, is a planning document preparation system for merging and storing several CUTTECH sessions to create a variant process plan for a part. CUTPLAN contains a module for estimating processing times from set-up and run-time constants specific to operations not supported in the CUTTECH module. With a data base of stored process plans, part characteristics and definitions are grouped using relational data base. This allows the module to take advantage of family-of-parts planning similarities. CUTPLAN also provides an external interface facility for integrating MetCUT's modules with other Computer Integrated Manufacturing (CIM) systems. The benefits of MetCAPP include planning accuracy, planning productivity, machining productivity, and tooling standardization.

Martin Marietta Company has designed a knowledge-based system to assist process engineers and technicians in evaluating the processability and moldability of poly-isocyanurate (PIR) formulations for the thermal protection system of the Space Shuttle external tank. The system consists of two segments. One segment is for reaction injection molding while the other is for process development. It takes advantage of both symbolic and numeric processing techniques. Process knowledge, consisting of heuristic knowledge acquired from domain experts (such as case histories of chemical formulations and their moldability in test mold configurations), and the knowledge of causal relationships derived from the empirical data aids the process engineer in two major ways:

(1). Identifying a startup set of mold schedules.

(2). Refining the mold schedules to remedy specific process problems diagnosed by the system.

The system, named RIM-PDA (Reaction Injection Molding - Process Development Advisor), takes advantage of conventional algorithmic approaches as well as state-of-the-art artificial intelligence methodologies to analyze the identified tasks. Mechanisms for switching between layers of reasoning based on the type of question asked of the system are also incorporated into the system.

An expert system developed by Parker Hannifin Corporation's Tube Fitting Division in Columbus, Ohio has been reported to sharply reduce the time required to match the proper tube and fitting connections in the design of fluid power systems. The system replaces several pages of the company's Tube Fitting catalog. It can perform the following functions:

(1). Pointing out design conflicts automatically.

(2). Noting incompatible data immediately.

(3). Referring the user to additional technical data if necessary.

(4). Printing out a listing of the properly sized tubing.

The task of selecting appropriate processes to produce each of the machined surfaces of a part is a complicated task. Nau and Chang (1983) utilized expert system techniques for automating the process selection activity. Process selection works in two steps. First, a group technology code is used to classify a part as being in a family of similar parts. Second, when a process plan for a part is desired, a human user enters the code for the part into the system and the system retrieves a process plan which was previously used for some part in the family.

In an automated process selection method, expert system techniques are used in accumulating the necessary information about each surface of the part by representing the part as frames. All the knowledge about a particular object or event is stored together in frames.

11.5 APPLICATIONS IN PROCESS CONTROL

Expert systems can be used for monitoring thousands of process variables. With such systems, a small crew of operators can regulate the operation of complex industrial processes. Waterman (1987) gives a description of two such systems: FALCON and PDS.

FALCON identifies probable causes of process disturbances in a chemical process plant by interpreting data consisting of numerical values from gauges and the status of alarms and switches. The system interprets the data by using knowledge of the effects induced by fault in a given component and how disturbances in the input of a component will lead to disturbances in the output. Knowledge is represented in the system in two ways: as a set of rules controlled by forward chaining and as a causal model in network form. The system, developed at the University of Delaware, is written in LISP.

PDS (Portable Diagnostic System) diagnoses malfunctions in machine processes by interpreting information from sensors attached to the process. The system uses diagnosis methods that relate sensor readings to component malfunctions. PDS uses a forward chaining, rule-based representation scheme implemented in SRL, a frame-based knowledge engineering language. This system was developed at Carnegie Mellon University in cooperation with Westinghouse Electric Corporation.

Miller (1985) describes a real-time expert system for process control, called PIPCON (Process Intelligent Control), marketed by LISP Machine, Inc. PIPCON can monitor up to 20,000 measurements and alarms and can assign priorities to alarms to assist an operator in dealing efficiently with a process interruption or fault. Another process control system is PTRANS which helps control the manufacture and distribution of Digital Equipment Corporation's computer systems. It uses customer order descriptions and information about plant activity to develop a plan for assembling and testing the order. PTRANS monitors the progress of technicians implementing the plan, diagnoses problems, suggests solutions, and predicts possible impending shortages or surpluses of materials.

An expert system used as a diagnostic tool for failures in semiconductor fabrication was developed jointly by the National Bureau of Standards and the Westinghouse Research and Development Center. The tool helps manufacturers pinpoint problems that could cause failures at various stages in the semiconductor fabrication process. The knowledge is based on the collective intelligence and experience of several fabrication experts. Specialists with considerable expertise are usually required to interpret fabrication test data, but such experts are not always readily available. The expert system allows nonexpert semiconductor process personnel to directly diagnose problems on a personal computer.

11.6 APPLICATIONS IN FACILITY PLANNING

Industrial facility layout is another candidate area for expert systems and can be used to combine judgmental rules of human experts with quantitative tools in order to develop good facilities design for a variety of manufacturing situations. Two such systems are FADES and IFLAPS. FADES is a facilities planning and design system. The knowledge in this system is represented in the form of rules implemented in logic procedures and first order predicates. The knowledge base comprises the areas of work station technology, economic investment analysis, development of relationship ratings among work stations, selection of assignment algorithms, input preparation and invocation of algorithm for layout planning, and retrieval of information needed by logic rules from an existing company data base. IFLAPS is a multicriteria facilities layout analysis and planning system. This is a rule-based system implemented in PROLOG. The system explains its reasoning through an efficient user interface and acquires new knowledge through rule-based learning.

The Interior Department of the Bureau of Mines has developed an expert system for environmental facility control of coal mines. The system helps in achieving better control of respirable dust and explosive methane gas in underground coal mines. It helps coal mine operators solve problems in dust control for continuous miners, longwall shearers, and methane control. It obtains input about a control problem from the user, analyzes the data, and then suggests approaches to a solution.

11.7 EXPERT SYSTEMS IN CAD/CAM

Expert systems have been applied to various intricate design tasks such as electronic circuits, and have been explored for CAD/CAM applications. General Electric (Schenectady, NY) developed an expert system capable of redesigning an existing design. This system can work on an existing design or it can generate a new one. HICLASS (Hughes Integrated Classification System) is an expert system operating at Hughes Aircraft Company. The system handles planning methods, processes, standards, cost estimates, scheduling, productivity management, and quality control. It supports productivity-based automation and integrated design of manufacturing systems. It is capable of deducing the required manufacturing process from engineering design data. The expert system involves three phases:

Definition: A problem definition phase;
The problem associated with an engineering design is presented.

Reasoning: A problem-solving phase;
Symbolic processing is done while requirements and constraints are being evaluated until a solution is reached.

Presentation: A recommendation phase;
The recommended solution is graphically presented to the user.

APPLICATIONS IN ENGINEERING DESIGN Expert systems can help engineers quickly track ongoing changes during the course of a product development cycle. An expert system can serve as a central repository for archiving different types of design data as well as providing shared access to that data. External programs may be interfaced with expert systems to provide capabilities for efficient design storage and data comprehension ability. With proper interface, expert systems can be used to archive and monitor changes to files created by such things as CASE (Computer-Aided Software Engineering) tools, CAD (Computer-Aided Design), and CAE (Computer-Aided Engineering) programs, compilers, debuggers, editors, word processors, and spreadsheets. Such interface is particularly useful in a manufacturing environment where the interface of design and manufacturing activities has been traditionally difficult to achieve.

TeamNet software from TeamOne Systems, Inc. is an example of a tool designed to provide efficient work groups interface. TeamNet can support work groups of as many as 100 users. It is being used at Martin Marietta Corp.'s Astronautics Division to create real-time systems in a software engineering environment. It manages the entire software development cycle from code, design models, and documentation to delivery stages.

Further details on the applications of expert systems in the engineering design environment can be found in the following references: Chandrasekaran (1990), Coyne (1990), Coyne et al (1989), Fisher (1986), Gero (1990), Gero (1987), Maher (1988a), Maher (1988b), Maher (1990), Mellichamp (1987), Sriram et al (1989), and Takeda et al (1990).

11.8 APPLICATIONS IN MAINTENANCE AND FAULT DIAGNOSIS

One area in which expert systems have been shown to be quite successful is the area of fault diagnosis and repairs. The maintenance of a complex item of equipment involves a diagnostic procedure incorporating many rules as well as judgment decision by the maintenance personnel. Experience is an important factor in determining the ease with which a mechanic can locate a failure in a component and implement the appropriate correction. Expert systems are now being utilized to assist maintenance personnel in performing complex repairs by presenting menu-driven instruction guides for the diagnostic task. These expert systems incorporate the knowledge of mechanics who are well experienced in the maintenance and repair of that item of equipment. The first maintenance expert system to become commercially available was CATS-1 which was later renamed DELTA. This expert system was introduced by General Electric Company in 1983. DELTA (Diesel-Electric Locomotive Troubleshooting Aid) is now being used in railroad repair shops to assist maintenance personnel in isolating and repairing a large variety of diesel-electric locomotive faults.

Expert systems such as CATS, DART, ACE (Miller 1986), COMPASS (Waterman 1987) have been used for the purpose of preventive maintenance. Bungers (1986) described an expert system called DEX.C3. The system is used for fault diagnosis in a three-gear automatic transmission found in Ford cars. DEX.C3 system was primarily developed to demonstrate the principles and potentials of expert systems to the Ford community and also as a means of supporting service stations operated by Ford Company. Piptone (1986) discusses an expert system named FIS (Fault Isolation System), used for providing assistance to technicians in diagnosing faults in electronic parts. Kumara et al (1986) also describe an expert system, called FOREST, used for fault isolation and diagnosis in automatic test equipment (ATE). The system attempts to emulate experienced field engineers whose speciality is diagnosing faults undetectable by existing ATE software.

At Hughes Aircraft Company, an expert system has been developed as a feasibility analysis tool. The expert system assists engineers in designing circuit cards by determining the testability of a card for the factory. The system also has links to external data bases for direct data inputs. The Oklahoma City plant of AT&T has also developed many expert systems for equipment troubleshooting. One of the systems, named OKIE (Oklahoma Interactive Expert System), was developed to troubleshoot AT&T 3B2 computers (Somby 1987).

Many Ford Motor Company dealers across the country no longer have to call Dearborn, Michigan to talk with company experts every time they run into difficult engine diagnosis problems. Instead, they simply tap into a nationwide computer system developed by Ford to duplicate the reasoning that the experts use to solve difficult engine problems.

At Xerox, an expert system named RIC (Remote Interactive Communications) is used for early-warning equipment diagnostics. The knowledge base for RIC is based on the reasoning of a special Xerox team of diagnosticians. The system reads data from a copier's internal instruments, senses when something is about to go wrong, and sends a report to a repairman. The repairman can then warn the customer that an imminent breakdown can be avoided by taking appropriate steps. In theory, RIC can prevent a Xerox copier from ever breaking down.

In 1986, IBM installed one of its first expert systems, called DEFT (Diagnostic Expert Final Test). The task of the system is to perform the mundane but critical job of diagnosing problems during the final testing of the giant disk drives that store information for IBM's mainframe computers. DEFT has been adapted as a diagnostic tool for IBM service experts and to perform a variety of different tests on much IBM equipment. The system, which cost about $100,000 initially, is said to have generated a payoff of around $12 million in annual savings. It should be mentioned that some of the savings that have been reported by companies are somewhat conservative. This is primarily because companies are cautious about letting competitors find out the details of their competitive edge.

An expert system for troubleshooting blast furnaces went into operation in 1987 at Kawasaki Steel's Mizushima Works in western Japan. The company reports that the system embodies both expert system technology and all the state-of-art technological know-how accumulated in the ironmaking area of steel operations over several decades. Using about 600 IF/THEN rules, the system covers all conceivable situations likely to develop inside a blast furnace. The system takes readings on up to 250 process variables.

One diagnostic application developed by Texas Instruments, Inc. involves a highly sophisticated machine used in the production of semiconductors (Herrod 1988). This application illustrates how an expert system can aid in significantly reducing error, avoiding costly waste and downtime. The machine, called an epitaxial reactor, is used to deposit thin layers of silicon on silicon wafers. The wafers, a few inches in diameter, are placed in vacuum chambers inside the reactors. The thin film (epitaxial layer) is grown at high temperature by controlling the flow rate and pattern of a mixture of silicon and other reactant gases.

The machine may process several wafers at a time. If it is set up improperly or a failure occurs while in process, thousands of dollars' worth of scrap may result and many hours of reactor time may be wasted. Because the reactors are very complex, only a few experts are skilled in diagnosing and fixing repair problems. Reactors could remain idle for several hours while waiting for a human expert to arrive. To reduce this expensive downtime, a panel of engineers created an expert system named Intelligent Machine Prognosticator (IMP). It consists of seven knowledge bases including three for faults, one for warnings, another for a hoist that forms part of the system, one for mechanical problems, and one for process problems. The combined knowledge bases contain up to 1000 rules to help the technician in diagnosing problems. Approximately 90 percent of the potential reactor problems are included in the expert system. It is reported that results with the system have been better than expected. The mean time to repair has decreased by 36 percent.

Another Texas Instruments product is an expert system that troubleshoots a complex electronic device. The device, containing several dozen state-of-the-art analog and digital circuit boards, is tested in an automated test equipment environment. The combination of possible symptoms, uncertainty of failure causes, and the frequent refinement and enhancement of both the product and test environment resulted in an enormous and complex domain. To tackle this large domain, a diagnostic expert system, called Expert Technician, was developed to provide a best-first troubleshooting procedure for junior and senior-level technicians.

A major component of the system is its ability to acquire and update symptom-action associations by which conditions, signs, and symptoms are linked to actions that eliminate the symptoms. These symptom-action links are integrated into the knowledge base as problems are discovered by the automated test equipment and are then strengthened as actions repeatedly result in stopping the symptom. A time-weighting factor is used to reduce the effect of older events. This way, the likelihood used by the system to infer the best-first action for a given set of symptoms is based both on frequency of association and recency of the association. This approach is very useful in dynamic domains where the need to identify failure trends is very critical. The final recommendations to the technicians are cost-weighted, using standard cost indices for performing the required tasks. The system is implemented in C programming language on minicomputers that interface with more than 50 computer-based automated test sets via a local area network.

One of the most frequently reported diagnostic expert systems is the one developed for the Campbell Soup Company of Camden, New Jersey by Texas Instruments. The expert system project involved solving a diagnostic problem for malfunctions in large soup sterilizers. The large, complex sterilizers are 72 feet high and hold up to 68,000 cans of soup. The soup is raised to a temperature of 250 degrees centigrade using pressurized steam to kill bacteria. Maintenance of these sterilizers is usually handled routinely by plant personnel. However, some problems could only be solved by an expert knowledgeable in the design and installation of the sterilizers.

Downtime is very expensive because of the large quantity of soup in a sterilizer at any given time and the potential effects of backlog. An expert system was created to capture the knowledge of the human expert who specializes in troubleshooting the sterilizers. The expert was close to retirement. So, the company wanted to retain his expertise and allow him to spend most of his remaining time in designing new equipment. The expert system that resulted from the effort can troubleshoot about 100 hydrostatic and rotary sterilizers. It also includes all of the start-up and shut-down procedures for the machines. The development of the system was completed in approximately seven months. It has been installed in several of Campbell's U.S. and Canadian plants. It has been found to operate successfully in diagnosing problems. On the basis of this success, similar systems have been developed to diagnose problems in the equipment that fills cans with soup and the equipment that seals the cans.

Eagle Technology, Inc. has developed a commercial maintenance expert system named EMM (Expert Maintenance Management). Standard modules of the system, designed to run on personal computers, include equipment records, preventive maintenance, work order management, parts inventory, and purchase orders. Users retrieve information and generate work orders using English language words and phrases. An enhancement schedule includes analysis of maintenance costs, maintenance/personnel scheduling, and preventive maintenance.

For nearly a decade, artificial intelligence technology has helped General Motors Corporation maintain its position as one of the world's largest automobile manufacturers. AI and expert systems have been used as strategic tools to meet GM's business needs. Expert systems, which now flourish at GM, allow scarce expertise to be captured, preserved, and improved across the organization. GM's earliest success with an intelligent system is credited to an employee named

Charley Amble. Amble was an experienced maintenance engineer, who, in 1987, was widely recognized throughout GM for his ability to identify problems in broken machine tools. Sometimes, Amble recognized problems before they occurred.

Amble and the Advanced Engineering Staff worked together to store Amble's precious knowledge and developed their first expert system for machine tool design. GM named the system "Charley." The expert system was so technically capable of identifying problems that even Charley, the human expert, was astonished by it. Designed for diagnosis and preventive maintenance, the system instructs less experienced individuals by providing an explanation capability. What used to take someone three years to learn, has been cut to three months. Reduced training costs attributed to "Charley," are estimated to generate a savings of $500,000 per year per plant for GM.

The U.S. Army has been applying AI techniques to logistics functions since the establishment of an Artificial Intelligence Office at the Army Logistics Center at Ft. Lee, New Jersey in 1984. Of the many applications of AI, expert systems are the type being used most by Army logisticians. Expert systems duplicate the human mental processes in solving problems and making predictions. The Directorate of Combat Developments at the Ordnance Missile and Munitions Center and School initiated an AI program to take advantage of the opportunities provided by expert systems. The first initiative of this AI program was to develop an expert system diagnostic tool to aid the mechanic in troubleshooting and repairing the Pulse Acquisition Radar (PAR) of the HAWK Missile System (Keller and Knutilla 1990). The expert system, called the Pulse Radar Intelligent Diagnostic Environment (PRIDE), is a tool built for soldiers by soldiers. So, the developers completely understood the needs of the users. This is a primary requirement of expert system development process.

The system assists a PAR mechanic in troubleshooting five basic faults. The system contains over 300 rules and combines technical manual procedures with the field experience of senior mechanics. It provides on-screen instructional assistance. It is intended to complement technical manual instructions and mechanic expertise, and not to replace either. The success of PRIDE led to the development of another expert system diagnostic tool to address the High Power Illuminator Radar of the HAWK missile system. The PRIDE effort grew from a grass roots endeavor to a major initiative in the Army's quest to provide the benefits of high technology to its soldiers. Several spinoff developments are expected to follow the implementation of PRIDE.

11.9 APPLICATIONS IN MATERIAL HANDLING AND SUPPLIES

A major challenge facing designers and materials engineers is the selection of engineering materials to satisfy product requirements under existing availability, supply, and production constraints. In an industrial environment, the control of various material handling activities by the computer is a very complex task. The process demands advanced strategic planning, high performance, high reliability, and precise timing. For example, a computer controlling a high-speed conveyor must make the correct decision before the next load reaches its diversion point or lose the load. Expert systems can be used for combining advanced logical processes with high-speed, multilocation decision making. Expert system techniques have been successfully implemented at the Digital Equipment Corporation facility at Marlboro, Massachusetts for controlling material handling processes. The utilization of expert systems has resulted in increased output, reduced cycle time, reduction of labor, improved equipment utilization, reduction of work-in-process, and improved scheduling (Wynot 1986).

At Daniel Industries of Houston, Texas, a fluid control and measurement device manufacturer, an expert system running on a personal computer produces dramatic increases in bill of material (BOM) and inventory accuracies. The system also enhances design productivity. The company produces some very complex products, consisting of many different parts. When an order is placed, design personnel search through a large number of possible configurations. Since each order is essentially a custom job, the number of possible configurations may run into several millions. Because of this complexity, the company needs a way to get very accurate bills of material. An accurate bill of material is crucial to their MRP II (Manufacturing Resource Planning) system. Since the installation of the system, productivity has increased and inventories have declined.

A similar expert system developed by InSol, Inc. (Jindia 1990), is designed to address the problem of generating accurate first level bills of material (BOM) for custom orders of a storage system. The design and layout of a storage system is based on customer's requirements and warehouse specifications. As a result, every order is a different order and it requires detailed calculations to determine the dimensions (length, width, and height) of a storage system. Also, the dimensions of different components of the system have to be determined. Depending on the nature of the order, it took a product expert about three to six hours to calculate and prepare a first level BOM. This BOM was then manually entered into an MRP system on a Hewlett Packard 3000 for expansion to produce purchasing and shop orders. The conventional process was prone to numerous errors in the final product shipped to the customer.

Due to the large size of the storage systems, it was not feasible to assemble the whole product before shipping. Consequently, problems that existed were observed only when the customer was ready to install the storage system in the warehouse. The following were concluded to be the major sources of errors in the order processing approach:

(1). Requirements as given by the customer to the company salesman.

(2). Requirements as documented by the salesman for the product expert.

(3). Manual calculation errors by the product expert.

(4). Data entry errors.

Due to the errors, the final product did not conform to the requirements. As a result, the client had to waste much time and money in correcting the problems. The conventional programming efforts did not succeed in solving the problems because of constantly changing customer requirements and changing product features provided in response to market conditions. An expert system solution was developed for the order processing system. The design of the expert system was executed from the point of view of the end user. Accordingly, the user interface for the expert system was developed based on the following guidelines:

- It must be an easy-to-use question-and-answer system.
- It must cover all product options.
- It must gather complete information about the product requirements.
- It must use a minimum set of questions for any set of customer requirements.

The expert system, developed with the aid of DCLASS development tool, helped to eliminate the errors that were common in the conventional manual system. Customer orders are collected in a series of question-and-answer prompts. After all the relevant data is collected, the processing of the data is done internally by the expert system and it is completely transparent to the user. The information collected from the client is stored in decision trees in the form of if-then-else logic. As questions are answered by the user, the expert system selects which trees to traverse to process the collected information. At the end of a session, the user sees a printout of all the major components and assemblies required to complete the order with their part numbers.

11.10 APPLICATIONS IN EQUIPMENT SELECTION AND OPERATING CONDITIONS

The task of selecting equipment or setting operating conditions to match product and production needs while achieving minimum cost requires extensive knowledge of facts, relationships, and rules that are specific to material handling. In addition, it requires consideration of complex equipment characteristics that can suggest many feasible alternatives. The selection process may have to accommodate multiple conflicting objectives. An expert system can provide the potential for solving this kind of selection problem. Malmborg et al (1987) developed a prototype expert system for selecting truck type. They define an industrial truck type as a collection of attributes that specify an industrial model in sufficient detail that one or more commercially available truck models could be associated with it. Based on the conditions specified, the expert system recommends the type of truck to use.

The engineers at COMSAT Corporation have developed an expert system that selects the correct heater warm-up time for in-orbit operation of the INTELSAT V Spacecraft electrothermal thrusters. When this task is performed by humans, it was prone to error and required constant cross-checking by an experienced engineer. The expert system provides reliable and quick selection of the correct warm-up time. It avoids potential human error and allows the operations staff to perform higher level tasks. Chrysler Corporation is developing an expert system to assist engineers and designers in selecting the best fasteners from among the estimated 30,000 types available for headlamp assembly. The fastener system is very complex because it must be developed for a large user base and it must incorporate the latest developments in fastener technology.

11.11 APPLICATIONS IN ROBOTICS

The area of robotics is a fertile one for the application of expert systems. Robots of the past were designed mainly for mechanical functions with preprogrammed instructions. Regardless of its changing environment, the robot would attempt to execute its tasks in the predetermined process. Nowadays, the increasing dynamism of production environments has necessitated the development of intelligent robots that react to their changing surroundings. The main functions of an intelligent robot include processing information, sensing, and motion. Information processing is primarily a brain function. Sensing (seeing and touching) and motion (moving and manipulations) are primarily body functions. The information processing function (thinking) is executed by a computer through an expert system technique. Some potential areas of using expert systems in robotics include:

- *Kinematics and design*: For the operation of a robot arm, the kinematic problem must be solved with respect to movement from one cartesian position and orientation to another. An expert system could be implemented to relieve the human expert in the symbolically tedious work of producing such solutions.

- *Robot selection*: Because of the shortage of experienced applications engineers, an expert system could distribute applications experience among a wider community of users. A knowledge base can be developed and periodically updated to reflect new developments in robot availability and utilization.

- *Workplace layout*: When robots are to be installed in a new workspace, an expert system can perform the necessary analysis to provide the optimum workspace requirements.

Machine vision, a critical component of robotics, is an area of AI that has been more successful in research laboratories than in actual practice. This is because laboratories operate under controlled conditions while actual practice is subject to all sorts of unanticipated environmental variations. An improvement in practical applications can be achieved by developing expert systems that use heuristics to guide machine vision system operations under various stimuli within a functional location. Schreiber (1985) discusses how ZapatA Industries (Frackville, Penn.), the largest U.S. manufacturer of bottle caps, switched to machine vision for quality control. The result of implementing the vision system was a 33 percent increase in productivity.

Researchers at McMaster University in Hamilton, Ontario, Canada have designed an expert system task planner to aid in the off-line programming of assembly robots. The system is used for automatic off-line programming of robots through specification of the goal state and the initial state. The robot planner uses a knowledge base for assembly sequences, geometric reasoning, and tooling. Software allows the user to describe the assembly task at a high level. The programmer does not need to specify moves or coordinates because the robot automatically converts its instructions into the detailed steps needed to execute the task.

Tou (1987) presents design concepts of expert systems for engineering design, production planning, and manufacturing. Expert systems can provide answers to problems that may be associated with integrated production automation in the future. The broad functional goals for using expert system techniques in the area of factory automation would be to provide expert assistance in the performance of professional and managerial tasks and in integrating and coordinating the management of the factory.

11.12 MACHINE TOOL APPLICATIONS

Expert system techniques can be used for managing the tool life in an FMS environment. An expert system can limit the occurrence of expensive tool failures as described by Villa et al (1985).

A diagnostic system for a machine tool controller is in operation at McDonnell Douglas Company. The primary function of this expert system is to allow maintenance people to easily identify problems that occur in the controller. The system performs an advisory role for a maintenance staff of about 35 people. Eventually, the system will hook up directly to the controller. It has been shown that the system will not reduce the number of employees needed in the plant, but will free them up for more creative tasks. The system is expected to help reduce downtime on the plant floor, allowing the company to produce in-house parts that otherwise would have to be contracted from outside manufacturers.

11.13 APPLICATIONS IN MANUFACTURING MANAGEMENT

IMACS (Intelligent Management Assistant for Computer System manufacturing) is an expert system built by Digital Equipment Corporation to assist managers in a manufacturing environment with paperwork, capacity planning, inventory management, and other tasks related to managing the manufacturing process. IMACS takes a customer's order and generates a rough build plan from which it can estimate the resource requirements for the order. Just before the computer system in the order is built, IMACS generates a detailed build plan and uses it to monitor the computer system's implementation.

The management of a complex processing plant is also a profitable area for the application of expert system technology. Many systems have been developed to assist with the interpretation of the numerous alarm conditions that can occur in large process plants. Given the complexity of many industrial processes, reliance on experienced and expert operators is very common. Figure 11.1 illustrates a conceptual model of the role of expert systems in enhancing the management of

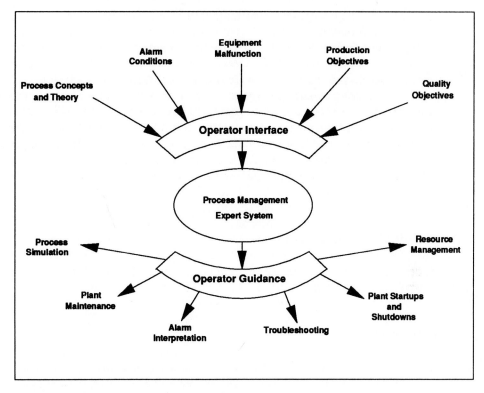

Figure 11.1. Model for process management expert system

complex processes. An expert system can provide guidance on the application of control strategies. In cases where the time cycle for operator response can span well over an eight-hour shift, it is important to maintain consistent operating conditions and operator actions. By offering consistent advice around the clock, an expert system could help maintain the required consistency. An example of this application is in operation at BHP (Broken Hill Proprietary) Central Research Laboratories in Shortland, New South Wales.

In another example of the application of expert systems in process management, an expert system (named WELD-SELECTOR) developed by the Colorado School of Mines (Golden, CO) helps engineers make welding decisions. Complexity in welding is growing. There are now hundreds of weldable metals, including specialized alloys. Some of these require highly specific procedures. In most shops, except the specialized ones, the increasing number of welding factors is making decisions about welding more and more difficult. The WELD-SELECTOR expert system helps in reducing the chances for decision errors. The system asks the user a series of questions about the welding to be performed. It searches through its knowledge base to find suitable welding electrodes and narrows down the possibilities to a final recommendation. The system considers chemical and physical properties of the base materials and the intended position of the weld. The expert system is marketed by the American Welding Institute in Knoxville, Tennessee.

Wright-Patterson Air Force Base (Aeronautical Systems Division) has developed an expert system which greatly reduces the time needed to manufacture composite aircraft parts. The system is used to run an autoclave (oven) which cures the composite parts. It controls several variables in the curing process to ensure that the finished composite parts will have the desired performance characteristics. Another expert system for the composite industry was developed by ABARIS company of Reno, Nevada under contract with the US Air Force Wright Aeronautical Materials Laboratory in Dayton, Ohio.

The system leads users through ultrasound inspection and repair of composite materials. Composite materials, used increasingly in aircraft parts, have partial failure modes that can cause problems in the field. Because the material is multilaminar and opaque, internal fracture or separation is difficult to identify. So, ultrasound inspection is used to find most of the internal damage. But each ply of lamination can cause discontinuities of signals that could be interpreted as damage. An expert system helps in analyzing the ultrasound data and obtaining correct interpretations.

11.14 EXERCISES

11.1 Conduct a survey of expert systems applications in your area of interest.

11.2 What specific problem in your area of interest has not been adequately covered by existing expert systems? How would you go about developing an expert system to solve the problem?

12

Case Studies: Samples of Expert System Developments

This chapter presents selected samples of expert systems applications to problems in engineering and manufacturing domains. The case samples were developed with the aid of the VP-Expert development tool by industrial engineering students in the Expert Systems Laboratory in the School of Industrial Engineering, University of Oklahoma. Complete or partial listing of the knowledge bases for some of the examples are presented in Appendix F. Even though the examples were developed with VP-Expert, the design structures can be easily extended for implementation with other development tools.

12.1 PROCESS-PLUS: AN EXPERT SYSTEM MODEL FOR GENERATIVE PROCESS PLANNING

Manufacturing process planning is a common task in small-batch, discrete-parts metalworking industries. It is a function within a manufacturing facility that establishes which machining processes and parameters are to be used to convert a raw material piece from its initial form to a final desired form. The final form is typically predetermined from an engineering drawing provided by a design engineer. After an understanding of the part features has been reached, an operation sheet containing operation details (e.g., appropriate sequence of processing operations, cut planning, speeds, feeds, and tooling) is prepared. Process planning represents a vital link between engineering design and the shop floor. There are many problems involved in process planning. These are outlined as follows:

(1). The conventional process planning approaches constitute a poor use of engineering skills because of the high clerical content of the procedures. Very often, records that have been kept to standardize methods of manufacturing or even record the existence of facilities within the plant are not kept up to date. Consequently, when reference is made to these records, the use of the information they contain generates inefficient or even inaccurate process planning.

(2). There is a problem in that the manufacturing logic for making the product may be applied differently by different process planners. This results in inconsistent use of the knowledge available in the organization. If the logic of manufacture is written down, it is often not even referred to because of the excessive clerical effort required to follow standard routines.

(3). Fewer and fewer engineers are engaged in the function of process planning. So, the available process records become even more out of date. Whenever an experienced process planner leaves an organization, considerable logic of manufacture can be lost.

The rate of change of design is increasing and the need to satisfy customer requirements more quickly is also increasing. The state of the manufacturing technology itself is becoming more volatile. This means that the existing skills of engineers must be used more effectively. This can be done by using the power of the computer to eliminate repetitive tasks and to improve level of service. The art of process planning can be enhanced by the technology of expert systems. A prototype expert system developed by Ajay Joshi to integrate CAD and CAM for generative process planning is presented here. The system, named PROCESS-plus, was developed by interfacing AUTOCAD with dBASE III-PLUS. The feature extraction was done through use of AUTOLISP. The knowledge base was written in VP-Expert, a rule-based shell. The input to the system is an engineering drawing and the system output is a detailed operation sheet for symmetrical rotational parts. The early attempts to implement computer-aided process planning were essentially computerized interactive retrieval systems. The systems were designed to assist the process planner in the planning and decision-making process. They provide storage of new designed parts, recall existing designs, identify and match existing designs to parts of similar nature, and provide editing capability for existing designs. There are two approaches to computer assisted process planning:

(1). The variant approach

(2). The generative approach

VARIANT APPROACH TO PROCESS PLANNING   Variant process planning uses data retrieval procedures to find standard plans for similar components. The basic analysis involved in part analysis description, classification, and coding is based on the concept of group technology. Group technology (GT) is used to form part families. The group technology approach enables data common to families of components to be reused when their individual process plans are generated. In order to benefit from this technique, an appropriate coding and classification system must be selected and implemented in a convenient format. This requires that parts be grouped into families satisfying the same basic shape. Once a variant process planning system has been set up, any desired modification might need to be carried out by an experienced process planner and a programming specialist. Thus, variant-based process planning systems typically lack flexibility. Any component that does not fall within a known part family may not have a convenient process plan. The cost and time required to set up a variant-based process planning system can represent a substantial investment. The biggest disadvantage of the approach is that an experienced process planner is required to construct, maintain, modify, and consistently edit the standard process plans.

GENERATIVE APPROACH TO PROCESS PLANNING Generative process planning generates a process plan automatically for a newly designed component. Instead of using existing standard plans, generative process planning utilizes built-in decision logic to uniquely select and develop a sequence of machining operations necessary to produce the desired part. Unlike the variant approach, no standard manufacturing plans are predefined or stored. The computer automatically generates a unique operation sheet for a part every time the part is ordered. Thus, the approach allows an organization to be responsive to the changing requirements of parts and the changing state of manufacturing technology. The generative process planning system essentially consists of two major components:

(1). A geometry-based coding scheme for translating physical features and engineering drawing specifications into computer-interpretable data.
(2). Software for managing the process planning activity.

The coding scheme defines all geometric features, feature sizes, locations, and feature tolerances for all process-related surfaces. The coding scheme not only describes the part in both the rough and finished states, but must also relate to the processes in terms of its capability to perform an operation and the available tooling. In effect, the coding scheme relates all the physical elements of the manufacturing process in a universal data language. The software comprises decision logic, formulas, and technological algorithms to compare the part geometry requirements to manufacturing capabilities and availabilities. This involves determination of the appropriate processing operations, tool speed, feed, tool geometry, cutting fluid, and so on. This component of generative process planning requires a thorough understanding of the operating modes and manufacturing capabilities for each of the available processes.

The generative approach to process planning has many advantages in terms of automating the manual activities involved in creating manufacturing routings and instructions. This approach produces results that are more accurate, consistent, and inexpensive. The approach can be fully automated and an up-to-date operation sheet can easily be generated each time a part is ordered. Except for major revisions in decision logic due to new equipment or processing capabilities, the system does not require much human intervention to construct, maintain, modify, or create consistent process plans. The development of a generative process planning system should be viewed in the light of future needs for integrated design and manufacturing functions.

EVOLUTION OF PROCESS-PLUS   With the preceding discussions in mind, an expert system was developed to achieve successful integration between design and manufacturing (Joshi 1989). The integration of design and manufacturing functions has been a major concern in industry. The expert system developed to achieve the desired integration is named PROCESS-PLUS. It is based on the generative approach of process planning. A methodology is used for combining a CAD software (AUTOCAD) with manufacturing decision logic so that process plans can be generated with little or no manual intervention. The rule-based technique of artificial intelligence is used to generate the desired process plans.

The user is asked to enter the part drawing in AUTOCAD. The coding scheme and the decision logic developed by using dBASE III-PLUS and VP-Expert will then generate the process plan. The system structure of PROCESS-PLUS is shown in Figure 12.1. The system is limited to symmetrical rotational parts. However, the technique can be easily adapted to systems that cover other part geometries. A comprehensive list of operations related to rotational parts is considered. The system was developed on the basis of three levels of effort:

(1). Data input and feature extraction using AUTOCAD.

(2). Data organization and extraction using dBASE III-PLUS.

(3). Construction of a knowledge base to generate process plans using VP-Expert.

FEATURE EXTRACTION   The main advantage of the generative approach to process planning is that little or no manual intervention is required for prepara-

Figure 12.1. PROCESS-PLUS system structure

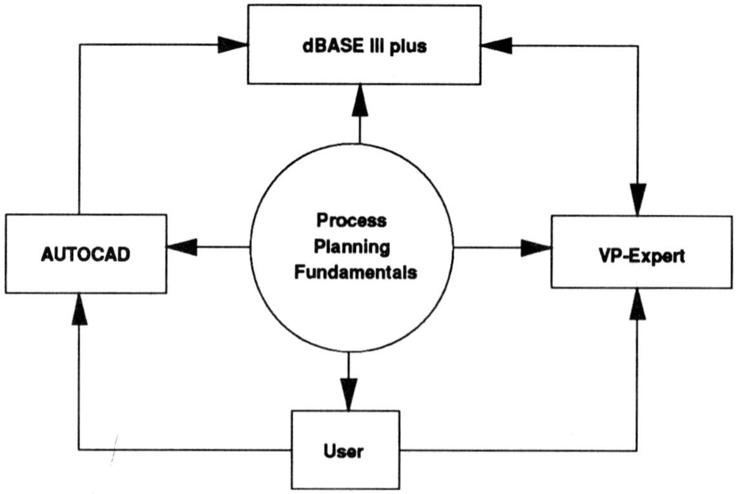

tion of a process plan. Many generative process planning systems have been developed, but very few of them can interface with CAD systems. There is a lack of smooth information flow between computer-aided design (CAD) systems and computer-aided manufacturing (CAM) systems. In the usual approach, the user has to enter the part coordinate data and the other necessary data by answering many questions, which takes more time. This nullifies whatever benefits are obtained through the elimination of manual intervention. To overcome this dilemma, PROCESS-PLUS was designed with the aim of developing a CAD interface with the knowledge base. The first step was to find a CAD software that is used extensively in industry. Since the expert system shell to be used was PC-based, it was necessary that the CAD software also be PC-based. Even though there are many microcomputer CAD systems available, AUTOCAD is by far the most prominent. One of the major reasons for AUTOCAD's position as the standard for PC-based CAD software is its adaptability. It also offers a high degree of flexibility and customization. It allows a user to tailor the software to his or her programming needs, and it can be modified to meet the needs of drafters and designers in many design situations.

Customization of AUTOCAD in PROCESS-PLUS was necessary because the input module for producing part drawings is designed for inexperienced users of AUTOCAD. Customized AUTOCAD benefits the user by presenting a more compact and familiar interface that reduces learning time. Most of the time spent producing and editing drawings in AUTOCAD is spent in selecting and/or typing commands in a precise order and then selecting the correct options within these commands. Customization allows a user to combine a long series of keystrokes into just a few. With customization, questions are posed to the user while the part drawing is made through use of the custom menu provided. A sample of the menu is shown in Figure 12.2. The descriptions of the items on the menu are presented below:

(1). LINE: This is used to draw straight surfaces on a part.

(2). CURVE: This is used to draw round fillets.

(3). DOTTED: This is used to draw internal machining surfaces.

Figure 12.2. PROCESS-PLUS screen menu

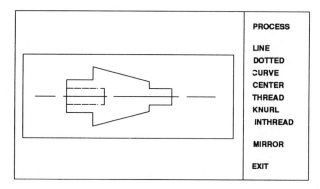

(4). CENTER: This is used to draw center lines.

(5). THREAD: This is used to draw external threaded surfaces.

(6). KNURL: This is used to draw knurling surfaces.

(7). INTHREAD: This is used to draw internal threaded surfaces.

(8). MIRROR: This is used to generate mirror images after drawing center lines.

(9). EXIT: This terminates the AUTOCAD module.

The code for the customized menu is stored in a file with the extension MNU. This file extension identifies an AUTOCAD screen menu file, which contains screen-menu prompts as well as the commands that are executed when options are selected for the printing device. Each line in a custom menu contains a specific command sequence, using one or more AUTOCAD commands along with whatever options may be appropriate. Each sequence begins at the leftmost position and can continue to the right indefinitely using a wraparound technique. A drawing data base is maintained simultaneously for each drawing. The only way to access this data is by using AUTOLISP. AUTOLISP is an implementation of the LISP programming language embedded within AUTOCAD. AUTOLISP allows AUTOCAD developers to write programs and functions in a powerful high level language that is well suited to graphics applications. It adheres closely to the syntax and conventions of common LISP. Even though it is a small subset of common LISP, it has many additional functions specific to AUTOCAD. AUTOCAD instructions that have been written in AUTOLISP are called LISP routines. LISP routines are contained in ASCII files that are called LISP files. LISP files can have any valid DOS file name and they always have the file extension LSP.

In AUTOCAD, each drawing element is considered as an entity. For example, a line is an entity. For each entity, there is an association list which contains dotted pairs of information about that entity. For example, an association list for a line drawn from (1.00, 2.00) to (6.00, 6.9) is as shown below:

```
((-1. 60000014)
(0. "LINE")
(8. "0")
(10. 1.00 2.00)
(11. 6.00 6.9)
)
```

The first number in the dotted pair is the code that represents a particular item. For example, -1 represents the entity name, 10 represents the starting point of the line. A comprehensive set of AUTOLISP functions provides access to AUTOCAD entities and to the graphics screen and input devices. A user can select entities, retrieve their values, and modify them. But no functions are provided for creating entities. An entity name is like a pointer into a file maintained by AUTOCAD's drawing editor, from which AUTOLISP can find the entity's data base record and its vectors (if on screen). This feature, by which the user can modify the entity data base, is used in PROCESS-PLUS for extracting the additional parameters of an entity such as tolerance, surface finish, threads per inch, and so on. When the user is drawing an entity on the screen using the menu provided, interactive questions are asked concerning relevant parameter values. There are some values in an association list which are not useful for the feature extraction. These values are searched in the entity data base and replaced by the parameter values entered by the user. A sample of this procedure is presented below.

In the association list for a threading surface, a dotted pair (38. 89) represents the layer name of an entity which is not useful since PROCESS-PLUS makes use of only one layer. So, in this case, the value 89 is replaced by a threads-per-inch value entered by the user. After this procedure is complete, the list associated with the threading surface contains all the information needed to select the machining parameters for that surface. After the part drawing is complete, the next job is to extract the required information from the entity data base. There are functions in AUTOLISP that can be used to access a particular piece of data. Through use of these functions, the required data is extracted. For example, the individual dotted pairs that represent the values can be retrieved by using the ASSOC command. To retrieve the values, the CDR command is used. The threads-per-inch value is retrieved by the following line:

```
(cdr(assoc 38 thr))
where
38 is the code which is a pointer for the parameter value
thr is the name of the list in which the entity data is stored
assoc locates the dotted pair which contains the value 38
cdr retrieves the second value in the selected dotted pair
```

All these commands are embedded in the AUTOLISP program which acts as a feature extractor of the input part drawing. The program is written in such a way that the output is in a format that can be interfaced with dBASE III-PLUS. The output of the LSP file is an ASCII file.

CONTROL STRUCTURE   After the data about the part drawing is extracted from AUTOCAD, the data obtained must be represented in a way that is suitable for processing by use of the available problem-solving knowledge. This is accomplished by a control structure written in dBASE III-PLUS. The output ASCII file from AUTOCAD is retrieved in dBASE III-PLUS and the piece of the data is stored as a field in a data base file.

There are many reasons why dBASE III-PLUS was chosen for developing the control structure. As discussed, the output of the AUTOCAD is an ASCII file which contains the numbers and characters associated with the part drawing. The control structure should be a tool which can take this data as input, convert it into a format that can be used by the knowledge base and can be interfaced with the chosen expert system shell (i.e., VP-Expert). Also, it should provide the necessary programming environment. All of this can be accomplished with dBASE III-PLUS. The three major components of this module are:

- Control structure
- Schemes of data representation
- Work space

Schemes of data representations are worked out for the part drawing entities. A sample of the profile description scheme is shown in Figure 12.3. Symmetric rotational parts are assumed to have two profiles, one external and one internal. Each profile is completely described by use of primitive segments "LINE" and "ARC." A "LINE" is a straight edge on a part and is specified by the coordinates of the endpoints of the line. Additional parameters are included in the description of a "LINE" to account for surface features, such as a threaded surface or a knurled surface. AN "ARC" is a curved surface on a part, such as groove or fillet. It is specified by the coordinates of the endpoints of the arc and the angle swept by the arc.

A reference point is defined for a part and the sequence of primitive segments is stored in the data base file. Parts that are produced on a lathe have the center point of the tool face as the reference point. The entity data is stored in the

Figure 12.3. Part profile description scheme

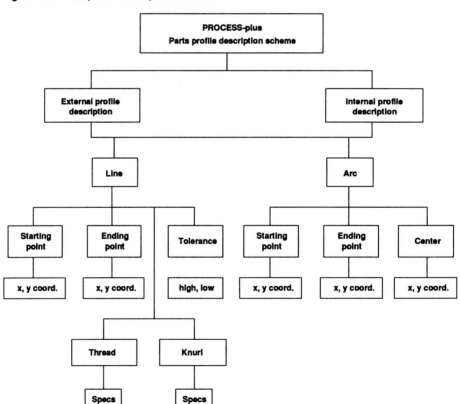

output ASCII file in an order in which the user has drawn the part drawing. Suppose a user draws an entity A followed by entities B,C, and D. If he later needs to make a change in entity A, he/she would need to replace A with a modified entity A′. In this case the order in which the output data is stored should be A′BCD, but it is actually stored as BCDA′. To find the machining operation sequence the data should be rearranged in the order A′BCD, which is the first step performed by the dBASE program.

Experienced operators play an important role in finding the operation sequence for parts. Operations associated with process planning are the various machining operations that change the shape of an object from a raw material form to a final desired form. Every machining operation has a unique way of changing the state of material and each one is called for, depending on the situation. Several factors may be evaluated as preconditions, such as the surface to be modified, the existence of certain features in raw materials, and so on. Not all operations are capable of generating desired shapes. For example, a turning operation is applicable only if the raw material is cylindrical and its dimensions are within the specified limits of the machine. A boring operation can be performed only if there exists a predrilled hole. Threading on a surface can be performed only if the part is cylindrical. For these reasons, it is very important to know the precedence of the required operations. The precedence logic used in PROCESS-PLUS is based on the developers' own experience as well as published guides.

PROBLEM-SOLVING STRATEGY   The process planner's job involves interpreting engineering drawing, reasoning about a component's geometry and quality, and finally making decisions about how the part can be best produced. This can be done by identifying the cutting precedences and by selecting processes, parameters, and tools to be used. If a computer-based system is to perform the task of process planning at a level comparable to humans, we need to supplement its numeric capabilities by providing logic that translates the piece-by-piece description into higher order relationships. This can be done by defining the interrelationships between the states of the production system.

In the approach used in PROCESS-PLUS, the part drawing is considered as a two-dimensional graph, which shows the area to be removed to get the final form of the part from the raw material bar stock. The area above a horizontal line is considered as a rectangle and the operation which removes the rectangular area is turning. Similarly, taper-turning is considered to remove a triangular area, which is the area above a slanted line. For finding out the number of passes in which the required material can be removed, it is necessary to find the depth of the area to be removed. Also for turning, drilling, and boring, the length of the cut is maximized. It is necessary to keep a record of the current (x,y) coordinates and the final coordinates. To achieve this, a special procedure was developed. For each edge of a surface, two records of x and y coordinates, (*xfinal, yfinal*) and (*xcurrent, ycurrent*) are maintained. After each operation or cut, the (*xcurrent, ycurrent*) are updated. An example is shown in Figure 12.4.

The figure shows two horizontal surfaces but at different levels. Before the machining is started (step1), the final coordinates for edges 1,2,3,4 are $(x1,y1)$,

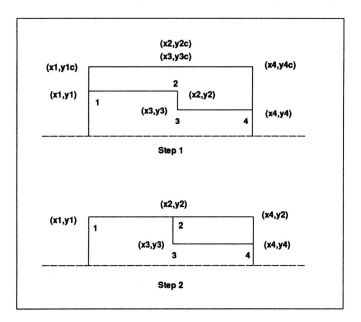

Figure 12.4. Path logic in PROCESS-PLUS

$(x2,y2)$, $(x3,y3)$ and $(x4y4)$, respectively. Similarly, the current coordinates for the edges 1,2,3,4 are $(x1,y1c)$, $(x2,y2c)$, $(x3,y3c)$ and $(x4,y4c)$, respectively. Note that $(x2,y2c)$ and $(x3,y3c)$ coincide initially. Starting from the left at $(x1,y1c)$, in order to maximize the cut, the first cut is made to $x4$ instead of $x2$. The depth of cut is $y1c\text{-}y1$. Because of this, the current coordinates of edges 1,2,3,4 change to $(x1,y1)$, $(x2,y2)$, $(x3,y1)$ and $(x4,y1)$, respectively. It is seen that the current coordinates for edges 1 and 2 are equal to the final coordinates (step 2). When this condition is satisfied, the machining of that portion of the surface is considered to be complete. To start the next machining operation, the current coordinates of the edges are updated and the process logic is repeated. Note that numerically, $y1c=y2c=y3c=y4c$, $y1=y2$, $y3=y4$, and $x2=x3$. The logic used for determining the operation sequence is given below.

(1). Find the maximum diameter of the part and determine the raw material diameter.

(2). Find the length of the part and suggest the required raw material length so that the part can be held in chuck while machining without affecting the actual part surface.

(3). Locate the center line and find the intersection point of the center line and the first external surface. That will be the starting point or reference point of machining.

(4). If the surface is horizontal and the operation is turning, then try to maximize the length of the material that can be removed in one pass.

(5). Threading, knurling, and so on are differentiated by the entity colors in PROCESS-PLUS. The colors are used for determining the operations.

(6). Before threading or knurling the part must be turned to a specific diameter.

(7). If the line is vertical, then there is a step involved.

(8). If the surface sequence is vertical downwards, horizontal and vertical upwards, then the operation can be turning, forming, or grooving depending on the width of the step.

(9). After completing the external operations, start internal operations.

(10). If the line is horizontal and dotted, then use drilling and try to maximize the length of the drilling cut.

(11). At the end of the process, perform any required parting operation at the required length.

After the part information is arranged in the required format and the sequence of operations is determined, there should be a way to store this information so that it can be interfaced with the knowledge base. The work space, which is the final data base file, stores the partial results obtained in the process planning. This information is used to decide the optimum machining parameters.

THE KNOWLEDGE BASE Process planning is a complex task. The main difficulty in process planning is the enormous amount of specialized information that must be processed within a restricted time frame. The process planner must search through several possibilities and develop a feasible plan. Apart from handling a large amount of information on the process planning, the process planner must also have considerable knowledge about the tools available, the capability of the machines, and how precisely the operation can be carried out on the machine. In practice, the expert process planner uses knowledge gained over several years of experience to develop feasible and effective process plans. With expert systems, the knowledge of such experienced process planners can be captured and implemented as a tool for nonexperts.

KNOWLEDGE ACQUISITION FOR PROCESS-PLUS Knowledge acquisition is a potential bottleneck in the development of knowledge-based systems. For process planning expert systems, the knowledge engineer should have a good understanding of the available processes, underlying expertise, and the required operations. The knowledge acquisition for PROCESS-PLUS was based on the developers' own previous experience and published guides and handbooks. The important considerations relevant for the selection of a development shell for process planning expert systems include:

(1). Types and capabilities of existing software in the process environment.

(2). Mode of knowledge acquisition: direct, indirect, manual, or automatic.

(3). Knowledge and data representation models most suitable for the problem domain (e.g., rules, examples, semantic networks).

(4). Final implementation constraints (e.g., hardware limitations, budget constraints).

(5). Required level of interface with external files and programs.

(6). The scope of the application of the expert system.

(7). Maintenance requirements for the expert system.

(8). Availability of experts to supervise knowledge update.

(9). Reasoning approach (e.g., forward chaining, backward chaining).

The VP-Expert development shell was chosen for PROCESS-PLUS because of its ease of use for rapid prototyping, reasonable cost, and accessibility of operating environment. In practice, a process planner first looks at the final part drawing and thinks of the methods and operations required to achieve the final form from the raw material stage. So, he goes back from the final drawing to the raw material. This is called backward chaining in expert system terminology. VP-Expert supports backward chaining. The VP-Expert knowledge base consists of three basic elements: Actions block, Rules, and Statements.

The ACTIONS block:
This defines the goals of the consultation and the sequence of their solution. In other words, the ACTIONS block tells the inference engine what it needs to find and in what order. This is accomplished with FIND clauses that instruct VP-Expert to find the value or values of one or more "goal variables." The goals are found in an order in which they are written in the ACTIONS block. The ACTIONS block also contains the clauses to get the data from the data base. An example of a part of the ACTIONS block in PROCESS-PLUS is shown below:

```
ACTIONS
    get all,c:\dbase\meter,all
    find material
    find tool
    find coolant;
```

The first statement "ACTIONS" represents the start of the ACTIONS block. The GET statement gets all the fields from the data base file named "meter" which is located in the directory called dBASE. The next three FIND statements contain the goals. Material is found first, then the tool, and finally the coolant.

RULES   IF-THEN rules convey the "knowledge" or "expertise" contained in the knowledge base. Each rule indicates that if a certain condition occurs, then a certain action should be taken. It can also represent the linkage of evidence and hypothesis. The use of IF-THEN rules has several advantages.

(1). The ease of acquiring knowledge from the expert because the IF-THEN format is similar to the way humans think.

(2). The ease of linking one rule inference to other rule inferences through the use of metarules.

(3). The ease of implementing backward reasoning.

(4). The expressibility of situation-action statements.

(5). The modularity of knowledge representation.

(6). The ease of maintenance and modification.

(7). The understandability of the knowledge represented.

An example of a rule in PROCESS-PLUS is presented below:

```
rule k
if operl = knurling
then tool = knurling_tool;
```

STATEMENTS   The statements such as ASK and CHOICES are used to present menu options or prompts to the user. An example of an ASK statement is:
     ASK material: "What is the raw material for the part?";
With this statement, the prompt "What is the raw material for the part?" is displayed on the screen for the user to respond to.

KNOWLEDGE BASE VERIFICATION AND VALIDATION   Verification involves the determination of whether or not a system is functioning as intended. This may involve program debugging, error analysis, input acceptance, output generation, reasonableness of operation, run time control, and problem scoping. Verification, in effect, ensures that an expert system does not contain technical errors. Validation concerns a diagnosis of how closely the expert system's solution matches a human expert's solution. Validation ensures that the system does not contain logic errors. If an expert system is valid, then the conclusions or recommendations it offers can substitute for those of a human expert. The cost savings associated with implementing the system may also be directly evaluated. The validation of PROCESS-PLUS was done by using different problem scenarios to simulate consultation sessions. Those who served as the domain experts during the system development played a very active role in the validation process. The three stages of PROCESS-PLUS (AUTOCAD module, dBASE III-PLUS module, and the VP-Expert module) were validated both independently during development as well as collectively after completing the development. Different part drawings were given and the answers provided by PROCESS-PLUS were checked with the answers of the domain experts. Iterative modifications of the system were undertaken until the final answers of the system matched the experts' answers to an acceptable level of confidence.

SAMPLE OUTPUT   A partial sample output of PROCESS-PLUS is presented below. The part represented by the process plan is shown in Figure 12.5.

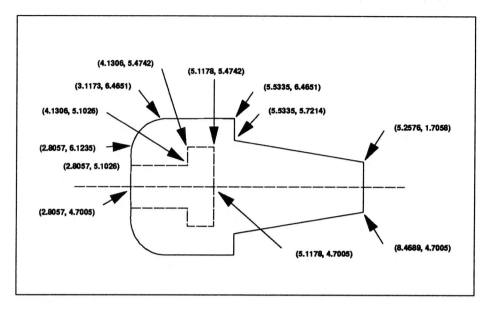

Figure 12.5. Sample input part drawing

General Information:

Part Name: CONNECTOR

Material: Free cutting steel (Diameter = 6.9634 inches; Length = 8.4689 inches)

For all operations except internal operations, hold one end of job in lathe head stock chuck and hold the other end of job in lathe tailstock.

Use countersunk drill for holding job in lathe tailstock.

STEP 1:

Operation:	Facing
Tool:	Parting tool
Tool material:	Carbide
Facing from:	x=2.8057, y=4.7005
To:	x=2.8057, y=6.1235
Coolant:	Water miscible dry

STEP 2:

Operation:	Filleting
Tool:	Form tool
Tool material:	Carbide
From:	2=2.8057, y=6.1235
To:	x=3.1173, y=6.4351
Coolant:	Water miscible dry

STEP 3:

Operation:	Turning
Tool:	Single point
Tool material:	Carbide
Total depth of cut	0.500
Rough cut:	0.25
Number of rough passes:	2
Speed:	350 to 450 rpm
Feed:	0.060 to 0.10 ipm
Coolant:	Water miscible dry
From:	x=5.5335, y=5.7214
To:	x=8.489, y=5.2576

.   .
.   .
.   .

STEP 8:

Operation:	Parting
Tool:	Parting tool
Tool material:	Carbide
From:	x=8.4689, y=4.7005
Coolant:	Water miscible dry

Another example of a complete process plan generated by PROCESS-PLUS is presented below:

INSTRUCTIONS

part name: testpart.1

1) Take the raw material with
Diameter = 7.5248 inches
Length = 9.6741 inches

2) Hold the job in the lathe head stock chuck

3) Hold the second part of the job in the lathe
tail stock for all operations except the
internal operations

4) For holding the job in the tail stock
use counter sunk drill

STEP 1

The operation is:	FACING
The tool is:	parting_tool
The tool material is:	carbide
FACING from:	x=8.1779,y=6.0797
to:	x= 9.6741, y=6.0797
The coolant to be used is:	water_miscible_dry

STEP 2

The operation is:	TAPERTURNING.
the tool is:	single_point
The tool material is:	carbide
The total depth of cut is:	1.4451
The rough cut is:	0.481700

The # of rough passes are: 3
The speed is: 175_to_350
The feed is: 0.060_to_0.18
The coolant to be used is: water_miscible_dry
TAPERTURNING from: x=8.2037,y=6.9933
to: x=8.1779, y=6.0797

STEP 3

The operation is: TAPERTURNING.
The tool is: single_point
The tool material is: carbide
The total depth of cut is: 0.5315
The rough cut is: 0.265750
The # of rough passes are: 2
The speed is: 350_to_450
The feed is: 0.060_to_0.10
The coolant to be used is: water_miscible_dry
TAPERTURNING from: x=4.4630,y=7.0248
to: x=8.2295, y=6.9933

STEP 4

The operation is: DRILLING
The tool is: twist_drill
The tool material is: HSS
The tool geometry:
Point angle: 125
Lip clearance angle: 10_12
Chisel point angle: 125_135
Helix angle: 24_32
The lubricant to be used: Lard_or_soluble_oil
The speed(sfpm):   50
The feed(ipm):   0.01
DRILLING from: x= 0.0000,   y= 100.0000
to: x= 6.8106,   y= 100.0000

12.2 JUSTEX: AN EXPERT SYSTEM FOR THE JUSTIFICATION OF ADVANCED MANUFACTURING TECHNOLOGY

Advanced manufacturing technology (AMT) has become an indispensable component in today's factories, both from a technological and economical point of view. However, justifying this manufacturing technology is not an easy task. Today's industries are not willing to take the risk involved in the implementation of advanced manufacturing technology. One of the main reasons for this is that top management fails to consider the qualitative factors involved in the justification process. As a result of this a number of projects have been abandoned. The failure to implement advanced manufacturing technology is not due to engineering shortcomings but due to setbacks in the managerial attitudes and policies. The basic problem is that many of the advantages of these advanced manufacturing technologies do not lie in the cost areas but in the more nebulous "strategic" areas such as shorter lead times, simpler scheduling, and more consistent quality.

The main objective of this expert system effort (Sundaram and Badiru 1990) is to develop a knowledge-based system that could be used by top management, engineers, and relevant managerial personnel as an aid in the justification process. The expert system, developed by Deepak Sundaram, is named JUSTEX (justification expert). The expert system provides a synergistic approach in that it combines tactical, economic, and strategic methods in the justification process. JUSTEX combines these strategies and recommends one of the following concerning the proposed technology:

GO: Go ahead with the proposed technology.

DEFER: Defer the implementation of the proposed technology.

NOGO: Reject the proposed technology.

The knowledge base is structured in the form of production rules. Four different knowledge bases are linked to form JUSTEX. The knowledge required for the development of this expert system was obtained from industry experts, books, journals, and other sources.

ADVANCED MANUFACTURING TECHNOLOGY   Advanced manufacturing technology (AMT) is a very broad area, generally used to include any computer or automated technology. It encompasses a wide area of design, manufacturing, service, and even decision support systems. Advanced manufacturing technology can extend from the implementation of software for an organization to a sophisticated CIM or group technology installation. For the purpose of JUSTEX, advanced manufacturing technology has been classified as follows:

(1). Design venture

(2). Specialized manufacturing venture

(3). Miscellaneous ventures

Under each of these headings there are further subheadings which narrow down the types of advanced manufacturing technology. For example under Design venture the subheadings are CAD, CAE, SIMULATION, and NC/CAM/CAD. The categories under Specialized manufacturing venture are MATERIAL HANDLING, FMS and ROBOTICS. Lastly the categories under Miscellaneous ventures are TOTAL QUALITY CONTROL and GROUP TECHNOLOGY. The categories are illustrated in the decision flow diagram shown in Figure 12.6. The above categories do not form a comprehensive list of advanced manufacturing technologies. However, the above can serve as a list for a prototype implementation venture. Hence, we see that advanced manufacturing technology can be defined as a computer- based installation that integrates manufacturing, design, and business operations. The business operations can include purchasing, distribution, accounting, and inventory control. The ideal AMT installation will design and manufacture parts from the raw material stage to the finished product stage.

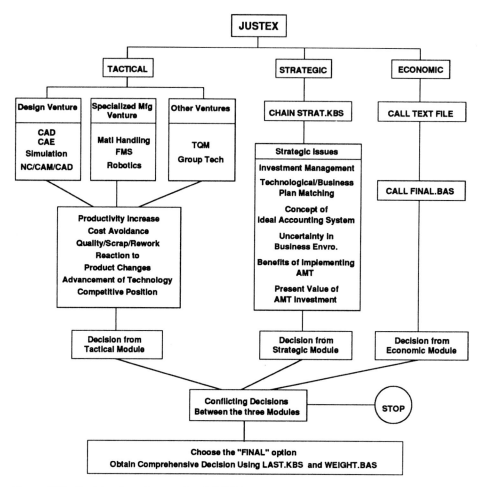

Figure 12.6. Decision flow diagram for JUSTEX

THE ROLE OF EXPERT SYSTEMS IN THE JUSTIFICATION PROCESS   The justification of AMT requires numerous disparate aspects of the investment opportunity to be considered. Long-term and short-term perspectives should be considered along with profitability, manufacturing flexibility, market uncertainty, and a wide array of qualitative factors. An expert system can serve as a valuable tool in combining these qualitative and quantitative factors and provide as an end result a justification methodology for AMT. The main role of the expert system is that it would offer the user more insight for capital investment decisions especially with strategic, nonquantifiable decision attributes that lend themselves well to heuristic analysis.

JUSTEX adopts a comprehensive approach to the justification problem and considers the total impact of factory automation on the organization itself. It also takes into account the interactions between the strategic components that play a vital role in the justification of any type of advanced manufacturing technology.

JUSTEX considers a tactical approach first. This enables the user to decide the specific areas or area of AMT that he is venturing into. The tactical approach is short term, but the decisions are based on the match between the company's objectives and the exact nature of the AMT venture. If these two do not match, then JUSTEX displays an appropriate decision on whether to implement AMT or not. The strategic approach is more long term in nature and takes into account several organizational aspects. The economical approach provides the quantitative aspects of the AMT investment. This approach will advise the user, from an economical standpoint, whether to go ahead with the implementation of AMT or not. The most important role of the expert system would be to combine the three different approaches so that a comprehensive decision is reached.

THE CHAINING AND REASONING STRATEGY IN JUSTEX   JUSTEX adopts a backward chaining strategy during the consultation process. Backward chaining is used to backtrack from a goal to the paths that lead to the goal. It is usually recommended when all outcomes are known and the number of possible outcomes are not large. The JUSTEX knowledge base consists of four separate knowledge bases linked together. In addition to this, the expert system has two BASIC programs that are linked from within the VP-Expert shell. Let us now consider the different modules in detail.

THE TACTICAL MODULE   The tactical module of JUSTEX has about 200 rules. The reasoning strategy is backward chaining. In this module of JUSTEX, AMT is classified as follows:

(1). Design venture

(2). Specialized manufacturing venture

(3). Miscellaneous applications

Under each of these subheadings there are other classifications that are listed below. Under Design venture the classifications are CAD, CAE, simulation and NC/CAM/CAD. This classification of design ventures is a fairly comprehensive classification and covers almost all possible design ventures.

The specialized manufacturing venture option is further classified into FMS, Material handling and Robotics. This classification however can be made more comprehensive in that there are other ventures that can fall into this category. However, the problems encountered as a result of memory restricted the classification to three. The miscellaneous applications were further classified into total quality control and group technology.

THE STRATEGIC MODULE   The strategic module consists of six issues that are vital to any growing organization. The strategic module also adopts a backward chaining strategy and is linked to the tactical module using the *chain* clause. The six issues are listed as follows:

(1). Effective management of hightech investment options.

(2). Match between the technological and business plans.

(3). Ideal accounting system.

(4). Uncertainty involved in the industrial environment.

(5). Benefits arising as a result of the implementation.

(6). Present worth of the investment.

The first issue is the effective management of high-tech investment options. Many strategic investment decisions can be postponed for a year or more, and under such circumstances the decision maker is afforded the time to resolve the uncertainty before making a commitment.

The second issue addressed in this expert system is the match between the technological and business plans. The long-range business plan must be consistent with the firm's technological resources. To have good investment alternatives the firm's technological and business portfolio must be integrated into the company's business policies.

The third issue considered in the strategic module is the concept of an ideal accounting system. Companies seeking to compete effectively must devise cost accounting systems that reflect their investment decisions and cost structures. Internal accounting practices should be guided by corporate strategies.

The fourth issue addressed in the strategic module is the uncertainty involved in the industrial environment. For the purpose of this paper, uncertainty reflects the subjectively assessed profitability of a proposed investment.

The fifth issue concerns the benefits arising as a result of the implementation. This issue attempts to capture the key benefits of AMT.

The sixth issue addressed in the strategic module is the present worth of the investment. This aspect of the justification process involves numbers; it has been added to combine monetary and nonmonetary aspects of the justification process. The DCF (discounted cash flow) method has been adopted to justify the venture economically, as this is the most commonly used economic justification tool.

THE ECONOMIC MODULE   In this module the DCF method was adopted as the justification tool. The DCF method presents a more pragmatic approach to the justification problem. It takes into account the time value of money and other factors such as inflation. The model used, is shown below.

$$PW = \sum_{j=0}^{N} P_j$$

$$PW = \sum_{j=0}^{N} C_j \left(\frac{1}{1+i}\right)^j$$

$$= \sum_{j=0}^{N} C'_j \left(\frac{1}{1+\theta}\right)^j \left(\frac{1}{1+i}\right)^j$$

$$= I + \sum_{j=1}^{j=N} S(1+k_1)^j + M(1+k_2)^j \left(\frac{1}{1+\theta}\right)^j \left(\frac{1}{1+i}\right)^j$$

where
I = Initial cash flow
S = Annual savings in present dollars
M = Annual cash flow due to O&M in present dollars
k_1 = Annual rate of increase in the relative value of annual savings due to price differentials
k_2 = Annual rate of increase in the relative cost of O&M due to price differentials
θ = Annual rate of general inflation
i = Inflation free discount rate (interest rate)
C'_j = Cash flow in period j in current (then) dollars
C_j = Equivalent cash flow in period j in present dollars
P_j = Present value of the amount located at period j
N = Number of periods

In the method mentioned above, the savings were classified as direct and indirect. The program starts with a display of selected text files, which gives the user an introduction to the system and its capabilities. The first step in the justification process is the tactical approach. In this module the user decides the exact nature and type of investment that he is venturing into. On the basis of user input, a decision is reached, depending on the match between the type of investment and the reasons for selecting that particular type of investment. The user then proceeds with the strategic module. Here, the user is presented with six issues vital to the justification process. Depending on the user's response to the six issues, the expert system provides a decision from a strategic standpoint.

The economic module was written in BASIC and is run from within the VP-Expert shell. This module deals with the monetary aspects of the investment. The user is asked to input numerical values for the capital, amount of savings, the inflation rate, and so on. The decision that results from this module is also generated from within the VP-Expert shell. The final knowledge base used in JUSTEX enables the user to arrive at a comprehensive decision when there are conflicting decisions from the three modules. This knowledge base also invokes a BASIC program from within the VP-Expert environment. Selected screen displays during JUSTEX consultation are presented in Figures 12–7 through 12–11.

12.3 RESISTOR: AN EXPERT SYSTEM
FOR RESISTOR CALCULATIONS

There is a large variety of resistors used in electronic devices such as computers and sophisticated machinery. An expert system was developed by Casey McDonough, Kirk Moore, Todd Howery, and Colin Doyle to help identify the numerous resistors that may be encountered in an electronic component. Resistors

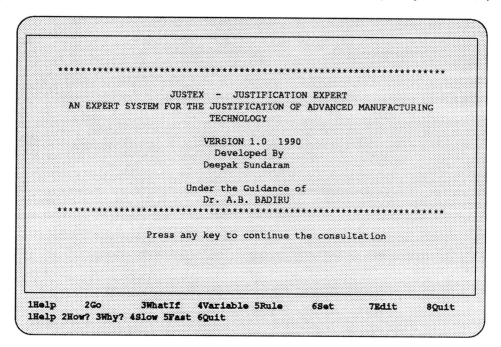

Figure 12.7. Introductory screen for JUSTEX

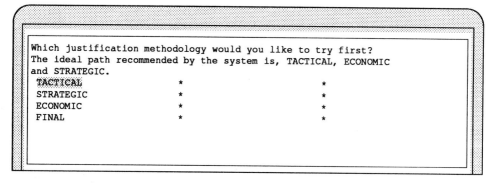

Figure 12.8. JUSTEX consultation screen

are identified by color coding. The tiny resistors have four color stripes on them and they are arranged in a specific order so that the resistance can be calculated. Ten colors are used in the coding. These ten colors can show up in any combination on the first three stripes and the fourth stripe determines the quality of the resistor. Each color has a corresponding numerical value so that when a black-green-yellow-silver combination occurs, the resistor will have a specific value. There are approximately 2000 different combinations. So, finding the values of resistors is a complex task. The expert system, named RESISTOR, was developed with VP-Expert.

```
Specialized Mfg            *                      *
Misc Applications          *                      *

  The following list shows some of the possible ventures. Please
  select the most appropriate application that best fits your
  choice.
CAD                        *                      *
CAE                        *                      *
Simulation                 *                      *
NC\CAM\CAD                 *                      *
```

Figure 12.9. JUSTEX consultation screen

```
The following list shows some of the areas which have scope for
improvement. Please identify the areas where you seek improvement
or change. Limit your choices to TWO (2). Press <End> after confirming
selection.
 Production Increase       *                      *
 Cost Avoidance            *                      *
 Quality Scrap Rework      *                      *
 React to Prod Change      *                      *
 Advancement of Tech       *                      *
 Competitive Position      *                      *
```

Figure 12.10. JUSTEX consultation screen

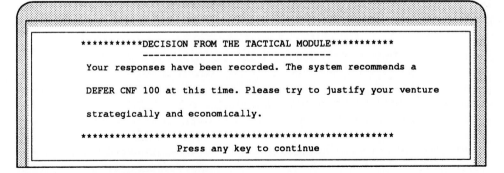

```
     **********DECISION FROM THE TACTICAL MODULE**********
     ---------------------------------
     Your responses have been recorded. The system recommends a

     DEFER CNF 100 at this time. Please try to justify your venture

     strategically and economically.

     ********************************************************
                     Press any key to continue
```

Figure 12.11. JUSTEX conclusion screen

INPUT REQUIREMENT   The user simply follows the instructions presented online and picks the corresponding color of the resistor to be identified. The expert system will show a sample resistor and label the color stripes one through four so that the user can give the desired information in the right order.

OUTPUT   The output of the program will generate a picture of the resistor with the user's color combination on it. It will then give the appropriate value of the resistor with proper tolerances. The system requires a color monitor and a video card capable of differentiating 16 colors. If a color monitor is not available, the system will calculate the resistor value without displaying a picture of the final resistor color code.

DESIGN METHODOLOGY   VP-Expert has good graphics capability that can be used to illustrate the color bands of a resistor. A BASIC program was written to perform the computations for the resistance value. Inputs from the user are shipped to an external text file. VP-Expert executes a batch file which runs the BASIC program. The batch file also stores the new values of the resistors to another text file. This text file is then used to display the current resistor picture.

IF-THEN rules are used to translate the input colors into their corresponding values and VP-Expert color codes. The first eleven rules of the knowledge base are used to set the resistor values that are shipped to the text files. The remaining rules find the color values of the four bands and fills the relevant bands with appropriate colors. This was done because a color value cannot be set to a variable name in graphics mode.

INTERFACE WITH OTHER ENGINEERING SYSTEMS   The simple task of identification performed by RESISTOR becomes very important when the expert system is interfaced with other engineering systems. For example, the system has been interfaced with an automated Circuit Design and Analysis program in a real-time mode.

12.4 ROBEX: AN EXPERT SYSTEM FOR MANUFACTURING ROBOT SYSTEM IMPLEMENTATION

Robotics is a branch of AI that has been very widely applied and is one of the more popular routes to automation. Though largely an American invention, robots are not as prevalent in American industry as they are abroad. This is mainly due to poor implementation strategies. Many companies have been reluctant to make the necessary investment, particularly when faced with surplus capacity and labor and there is no pressure to hold down prices. However, increased competition in many industries previously believed to be protected against foreign encroachment has led to more aggressive pursuit of robotics. Over the past few years, robotics has been embraced in many phases of manufacturing. The discouraging results in many instances are caused by improper planning and misplaced implementations in the wrong processes. Many people think that robots can do everything, but that is not true. A careful analysis of what robots can do or cannot do is essential.

An expert system, named ROBEX (Robot Expert), has been developed to serve as a consultant to manufacturing engineers concerning the planning and implementation of robots (Sunku and Badiru 1990). The system was developed with the VP-Expert inference engine. ROBEX was developed as an extension of ROBCON (Robot Consultant) developed by Neetin Datar (1989). ROBCON, developed with Texas Instrument's Personal Consultant Plus inference engine, deals with robots as an individual item and not as a system. ROBEX goes further than ROBCON by finding out whether there is an environment suitable for implementing robots, developing a comprehensive specification sheet, and developing a system implementation schedule. It also conducts a system safety review. Ralph Heinze, a manufacturing automation manager at Seagate Corporation in Oklahoma City, served as the primary domain expert for both ROBCON and ROBEX.

DESIGN STRUCTURE   ROBEX consists of 15 knowledge bases chained together to facilitate the sequential execution of the consultation without exiting the system. It contains 521 rules and 369 variables which can be instantiated with 989 different values. The rules are written in ARL (Abbreviated Rule Language) and they are executed in a backward chaining search process. Outputs can be generated to the screen or directly to a printer. Figure 12.12 shows the personnel, hardware, and software organization for the development and implementation of ROBEX. Figure 12.13 shows an example of a ROBEX consultation interaction. The knowledge bases are chained in the same sequence of tasks that would constitute any robot system implementation project.

The overall capabilities of ROBEX are summarized as follows:

Figure 12.12. Development and implementation of ROBEX

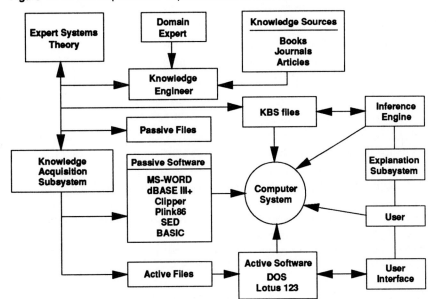

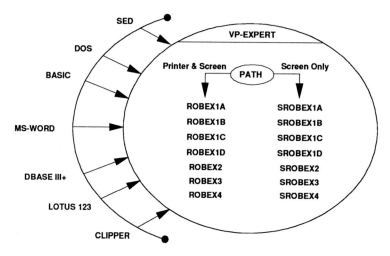

Figure 12.13. Consultation interface for ROBEX

- It evaluates the manufacturing environment (users, processes, management, etc.) for its suitability for potential robot applications.
- It develops a *work station information* sheet that can be used to survey the plant to identify potential application areas.
- It reviews the robot system concept design and provides recommendations.
- It develops an *application information sheet* that contains information about general description, unique considerations, and justification.
- It aids the user in the development of a *robot system specification sheet* that can be used to get quotations from vendors.
- It provides guidance on some of the required preimplementation tasks.
- It generates an *implementation involvement sheet* that can help a user determine the type of involvement needed from each member of the implementation team.
- It helps the user in the development of a *robot implementation schedule.*
- It reviews the robot system safety measures and provides recommendations to ensure the safe operation of a robot system.

ROBEX was validated by an industry expert. It has been found to aid engineers in learning more about the capabilities of robots. Future enhancements to the system include the addition of an economic module to perform economic analysis based on the contents of the specification sheet, the provision of an interface to a CAD system in order to conduct a robot work area design, and the inclusion of Gantt chart for the implementation process as a part of the expert system output.

12.5 BALA: BICYCLE ASSEMBLY LINE ADVISOR

BALA is an expert system developed to manage bicycle assembly operations. The system was developed by Khek Cuon Yong and executed in VP-Expert. The system serves two main functions. The first function is to educate new operators about the procedures involved in the assembly of a bicycle. The tools required for specific operations and the relevant safety aspects are addressed by the system. The second function of the system is to enable design engineers to perform economic analysis so as to determine the value-added measure associated with each operation involved in the complete design of a bicycle. The value-added measure is the value added to a complete bicycle by a specific operation in the assembly process. The minimum requirements and specifications for BALA are:

A. System Output Requirements:
   1. Cost of each operation
   2. Total cost of producing a bicycle
   3. Total value-added for a bicycle

B. User Interface Requirements:
   1. Delete or add specific operations
   2. Change specific operation costs

C. Text files:
   Whenever the system is activated, user instructions and system descriptions appear on the screen. Both the instructions and descriptions are read from text files.

D. Data Base File:
   A data base file contains such information as operations, description of tools, and related safety considerations.

E. Lotus 1-2-3 File:
   A spreadsheet file was designed to provide such information as cost of an operation and total assembly cost.

F. VP-Expert Control:
   VP-Expert serves as the main controller for the consultation process. During consultation, a user is able to read information from the data base and spreadsheet files.

   METHODOLOGY   The knowledge base starts with a routine that creates a set of arrays with names that correspond to the actual position of the work cells in a worksheet. This is done by reading columns of a special worksheet that has each individual cell filled with a name label that corresponds to its location in the worksheet as illustrated in Figure 12.14.

   After the creation of the arrays shown in Figure 12.14, BALA can reference any cell, column, or row in a worksheet directly by using the array with a suitable index. The motivation for using an index counter to reference a row in the worksheet is that a row can be referenced directly without the need to search for it

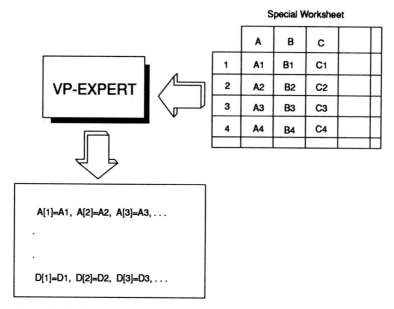

Figure 12.14. Special worksheet design for BALA

in the worksheet, and hence, reduces the disk access time. In addition, the counter makes the function of deleting, adding, and updating information in the worksheet much easier. An example of referencing rows in a worksheet through use of an index counter is presented below:

```
FOR INDEX = 1 TO number-of-operation
    WKS OPERATION, @A[INDEX] .. @D[INDEX], WORKSHT
    DISPLAY "LINE NUMBER  := {OPERATION[1]}"
    DISPLAY "NAME     := {OPERATION[2]}"
    DISPLAY "COST     := {OPERATION[3]}"
    DISPLAY "ESTIMATED VALUE  := {OPERATION[4]}"
END
```

Both the user's instructions and system descriptions are displayed from a text file named INITSCRN.TXT. After the user has read the instructions, he is required to select either to perform an economic analysis on an assembly line, or to get to know more about the procedures involved in an assembly line. He or she is then required to pick an assembly line from one of the three assembly lines namely: the Head, the Body, and the Tail assembly lines. The flow of options is shown in Figure 12.15.

INFORMATION MODE In the information mode, the user will first see a description of the selected assembly line. The information on the assembly line is displayed from a text file. The user can then pick one operation from the list of operations in the assembly line in order to learn more about any one of the procedures. The user is prompted to select one of the tools used in the operation. The

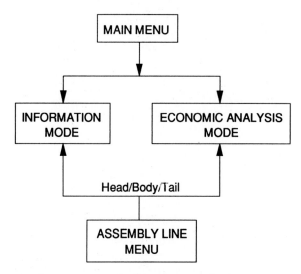

Figure 12.15. BALA consultation menu options

system will conclude the session by showing the safety precautions pertaining to the use of the tool selected by the user. Figure 12.16 shows the file interfaces in the information mode.

   ECONOMIC ANALYSIS MODE   In the economic mode, the user is presented with four major options: Display operation cost, Add operation, Delete operation, and Edit operation. The specific options are described as follows.

Figure 12.16. File interfaces in information mode for BALA

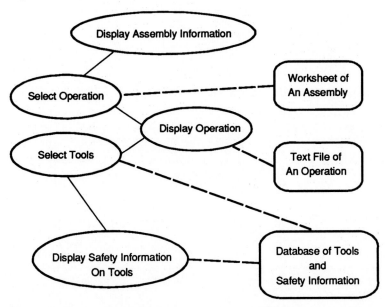

```
Select an Assembly of your interest..
Head ◄                    Body                    Tail

Select an Option which you want to perform..
Economic Analysis        Display Information
```

Figure 12.17. Screen display for BALA consultation

Display operation cost: This option shows the operation name together with the corresponding operation cost and estimated value. The user will see the total cost and the value-added measure of the assembly line.

Add operation: This option allows the user to add an operation to the existing list of operations in the assembly line. The user is required to specify the name, the cost, the estimated value, and the relative position of the operation to be added. The system will then add this operation to the existing list. It will recalculate the total cost and value added measure of the assembly line.

Delete operation: This option allows the user to delete an operation from the existing list of operations in the assembly process. After the user has specified which operation to delete, BALA will delete the operation and recalculate the total cost and the value added measure for total assembly.

Figure 12.18. Screen display for BALA consultation

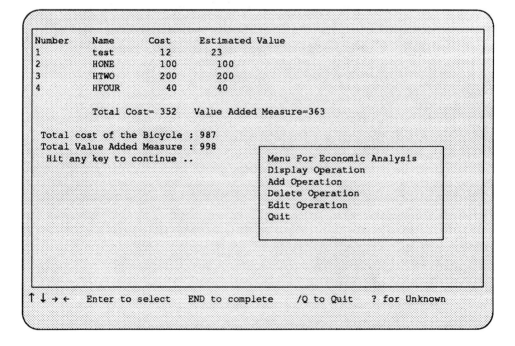

```
Number     Name      Cost      Estimated Value
1          test      12        23
2          HONE      100       100
3          HTWO      200       200
4          HFOUR     40        40

           Total Cost= 352   Value Added Measure=363

 Total cost of the Bicycle : 987
 Total Value Added Measure : 998
  Hit any key to continue ..          ┌─────────────────────────────┐
                                       │ Menu For Economic Analysis  │
                                       │ Display Operation           │
                                       │ Add Operation               │
                                       │ Delete Operation            │
                                       │ Edit Operation              │
                                       │ Quit                        │
                                       └─────────────────────────────┘


 ↑ ↓ → ←   Enter to select   END to complete   /Q to Quit   ? for Unknown
```

Edit operation: This option allows the user to update information concerning specific operations. The user is presented the existing information for the operation. Prompts are then used to ask the user for the desired changes. The information that can be edited includes the operation name, cost, and estimated value added.

Samples of screen displays during a BALA consultation are presented in Figure 12.17 and Figure 12.18. A listing of the complete knowledge base for BALA is presented in Appendix F.

12.6 TRANSPERT: EXPERT SYSTEM FOR SELECTING PROPER TRANSFORMER FOR A BUILDING COMPLEX

Establishing and maintaining any facility, residential, commercial, or industrial, requires electrical power. The incoming electrical power from the source in almost all the cases does not match the voltage requirements of the equipment contained in the target facilities. In order to run this equipment, one needs a device which can step down the incoming high electrical voltage to a desired low voltage. This device is known as a transformer. A transformer is an essential component of the supply of electrical power to any facility. There are various kinds of transformers to suit specific requirements. Thus, the selection of a proper transformer to meet particular needs is vital. The selection often requires some background in electrical engineering or a consultation with a professional, both of which are time consuming and cost oriented.

To aid the transformer selection process, an expert system was developed. The system, named TRANSPERT, was developed with VP-Expert by a team consisting of Biswas Bhismadeva, Katti Ranganath, Rao Viswanatha, and Samanta Shantanu. TRANSPERT selects the proper size of a distribution transformer to feed an electrical power supply (1/3 Phase) to a building complex. It also gives an estimate of the annual energy cost resulting from the installation of the particular transformer recommended. A variable tariff rate of 5.5 cents per kilowatt-hour of energy consumption is assumed for the cost analysis. The system was developed in conformity with the National Electrical Code (USA) and the guidelines of the American Society of Refrigeration and Air Conditioning Engineers (ASHRAE).

The selection of a transformer by TRANSPERT is limited to distribution type used to step down incoming voltage and feed a facility. It can handle both single and three phase loads. TRANSPERT cannot be used to select power transformers for transmitting power. The size of transformer is expressed in kilo-volt-amps (KVA). The maximum size of transformer that can be handled by TRANSPERT is 10,000 KVA, applicable for a distribution transformer. Typical questions asked by TRANSPERT during a consultation include:

(1). Total floor space (including floor levels):
   - Ceiling height is set at 9 feet.
   - Lighting load of 2 watts per square feet is assumed (American National Code).

(2). Central air conditioning or window air conditioning units:
   If window air conditioning is specified, the user will need to provide the area
   to be covered by the unit. In the case of central air conditioning, the total
   floor area of the building is assumed. On the basis of this information, watts
   consumption per square feet recommended by American Society of Heating,
   Refrigeration and Air Conditioning Engineers is calculated.

(3). Total wattage of installed equipment.

In case exhaust fans are contemplated, the program asks the user to provide
the floor area for which exhaust fans are required. Watts per square feet required
for exhaust is assumed (value chosen from ASHRAE) and total wattage is computed. Elevators are classified on the basis of passenger carrying–capacity of zero
to 12 and zero to 24. Different wattages are calculated for each type depending
upon the user requirement. Since all the types of loads specified for a facility will
not be in operation at the same time or around the clock, a load factor of 60% is
used by TRANSPERT to rate the calculated wattage. The transformer size is selected based on the rated wattage. The type of transformer cooling is also recommended depending upon the size of the transformer (KVA rating). TRANSPERT
can also calculate the floor space required to install the recommended transformer if the user chooses to install it indoors.

In order to calculate the energy cost, the user has to provide the number of
working days per year. The cost of one kilowatt hour of energy is assumed to be
5.5 cents. The energy cost in dollars is computed as:

Cost = KWH*(Diversity Factor)*(Working Days)*(Hours Per Day)*($/KWH).

Abbreviated portions of the knowledge base for TRANSPERT are presented
below:

```
BKCOLOR=1;
RUNTIME;
ENDOFF;
ACTIONS
   COLOR=4
   WOPEN 1,2,2,19,75,2
   WOPEN 2,4,6,15,66,5
   WOPEN 3,6,11,11,56,6
   WOPEN 4,8,16,7,46,7
   ACTIVE 4
   DISPLAY "


   T  R  A  N  S  P  E  R  T


~"
   WCLOSE 1
   WCLOSE 2
   WCLOSE 3
```

```
WCLOSE 4
COLOR=15
WOPEN 5,2,6,18,66,4
ACTIVE 5
DISPLAY "
WELCOME TO T  R  A  N  S  P  E  R  T - AN EXPERT SYSTEM
DESIGNED TO SELECT PROPER SIZE OF A DISTRIBUTION
TRANSFORMER FOR A COMPLEX.
TRANSPERT IS DEVELOPED BY:
        SAMANTA SHANTANU
        RAO VISWANATHA
        KATTI RANGANATH
        BISWAS BHISMADEVA
TRANSPERT IS PRESENTED TO:
        DR. A. B. BADIRU
        (PRESS ANY KEY TO BEGIN CONSULTATION)~"
WCLOSE 5
WOPEN 6,2,6,19,66,5
ACTIVE 6
CLS
DISPLAY "
        T_R_A_N_S_P_E_R_T
TRANSPERT HAS BEEN DEVELOPED IN CONFORMITY WITH NATIONAL
ELECTRICAL CODE (USA) AND THE AMERICAN SOCIETY OF
REFRIGERATION AND AIR CONDITIONING ENGINEERS.
TRANSPERT SELECTS THE PROPER SIZE OF A DISTRIBUTION
TRANSFORMER TO FEED ELECTRICAL POWER SUPPLY (1/3 PHASE)
TO A COMPLEX. COMPLEX IN THIS CASE CAN BE A GROUP OF
BUILDINGS TO SERVE EDUCATIONAL, RECREATIONAL, OR ANY
INDUSTRIAL ESTABLISHMENTS. THE SIZE OF TRANSFORMER IS
EXPRESSED IN ELECTRICAL POWER RATING KILO-VOLT-AMPS.
THE APPLICATION OF THIS SYSTEM IS LIMITED BY :
(1) DISTRIBUTION TRANSFORMER OF SIZE LESS THAN OR EQUAL
    TO 10000 KILO VOLTS-AMPS.
(2) TYPE OF USAGE (DISTRIBUTION OF POWER AND NOT FOR
    TRANSMISSION).
        (PRESS ANY KEY TO CONTINUE)~"
WCLOSE 6
CLS
COLOR=15
FIND LLOAD
FIND CALOAD
FIND WALOAD
FIND RHL
FIND WSL
.

.
FIND RECO
FIND COOL
FIND WD
FIND Z;
```

```
RULE 1
IF   TAREA>=0
THEN LLOAD=(TAREA*2.0/1000.0);
RULE 2
IF   C=CENTRL_AIR_CONDITIONING
THEN CALOAD=(TAREA*0.003);
RULE 3
IF   C=WINDOW_AIR_CONDITIONING_UNITS AND
     TAREAW>=0
THEN WALOAD=(TAREAW*12000.0/957600.0);
RULE 4
IF   RH >=0
THEN RHL=(RH*1);
RULE 5
IF   WS>=0
THEN WSL=(WS*2.0);
RULE 6
IF   DR>=0
THEN DRL=(DR*3.0);
RULE 7
IF   TV>=0
THEN TVL=(TV*0.5);
RULE 8
IF   VCR>=0
THEN VCRL=(VCR*0.4);
RULE 9
IF   RA>=0
THEN RAL=(RA*4.0);
RULE 10
IF   EF=YES AND
     TEXAREA>=0
THEN EFL=(TEXAREA*0.3);

     .
     .
     .
     .


RULE 55
IF   LOCA=INDOOR AND
     RECO>=750 OR
     RECO<=5000
THEN RS=20;
RULE 56
IF   LOCA=INDOOR AND
     RECO>=75000 OR
     RECO<=10000
THEN RS=25;
RULE 57
IF   LOCA=OUTDOOR
THEN RS=CASING;
```

RULE 58
IF   AEB=YES AND
     WD>=0
THEN EB=(TL*0.2*24.0*WD*0.05);
RULE 59
IF   AEB=NO
THEN WD=0;
RULE 60
IF   RECO<=1000
THEN COOL=OIL_COOLED;
RULE 61
IF   RECO>1000 OR
     RECO<10000
THEN COOL=FORCED_AIR_OR_OIL_COOLED;
RULE 62
IF   AEB=YES AND
     LOCA=INDOOR AND
     RECO<=10000
THEN Z=K
WOPEN 6,1,2,20,75,4
ACTIVE 6

DISPLAY "
* *
                              RECOMMENDATION

USE 3 PHASE , {RECO} KVA ,{PPV} V - 120/208 TRANSFORMER
THE TRANSFORMER SELECTED IS OF {RECO} KVA RATING.
ANNUAL ENERGY BILL IS $ {EB}.
TOTAL FLOOR AREA REQUIRED FOR THE ABOVE TRANSFORMER IS {RS} FEET BY {RS} FEET.
TYPE OF COOLING :{COOL}

                              END OF CONSULTATION
* *
~";
RULE 63
IF   AEB=YES AND
     LOCA=OUTDOOR AND
     RECO<=10000
THEN Z=K1
WOPEN 6,1,2,20,75,4
ACTIVE 6
DISPLAY "

* *
                              RECOMMENDATION

USE 3 PHASE, {RECO} KVA , {PPV} V -120/208 TRANSFORMER.
THE TRANSFORMER SELECTED IS OF {RECO} KVA RATING.
ANNUAL ENERGY BILL IS $ {EB}
THE ABOVE TRANSFORMER SHOULD BE ENCLOSED IN A WEATHERPROOF CASING.
TYPE OF COOLING : {COOL}

                          END OF CONSULTATION
* *~";
RULE 64
IF   AEB=NO AND
     LOCA=INDOOR AND
     RECO<=10000
THEN Z=K2
WOPEN 6,1,2,20,75,4
ACTIVE 6
DISPLAY "
* *
                          RECOMMENDATION

USE 3 PHASE , {RECO} KVA , {PPV} V -120/208 TRANSFORMER.
THE TRANSFORMER SELECTED IS OF {RECO} KVA RATING.
TOTAL FLOOR AREA REQUIRED FOR THE ABOVE TRANSFORMER IS {RS} FEET BY {RS} FEET.
TYPE OF COOLING : {COOL}

                          END OF CONSULTATION
* ~";
RULE 65
IF   AEB=NO AND
     LOCA=OUTDOOR AND
     RECO<=10000
THEN Z=K3
WOPEN 6,1,2,20,75,4
ACTIVE 6
DISPLAY "
* *
                          RECOMMENDATION

USE 3 PHASE , {RECO} KVA , {PPV} V -120/208 TRANSFORMER
THE TRANSFORMER SELECTED IS OF {RECO} KVA RATING.
TRANSFORMER SHOULD BE ENCLOSED IN WEATHERPROOF CASING.
TYPE OF COOLING : {COOL}.

END OF CONSULTATION

* *~";

RULE 66
IF RECO>10000
THEN Z=K5
DISPLAY "

* *

RECOMMENDATION

SORRY THIS EXPERT SYSTEM HAS TO BE UPDATED FOR KVA RATING OF MORE THAN 10000

END OF CONSULTATION

* ";

ASK TAREA:"

* *

START OF CONSULTATION

WHAT IS THE TOTAL FLOOR AREA OF THE BUILDING
(in square feet)?
";
ASK C: " WHAT TYPE OF AIR CONDITIONING DO YOU NEED ?
";
CHOICES C: CENTRL_AIR_CONDITIONING,WINDOW_AIR_CONDITIONING_UNITS;

ASK TAREAW: "
WHAT IS THE TOTAL FLOOR AREA IN THE BUILDING FOR WHICH
WINDOW AIR CONDITIONING UNITS ARE REQUIRED (in square feet) ?
";
ASK RH: "
WHAT IS THE TOTAL NUMBER OF ROOM HEATERS REQUIRED ?
";
ASK WS: " WHAT IS THE TOTAL NUMBER OF WASHING MACHINES REQUIRED ?
";
ASK DR: " WHAT IS THE TOTAL NUMBER OF DRYERS REQUIRED ?
";
ASK TV: " WHAT IS THE TOTAL NUMBER OF TELEVISIONS REQUIRED ?
";
ASK VCR: " WHAT IS THE TOTAL NUMBER OF VCR's REQUIRED ?
";
ASK RA: " WHAT IS THE TOTAL NUMBER OF COOKING RANGES REQUIRED ?
";
ASK EF: " ARE EXHAUST FANS REQUIRED ?
";
CHOICES EF: YES,NO;
ASK TEXAREA: " WHAT IS THE TOTAL FLOOR AREA IN THE BUILDING FOR
WHICH EXHAUST FANS ARE REQUIRED ?
";

ASK CM: " WHAT IS THE TOTAL NUMBER OF COFFEE MACHINES REQUIRED ?
";
ASK MW: " WHAT IS THE TOTAL NUMBER OF MICROWAVE OVENS REQUIRED ?
";
ASK WH: " WHAT IS THE TOTAL NUMBER OF WATER HEATERS REQUIRED ?
";
ASK OV: " WHAT IS THE TOTAL NUMBER OF OVENS REQUIRED ?
";
ASK VC: " WHAT IS THE TOTAL NUMBER OF VACUUM CLEANERS REQUIRED ?
";
ASK PC: " WHAT IS THE TOTAL NUMBER OF COMPUTER PC's REQUIRED ?
";
ASK PRD: " WHAT IS THE TOTAL NUMBER OF PRINTERS (DOT MATRIX) REQUIRED ?
";
ASK PRL: " WHAT IS THE TOTAL NUMBER OF PRINTERS (LASER) REQUIRED ?
";
ASK XOX: " WHAT IS THE TOTAL NUMBER OF PHOTOCOPY MACHINES REQUIRED ?
";
ASK SAC: " WHAT IS THE TOTAL NUMBER OF SMALL APPLIANCE CIRCUITS REQUIRED ?
";
ASK EL: " DOES THE BUILDING HAVE ELEVATORS ?
";
CHOICES EL: YES,NO;
ASK EL1: "
WHAT IS THE NUMBER OF ELEVATORS WITH CARRYING CAPACITY UP TO 12 ?
";
ASK EL2: " WHAT IS THE NUMBER OF ELEVATORS WITH CARRYING CAPACITY UP TO 24 ?
";
ASK OL: " ARE ANY OTHER LARGE LOADS GOING TO BE INSTALLED
IN THE BUILDING ?
";
CHOICES OL: YES,NO;
ASK OTL: " GIVE THE TOTAL LOAD IN KILOWATTS AS PROVIDED BY THE
MANUFACTURER.
";
ASK PV: " WHAT IS THE INCOMING SUPPLY VOLTAGE TO YOUR BUILDING ?
(IF NOT KNOWN, CONTACT THE ENERGY SUPPLY AGENCY.)
";
ASK AEB: "
DO YOU NEED TO KNOW THE EXPECTED ANNUAL ENERGY BILLS ?
";
CHOICES AEB: YES, NO;
ASK WD: " WHAT IS THE TOTAL ANNUAL WORKING DAYS ?
";
ASK LOCA: " WHERE WOULD YOU LIKE TO INSTALL THE TRANSFORMER ?
";
CHOICES LOCA: INDOOR,OUTDOOR;

12.7 OTHER SYSTEMS

Many other expert system case samples have been developed in the Expert Systems Laboratory in the School of Industrial Engineering, University of Oklahoma. Space limitation makes it impossible to present many of them in this book. A brief overview of other recent developments is presented below:

EHSS: Expert Heuristic Selection System for Project Scheduling (Khuzema 1988):

This is an expert system developed to help project managers select appropriate scheduling heuristics for different types of projects. A project network complexity criterion was used to categorize project types. Rule efficiency ratios are used to evaluate heuristic performance. The results of heuristic network analysis are utilized as expertise for the expert system.

XMEDIA: Multimedia Expert System for Design for Manufacturability (Nowland 1989):

This expert system uses a multimedia-based knowledge base to present design guidelines in a manufacturing environment. It is used as a training and a correspondence tool between design and manufacturing groups. The system incorporates images and textual knowledge. Standard textual information is presented to the user through a series of windows. Nontextual information (e.g., graphics) is used to present knowledge that cannot be clearly defined in words.

INFOGUIDE: An Expert System for Computer Automation Test Systems:

This expert system was developed to provide information regarding the setup and testing of circuit boards. The system was developed by Joel Haines and David Ruedy and installed at a local manufacturing plant.

FIRES-II: Fault Isolation and Repair using an Expert System:

This expert system was developed by Stan Reisman and John Lambert. It was designed for use in the fault diagnosis of highly integrated computer circuit boards in a high volume production facility.

ASRS: An Expert System for Automated Storage and Retrieval System:

This system was developed by Don Birdwell to serve as an aid in troubleshooting ASRS systems. ASRS provides a set of decision tools for operators and maintenance personnel. The benefits of the system include the following:

- Reducing the time for error diagnosis and correction.
- Providing on-line error and performance reports.
- Providing error history files.
- Providing on-line preventive maintenance scheduling.
- Documenting an engineer's knowledge about error correction.

- Reducing the learning curve for operators and maintenance personnel.
- Formalizing requests for crane maintenance.
- Improving communication between engineering, maintenance, and the shop.

PROJECT-SIMULATOR: An Expert System for Simulation Modeling of Project Networks (Dhanushkodi 1989):
This expert system was developed to aid a user in constructing SLAM simulation models of project networks. The user interacts with the system in two stages. In the first stage, the user draws the network using the customized menu available in AUTOCAD. As the user draws the network, the network structure is extracted. In the second stage, the user interacts with an external program to edit activity durations and to add or edit resource information.

LOCATOR: Trouble Locating Expert System for 3B2 Peripheral Modules:
This expert system was developed by Dan Foresee as a diagnostic tool for 3B2 computer and its associated peripherals. The system helps in reducing confusion associated with troubleshooting. It also minimizes troubleshooting time by reducing wrong guesses.

GRINDALL: An Expert System for Grinding Wheel Selection:
This expert system was developed by Anjan Kumar Bellur and S. Somasundaram. It is a rule-based system for selecting the correct grinding wheel and process parameters for a given work material and desired accuracy.

APPENDIX A

Introduction to VP-Expert

VP-Expert is one of the first low-cost PC-based expert system tools offered by a major software company, Paperback Software International of Berkeley, California. The rule-based program is easy to use and relatively inexpensive. The student version of the program is offered at a price that fits the budget of most college students. The considerate pricing of the student version has helped to make the program one of the most dominant expert systems tools on college campuses.

VP-Expert has good interface capabilities to external programs such as spreadsheets, data bases, DOS executable (.EXE) programs, batch (.BAT) files, and DOS command (.COM) files. The program also has built-in graphics capability and hypertext structure. The program uses a combination of backward chaining and forward chaining search strategy.

The user's guide that comes with VP-Expert is straightforward with numerous examples for the beginner. The purpose of the introduction in this Appendix is not to provide a comprehensive user's guide to VP-Expert, but rather to highlight some of the basic features of the program. Readers interested in third-party guides to VP-Expert should consult the following references:

Friederich, Sylvia and Michael Gargano, *Expert Systems Design and Development Using VP-Expert,* John Wiley, New York, 1989.

Wang, Wally and John Mueller, *Illustrated VP-Expert,* Wordware Publishing, Inc., Plano, TX, 1989.

Hicks, Richard and Ronald Lee, *VP-Expert for Business Applications,* Holden-Day, Inc., Oakland, CA, 1988.

VP—EXPERT CONSULTATION   The user interface for VP-Expert is very simple. The steps below show the procedure for running a sample consultation with VP-Expert. It is assumed that VP-Expert has been successfully installed on your computer and that sample knowledge bases exist for running the example shown here.

(1). Type VPX and press ⏎ to start the program. The startup screen shown in Figure A.1 will appear. You may select an option from any VP-Expert Command Menu in any of the four ways below:

- Type the first letter of the command.
- Type the command number.
- Type the function key listed for the command.
- Move cursor to the command and press Enter.

(2). Select PATH by pressing F7, 7, or P to specify the directory path where the desired knowledge base for the consultation is located. Figure A.2 shows the screen for specifying the path.

(3). Select FILE by pressing F6, 6, or F to specify the filename to be loaded. Figure A.3 shows the screen for knowledge base listing.

(4). Move the cursor to the desired filename or type the name of the file and then press ⏎ .

(5). Select CONSULT by pressing F4, 4, or C to load the selected file. After the file is loaded, the screen in Figure A.4 is displayed.

Figure A.1. VP-expert startup screen

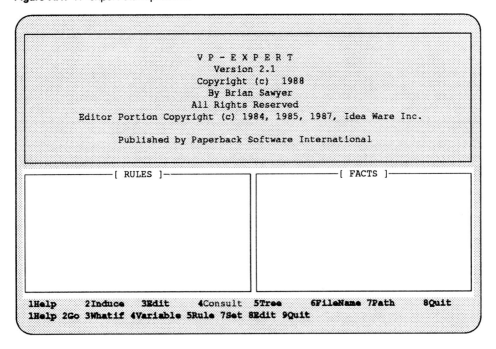

```
                         V P - E X P E R T
                            Version 2.1
                         Copyright (c)  1988
                          By Brian Sawyer
                         All Rights Reserved
          Editor Portion Copyright (c) 1984, 1985, 1987, Idea Ware Inc.

                   Published by Paperback Software International
```

```
──────[ RULES ]────────                    ──────[ FACTS ]──────
```

```
1Help     2Induce    3Edit      4Consult   5Tree      6FileName 7Path      8Quit
1Help 2Go 3Whatif 4Variable 5Rule 7Set 8Edit 9Quit
```

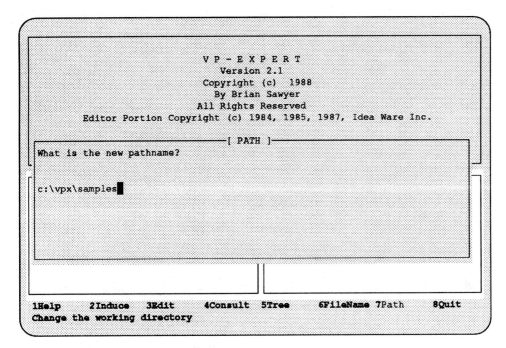

Figure A.2. Knowledge base directory path

Figure A.3. Listing of knowledge base files

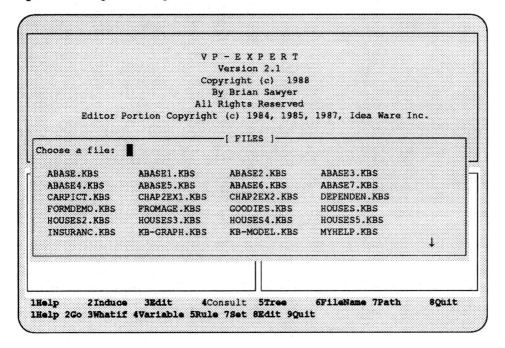

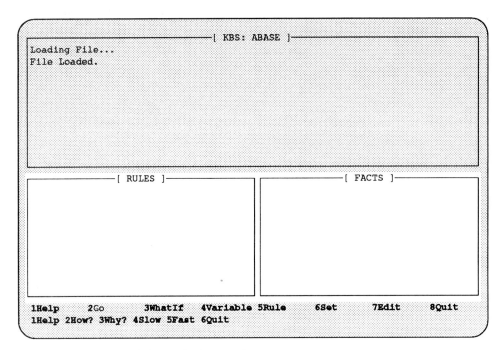

Figure A.4. Initial VP-expert consultation screen

(6). Select GO by pressing F2, 2, or G to begin the connsultation. From this point on, the specific screen displays built into the knowledge base will appear. An example of a consultation screen is shown in Figure A.5.

The other command options shown in Figure A.1 are explained below:

F1 *(HELP)*

Press this key to get online help on various topics regarding the use of VP-Expert. The help command is available on all VP-Expert command menus and provides onscreen information about the command offered by the currently active menu.

F2 *(INDUCE)*

This command creates a working knowledge base directly from a previously created induction table. Induction tables can be created online with the help of the CREATE command available in VP-Expert or can be predeveloped as Text, Worksheet, or Database files. After the Induce command is invoked, a submenu appears with the choices: Create, Text, Worksht, Database.

F3 *(EDIT)*

The Edit command invokes the VP-Expert Editor and loads the currently active knowledge base for editing. If no file is currently active, a new one can be

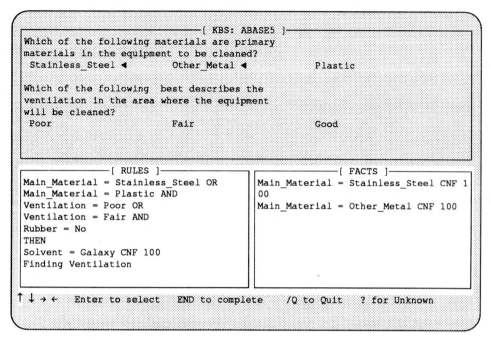

Figure A.5. Problem consultation screen

created in the editor. VP-Expert assumes the extension .KBS if none is typed in by the user.

F5 *(TREE)*

The Tree Command permits the viewing of the file created by the last execution of the Trace command. The Trace command records the implicit search pattern followed during a consultation.

F8 *(QUIT)*

The Quit command is used to exit from VP-Expert.

CODING A KNOWLEDGE BASE The coding of a knowledge base is done after proper knowledge acquisition and representation have been completed. Knowledge that is represented in terms of rules is the only type of knowledge that VP-Expert can handle. The knowledge base can be coded by typing the rules externally as a text file through use of any ASCII text editor, coded directly by using VP-Expert editor, or induced from a previously constructed induction table. The VP-Expert knowledge base consists of three basic elements: Actions block, Rules, and Statements.

ACTIONS BLOCK This defines the goals of the consultation and the sequence of their solution. In other words, the ACTIONS block tells the inference engine what it needs to find and in what order. This is accomplished with FIND clauses that instruct VP-Expert to find the value or values of one or more "goal varia-bles." The goals are found in an order in which they are written in the ACTIONS block. An example of an ACTIONS blocks is presented below:

```
ACTIONS

DISPLAY "This is a sample knowledge base"
FIND var1
FIND var2
FIND ending;
```

RULES   IF-THEN rules convey the "knowledge" or "expertise" contained in the knowledge base. Each rule indicates that if a certain condition occurs, then a certain action should be taken. It can also represent the linkage of evidence and hypothesis. An example of a VP-Expert rule is presented below:

```
RULE1
IF        Scsi_msg = Yes AND
          Pup = Disk
THENDM = 4
          SAVEFACTS pupfacts
          CHAIN pup_dm
          Ending = True;
```

STATEMENTS   The statements such as ASK and CHOICES are used to pres-ent menu options or prompts to the user. An example of an ASK statement is:
ASK material: "What is the raw material for the part?";
An example of a CHOICES statement is:
CHOICES answer: Yes, No, Unknown

Several sample knowledge base files are provided with the VP-Expert software. One of the samples is presented below:

```
RUNTIME;
ENDOFF;
BKCOLOR = 1;
ACTIONS
 COLOR = 15
 DISPLAY " FROMAGE.KBS
```

This VP-Expert release 2.1 sample file demonstrates the use of the FORMFIELD statement combined with the CHOICES statement to create a dynamic consultation.

You must have a Microsoft-compatible mouse and an EGA display installed to properly use this demonstration rule base. You need to modify the rule base in order to have it support other display types.

Find Continue
; ! — [End of Actions]
Ask Reponse:"
Do you wish to procede?";
Choices Response: Yes, No;

Rule Show_Sample
If   Response = Yes
THENContinue = Yes
          CLS
          MOUSEON
          GMODE 16
          Done = NO
          Course = ?
          Preference = ?
          Consistency = ?
          The_Cheese = na
          WHILETRUE Done = NO THEN END
ELSEContinue = no;

WHENEVER 1
IF   Complement = Bread AND
          Preference = Mild OR
          Preference = Flavorful AND
          Consistency = Soft
THENThe_Cheese = Brie
BECAUSE "Your preferences in taste and consistency determine the most appropriate
cheese for the course you have selected.";

WHENEVER 2
IF   Complement = Bread AND
          Preference = Pungent AND
          Consistency = Soft
THENThe_Cheese = Chevres
BECAUSE "Your preferences in taste and consistency determine the most appropriate
cheese for the course you have selected.";

WHENEVER 3
IF   Complement = Bread AND
          Preference = Mild OR
          Preference = Flavorful AND
          Consistency = Firm
THENThe_Cheese = Gouda
BECAUSE "Your preferences in taste and consistency determine the most appropriate
cheese for the course you have selected.";

WHENEVER 4
IF   Complement = Bread AND
          Preference = Pungent AND
          Consistency = FIRM
THENThe_Cheese = Asiago
BECAUSE "Your preferences in taste and consistency determine the most appropriate
cheese for the course you have selected.";

WHENEVER 5
IF   Complement = Bread_and_Fruit AND
            Preference = Mild OR
            Preference = Flavorful AND
            Consistency = Soft
THENThe_Cheese = Camembert
BECAUSE"Your preferences in taste and consistency determine the most appropriate
cheese for the course you have selected.";

WHENEVER 6
IF   Complement = Bread_and_Fruit AND
            Preference = Pungent AND
            Consistency = Soft
THENThe_Cheese = Tallegio
BECAUSE"Your preferences in taste and consistency determine the most appropriate
cheese for the course you have selected.";

WHENEVER 7
IF   Complement = Bread_and_Fruit AND
            Preference = Mild OR
            Preference = Flavorful AND
            Consistency = Firm
THENThe_Cheese = Italian_Fontina
BECAUSE "Your preferences in taste and consistency determine the most appropriate
cheese for the course you have selected.";

WHENEVER 8
IF   Complement = Bread_and_Fruit AND
            Preference = Pungent AND
            Consistency = Firm
THENThe_Cheese = Appenzeller
BECAUSE "Your preferences in taste and consistency determine the most appropriate
cheese for the course you have selected.";

WHENEVER 9
IF   Complement = Crackers_and_Bread AND
            Preference = Mild OR
            Preference = Flavorful AND
            Consistency = Soft
THENThe_Cheese = Montrachet
BECAUSE "Your preferences in taste and consistency determine the most appropriate
cheese for the course you have selected.";

WHENEVER 10
IF   Complement = Crackers_and_Bread AND
            Preference = Pungent AND
            Consistency = Soft
THENThe_Cheese = Gorgonzola
BECAUSE "Your preferences in taste and consistency determine the most appropriate
cheese for the course you have selected.";

WHENEVER 11
IF   Complement = Crackers_and_Bread AND
           Preference = Mild OR
           Preference = Flavorful AND
           Consistency = Firm
THENThe_Cheese = Stilton
BECAUSE "Your preferences in taste and consistency determine the most appropriate cheese for the course you have selected.";

WHENEVER 12
IF   Complement = Crackers_and_Bread AND
           Preference = Pungent AND
           Consistency = firm
THENThe_Cheese = Kasseri
BECAUSE "Your preferences in taste and consistency determine the most appropriate cheese for the course you have selected.";

WHENEVER 13
IF   Course = Dessert AND
           Course = Appetizer OR
           Course = Salad
THENComplement = Bread
BECAUSE "The type of cheese and its complement are determined by the course the cheese will be served with.";

WHENEVER 14
IF   Course = Dessert AND
           Course <> Appetizer AND
           Course <> Salad
THENComplement = Bread_and_Fruit
BECAUSE "The type of cheese and its complement are determined by the course the cheese will be served with.";

WHENEVER 15
IF   Course = Appetizer OR
           Course = Salad AND
           Course <> Dessert
THENComplement = Crackers_and_Bread
BECAUSE "The type of cheese and its complement are determined by the course the cheese will be served with.";
ASK Course: "With what course will you be serving cheese?";
CHOICES Course: Appetizer, Salad, Dessert;
ASK Preference: "What is your preference in cheese?";
CHOICES Preference: Mild, Flavorful, Pungent;
ASK Consistency: "What consistency of cheese would you prefer?";
CHOICES Consistency: Soft, Firm;
ASK The_Cheese: "Recommended cheese:";
ASK Complement: "Served with:";
PLURAL: Course;
LBUTTON Done: 65, 2, 4, 14, Done;
FORMFIELD Course: 60, 5, 16, 0;

```
FORMFIELD Preference: 60, 9, 16, 0;
FORMFIELD Consistency: 60, 13, 16, 0;
FORMFIELD The_Cheese: 50, 18, 26, 0;
FORMFIELD Complement: 50, 21, 26, 0;
```

Instead of typing the knowledge base rules directly, the user may employ an induction table. An induction table can be created in any of several different environments. It can be created in a text editor, in a VP-info or dBASE data base file, or in a VP-Planner Plus or Lotus 1-2-3 worksheet. An example of an induction table created as a text file is presented below:

Main_Material	Rubber	Solvent
Stainless_Steel	No	ACD_500
Stainless_Steel	Yes	D_Grease
Other_Metal	No	Cloripro_I
Other_Metal	Yes	MTZ_80

The first row of the induction table identifies the variables to be contained in the knowledge base. The last column of the table shows the goal variable. The preceding columns show the condition variables and their expected parameter values needed to achieve the goal variable. For example, the second row of the table will generate the following rule:

```
IF      Main_Material = Stainless_Steel
        and Rubber = No
THEN    Solvent = ACD_500
```

An asterisk (*) is used to indicate that a particular variable is not to be included in the rule generated by a row of the induction table. For example, if the second row of the induction table contained an asterisk as shown below, then the rule generated by the row would not contain the rubber variable:

```
Main_Material  Rubber  Solvent
Stainless_Steel   *       ACD_500
```

```
Associated rule:
IF Main_Material = Stainless_Steel
THEN Solvent = ACD_500
```

The knowledge base induced from the induction table presented earlier is presented below:

```
ACTIONS
        FIND Solvent;
```

```
RULE 0
IF          Main_Material = Stainless_Steel AND
            Rubber = NO
THEN
            Solvent = ACD_500;
RULE 1
IF          Main_Material = Stainless_Steel AND
            Rubber = Yes
THEN
            Solvent = D_Grease;
RULE 2
IF          Main_Material = Other_Metal AND
            Rubber = No
THEN
            Solvent = Cloripro_I;
RULE 3
IF          Main_Material = Other_Metal AND
            Rubber = Yes
THEN
            Solvent = MTZ_80;
ASK Main_Material: "What is the value of Main_Material?";
CHOICES Main_Material: Stainless_Steel, Other_Metal;

ASK Rubber: "What is the value of Rubber?";
CHOICES Rubber: No, Yes;
```

If desired, the knowledge base can be edited to enhance it or to change the context of the prompts (ASK statements) generated by the Induce command.

A summary of the VP-Expert editor commands is presented below. Note that the functions of the keys presented here are valid only when using the editor to create or edit a knowledge base file. The same function keys have different functions when using the consultation menus.

F1   HELP SYSTEM

F2   REFORMATS A PARAGRAPH

F3   TAB SET OR REMOVE

F4   DISPLAYS SCREEN FOR MARGIN/JUSTIFY SETTINGS

F5   CENTERS CURRENT LINE

F7   BOLDFACE ON/OFF

F8   UNDERLINE ON/OFF

F9   DOCUMENT MODE ON/OFF

F10   PRINT MENU OPTIONS

ALT- 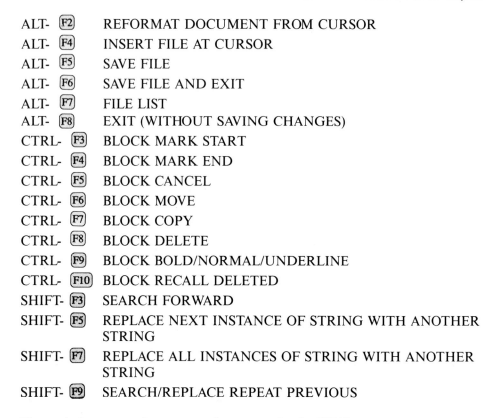	REFORMAT DOCUMENT FROM CURSOR

ALT- F2   REFORMAT DOCUMENT FROM CURSOR

ALT- F4   INSERT FILE AT CURSOR

ALT- F5   SAVE FILE

ALT- F6   SAVE FILE AND EXIT

ALT- F7   FILE LIST

ALT- F8   EXIT (WITHOUT SAVING CHANGES)

CTRL- F3   BLOCK MARK START

CTRL- F4   BLOCK MARK END

CTRL- F5   BLOCK CANCEL

CTRL- F6   BLOCK MOVE

CTRL- F7   BLOCK COPY

CTRL- F8   BLOCK DELETE

CTRL- F9   BLOCK BOLD/NORMAL/UNDERLINE

CTRL- F10   BLOCK RECALL DELETED

SHIFT- F3   SEARCH FORWARD

SHIFT- F5   REPLACE NEXT INSTANCE OF STRING WITH ANOTHER
             STRING

SHIFT- F7   REPLACE ALL INSTANCES OF STRING WITH ANOTHER
             STRING

SHIFT- F9   SEARCH/REPLACE REPEAT PREVIOUS

Figure A.6 presents the command menu paths for VP-Expert.

MODEL FOR VP-EXPERT KNOWLEDGE BASE ORGANIZATION   The model presented below is intended to serve as a template for organizing the VP-Expert knowledge base. The organization shown in the model is optional. This general structure should work for most knowledge bases. In some cases, the order of the contents of the model may be changed. For example, *statements* may precede the *ACTIONS* block or follow the *rules* section. A VP-Expert user can just copy the model presented and then fill in the appropriate actions, rules, and statements for the problem being addressed.

```
! Knowledge Base:   [descriptive title]
! Filename:         [desired filename]
! Revision Date:    [current date]
! Author:           [developer's name]
! Description:      [brief problem description]
! Requirements:     [special hardware/software requirements; e.g., mouse, EGA]
! VPX Release:      [version of VP-Expert used]
```

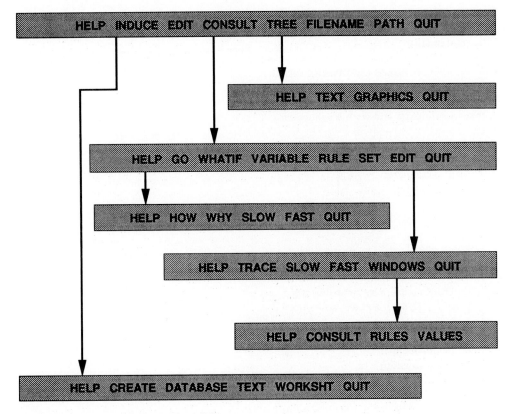

Figure A.6. Command menu paths for VP-expert

```
RUNTIME;

!............ACTIONS BLOCK (PROCEDURES)............
! Syntax notes:
! A single semicolon indicates the end of the ACTIONS block
! Clauses within the ACTIONS block contain no punctuation


ACTIONS
!  [action clause]
!  [action clause]
!  [action clause]
TMODE;   ! End of Actions


!............STATEMENTS BLOCK (DEFINITIONS)............

! Syntax notes:
! Each statement must end with a semicolon
```

```
!  [statement;]
!  [statement;]
!  [statement;]


!............RULES (BACKWARD CHAIN)............

! Syntax notes:
! Each rule must end with a semicolon

! RULE ruleID
!   IF   condition[s]
!   THENconclusion
        [actions];


!............WHENEVER RULES (FORWARD CHAIN)............

! Syntax notes:
! Each WHENEVER rule must end with a semicolon
! WHENEVER rules do not require a conclusion
! The THEN clause may refer directly to an action
!   (e.g. .... THEN DISPLAY "some text")


! WHENEVER wheneverID
!   IF   condition[s]
!   THEN[conclusion]
!       [actions];


!............END OF KNOWLEDGE BASE FILE............
```

APPENDIX B

Guide to Expert Systems Tools

EXPERT SYSTEMS

Product	Company	Environment	Features	Price
Alacrity Strategy	Alacritous, Inc. 120 Front Street E, Suite 208 Toronto, Ontario M5A 1E2 Canada	MS-DOS, Netbios Networks	Intelligent business planning workbook, 3000 rules with 2900 recommendations	$4000
BuySmart	Expert Systems Buying, Inc. 2040 Polk Street, Suite 317 San Francisco, CA 94109	MS-DOS	Guide for acquisition of manufacturing systems	Contact vendor
EXPERIMENTAL DESIGN	Statistical Programs 9941 Rowlett, Suite 6 Houston, TX 77075	MS-DOS	Statistical consulting, design of experimental model	$295
Expert Controller	Umecorp 45 San Clemente Dr Corte Madgra, CA 94925	IBM PC/AT, Mac II	Process monitoring and control	$10,000
Expert Voice	J Soft, Inc 21414 West Honey Lane Lake Villa, IL 60046	PC-DOS, PS2	Voice selection expert in disk, hypertext	$295
HyperEstimator	Turtle Creek Software 651 Halsey Valley Road Spencer, NY 14883	Macintosh Plus, SE or any II	Estimator for builders and architects	$95
Logic Gem	Sterling Castle Software 702 Washington St, Ste 174 Marina Del Rey, CA 90292	IBM PC	Translates a table into source code in C, BASIC, FORTRAN, dBase, Pascal, English	$99

Mortgage Broker	Synthetic Intelligence Comp 286 Fifth Avenue, #707 New York, NY 10001	MS-DOS	Mortgage servicing, statistics, budget control, broker best match	$1700
Operations Planner	Carnegie Group, Inc.	MS-DOS	Operations planning system	$3900
PC Purchase Advisor	Thinking Software, Inc 46-16 Sixty-Fifth Place Woodside, NY 11377	MS-DOS	Assists in configuration of PC AT	$59.95
PC Therapist	Thinking Software, Inc	MS-DOS	Natural language processing, speech synthesis, machine learning, animated talking head	$59.95
People-Planner	Information Marketing Business, Inc. 18 Hurley Street Cambridge, MA 02141	MS-DOS	Records time, labor requirements, work schedules, costs	$2200
Performance Advisor	Domanski Sciences, Inc. 16 Colonial Court Howell, NJ 07731	IBM PC, XT, AT, PS2	Tuning advice for MVS, CDICS, DB2, IMS	$995
PIUS	COGENSYS 9665 Chesapeake Dr, Suite 401 San Diego, CA 92123	PC, PS2	Personal insurance underwriting	Contact vendor
ROI EXPERT	Microtext Services Co. 1312 Kyle Drive St Charles, MO 63303	PC DOS	Financial expertise, project analysis, business accounting	$69.95
StreetSmart	Street Map Software 1014 Boston Circle Schaumburg, IL 60193	MS-DOS	Finds the best route considering distances, speed limits, one-way street, etc.	$349
Symbologic	Symbologic Corp 14379 North East 90th St Tedmond, WA 98052	MS-DOS, Microsoft Windows	Graphical knowledge representation	$1995
TeckChek	Bookman Consulting, Inc 67 Wall Street, Suite 2411 New York, NY 10005	IBM PC	Hiring and training aids	$999 per month
TestBench	Carnegie Group, Inc.	TI Explorer, PC/AT	Process and machine troubleshooting	$42,000
Traveler's Guide	Traveler's Guild 1900 Clark Marquette, MI 49855	PC	Hypertext language reference, point and click learning exercises, pop-up dictionary	$139
TRILOGY	Metavision, Inc 307 Ste Catherine St West, #720 Montreal Quebec H2X 2A3	IBM PC	Intelligent tutoring system, courseware construction	$2000
Turbo Spring Stat	SPRING SYSTEMS P. O. Box 10073 Chicago, IL 60610	IBM PC	Modular design, custom configuration	$469.95

DEVELOPMENT ENVIRONMENTS

Product	Company	Environment	Features	Price
1st Class Fusion HT	AICorp	PC	Induction, Hypertext	$995
Aion Development System	Aion Corp	IBM PC/XT/AT, PS2	Object-oriented program, data base integration, pattern matching, backward chaining, text substitution	$7000 up
Application Software Expert	Software Artistry, Inc	MS-DOS, IBM AS/400, RS/6000	General Development environment	$5000 up
ART-IM	Inference Corporation	MS-DOS	High-end tool for developing information-intensive applications, portability to IBM mainframes	$8000
AutoIntelligence	Intelligence Ware, Inc.	MS-DOS	Captures and distills knowledge of an expert to generate an expert system, knowledge discovery model	$490 up
COGITO	Logic Lab	Macintosh Plus, SE, II	Hyperresolution, algebraic operations, PROLOG	$59
Crystal Induction System	Intelligent Environments, Inc.	IBM PC	Generates rules from a series of examples entered in text or spreadsheet form	$295
EasyExpert	Park Row Software 4640 Jewell St, #232 San Diego, CA 92109-3178	MS-DOS	Menu-driven editor, online help, example rule sets, consistency checker	$49.95
Expert System Environment	IBM KBSC 101 California Av, M/S 6 Palo Alto, CA 94304	PC, XT, AT, PS2	Forward and backward chaining, designer screens, integrated relational data base interface	$594 up
EXSYS Professional	EXSYS, Inc.	MS-DOS, PS2	Command language, rules, custom frames, hypertext, blackboarding, direct dBase III, Lotus, LINDO, linear programming access	$795
Goldworks	Gold Hill Computers Co.	PC, AT, PS2	Frames, object oriented programming, forward and backward chaining, external interfaces	$7500
GURU	Mdbs, Inc KG Software Div P. O. Box 5268 Lafayette, IN 47903-5268	MS-DOS, OS2, VAX, VMS, Sun	Case save and replay, metarules, dependency diagram, spreadsheet, mixed forward and backward chaining, built-in relational database manager	$6500
Intelligence Compiler	Intelligence Ware, Inc.	MS-DOS, PS2, DEC VAX/VMS	Integrates relational data bases, logic programming, object oriented programming, dBase, Lotus 1-2-3 link	$490 up

IXL	Intelligence Ware, Inc.	MS-DOS, PS2	Generates rules from a set of hypotheses using a proprietary induction algorithm, dBase, Lotus, ASCII text file interfaces	$490 up
K-Base Builder	The GINESYS Corp 1200 Woodruff Road, Ste C-9 Greenville, SC 29607	MS-DOS, PS2	Natural language, tutorial, backward and forward chaining, compiler, EMS support, debugging, tracing	$795
KAPPA	IntelliCorp	IBM PC/AT	Object-oriented development environment, OOP- and C-based procedures, rule base, presentation graphics	$3500 up
KBMS/PC	AICorp	286, 386	Natural language, compatible with VAX, IBM mainframe	$5000 up
KDS	KDS Corporation	MS-DOS, PS2	User-directed chaining, forward and backward chaining, graphics	$1495
KEE	IntelliCorp	Compaq 386, PS2	UNIX system, V386 operating system, Macintosh version	$9900
KES	Software Architecture & Engineering 1600 Wilson Blvd, Ste 500 Arlington, VA 22209-2403	Variety of operating systems	Written in C, goal-directed, backward and forward chaining, class inheritance	$4000 up
KnowledgePro	Knowledge Garden, Inc	IBM PC, XT, AT, PS2	Training, intelligent hypertext, diagnostic systems, forward and backward chaining, object oriented, procedural, hypertext, Microsoft Windows version available	$495
LEVEL5	Information Builders, Inc 1250 Broadway New York, NY 10001	PC, PS2, DEC VAX, Macintosh, IBM mainframe	Expertise transfer, external data base interface	Contact vendor
MAGELLAN	Emerald Intelligence 3915 AI Research Park Dr Ann Arbor, MI 48108	Commodore Amiga	Rule-based, graphic oriented, windowing	$69
MAHOGANY Professional	Emerald Intelligence	IBM PC	Hybrid object oriented, rule base, mouse, window interface	$495
NEMO	Expert Knowledge Co.	Sun 3, 4, SPARC, PC 386 with UNIX	Continuous application handling, temporal logic, dynamic graphical interface	$12,195 up
NEXPERT OBJECT	Neuron Data 444 High Street Palo Alto, CA 94710	PC, Mac, Sun, HP, IBM mainframes, DEC, UNIX, OS2	Rules and objects, C, embedded AI library, data base interface, compatible across standard platforms	$5000 up
OPS 83	Production Systems Technologies Co	MS-DOS, Dec, Sun, OS2	Computer vision, design applications, diagnosis, simulation, planning, requires Pascal or C programming experience, forward and backward chaining	$1950 up

PC Expert	Software Artistry, Inc 3500 Depauw Blvd, Ste 2021 Indianapolis, IN 46268	MS-DOS, IBM AS/400, IBM RS/6000	Hypermedia using text, graphics, images, data bases, portable across IBM platforms	$495 up
Personal Consultant Plus	Texas Instruments Data Systems Group P. O. Box 809063 Dallas, TX 75380-9063	PC, MS-DOS, TI Explorer	Power development tool, combines frames with rules, LISP based, external interfaces	$2950
Turbo Shell	Berkshire Software Co	MS-DOS	Uses confidence factors and fuzzy logic	Contact vendor
VP-Expert	Paperback Software	MS-DOS	Backward and forward chaining, hypertext, dBase and spreadsheet access, dynamic graphic images	$249
VP-Expert/SQL	Paperback Software	MS-DOS	All VPX features plus access to SQL data bases, access to DB2 files	$695

NEURAL NETWORKS

Product	Company	Environment	Features	Price
AIM Professional	AbTech Corp. 700 Harris Street Charlottesville, VA 22901	MS-DOS, VAX, Macintosh	Automatically determines best network structure, good for estimation and classification	$995
Brain Simulator	Abbot, Foster, & Hauserman 44 Montgomery St, 5th Floor San Francisco, CA 94104	MS-DOS	Emulates human brain, shows how neuron circuitry works	$999
BrainMaker	California Scientific Software 10141 Evening Star Dr, #6 Grass Valley, CA 95941	IBM PC, XT, AT, PS2	Designing, building neural networks, menu-driven batch processing, reads data from Lotus, dBase, Excel, ASCII	$195
DESIRE/ NEUNET	Korn Industrial Consultants 6801 Opatas Street Tucson, AZ 85715	AT, 386	Neural Networks with up to 16,380 neurons	$695
GENESIS	Neural Systems, Inc 2827 West 43rd Av Vancouver, British Columbia V6N 3H9 CANADA	PC, MS-DOS	Development environment for interfacing neural networks to application software, up to 62 layers networks for embedded use	$1095
Hyperbrain	Neurix	Macintosh Plus, SE, II	Creates advanced custom applications by utilizing the power of hypercard	$200
K-Induction	The GINESYS Corp 1200 Woodruff Road, Ste C-9 Greenville, SC 29607	MS-DOS, PS2	Builds rule base from data table, allows for conflicting and incomplete data, fast learning	$1295

MacBrain	Neurix One Kendall Square, Ste 2200 Cambridge, MA 02139	Macintosh Plus, SE, II	Adjustable neural connections, menu-selected learning rules, activation rules, graphics animation	$995
N-NET 210	AI Ware, Inc	PS2, 286 PC	User and programming interfaces, link network, associative recall, supervised and unsupervised learning	$1495
Neuralog	Berkshire Software Co	MS-DOS	Back propagation, includes PROLOG source, pattern recognitions, graphics examples	$149
NeuralWorks	NeuralWare, Inc	IBM PC/XT/AT/PS2, RS6000, Mac, Sun	Generates network types from an extensive library, creates network diagnostic tools, several examples	$1495
NeuralShell	Ward Systems Group, Inc 245 West Patrick Street Frederick, MD 21701	MS-DOS	Easy to use shell to apply neural nets to many practical applications, designed for the expert systems domain	$195
Neuron Expert Professional	Thinking Software, Inc 46-16 65th Place Woodside, NY 11377	MS-DOS	Easy neural network toolkit, learn in one session	$99.95
Neurosoft	HNC, Inc 5501 Oberlin Dr San Diego, CA 92121	Link between neural networks and programs written in C, 18 neural net paradigms		Contact vendor
NeuroSym	NeuroSym Corporation P.O. Box 980683 Houston, TX 77098-0683	IBM PC	Allows neural networks to be added to C programs, supports 10 paradigms, multiple nets and multiple paradigms	$179
Plexi	Lucid, Inc 707 Laurel Street Menlo Park, CA 94025	Sun3, Sun4, SPARC workstation	Powerful graphical interactive interface, delivery capabilities	Contact vendor
SYSPRO	Martingale Research Corp 100 Allentown Parkway, Allen, TX 75002		FORTRAN-based neural network simulation and prototyping tool	Contact vendor

Names and Addresses
of Expert Systems Companies

AbTech Corporation
700 Harris Street
Charlottesville, VA 22901
(804) 977-0686
Product(s): AIM neural network
system

Acquired Intelligence, Inc.
P. O. Box 2091
Davis, CA 95617
(916) 753-4704

AI Corp, Inc.
138 Technology Drive
Waltham, MA 02254
(617) 891-6500
Product(s): Knowledge Base
Management System (KBMS),
1st-CLASS

AI Ware, Inc.
11000 Cedar Avenue, #212
Cleveland, OH 44106

Aion Corporation
101 University Avenue
Palo Alto, CA 94301
(415) 328-9595
Product(s): Aion development
system (ADS)

Arity Corporation
29 Domino Drive
Concord, MA 01742
(508) 371-1243
Product(s): Software tools, PROLOG

Artificial Intelligence Technologies,
Inc.
40 Saw Mill River Road
Hawthorne, NY 10532
(914) 347-6860
Product(s): Consulting, training,
general services

Automated Reasoning Corporation
25 Davids Drive
Hauppauge, NY 11788
(516) 231-7777
Product(s): I-CAT (Intelligent
Computer Aided Troubleshooting)
system

Bell Atlantic Knowledge Systems,
Inc.
P. O. Box 3528
Princeton, NJ 08543-3528
(609) 275-4545
Product(s): Software tools, LASER
development environment

Berkshire Software Co.
44 Madison Street
Lynbrook, NY 11563
(516) 593-8019
Product(s): AI and PROLOG
products

Blackboard Technology Group
P. O. Box 44
Amherst, MA 01004
(413) 256-4240
Product(s): GBB generic framework
for blackboard applications

Bolesian, Inc.
One Kendall Square, Suite 2200
Cambridge, MA 02139
(617) 621-7181
Product(s): Structured Knowledge
Engineering (SKE) methodology

California Intelligence
912 Powell Street
San Francisco, CA 94108

CAM Software, Inc.
Westpark Building, Suite 208
750 North 200 West
Provo, UT 84601
(801) 373-4080
Product(s): LogicTree expert system
tool

Carnegie Group
Five PPG Place
Pittsburg, PA 15222
(412) 642-6900
Product(s): Consulting services,
expert systems development

Chestnut Software, Inc.
636 Beacon Street
Boston, MA 02215
(617) 262-0914
Product(s): LISP-to-C Translator,
dBLISP, FOXLISP

CIM Solutions
P. O. Box 7041
Provo, UT 84604
(801) 374-5626
Product(s): Socrates

CMD (Consultants for Management
Decisions)
One Main Street
Cambridge, MA 02142
(617) 225-2200
Product(s): Software tools,
consulting services

Cognition Technology Corp.
55 Wheeler Street
Cambridge, MA 02138
(617) 492-0246

Cognitive Systems, Inc.
234 Church Street
New Haven, CT 06510
(203) 773-0726
Product(s): Software development
services

Cutter Information Corporation
1100 Massachusetts Avenue
Arlington, MA 02174
(617) 648-8700
Product(s): AI publications,
Newsletter
(Expert Systems Strategies)

Digital Equipment Corporation
290 Donald Lynch Boulevard
Marlboro, MA 01752
(508) 490-8513
Product(s): Hardware tools

Emerald Intelligence, Inc.
3915 AI Research Park Drive
Ann Arbor, MI 48108
(313) 663-8757
Product(s): Mahogany family of
expert systems development tool

Expert Knowledge
1801 Avenue of the Stars, Suite 507
Los Angeles, CA 90067

Expert Systems International
1700 Walnut Street
Philadelphia, PA 19103
(215) 735-8510
Product(s): Prolog products

Expertech, Inc.
P. O. AS
Incline Village, NV 89540
(702) 831-0136

ExperTelligence
5638 Hollister Avenue
Goleta, CA 93117
(805) 967-1797
Product(s): Procyon Common LISP,
CLOS, SPOKE

EXSYS, Inc.
7800 Marble NE, Suite 2
Albuquerque, NM 87110
(505) 256-8356
Product(s): EXSYS expert systems
development tool

Foundation Technologies, Inc.
One Kendall Square, Suite 2200
Cambridge, MA 02139
(617) 720-2760
Product(s): General consulting
services

Franz, Inc.
1995 University Avenue
Berkeley, CA 94704
(415) 548-3600
Product(s): LISP implementations

GENSYM Corporation
125 Cambridge Park Drive
Cambridge, MA 02140
(617) 547-9606
Product(s): Expert systems products,
development services

Gold Hill Computers
26 Landsdowne Street
Cambridge, MA 02139
(617) 621-3300
Product(s): GoldWorks

HNC, Inc.
5501 Oberlin Drive
San Diego, CA 92121
(619) 546-8877
Product(s): IDEPT (Image
Document Entry Processing
Terminal) workstation

IBM Knowledge Based Systems
Center
1501 California Avenue
Palo Alto, CA 94304
(415) 465-4004
Product(s): Expert system
development tools, hardware,
software

IBUKI
1447 North Shoreline Boulevard
Mountain View, CA 94043
(415) 961-4996
Product(s): IBUKI Common LISP
(IBCL)

Inference Corporation
550 North Continental Boulevard
El Segundo, CA 90245
(213) 322-0200
Product(s): ART-IM (Automated
Reasoning Tool for Information
Management)

Information Builders, Inc.
1250 Broadway
New York, NY 10001
(212) 736-4433
Product(s): LEVEL5 expert systems
development tool

IntelliCorp
1975 El Camino Real West
Mountain View, CA 94940
(415) 965-5500
Product(s): Development tools,
KAPPA

IntelligenceWare, Inc.
9800 S. Sepulveda Blvd, Suite 730
Los Angeles, CA 90045
(213) 417-8896

Intelligent Environments, Inc.
2 Highwood Drive
Tewksbury, MA 01876

International Chip Corporation
AT&T Building
1201 Main Street, Suite 2000
Columbia, SC 29201
(803) 779-2504
Product(s): REX and CAKE
development tools

KDS Corp
934 Hunter Road
Wilmette, IL 60091
(312) 251-2621

Knowledge Garden, Inc.
473A Malden Bridge Road
Nassau, NY 12123
(518) 766-3000
Product(s): KnowledgePro

Logic Lab
720 Calmar Avenue
Oakland, CA 94610

Logicware International
2065 Dundas Street E, Suite 204
Mississauga, Ontario
Canada L4V 1T1
(416) 672-0300

Lucid, Inc.
707 Laurel Street
Menlo Park, CA 94025
(415) 329-8400
Product(s): LISP implementations

Micro Data Base Systems
P. O. Box 248
Lafayette, IN 47902-0248
(317) 447-1122
Product(s): GURU development tool

NeuralWare, Inc.
Penn Center West
Building IV, Suite 227
Pittsburg, PA 15276
(412) 787-8222
Product(s): Neural network
computing software, seminars,
consulting

Neuron Data, Inc.
444 High Street
Palo Alto, CA 94301
(415) 321-4488
Product(s): NEXPERT development
tool

New Science Associates, Inc.
167 Old Post Road
Southport, CT 06490
(203) 259-1661
Product(s): Research and consulting
services

Paperback Software International
2830 Ninth Street
Berkeley, CA 94710
(415) 644-2116
Product(s): VP-Expert

Paralogic, Inc.
NET Ben Franklin Technology
Center
115 Research Drive
Bethlehem, PA 18015
(215) 861-6960
Product(s): PROLOG
implementations

Production Systems Technologies,
Inc.
5001 Baum Boulevard
Pittsburg, PA 15213
(412) 683-4000
Product(s): OPS83

Quintus Computer Systems
1310 Villa Street
Mountain View, CA 94041
(415) 965-7700
Product(s): PROLOG-based
development tools

Radian Corp
8501 Mo-Pac Blvd
P. O. Box 201088
Austin, TX 87820-1088
(512) 454-4797

Science Applications International
Corporation
10260 Campus Point Drive
San Diego, CA 92121
(619) 546-6148
Product(s): General services,
consulting, training

SGS-Thomson INMOS Division
INMOS Business Center
Headquarters
2225 Executive Circle
P. O. Box 16000
Colorado Springs, CO 80935-6000
(719) 630-4000
Product(s): Hardware and software
tools

Software Artistry, Inc.
3500 DePauw Boulevard, Suite 1100
Indianapolis, IN 46268
(317) 876-3042
Product(s): Application Software
Expert (ASE) development tool

Symbolics, Inc.
8 New England Executive Park
Burlington, MA 01803
(617) 221-1000
Product(s): Hardware and software
tools

Symbologic Corporation
15379 NE 90th Street
Redmond, WA 98052
(206) 881-3938
Product(s): General services, expert
systems

Synchronetics, Inc.
301 North Front Street
Baltimore, MD 21202
(301) 752-1065
Product(s): Natural language text
processing systems

Texas Instruments
Advance Systems Division
P. O. Box 809063
Dallas, TX 75380-9063
(800) 527-3500

The Schwartz Associates
801 West El Camino Real, Suite 150
Mountain View, CA 94040
(415) 965-4561
Product(s): Consulting services,
expert systems, neural networks

Top Level
196 North Pleasant Street
Amherst, MA 01002
(413) 256-6405
Product(s): Top level common Lisp
(TopCL)

Glossary of Expert Systems Terms

AI. Artificial intelligence.

AI paradigm. A mechanism that can be used to represent knowledge in an expert system program; for example: production rules, frames, and object-oriented programming techniques.

AI programming language. A programming language specifically designed for use in artificial intelligence. Such specialized languages provide mechanisms and structures that facilitate symbolic reasoning. The two most common of these languages are LISP and PROLOG.

AI workstation. A LISP machine.

Algorithm. A step-by-step procedure that has a specific beginning and end and is guaranteed to solve a specific problem.

Allophone. A unit of speech that represents a particular sound as it actually occurs in a word.

Analogical inference. Mapping of a known event, object, or description to a similar event, object, or description.

Antecedent. The left-hand side—the if clause—of a production rule. This is the pattern that must be satisfied for the rule to be applicable.

Artificial intelligence (AI). The science of making machines behave in a way that would generally be accepted as requiring human intelligence. Important subfields of artificial intelligence include robotics, computer vision, speech synthesis and recognition, automated reasoning and theorem proving, natural language processing, automatic programming, automated learning, neural networks, and expert systems.

ASCII. American Standard Code for Information Interchange. This is a standard code used to represent letters, numbers, and special functions as a series of zeros and ones.

Assembly language. A low-level language in which each instruction is assembled into one machine-language instruction.

Atom. A number or symbol.

Atomic formulas. Simple relations between things (predicates); also called propositions.

Attribute hierarchy. A structure that shows the hierarchical relationship of attributes used in constructing the knowledge base.

Attributes. Properties associated with objects.

Automatic programming. An area of AI research involved in creating AI software that can generate programs from a programmer's specifications.

Backward chaining. A search technique that starts in a goal state and works toward an initial state.

Bayesian statistics. Encompasses Bayes' theorem for handling uncertainty in expert systems.

Belief. The confidence in how reliable a statement is perceived.

Bit-mapped display. A display screen that allows a programmer to turn each individual pixel on or off.

Blackboard. A system architecture that uses multiple accessible processes, called knowledge sources, within its data base.

Breadth-first search. A search technique that evaluates every node at a given level of the search space before moving to the next level.

Cell. The structure used in a computer to represent a list. Each cell has two fields for storing data and pointing to other cells in the list.

Certainty factor. A number attached to a rule of fact that denotes the degree of certainty that is assigned to it. The use of certainty factors is a common approach for representing uncertainty in production rule systems.

Chaining. A technique for reproducing or approximating part of an expert's reasoning processes by utilizing a sequence of rules from a set of production rules. This can involve forward, backward, or mixed chaining.

Cognitive science. The field that investigates the details of the mechanics of human intelligence to determine the processes that produce intelligence in a given situation.

Common LISP. A standardized version of "East Coast" LISP.

Compiler. A program that converts an entire high-level language program into machine language.

Computer vision. An area of AI research that is attempting to enable computers to understand visual images.

Conclusion. Consequent of a production rule.

Condition. Antecedent of a production rule.

Conflict resolution. The mechanism in forward or backward chaining that determines which rule should actuate or fire when there is more than one rule in the conflict set.

Conflict set. In forward and backward chaining the set of rules applicable at any one time. When there is more than one rule in the conflict set, conflict-resolution techniques are utilized to determine which rule should fire.

Connected word recognition. An approach to speech recognition that recognizes words spoken in normal context.

Consequent. Refers to the conclusion of a production rule if the conditions or antecedents of that rule are met.

Constraint propagation. A search technique for moving information between subproblems.

Constraints. Facts that restrict the solution of a problem.

Continuous speech recognition. An approach to speech recognition that understands speech in typical conversations of normal durations.

Control. Procedure(s) that affects the order of problem-solving tasks in expert systems.

Control knowledge. Facts that influence the selection of the control strategy.

Control strategy. Selecting the next course of action given many problem-solving tasks.

Dialog structure. The language interface between the user and the expert system in order to get answers from the expert system and challenge the results.

Data-driven reasoning. *See* forward chaining.

Data driven. Refers to forward chaining.

Data base. Information stored in a computer for subsequent retrieval.

Declarative knowledge. Knowledge that can't be immediately executed but can be retrieved and stored.

Default value. A value that is used if no other value is specified.

Degrees of Freedom (DOF). The "joints" in a robot arm.

Demon. In a frame system, a program that is triggered when a particular action related to a slot occurs. Actions that might trigger a demon include the initial insertion, the change, or the retrieval of a slot value.

Dependency-directed backtracking. A search method that traces back errors and inconsistencies to the inference rules that created them.

Depth-first search. A search technique that advances from the first level to a terminal node. If the terminal node is a goal state, the search is finished. If not, the process is repeated.

Development environment. The computer and the knowledge engineering software tools that are used during the development of an expert system.

Development tool. A program designed to assist programmers in the development of software. Intelligent tools incorporate AI techniques.

Domain. The application area of an expert system—the problem area of interest; or, the application area in which an expert system is being developed; or, a person with expertise in the domain of the expert system being developed. The domain expert works closely with the knowledge engineer.

Domain knowledge. The facts and rules of thumb of a problem area of application.

Edge detection. A computer vision technique which helps the computer understand the visual images it receives by locating the edges of an object.

End effector. Another name for a robot hand. It also is called a gripper.

Event driven. Same as forward chaining.

Exhaustive search. Searching technique that tests every alternative one at a time.

Expert system. An advanced computer program that can, at an acceptable level of competence, solve difficult problems requiring the use of expertise and experience.

Expert system shell. A building kit to aid in the construction of expert systems; also referred to as an expert system application generator.

Expert systems. A subfield of AI involving the development and application of expert system programs.

Explanation. The process of describing how and why an expert system reached a particular conclusion.

Explanation facility. The component of an expert system that can explain the system's reasoning, such as how a conclusion was reached or why a particular question was asked.

Facet. A part of a slot that contains a piece of information related to the slot, such as the range of acceptable values for the slot, the default value, or the slot's value itself.

Fifth generation. The generation of computers that will be built on knowledge-based systems and natural language concepts.

Fire. To actuate or trigger a rule in a production rule system.

First-order predicate calculus. A system of formal logic that is based on predicate calculus with the addition of functions and other analytical features.

Forward chaining. A search control strategy that starts from facts to arrive at a conclusion.

Frame-based CAI. A computer-assisted instruction technique based on the method used in a programmed instruction text. The material presented to the student depends on how the questions asked are answered.

Frames. A way of representing knowledge that stores a list of an object's typical attributes with the object. Each attribute is stored in a separate slot.

Fuzzy logic. Uses imprecise or possibility knowledge, based on fuzzy set theory, to handle uncertainty in expert systems.

Generate and test. State-space search that generates a solution and tests that solution to see if it meets constraints.

Goal driven reasoning. Same as backward chaining.

Hardware. The computer(s) on which an expert system (or any computer program) is developed or deployed.

Heuristic. A rule of thumb usually developed through professional experience.

Hierarchical plan. One category of AI techniques used for planning. A hierarchical plan starts at a general level of planning and moves down to a specific, detailed plan.

Hierarchical planning. A search technique that produces a hierarchy of abstraction spaces, in each of which preconditions at a lower level of abstraction are ignored.

High-level language. A language in which the computer instructions closely resemble English. One high-level language instruction is normally converted into several machine-language instructions.

Human factors. This refers to all interfaces between man, machine, and the environment in which they operate.

Hypothesis-driven reasoning. *See* backward chaining.

Inductive learning. The ability to make inductive inference from facts provided by the environment.

Inference engine. The component of an expert system that controls its operation by selecting the rules to use, accessing and executing those rules, and determining when a solution has been found. This component is known also as the control structure or rule interpreter.

Inheritance. A mechanism in a frame or object-oriented system that allows all the information known in general about all members of a class to be considered true for each individual member of the class.

Integrated circuit. An electronic circuit containing multiple electronic components fabricated at the same time in steps on a single slice or wafer of semiconductor material. When separated into individually packaged integrated circuits, they are known also as IC's or chips.

Intelligent Computer-Assisted Instruction (ICAI). An area of AI research with the goal of creating training programs that can analyze a student's learning pattern and modify their teaching techniques accordingly. The components of an ICAI program are problem-solving expertise, student model, and tutoring module.

Intelligent robot. A robot that includes AI techniques to allow it to understand its environment and change its actions on the basis of external situations. An intelligent robot is known also as a sensor-controlled robot.

IPL (Information Processing Language). An AI programming language and a forerunner of LISP.

Isolated word recognition. An approach to speech recognition that uses pattern-matching techniques to recognize isolated words.

Knowledge document. A document in which the knowledge obtained from experts during knowledge acquisition is recorded. The document is updated as new pieces of knowledge are found and as previously found knowledge is revised.

Knowledge-based system. Another name for "expert system."

Knowledge-engineering software tool. *See* software tool.

Knowledge acquisition. The process of extracting knowledge from the domain expert for developing the knowledge base. This is typically performed by interviewing, scenario-building, and questionnaires.

Knowledge base. A set of facts and heuristics specially encoded into an expert system.

Knowledge elicitation. *See* knowledge acquisition.

Knowledge engineer. The individual who is responsible for the knowledge acquisition, representation, programming, and refinement phases of developing an expert system.

Knowledge engineering. The process of developing an expert system. The term knowledge engineering, used broadly, indicates all the technical aspects involved with developing an expert system. Sometimes the term is confined to the task of acquiring knowledge from an expert.

Knowledge implementation. The process of taking the knowledge found during knowledge acquisition and translating it into an operational expert system program.

Knowledge programming. Refers to the process of encoding the knowledge into a knowledge base.

Knowledge representation. The process of defining the approach that will be used in an expert system program to represent the domain knowledge found during knowledge acquisition.

Knowledge representational paradigm. *See* AI paradigm.

Knowledge source. A set of related rules used in a blackboard architecture.

Knowledge system. An expert system.

Knowledge testing. Refinement of the knowledge base, usually accomplished by verification studies.

Learning. The cognitive activities involved in acquiring and applying knowledge.

LISP. LISt Processor. An AI programming language that is especially popular in the United States.

LISP Machine. A single-user computer designed primarily for the development of AI programs. LISP machines also are known as AI workstations.

List. A sequence of elements enclosed in parentheses, in which each element is either an atom or another list.

List processing. The execution of symbols (strings of characters) and symbol structures (data structures).

Local Area Network (LAN). A means of computer communication in which the computers are physically connected to share resources.

Logic programming. Languages, like PROLOG, based on first-order predicate calculus.

Logical Inferences Per Second (LIPS). A means of measuring the speed of computers used for AI applications.

Machine language. The language in binary code that the computer understands.

Machine learning. The field devoted to building models of human learning and to understanding how machines might be endowed with the ability to learn.

Machine translation. An area of AI research that is attempting to use computers to translate text from one language to another. These programs often use a combination of natural language understanding and generation.

Manipulator. Another name for a robot arm.

Menus. A list of the options available at a particular place in a computer program.

Message. In an object-oriented programming system, a communication sent from one object to another (or to itself). It contains information for the receiving object on which method to invoke and also contains any necessary parameters for the method.

Metarule. A rule about a rule. Metarules are a type of production rule used in expert systems to specify the conditions under which certain rules should be followed instead of others.

Metaknowledge. Knowledge about knowledge.

Method. A procedure related to an object in an object-oriented programming system.

Mixed chaining. A reasoning technique used in a production rule system that allows both forward and backward chaining to be used for different parts of the same problem.

Model-based system. A type of expert system based on a model of the structure and behavior of the device it is designed to understand.

Model-based vision. A computer vision technique in which image templates or descriptions of features of objects are stored to help the computer identify an object.

Modus ponens. The part of predicate calculus that refers to rules of inference.

Monotonic logic. A special type of logic in which the set of theorems and facts does not change when new axioms are added to a set of axioms.

Mouse. A small, sliding, handheld pointing device that controls the movement of a pointer on the computer screen. The two types of mouse devices are mechanical and optical.

Multiple inheritance. Inheritance from more than one source. It can be used to give an individual that is a member of more than one class the attributes of each class.

Multiple worlds. The process of creating additional contexts in which to test alternative hypotheses.

Natural language. An application of artificial intelligence in which the focus is programming the computer to understand language and linguistics.

Natural language generation. The part of natural language processing research that is attempting to have computers present information in English. Natural language generation programs must decide when to say something, what to say, and how to say it.

Natural language understanding. The part of natural language processing research that is investigating methods of allowing computers to understand instructions given in English.

Nodes. Objects in a linked graph.

Nonhierarchical plan. One category of AI techniques used for planning. A non-hierarchical plan represents a plan on one level only.

Nonalgorithmic. A problem-solving approach that does not follow a step-by-step procedure.

Object-oriented language. A programming language that manipulates objects used for declarative knowledge.

Object-oriented programming. A set of techniques that allows programs to be built using object as the basic data-items and actions on objects as the active mechanisms.

Object. A data structure that contains all the information related to a particular entity. It might be considered a frame with additional features allowing it to contain and invoke methods and to send and receive messages.

Object. An entity for denoting declarative (and sometimes procedural) knowledge.

Paradigm. *See* AI paradigm.

Parallel processing. The computer technique of performing several processing actions at the same time.

Parsing. The process of applying a body of syntactic knowledge and procedure for using the knowledge.

Pattern-matching. An AI technique that recognizes relationships and patterns in objects, events, and processes.

Pattern recognition. The process of matching and identifying patterns.

Phoneme. A unit of speech that is the sound of an individual consonant or vowel.

Pixels. The individual dots on a computer screen. Letters, numbers, and symbols consist of pixels arranged in a matrix.

Planning and decision support. An area of AI research that is applying AI techniques to the planning and decision-making process to help managers who have decision-making responsibilities.

Plausible reasoning. A form of guessing where, in deciding between two nodes, a search path is followed on an arbitrary basis.

Predicate calculus. A system of formal logic that is based on propositional calculus with the added capabilities of specifying relationships and making generalizations.

Problem-solving expertise. The component of an ICAI program that contains the information being presented to the student.

Problem space. States that can be reached from the initial state by application of the rules in all possible ways.

Procedural knowledge. Knowledge that can be executed.

Production rule. A rule in the form of an "if-then" or "condition-action" statement, often used in expert systems. A production rule represents a heuristic.

Production rule. An antecedent-consequent rule; SITUATION-ACTION rule; IF-THEN rule.

Production system. A problem-solving architecture using a rule-based structure.

PROLOG. PROgramming in LOGic. An AI programming language that is especially popular in Europe and Japan.

Propositional calculus. A system of formal logic that provides a step-by-step inference system for determining whether a given proposition is true or false.

Propositional calculus. Refers to predicate calculus involving a set of logical axioms and theorems.

Prototyping. Developing a scaled-down version of the expert system and iteratively refining each version.

Pruning. A means of reducing the size of a search space, usually accomplished with heuristic rules.

Random Access Memory (RAM). A memory into which data can be placed (written) and from which data can be retrieved (read).

Reasoning by analogy. Employing analogical inference in solving problems.

Recursion. Defining an item in terms of itself.

Recursive. Operations that are defined in terms of themselves.

Robotics. An area of AI research involved in developing intelligent robots.

Rule-based system. An expert system made up of production rules; also called a production system.

Rule interpreter. The part of a production system that executes the rules.

Scheduler. The program in a blackboard architecture that selects the most likely processing event that will lead to a complete problem solution.

Schema. Same as a frame.

Script. A special form of a frame that includes scenes of activities.

Scripts. A way of representing knowledge that stores the events that take place in familiar situations in a series of slots. A script is composed of a series of scenes composed of a series of events.

Search. The process of starting in some initial state and attempting to reach a goal state by evaluating possible alternative solutions.

Search space. All of the possible states that could be evaluated during a search. The search space often is represented as an inverted tree, called a search tree.

Second-order predicate calculus. Logic that permits variables to represent predicates.

Semantic network. A knowledge representation scheme in which the objects are portrayed as nodes and relationships between them are arcs.

Semantic network. A means of representing facts as nodes in a graph and their relationships to other facts as the links or arcs.

Sequential processing. The computer technique of performing actions one at a time in sequence.

Servomechanism. A device that can correct a robot's performance.

Shell. An extensive package of software facilities used in the development of expert systems. *See* software tool.

Simulation. An AI technique that uses a model of intelligent human behavior to determine if the computer will exhibit the same intelligent behavior as a human.

Slot. A component of a frame that refers to a specific attribute of the frame entity and contains the value of the attribute if the value is known. A slot can contain fixed information, for the problem at hand, or information that can vary during a program run.

Slot filling. The process of putting values in frames.

Software tool (for knowledge engineering). A software package that provides facilities to aid in expert system development.

Speaker-dependent recognition. An approach to speech recognition that recognizes the speech of any speaker.

Speech recognition. An area of AI research with the ultimate goal of allowing computers to recognize and understand human speech, regardless of the speaker; use of computers to identify speech patterns.

Speech synthesis. The generation of speech by a computer.

Speech understanding. Writing programs that understand the spoken language.

Student model. The component of an ICAI program that analyzes the student's performance to determine why the student is having difficulty.

Syllable. A unit of speech consisting of a vowel and the surrounding consonants that are pronounced together.

Telecommunication. A means of communication in which computers use telephone lines to transmit and receive information.

Time sharing. An approach to using computers that allows many people to share the resources of a computer at the same time.

Truth maintenance. A system that records justification for assertions.

Turing test. An "imitation game" devised by Alan Turing, used to experiment if a computer can think. An interrogator attempts to discover which of two respondents is a person and which is a computer by engaging both of them in thoughtful conversation.

Tutoring module. The component of an ICAI program that selects the strategies for presenting tutorial information to a student.

Uncertainty. The situation in which knowledge or data in an expert system is not completely certain.

User interface. The component of an expert system that allows bidirectional communication between the expert system and its user.

Very Large Scale Integration (VLSI). The process of combining several hundred thousand electronic components on a single chip of semiconductor material.

Virtual memory. A system of managing RAM and disk space so that a computer appears to have more memory than it really does.

Well-formed formulas. Formulas that use connectives and quantifiers composed of terms and atomic formulas.

Windowing. A means of dividing the computer screen into several areas so that a variety of information can be displayed simultaneously.

Working memory. The part of an expert system program that contains the data the system has received about the current problem. In addition, any information that the expert system derives about the present problem is stored in the working memory.

APPENDIX E

Conversion Factors for Engineering and Manufacturing

NUMBER PREFIXES

Prefix	SI Symbol	Multiplication Factors	Example
tera	T	$1\ 000\ 000\ 000\ 000 = 10^{12}$	tera fortune
giga	G	$1\ 000\ 000\ 000 = 10^{9}$	giga byte
mega	M	$1\ 000\ 000 = 10^{6}$	mega bucks
kilo	k	$1\ 000 = 10^{3}$	kilo byte
hecto	h	$100 = 10^{2}$	hectogram
deca	da	$10 = 10^{1}$	decade
deci	d	$0.1 = 10^{-1}$	decimal
centi	c	$0.01 = 10^{-2}$	centimeter
milli	m	$0.001 = 10^{-3}$	millimicron
micro	μ	$0.000\ 001 = 10^{-6}$	microcomputer
nano	n	$0.000\ 0.000\ 001 = 10^{-9}$	nanosecond
pico	p	$0.000\ 0.000\ 000\ 001 = 10^{-12}$	picosecond
femto	f	$0.000\ 0.000\ 000\ 000\ 001 = 10^{-15}$	femto chance
atto	a	$0.000\ 0.000\ 000\ 000\ 000\ 001 = 10^{-18}$	atto likelihood

AREA

Multiply	by	to obtain
acres	43,560	sq feet
	4,047	sq meters
	4,840	sq yards
	0.405	hectare
sq cm	0.155	sq inches
sq feet	144	sq inches
	0.09290	sq meters
	0.1111	sq yards
sq inches	645.16	sq millimeters
sq kilometers	0.3861	sq miles
sq meters	10.764	sq feet
	1.196	sq yards
sq miles	640	acres
	2.590	sq kilometers

VOLUME

Multiply	by	to obtain
acre-foot	1233.5	cubic meters
cubic cm	0.06102	cubic inches
cubic feet	1728	cubic inches
	7.480	gallons (US)
	0.02832	cubic meters
	0.03704	cubic yards
liter	1.057	liquid quarts
	0.908	dry quart
	61.024	cubic inches
gallons (US)	231	cubic inches
	3.7854	liters
	4	quarts
	0.833	British gallons
	128	U.S. fluid ounces
quarts (US)	0.9463	liters

ENERGY, HEAT, POWER

Multiply	by	to obtain
BTU	1055.9	joules
	0.2520	kg-calories
watt-hour	3600	joules
	3.409	BTU
HP (electric)	746	watts
BTU/second	1055.9	watts
watt-second	1.00	joules

MASS

Multiply	by	to obtain
carat	0.200	cubic grams
grams	0.03527	ounces
kilograms	2.2046	pounds
ounces	28.350	grams
pound	16	ounces
	453.6	grams
stone (UK)	6.35	kilograms
	14	pounds
ton (net)	907.2	kilograms
	2000	pounds
	0.893	gross ton
	0.907	metric ton
ton (gross)	2240	pounds
	1.12	net tons
	1.016	metric tons
tonne (metric)	2,204.623	pounds
	0.984	gross ton
	1000	kilograms

TEMPERATURE

Conversion formulas	
Celsius to Kelvin	$K = C + 273.15$
Celsius to Fahrenheit	$F = (9/5)C + 32$
Fahrenheit to Celsius	$C = (5/9)(F - 32)$
Fahrenheit to Kelvin	$K = (5/9)(F + 459.67)$
Fahrenheit to Rankin	$R = F + 459.67$
Rankin to Kelvin	$K = (5/9)R$

VELOCITY

Multiply	by	to obtain
feet/minute	5.080	mm/second
feet/second	0.3048	meters/second
inches/second	0.0254	meters/second
km/hour	0.6214	miles/hour
meters/second	3.2808	feet/second
	2.237	miles/hour
miles/hour	88.0	feet/minute
	0.44704	meters/second
	1.6093	km/hour
	0.8684	knots
knot	1.151	miles/hour

PRESSURE

Multiply	by	to obtain
atmospheres	1.01325	bars
	33.90	feet of water
	29.92	inches of mercury
	760.0	mm of mercury
bar	75.01	cm of mercury
	14.50	pounds/sq inch
dyne/sq cm	0.1	N/sq meter
newtons/sq cm	1.450	pounds/sq inch
pounds/sq inch	0.06805	atmospheres
	2.036	inches of mercury
	27.708	inches of water
	68.948	millibars
	51.72	mm of mercury

CONSTANTS

speed of light	$2.997,925 \times 10^{10}$ cm/sec
	983.6×10^6 ft/sec
	186,284 miles/sec
velocity of sound	340.3 meters/sec
	1116 ft sec
gravity	9.80665 m/sec square
(acceleration)	32.174 ft/sec square
	386.089 inches/sec square

LENGTH

Multiply	by	to obtain
angstrom	10^{-10}	meters
feet	0.30480	meters
	12	inches
inches	25.40	millimeters
	0.02540	meters
	0.08333	feet
kilometers	3280.8	feet
	0.6214	miles
	1094	yards
meters	39.370	inches
	3.2808	feet
	1.094	yards
miles	5280	feet
	1.6093	kilometers
	0.8694	nautical miles
millimeters	0.03937	inches
nautical miles	6076	feet
	1.852	kilometers
yards	0.9144	meters
	3	feet
	36	inches

Knowledge Base Listings

PROCESS-PLUS KNOWLEDGE BASE

```
RUNTIME;
EXECUTE;
BKCOLOR = 7;
ACTIONS
    color = 4
    get all,c:\dbase\meter,all
    display"


                PROCESS plus
        This prototype expert system prepares the
process
        plan for the given part using the generative
        approach



        Press any key to proceed...~"
    cls
    wopen 1,2,2,10,73,7
        active 1
        find part
        cls
        wclose 1
        printon
        find inst
        cls
    wopen 2,2,2,10,73,7
        active 2
        menu material,all,mate,material
        find material
        cls
        step = 1
        whileknown mark
        wopen 3,2,2,20,73,7
        active 3
        reset coolant
        reset tool1
        reset tool2
        reset dis
        reset made
        reset tool
        reset done
        reset name
        reset finish
```

```
        reset zone
        reset rod
        reset depth
        reset roughcut
        reset roughpass
        reset oper1
        reset speed
        reset game
        get all,c:\dbase\ca,all
        find tool
        find game
        find name
        find finish
        find done
        find made
        find rod
        find coolant
        find zone
        find dis
    step = (step + 1)
    cls
    end;
rule 1
if    oper1 = turning or
      oper1 = taperturning and
      oper2 = otwo
then  tool = single_point
      toolmat = carbide;
rule 2
if    dia <> unknown
then  inst = yes
      display"
                INSTRUCTIONS
        Part name: {part}
    1) Take the raw material with
        Diameter = {dia}    inches
        Length   = {length} inches
    2) Hold the job in the lathe head stock chuck
    3) Hold the second part of the job in the
        lathe tailstock for all operations
        except the internal operations
    4) For holding the job in the tailstock
        use countersunk drill
```

Press any key to proceed..~";
rule 3
if   ag <> unknown
then   cont = yes;
rule 4
if   oper1 = turning or
       oper1 = taperturning and
       oper2 = threading
then   tool = yes
       tool1 = single_point
       tool2= v_tool
       toolmat = carbide;
rule 5
if   oper1 = boring and
       oper2 = inthreading
then   tool = yes
       tool1 = boring_tool
       tool2 = boring_v_tool
       toolmat = carbide_bit;
rule 6
if   oper1 = intthreading and
       oper2 = otwo
then   tool = boring_v_tool
       toolmat = carbide_bit;
rule 7
if   oper1 = turning or
       oper1 = taperturning and
       oper2 = knurling
then   tool = yes
       tool1 = single_point
       tool2 = knurling_tool
       toolmat = carbide;
rule 8
if   oper1 = parting or
       oper1 = grooving
then   tool = parting_tool
       toolmat = carbide;
rule 9
if   oper1 = drilling
then   tool = twist_drill
       toolmat = HSS;
rule 10
if   oper1 = filleting or
       oper1 = forming
then   tool = form_tool
       toolmat = carbide;
rule 11
if   oper1 = boring and
       oper2 = otwo
then   tool = boring_tool
       toolmat = carbide_bit;

rule 12
if   oper1 = facing
then   tool = parting_tool
       toolmat = carbide;
rule 13
if   oper1 = threading
then   tool = v_tool;
rule 14
if   oper1 = knurling
then   tool = knurling_tool;

rule 15
if   oper2 <> threading and
       oper1 <> threading and
       oper1 <> drilling
then   game = hh;
rule 16
if   material = free_cutting_steel and
     tool = single_point or
     tool1 = single_point
then name = yes
       sp1 = 175_to_350
       sp2 = 350_to_450
       sp3 = 450_to_600
       sp4 = 600_to_750
       sp5 = 750_to_1500;
rule 17
if   material = low_alloy_csteel and
     tool = single_point or
     tool1 = single_point
then name = yes
       sp1 = 150_to_300
       sp2 = 300_to_400
       sp3 = 400_to_550
       sp4 = 550_to_700
       sp5 = 700_to_1200;
rule 18
if   material = medium_alloy_steel and
     tool = single_point or
     tool1 = single_point
then name = yes
       sp1 = 125_to_250
       sp2 = 250_to_350
       sp3 = 350_to_450
       sp4 = 450_to_600
       sp5 = 600_to_1000;
rule 19
if   material = high_alloy_steel and
     tool = single_point or
     tool1 = single_point
then name = yes

```
    sp1 = 100_to_300
    sp2 = 200_to_300
    sp3 = 300_to_400
    sp4 = 400_to_500
    sp5 = 500_to_750;
rule 20
if   material = cast_iron and
     tool = single_point or
     tool1 = single_point
then name = yes
    sp1 = 100_to_200
    sp2 = 200_to_250
    sp3 = 250_to_350
    sp4 = 350_to_450
    sp5 = 450_to_600;

rule 21
if   material = tungstan_steel and
     tool = single_point or
     tool1 = single_point
then name = yes
    sp1 = 50_to_150
    sp2 = 150_to_200
    sp3 = 200_to_250
    sp4 = 250_to_325
    sp5 = 325_to_400;
rule 22
if   material = copper_alloy and
     tool = single_point or
     tool1 = single_point
then name = yes
    sp1 = 300_to_500
    sp2 = 500_to_650
    sp3 = 650_to_800
    sp4 = 800_to_1000
    sp5 = 1000_to_1250;
rule 23
if   material = Mg_alloy and
     tool = single_point or
     tool1 = single_point
then name = yes
    sp1 = 300_to_500
    sp2 = 500_to_600
    sp3 = 600_to_800
    sp4 = 800_to_1250
    sp5 = 1250_to_2000;

rule 24
if   material = Al_alloy and
     tool = single_point or
     tool1 = single_point
```

```
then name = yes
    sp1 = 100_to_200
    sp2 = 200_to_300
    sp3 = 300_to_450
    sp4 = 450_to_700
    sp5 = 700_to_1000;

rule 25
if   tomin <= 0.005
then finish = yes
    depth2 = ((depth) - 0.005)
    finishcut = 0.005
    feed1 = 0.004_to_0.005
    speed1 = (sp5)
    finishpass = 1;
rule 26
if   tomin > 0.005
then finish = yes
    depth2 = (depth);
rule 27
if   depth2 < 0.5
then done = yes
    depth1 = (depth2)
    roughpass = 1;
rule 28
if   depth2 >= 0.5 and
     depth2 <= 1.0
then done = yes
    depth1 = (depth2/2)
    roughpass = 2;
rule 29
if   depth2 > 1.0 and
     depth2 <= 1.5
then done = yes
    depth1 = (depth2/3)
    roughpass = 3;
rule 30
if   depth2 > 1.5 and
     depth2 <= 2.0
then done = yes
    depth1 = (depth2/4)
    roughpass = 4;
rule 31
if   tool = single_point
then made = yes;
rule 32
if   tool = noo
then made = no;
```

rule 33
if   tool = parting_tool
then made = rt
  finish = yes
  rod = no;
rule 34
if   tool = form_tool
then made = ft
  finish = yes
  name = yes
  game = yes
  done = yes
  rod = ko;
rule 35
if   rod = ko
then dis = yes
  display " STEP {step}

      The operation is: {oper1}
      The tool is: {tool}
      The tool material is: {toolmat}
      from: x= {fromx}, y= {fromy}
      to: x= {tox}   , y= {toy}
      The coolant to be used: {coolant}

      Press any key to continue ..~";
rule 36
if   tool1 = single_point
then made = yes;
rule 37
if   made = yes and
  depth1 > 0.375
then rod = yes
  feed = 0.060_to_0.18
  speed = (sp1)
  roughcut = (depth1);
rule 38
if   made = yes and
  depth1 <= 0.375 and
  depth1 > 0.187
then rod = yes
  feed = 0.060_to_0.10
  speed = (sp2)
  roughcut = (depth1);
rule 39
if   made = yes and
  depth1 <= 0.187 and
  depth1 > 0.094
then rod = yes
  feed = 0.030_to_0.060
  speed = (sp3)
  roughcut = (depth1);

rule 40
if   made = yes and
  depth1 <= 0.094 and
  depth1 > 0.015
then rod = yes
  feed = 0.01_to_0.030
  speed = (sp4)
  roughcut = (depth1);
rule 41
if   made = yes and
  depth1 <= 0.015 and
  depth1 > 0.005
then rod = yes
  feed = 0.008_to_0.010
  speed = (sp5)
  roughcut = (depth1);
rule 42
if   rod = yes and
  tool = single_point
then dis = yes
    display " STEP {step}
    The operation is: {oper1}.
    The tool is: {tool}
    The tool material is: {toolmat}
    The total depth of cut is: {depth}
    The rough cut is: {roughcut}
    The # of rough passes are: {roughpass}
    The speed is: {speed}
    The feed is: {feed}
    The coolant to be used is: {coolant}
  {oper1} from: x={fromx},y={fromy}
        to: x={tox}, y={toy}
    Press any key to continue ..~";
rule 43
if   rod = no
then dis = yes
  display " STEP {step}
    The operation is: {oper1}
    The tool is: {tool}
    The tool material is: {toolmat}
  {oper1}from: x={fromx},y={fromy}
    to: x= {tox}, y={toy}
    The coolant to be used is: {coolant}

    Press any key to continue..~";
rule 44
if   rod = yes and
  tool2 = v_tool and
  done = yes and
  gone = yes
then dis = yes

display " STEP {step}
    The operation # 1 is: {oper1}
    The tool is: {tool1}
    The tool material is: {toolmat}
    The total depth of cut is: {depth}
    The rough cut is: {roughcut}
    The # of roughpasses are: {roughpass}
    The speed is: {speed}
    The feed is: {feed}
{oper1} from:x={fromx},y={fromy} to:x={tox},
y={toy}
    Press any key to continue..~"
    display"
    The operation # 2 is: {oper2}
    The tool is: {tool2}
    The tool material is: {toolmat}
    The speed in rpm is: {speed1}
    The surface speed is: {feed1}
    The coolant to be used is: {coolant}
{oper2}from:x={x1},y={y1} to: x={x2}, y={y2}
    Press any key to continue..~";

rule 45
if rod = yes and
    tool2 = knurling_tool
then dis = yes
    display " STEP {step}
    The operation # 1 is: {oper1}
    The tool is: {tool1}
    The tool material is: {toolmat}
    The total depth of cut is: {depth}
    The rough cut is: {roughcut}
    The # of roughpasses are: {roughpass}
    The speed is: {speed}
    The feed is: {feed}
    The coolant to be used is: {coolant}
{oper1} from: x={fromx},y={fromy}
    to: x={tox}, y={toy}
    Press any key to continue..~"
    display "
    The operation # 2 is: {oper2}
    The tool is: {tool2}
    The tool material is: {toolmat}
    The coolant to be used is: {coolant}
{oper2} from: x={x1},y={y1}
    to: x={x2}, y={y2}
    Press any key to continue..~";

rule 46
if tool = boring_v_tool
then made = ih
    finish = yes
    rod = it;
rule 47
if rod = it and
    gone = yes
then dis = yes
    display"STEP {step}
    The operation is: {oper1}
    The tool is: {tool}
    The tool material is: {toolmat}
    The coolant to be used is: {coolant}
{oper1} from: x={fromx},y={fromy}
    to: x={tox}, y={toy}
    Press any key to continue..~";
rule 48
if tool = v_tool
then made = th
    finish = yes
    rod = ht;
rule 49
if rod = ht and
    gone = yes
then dis = yes
    display" The operation is {oper1}
    The tool is {tool}
    The tool material is {toolmat}
    The threads per inch {tolplus}
    The speed in rpm is {speed}
    The surface speed is {feed}
    The coolant to be used is {coolant}
    {oper1} from x={fromx},y={fromy}
    to x={tox}, y={toy}";
rule 50
if tool = knurling_tool
then made = yt
    finish = yes
    rod = tt;
rule 51
if rod = yt
then dis = yes
    display" The operation is {oper1}
    The tool is {tool}
    The tool material is {toolmat}
    The coolant to be used is {coolant}
    The turns per inch {tolplus}
    {oper1} from x={fromx},y={fromy}
    to x={tox}, y={toy}";

rule 52
if material = free_cutting_steel and
   tool = v_tool or
   tool2 = v_tool
then game = thr
   rp1 = 700
   sf1 = 50
   rp2 = 400
   sf2 = 45
   rp3 = 270
   sf3 = 40
   rp4 = 150
   sf4 = 35
   rp5 = 80
   sf5 = 30
   rp6 = 40
   sf6 = 25
   rp7 = 26
   sf7 = 20;
rule 53
if material = low_alloy_csteel or
   material = medium_alloy_ateel or
   material = high_alloy_steel or
   material = tungstan_steel and
   tool = v_tool or
   tool2 = v_tool
then game = thr
   rp1 = 275
   sf1 = 20
   rp2 = 160
   sf2 = 18
   rp3 = 100
   sf3 = 15
   rp4 = 50
   sf4 = 12
   rp5 = 30
   sf5 = 10
   rp6 = 15
   sf6 = 8
   rp7 = 10
   sf7 = 8;

rule 54
if material = cast_iron and
   tool = v_tool or
   tool2 = v_tool
then game = thr
   rp1 = 850
   sf1 = 60
   rp2 = 500
   sf2 = 55

   rp3 = 340
   sf3 = 50
   rp4 = 200
   sf4 = 45
   rp5 = 100
   sf5 = 40
   rp6 = 50
   sf6 = 35
   rp7 = 38
   sf7 = 30;

rule 55
if material = copper_alloy and
   tool = v_tool or
   tool2 = v_tool
then game = thr
   rp1 = 975
   sf1 = 70
   rp2 = 600
   sf2 = 65
   rp3 = 400
   sf3 = 60
   rp4 = 250
   sf4 = 55
   rp5 = 130
   sf5 = 50
   rp6 = 70
   sf6 = 45
   rp7 = 51
   sf7 = 40;
rule 56
if material = Al_alloy or
   material = Mg_alloy and
   tool = v_tool or
   tool2 = v_tool
then game = thr
   rp1 = 1100
   sf1 = 80
   rp2 = 700
   sf2 = 75
   rp3 = 475
   sf3 = 70
   rp4 = 280
   sf4 = 65
   rp5 = 150
   sf5 = 60
   rp6 = 100
   sf6 = 55
   rp7 = 64
   sf7 = 50;

rule 57
if y1 <= 0.3125 and
    game = thr
then done = yes
    gone = yes
    speed1 = (rp1)
    feed1 = (sf1);
rule 58
if y1 > 0.3125 and
    y1 <= 0.4375 and
    game = thr
then done = yes
    gone = yes
    speed1 = (rp2)
    feed1 = (sf1);
rule 59
if tool = boring_v_tool or
    tool2 = boring_v_tool
then game = thr;
rule 60
if game = thr
then gone = yes;
rule 61
if depth = 0
then zone = yes
    depth = 0.005
    roughcut = 0.005;
rule 62
if depth <> 0
then zone = no;
rule 63
if rod = yes and
    tool2 = boring_v_tool and
    done = yes and
    gone = yes
then dis = yes
    display " STEP {step}
    The operation # 1 is: {oper1}
    The tool is: {tool1}
    The tool material is: {toolmat}
    The total depth of cut is: {depth}
    The rough cut is: {roughcut}
    The # of roughpasses are: {roughpass}
    The speed is: {speed}
    The feed is: {feed}
    The coolant to be used is: {coolant}
{oper1} from: x={fromx},y={fromy}
    to: x={tox}, y={toy}
    Press any key to continue..~"
  display "
    The operation # 2 is: {oper2}

    The tool is: {tool2}
    The tool material is: {toolmat}
    The coolant to be used is: {coolant}
  {oper2} from x={x1},y={y1}
      to x={x2}, y={y2}
    Press any key to continue..~";
rule 64
if y1 > 0.4375 and
    y1 <= 0.625 and
    game = thr
then done = yes
    gone = yes
    speed1 = (rp3)
    feed1 = (sf3);
rule 65
if y1 > 0.625 and
    y1 <= 1.125 and
    game = thr
then done = yes
    gone = yes
    speed1 = (rp4)
    feed1 = (sf4);
rule 66
if y1 > 1.125 and
    y1 <= 1.75 and
    game = thr
then done = yes
    gone = yes
    speed1 = (rp5)
    feed1 = (sf5);
rule 67
if y1 > 1.75 and
    y1 <= 2.75 and
    game = thr
then done = yes
    gone = yes
    speed1 = (rp6)
    feed1 = (sf6);
rule 68
if y1 > 2.75 and
    game = thr
then done = yes
    gone = yes
    speed1 = (rp7)
    feed1 = (sf7);

rule 69
if material = free_cutting_steel or
    material = tungstan_steel and
    tool = twist_drill
then game = yes

name = yes
made = yes
finish = yes
done = yes
rod = yes
speed2 = 50
feed2 = 0.01
coolant = Lard_or_soluble_oil
point = 125
lip = 10_12
chisel = 125_135
helix = 24_32;
rule 70
if   material = low_alloy_steel and
     material = medium_alloy_steel and
     tool = twist_drill
then game = yes
     name = yes
     made = yes
     finish = yes
     done = yes
     rod = yes
     speed2 = 110_120
     feed2 = 0.020
     coolant = soluble_oil
     point = 118
     lip = 12_15
     chisel = 125_135
     helix = 24_32;
rule 71
if   material = high_alloy_steel and
     tool = twist_drill
then game = yes
     name = yes
     made = yes
     finish = yes
     done = yes
     rod = yes
     speed2 = 80
     feed2 = 0.010
     coolant = soluble_oil
     point = 118
     lip = 12_15
     chisel = 125_135
     helix = 24_32;
rule 72
if   material = cast_iron and
     tool = twist_drill
then game = yes
     name = yes
     made = yes

finish = yes
done = yes
rod = yes
speed2 = 80_100
feed2 = 0.020
coolant = none
point = 90_100
lip = 12
chisel = 125_135
helix = 24_32;
rule 73
if   material = copper_alloy and
     tool = twist_drill
then game = yes
     name = yes
     made = yes
     finish = yes
     done = yes
     rod = yes
     speed2 = 200
     feed2 = 0.003_0.020
     coolant = none
     point = 118
     lip = 12_15
     chisel = 0
     helix = 10_22;
rule 74
if   material = Mg_alloy and
     tool = twist_drill
then game = yes
     name = yes
     made = yes
     finish = yes
     done = yes
     rod = yes
     speed2 = 300_2000
     feed2 = 0.004_0.050
     coolant = none
     point = 70_118
     lip = 12
     chisel = 120_135
     helix = 10_30;
rule 75
if   material = Al_alloy and
     tool = twist_drill
then game = yes
     name = yes
     made = yes
     finish = yes
     done = yes
     rod = yes

speed2 = 60
feed2 = 0.010
coolant = 0.66_lard_and_0.33oil_and_kerosene
point = 118
lip = 7_10
chisel = 120_130
helix = 15_30;
rule 76
if   tool = twist_drill and
     game = yes
then dis = yes
     display " STEP {step}
      The operation is: {oper1}
      The tool is: {tool}
      The tool material is: {toolmat}
      The tool geometry:
      Point angle: {point}
      Lip clearance angle: {lip}
      Chisel point angle: {chisel}
      Helix angle: {helix}
      The lubricant to be used: {coolant}
      The speed(sfpm):   {speed2}
      The feed(ipm):   {feed2}
     {oper1} from: x= {fromx}, y= {fromy}
          to: x= {tox}, y= {toy}
      Press any key to continue..~";
rule 77
if   material = free_cutting_steel and
     oper1 <> drilling
then coolant = water_miscible_Dry;
rule 78
if   material = low_alloy_csteel or
     material = medium_alloy_steel and
     oper1 <> drilling
then coolant = water_miscible_Dry;
rule 79
if   material = high_alloy_steel or
     material = tungstan_steel and
     oper1 <> drilling
then coolant = HD_water_miscible;
rule 80
if   material = cast_iron and
     oper1 <> drilling
then coolant = GP_water_miscible_Dry;
rule 81
if   material = copper_alloy and
     oper1 <> drilling
then coolant = water_miscible;

rule 82
if   material = Mg_alloy and
     oper1 <> drilling
then coolant = LD_cutting_oil_or_speciality_fluids;
rule 83
if   material = Al_alloy and
     oper1 <> drilling
then   coolant = Water_miscible_Dry;
rule 84
if   material = free_cutting_steel and
     tool = boring_tool or
     tool1 = boring_tool
then name = yes
     s1 = 275_to_475
     f1 = 0.010_to_0.020
     s2 = 350_to_625
     f2 = 0.008_to_0.012
     s3 = 500_to_1500
     f3 = 0.002_to_0.008;
rule 85
if   material = low_alloy_csteel or
     material = medium_alloy_steel or
     material = high_alloy_steel and
     tool = boring_tool or
     tool1 = boring_tool
then name = yes
     s1 = 200_to_475
     f1 = 0.010_to_0.020
     s2 = 300_to_675
     f2 = 0.008_to_0.012
     s3 = 500_to_1500
     f3 = 0.002_to_0.008;

rule 86
if   material = cast_iron and
     tool = boring_tool or
     tool1 = boring_tool
then name = yes
     s1 = 250
     f1 = 0.010_to_0.020
     s2 = 275
     f2 = 0.008_to_0.012
     s3 = 300
     f3 = 0.002_to_0.008;
rule 87
if   material = tungstan_steel and
     tool = boring_tool or
     tool1 = boring_tool
then name = yes
     s1 = 150_to_350
     f1 = 0.010_to_0.020

s2 = 250_to_450
f2 = 0.008_to_0.012
s3 = 300_to_800
f3 = 0.002_to_0.008;
rule 88
if   material = copper_alloy and
     tool = boring_tool or
     tool1 = boring_tool
then name = yes
     s1 = 200_to_500
     f1 = 0.010_to_0.020
     s2 = 300_to_600
     f2 = 0.008_to_0.012
     s3 = 400_to_1000
     f3 = 0.002_to_0.008;
rule 89
if   material = Al_alloy or
     material = Mg_alloy and
     tool = boring_tool or
     tool1 = boring_tool
then name = yes
     s1 = 250_to_600
     f1 = 0.010_to_0.020
     s2 = 300_to_1000
     f2 = 0.008_to_0.012
     s3 = 400_to_1500
     f3 = 0.002_to_0.008;
rule 90
if   tool = boring_tool
then made = yes;
rule 91
if   made = yes and
     depth1 > 0.15625
then rod = yes
     speed = (s1)
     feed = (f1)
     roughcut = (depth1);
rule 92
if   made = yes and
     depth1 <= 0.15625 and
     depth1 > 0.0625
then rod = yes
     speed = (s2)
     feed = (f2)
     roughcut = (depth1);
rule 93
if   made = yes and
     depth1 <= 0.0625
then rod = yes

speed = (s3)
feed = (f3)
roughcut = (depth1);
rule 94
if   rod = yes and
     tool = boring_tool
then dis = yes
     display " STEP {step}
     The operation is: {oper1}.
     The tool is: {tool}
     The tool material is: {toolmat}
     The total depth of cut is: {depth}
     The rough cut is: {roughcut}
     The # of rough passes are: {roughpass}
     The speed is: {speed}
     The feed is: {feed}
     The coolant to be used is: {coolant}
     {oper1} from x={fromx},y={fromy}
          to x={tox}, y={toy}
     Press any key to continue..~";
ask material: " What is the raw material for the part?";
ask part:" What is the name of the part?";

JUSTEX KNOWLEDGE BASE

RUNTIME;
ENDOFF;
ACTIONS
bkcolor=4
color=14
wopen 1,1,2,16,75,4
active 1
        FIND proceed
        FIND stratdec
wclose 1
bkcolor=5
color=14
wopen 2,1,2,10,70,5
active 2
PRINTON
DISPLAY "
        *****DECISION FROM THE STRATEGIC
MODULE*****

  Your responses have been recorded. From a strategic
standpoint the
  system recommends a {stratdec}.
  If there are conflicting results from the three modules
then please
  choose the FINAL option from the main menu.

****
        Press any key to continue~"
PRINTOFF
EJECT
wclose 2
    CHAIN tactical;

RULE 1
    IF proceed = yes
    THEN sdummy = found
    FIND iss1
    CLS
    FIND iss2
    CLS
    FIND iss3
    CLS
    FIND iss4
    CLS

FIND iss5
CLS
FIND iss6;

RULE 2
IF proceed = no
THEN stratdec = CONSULTATION_WITH_THE_EC
ONOMIC_MODULE;

RULE 3
IF proceed = yes AND
    iss1 = first AND
    iss2 = forth AND
    iss3 = second AND
    iss4 = second AND
    iss5 = third AND
    iss6 = second
THEN   stratdec = GO;

RULE 4
    IF iss1 = first AND
      iss2 = third AND
      iss3 = second AND
      iss4 = third AND
      iss5 = second AND
      iss6 = second
THEN   stratdec = GO;
RULE 5
    IF iss1 = second AND
      iss2 = second AND
      iss3 = second AND
      iss4 = second AND
      iss5 = third AND
      iss6 = second
THEN   stratdec = GO;
RULE 6
    IF iss1 = second AND
      iss2 = third AND
      iss3 = second AND
      iss4 = second AND
      iss5 = third AND
      iss6 = second
THEN   stratdec = GO;

RULE 7
 IF iss1 = second AND
  iss2 = forth AND
  iss3 = second AND
  iss4 = second AND
  iss5 = third AND
  iss6 = second
THEN stratdec = GO;

RULE 8
 IF iss1 = third AND
  iss2 = first AND
  iss3 = third AND
  iss4 = third AND
  iss5 = third AND
  iss6 = second
THEN stratdec = GO;

RULE 9
 IF iss1 = third AND
  iss2 = second AND
  iss3 = second AND
  iss4 = third AND
  iss5 = third AND
  iss6 = second
THEN stratdec = GO;

RULE 10
 IF iss1 = third AND
  iss2 = third AND
  iss3 = second AND
  iss4 = second AND
  iss5 = third AND
  iss6 = second
THEN stratdec = GO;

RULE 11
 IF iss1 = third AND
  iss2 = forth AND
  iss3 = second AND
  iss4 = second AND
  iss5 = third AND
  iss6 = second
THEN stratdec = GO;

RULE 12
 IF iss1 = first AND
  iss2 = forth AND
  iss3 = third AND
  iss4 = first AND
  iss5 = third AND
  iss6 = second
THEN stratdec = GO;

RULE 13
 IF iss1 = first AND
  iss2 = third AND
  iss3 = third AND
  iss4 = first AND
  iss5 = third AND
  iss6 = second
THEN stratdec = GO;

RULE 14
 IF iss1 = second AND
  iss2 = second AND
  iss3 = third AND
  iss4 = second AND
  iss5 = third AND
  iss6 = second
THEN stratdec = GO;

RULE 15
 IF iss1 = second AND
  iss2 = forth AND
  iss3 = third AND
  iss4 = first AND
  iss5 = third AND
  iss6 = second
THEN stratdec = GO;

RULE 16
 IF iss1 = third AND
  iss2 = second AND
  iss3 = third AND
  iss4 = second AND
  iss5 = third AND
  iss6 = second
THEN stratdec = GO;

RULE 17
 IF iss1 = third AND
  iss2 = third AND
  iss3 = third AND
  iss4 = first AND
  iss5 = third AND
  iss6 = second
THEN stratdec = GO;

RULE 18
 IF iss1 = third AND
  iss2 = forth AND
  iss3 = third AND
  iss4 = first AND
  iss5 = third AND
  iss6 = second
THEN stratdec = GO;

RULE 19
  IF iss1 = third AND
    iss2 = forth AND
    iss3 = third AND
    iss4 = second AND
    iss5 = first AND
    iss6 = second
THEN   stratdec = GO;
RULE 20
  IF iss1 = third AND
    iss2 = forth AND
    iss3 = third AND
    iss4 = third AND
    iss5 = first AND
    iss6 = second
THEN   stratdec = GO;
RULE 21
  IF iss1 = first AND
    iss2 = third AND
    iss3 = second AND
    iss4 = third AND
    iss5 = third AND
    iss6 = second
THEN   stratdec = GO;
RULE 22
  IF iss1 = third AND
    iss2 = third AND
    iss3 = second AND
    iss4 = third AND
    iss5 = third AND
    iss6 = second
THEN   stratdec = GO;
RULE 23
  IF iss1 = third AND
    iss2 = forth AND
    iss3 = second AND
    iss4 = third AND
    iss5 = third AND
    iss6 = second
THEN   stratdec = GO;
RULE 24
  IF iss1 = first AND
    iss2 = forth AND
    iss3 = third AND
    iss4 = second AND
    iss5 = third AND
    iss6 = second
THEN   stratdec = GO;

RULE 25
  IF iss1 = first AND
    iss2 = forth AND
    iss3 = third AND
    iss4 = third AND
    iss5 = second AND
    iss6 = second
THEN   stratdec = GO;
RULE 26
  IF iss1 = first AND
    iss2 = forth AND
    iss3 = third aND
    iss4 = third AND
    iss5 = third AND
    iss6 = second
THEN   stratdec = GO;
RULE 27
  IF iss1 = first AND
    iss2 = third AND
    iss3 = third AND
    iss4 = second AND
    iss5 = third AND
    iss6 = second
THEN   stratdec = GO;
RULE 28
  IF iss1 = first AND
    iss2 = third AND
    iss3 = third AND
    iss4 = third AND
    iss5 = second AND
    iss6 = second
THEN   stratdec = GO;
RULE 29
  IF iss1 = first AND
    iss2 = third AND
    iss3 = third AND
    iss4 = third AND
    iss5 = third AND
    iss6 = second
THEN   stratdec = GO;
RULE 30
  IF iss1 = second AND
    iss2 = second AND
    iss3 = third AND
    iss4 = third AND
    iss5 = third AND
    iss6 = second
THEN   stratdec = GO;

RULE 31
    IF iss1 = second AND
    iss2 = forth AND
    iss3 = third AND
    iss4 = second AND
    iss5 = third AND
    iss6 = second
THEN   stratdec = GO;
RULE 32
    IF iss1 = second AND
    iss2 = forth AND
    iss3 = third AND
    iss4 = third AND
    iss5 = second AND
    iss6 = second
THEN   stratdec = GO;
RULE 33
    IF iss1 = second AND
    iss2 = forth AND
    iss3 = third AND
    iss4 = third AND
    iss5 = third AND
    iss6 = second
THEN   stratdec = GO;
RULE 34
    IF iss1 = third AND
    iss2 = third AND
    iss3 = third AND
    iss4 = second AND
    iss5 = third AND
    iss6 = second
THEN   stratdec = GO;
RULE 35
    IF iss1 = first AND
    iss2 = forth AND
    iss3 = second AND
    iss4 = third AND
    iss5 = third AND
    iss6 = second
THEN   stratdec = GO;
RULE 36
    IF iss1 = second AND
    iss2 = second AND
    iss3 = second AND
    iss4 = third AND
    iss5 = third AND
    iss6 = second
THEN   stratdec = GO;

RULE 37
    IF iss1 = second AND
    iss2 = third AND
    iss3 = second AND
    iss4 = third AND
    iss5 = third AND
    iss6 = second
THEN   stratdec = GO;
RULE 38
    IF iss1 = second AND
    iss2 = forth AND
    iss3 = second AND
    iss4 = third AND
    iss5 = third AND
    iss6 = second
THEN   stratdec = GO;
RULE 39
    IF iss1 = third AND
    iss2 = third AND
    iss3 = second AND
    iss4 = third AND
    iss5 = second AND
    iss6 = second
THEN   stratdec = GO;
RULE 40
    IF iss1 = third AND
    iss2 = forth AND
    iss3 = second AND
    iss4 = third AND
    iss5 = second AND
    iss6 = second
THEN   stratdec = GO;
RULE 41
    IF iss1 = first AND
    iss2 = forth AND
    iss3 = third AND
    iss4 = second AND
    iss5 = second AND
    iss6 = second
THEN   stratdec = GO;
RULE 42
    IF iss1 = first AND
    iss2 = forth AND
    iss3 = third AND
    iss4 = third AND
    iss5 = first AND
    iss6 = second
THEN   stratdec = GO;

RULE 43
IF iss1 = first AND
    iss2 = third AND
    iss3 = third AND
    iss4 = second AND
    iss5 = second AND
    iss6 = second
THEN   stratdec = GO;
RULE 44
IF iss1 = first AND
    iss2 = third AND
    iss3 = third AND
    iss4 = third AND
    iss5 = first AND
    iss6 = second
THEN   stratdec = GO;
RULE 45
IF iss1 = second AND
    iss2 = second AND
    iss3 = third AND
    iss4 = third AND
    iss5 = second AND
    iss6 = second
THEN   stratdec = GO;
RULE 46
IF iss1 = second AND
    iss2 = forth AND
    iss3 = third AND
    iss4 = second AND
    iss5 = second AND
    iss6 = second
THEN   stratdec = GO;
RULE 47
IF iss1 = second AND
    iss2 = forth AND
    iss3 = third AND
    iss4 = third AND
    iss5 = first AND
    iss6 = second
THEN   stratdec = GO;
RULE 48
IF iss1 = third AND
    iss2 = second AND
    iss3 = third AND
    iss4 = third AND
    iss5 = third AND
    iss6 = second
THEN   stratdec = GO;

RULE 49
IF iss1 = third AND
    iss2 = third AND
    iss3 = third AND
    iss4 = second AND
    iss5 = second AND
    iss6 = second
THEN   stratdec = GO;
RULE 50
IF iss1 = third AND
    iss2 = third AND
    iss3 = third AND
    iss4 = third AND
    iss5 = first AND
    iss6 = second
THEN   stratdec = GO;
RULE 51
IF iss1 = third AND
    iss2 = third AND
    iss3 = third AND
    iss4 = third AND
    iss5 = second AND
    iss6 = second
THEN   stratdec = GO;
RULE 52
IF iss1 = third AND
    iss2 = third AND
    iss3 = third AND
    iss4 = third AND
    iss5 = third AND
    iss6 = second
THEN   stratdec = GO;
RULE 53
IF iss1 = third AND
    iss2 = forth AND
    iss3 = third AND
    iss4 = second AnD
    iss5 = second AND
    iss6 = second
THEN   stratdec = GO;
RULE 54
IF iss1 = third AND
    iss2 = forth AND
    iss3 = third aND
    iss4 = third AND
    iss5 = third AND
    iss6 = second
THEN   stratdec = GO;

RULE 55
  IF iss1 = third AND
      iss2 = forth AND
      iss3 = third AND
      iss4 = third AND
      iss5 = second AND
      iss6 = second
THEN   stratdec = GO;
RULE 56
  IF iss1 = third AND
      iss2 = forth AND
      iss3 = third AND
      iss4 = third AND
      iss5 = third AND
      iss6 = second
THEN   stratdec = GO;
RULE 57
  IF iss1 = first AND
      iss2 = forth AND
      iss3 = third AND
      iss4 = third AND
      iss5 = first AND
      iss6 = first
THEN   stratdec = DEFER;
RULE 58
  IF iss1 = first AND
      iss2 = third AND
      iss3 = third AND
      iss4 = third AND
      iss5 = first AND
      iss6 = first
THEN   stratdec = DEFER;
RULE 59
  IF iss1 = third AND
      iss2 = forth AND
      iss3 = third AND
      iss4 = third AND
      iss5 = first AND
      iss6 = first
THEN   stratdec = DEFER;
RULE 60
  IF iss1 = first AND
      iss2 = forth AND
      iss3 = third AND
      iss4 = third AND
      iss5 = second AND
      iss6 = first
THEN   stratdec = DEFER;

RULE 61
  IF iss1 = first AND
      iss2 = forth AND
      iss3 = third AND
      iss4 = third AND
      iss5 = third AND
      iss6 = first
THEN   stratdec = DEFER;
RULE 62
  IF iss1 = first AND
      iss2 = third AND
      iss3 = third AND
      iss4 = third AND
      iss5 = third AND
      iss6 = first
THEN   stratdec = DEFER;
RULE 63
  IF iss1 = second AND
      iss2 = forth AND
      iss3 = third AND
      iss4 = third AND
      iss5 = second AND
      iss6 = first
THEN   stratdec = DEFER;
RULE 64
  IF iss1 = second AND
      iss2 = forth AND
      iss3 = third AND
      iss4 = third AND
      iss5 = third AND
      iss6 = first
THEN   stratdec = DEFER;
RULE 65
  IF iss1 = third AND
      iss2 = third AND
      iss3 = third AND
      iss4 = third AND
      iss5 = third AND
      iss6 = first
THEN   stratdec = DEFER;
RULE 66
  IF iss1 = third AND
      iss2 = forth AND
      iss3 = third AND
      iss4 = third AND
      iss5 = third AND
      iss6 = first
THEN   stratdec = DEFER;

RULE 67
  IF iss1 = third AND
      iss2 = forth AND
      iss3 = third AND
      iss4 = third AND
      iss5 = second AND
      iss6 = first
THEN   stratdec = DEFER;
RULE 68
  IF iss1 = third AND
      iss2 = forth AND
      iss3 = third AND
      iss4 = third AND
      iss5 = third AND
      iss6 = first
THEN   stratdec = DEFER
ELSE   stratdec = NOGO;

ASK proceed:
"The strategic justification module involves six (6) basic issues. It
is advisable to run this module as the last part of the consultation,
since there are questions related to the economical justification module.
The Knowledge base is designed in such a way that the user may not have
to answer all six (6) questions if the strategic decision is headed for
NOGO.
Hence the user may return to the main menu after answering three
responses. Are you ready?";
CHOICES proceed:
YES, NO;
ASK iss1:
" High Technology investment options must be effectively managed for
 future growth. Which of the following three options best describes
 the investment option being considered?
   1. Technology is immediately available.
   2. Technology will be available for years and is not proprietary.
   3. Technology will be available for years and is proprietary.";
CHOICES iss1: first, second, third;

ASK iss2:
" The organizations technological plan should match its business plan
 for the next five years, else success of new technology is questionable.
   Which of the following best describes the firms technological/business
   match with respect to this investment.
     1. The two plans will never agree.
     2. They do not agree now but will in 1-2 years.
     3. They do now, but may not in 1-2 years.
     4. They match perfectly and will remain that way.";
CHOICES iss2: first, second, third, forth;
ASK iss3:
" The third issue relates to the organizations accounting system.
   The ideal accounting system would be one that considers direct and
   indirect labor to be fixed and an AMT investment to be variable based
   on the utilization. Which of the following best describes a scenario of
   a future ideal cost accounting system.
     1. Impossible in the near future.
     2. Management is reluctant but will give this idea a fair review.
     3. Possible, and this system currently exists or is being developed.";
CHOICES iss3: first, second, third;
ASK iss4:
" Which of the following three statements best describes the complexity
 of the AMT investment and the uncertainty (technological/environmental)
 involved.
     1. Investment is of high complexity and is also highly uncertain.
     2. Investment is of moderate complexity and is also moderately
         uncertain.
     3. Investment is simple and there is no uncertainty.";
CHOICES iss4: first, second, third;
ASK iss5:
" The Advanced Manufacturing Technology must be highly flexible in
 terms of capacity and must promote better product quality and
 improved productivity.
   Which of the following best describes the investment's impact on the
   above.

1. There is very little or no improvement in the long
run.
2. The investment can make marginal
improvements.
3. The investment can make significant/marked long
term
    improvements.";
CHOICES iss5: first, second, third;
ASK iss6:
" The sixth issue relates to the decision obtained from
the economic
  justification module. Which of the following
statements best describes
  the decision obtained from the economic justification
module.
1. Present Worth is greater than or equal to zero.
2. Present Worth is less than zero.";
CHOICES iss6: first, second;

BALA KNOWLEDGE BASE

Runtime;
bkcolor= 1;
!
!This knowledge base is designed to familiarise new operaters with the different
!assembly lines that the ABC bicycle manufacturing company has on its production
!line. The knowledge base has also catered for users who wish to update the present
!information base which contains information about the assembly lines of the
!company
!
!The primary objective of this knowledge base is to provide an overview of
!the different assembly lines and operations involved in manufacturing a bicycle
!to a newly hired assembly line operator. Another objective of the knowledge
!base is to facilitate information update, whenever necessary, so that software
!maintenance of the expert system is kept to a minimum.
!
!Software Description:
!---------------------
!
!The program starts by displaying introductory information on how the software
!is structured to offer consultaion to the user; this would help the user to use
!this package more effectively
!
!User is asked if he wishes to learn about a particular assembly line or to
!perform economic analysis on one of the three assembly lines. He is then
!asked to select one from the three assembly lines in the production line of the
!company.
!Display information on a particular assembly line
!--
!If the user selected this option, he will see a brief description of the
!assembly line he selected and he will then be asked to pick a particular operation
!from the assembly line which he wishes to know more about. After he selected an
!operation, the information and safety precaution pertaining to the operation
!will be displayed on the screen. This concludes the display information option
!
!Economic Analysis on a particular assembly line
!--
!When the user selects this option, A list of operations pertaining to the
!assembly line(selected ealier by the user) is displayed on the screen.
!The list seen on the screen will include the information on all the operations
!in the assembly line: such as operation name, cost of the operation and an estimated
!value of the operation. The list ends with a total of all operation costs and
!a total of all of the operation's estimated values.
!Edit, Delete and Add operation to a particular assembly line
!---
!This option is provided to facilitate updating of the existing information
!base about the production line of the company. The user is allowed to add to,
!delete from and update on the assembly line record an operation's information.
!
!
!_____

_____

!
!This routine is provided to stop a scrolling page..maximum lines per page can
!be adjusted and set individually on the calling routine whenever LineIndex
if PageLineIndex > (LinesPerPage) then
    color=14
    display " ====> more on next page... (Lines per page can be adjusted!) ~ "
    color=11
    PageLineIndex=1
;

! *********** Start Main Action Block ..
ACTIONS

```
Start=Yes
bcall Xpath        !Establish correct path using batchfile
Xpath..
Find InitIndex      !Rule 0
wopen 6,1,1,23,78,0


whiletrue Done<>Yes then
cls
WindowNumbr=1         !inittailise window numbr
   color = 11
   Reset DisplayStartScrn
   Find  DisplayStartScrn   !display Starting screen
now..(Rule 2,1)
   wopen 2,2,1,10,75,1


   color=11
   Reset ChooseAssembly
   Find  ChooseAssembly    !Every Assembly has a
spread sheet to represent it
                   !(Rule 2a)
   Reset SelectOption
   Find SelectOption  ! Either to Display Instruciton or
do Economic analysis
              !(Rule 2b)
   wclose 2
   cls
   color=11
   Reset DisplayInstruction
   Find  DisplayInstruction  !(Rule 5)
   Reset EconomicAnalysis
   Find  EconomicAnalysis   !(Rule 6)
   display " Exiting Main Program.. "
   reset Done
   find Done
   Wclose All
   Close All
end
;
!*********** End Of Main Action Block

Rule 0
if Start=Yes then          ! This routine creates arrays
that have name
   InitIndex=Initialise_now    ! which correspond a
position of work cells :
   wks A,A1..A20,Row1Ind       !
A[1]=A1....A[20]=A20
   wks B,B1..B20,Row1ind       !
B[1]=B1....B[20]=B20
   wks C,C1..C20,Row1ind       ! ..
```

```
   wks D,D1..D20,Row1ind       !
D[1]=D1....D[20]=D20
;


Rule 1
if WindowNumbr < 14    !This Routine display
contents of a specified text file
   then                     !TextFileName contains the
filename
   DisplayText=Display_Text_now      !of the file that
is to be displayed
   PageLineIndex=0
   whileknown currline
     PageLineIndex=(PageLineIndex + 1)
     reset currline
     receive @TextFileName,currline
     display "{currline}"
   end
   display "~"
;
Rule 2
if WindowNumbr <14 then
DisplayStartScrn=Display_Starting_Screen_Now
   LinesPerPage=10            !numbr of lines per page
(for use in paging)
   TextFileName=Mess          !name of the text file to
be displayed
   wopen 1,5,1,12,78,1
   Reset DisplayText
   Find  DisplayText
   wclose 1
;


Rule 3a
if WindowNumbr <14
then
   ChooseAssembly=Choosing_now      !Select from
Head, Body, and Tail assembly
   reset Assembly
   Find  Assembly   !see ask assembly..
;
Rule 3b
if WindowNumbr < 14
then
   SelectOption=Selecting_now     !Select to perform
Economic Analysis or
   reset MainOption              !to know more about
assembly operations
   Find  MainOption   !see ask MainOption..
;
```

Rule 5
if MainOption=Display_Information !Selected to Know
more about assembly
then   !operations.
  DisplayInstruction=Display_Instruction_Now
  Reset DisplayIntroInstruction !Display information
of assembly line
  Find DisplayIntroInstruction   !(Rule 5 b)
  whiletrue Done<>Yes then
    cls
    Reset DisplayOperation   !
    Find DisplayOperation   !(Rule 5 c)
    cls
    Reset DisplaySafety   !
    Find DisplaySafety   !(Rule 5 f)
    display " Exiting the Display Instruction Option "
    Reset Done
    Find Done
  end
else
  DisplayInstruction=Not_Selected
!MainOption=something
;

Rule 5b
if WindowNumbr < 14 then   !Display Information of
assembly
  DisplayIntroInstruction=Display_Instrction_Now
  LinesPerPage=15
  TextFileName=(Assembly)
  Reset DisplayText
  Find DisplayText
;
Rule 5c
 if WindowNumbr < 14 then
  DisplayOperation=DisplayOperationNow
  reset OperationNumbr
  Find OperationNumbr   !Pick one operation from
assembly line.. Rule 5b
  reset DisplayOperatn
  Find DisplayOperatn   !Display operation's
information.. Rule 5d
;
Rule 5d
if WindowNumbr < 14 then
  OperationNumbr=Selecting_Now
  wks NumbrOfOperation,F1,@Assembly
  display " This Option allows you to know more about
any individual operation"
  display " in the {Assembly} assembly line. You can
select any of the operation"

display " in this assembly to find out more about the
operation and safety "
display " precautions in using the tools needed for the
operation. "
  RowNumbr=1
  for LindIndex=1 to @NumbrOfOperation
    RowNumbr=(RowNumbr+1)
    wks
OpNumbr[LineIndex],@A[RowNumbr],@Assembly
    wks OpName,@B[RowNumbr],@Assembly
    OprName[LineIndex]=(OpName)
    display " #{OpNumbr[LineIndex]}
{OprName[LineIndex]}"
  end
  NewOpNumbr=0
  LastOperation=(NumbrOfOperation)
  whiletrue NewOpNumbr<1 or
NewOpNumbr>(LastOperation) then
      reset AskOpNumbr
      Find AskOpNumbr
      NewOpNumbr=(AskOpNumbr)
  end
  OperationNumbr=(NewOpNumbr)
  RowNumbr=(OperationNumbr+1)
  wks PickedOp,@B[RowNumbr],@Assembly
;
Rule 5e
if WindowNumbr <14 then
  DisplayOperatn=Display_Op_Now
  LinesPerPage=15
  TextFileName=(PickedOp)
  wopen 7,5,1,17,78,1
  color=11
  reset DisplayText
  find DisplayText
  wclose 7
;
Rule 5f
if WindowNumbr < 14 then
  DisplaySafety=Display_Safety_Now
  reset pickTools
  menu pickTools,PickedOp=Op_Name,Tools,tools
  Find pickTools
  LinesPerPage=15
  TextFileName=(pickTools)
  wopen 8,5,1,17,78,1
  color=11
  reset DisplayText
  Find DisplayText
  wclose 8
;

Rule 6
if MainOption=Economic_Analysis then
  EconomicAnalysis=Doing_Economic_Analysis_Now
  reset EconOption
  whiletrue EconOption<>Quit then
    wopen 2,10,40,8,32,1
    reset EconOption
    Find EconOption
    wclose 2
    cls
    color=11
    reset ServeEconOption
    Find ServeEconOption
  end
else
  EconomicAnalysis=Not_Selected !
MainOption<>Economic_Analysis
;
Rule 6b
if EconOption=Display_Operation then
  ServeEconOption=Display_Operatin
  !Find the total Numbr of operations in this assembly
  wks NumbrOfOperation,F1,@Assembly   !Cell F1
stores that parameter..
  TotalCost=0
  ValueAdded=0
  RowNumbr=1
  display "Number   Name   Cost   Estimated Value
"
  for LineIndex = 1 to @NumbrOfOperation
    RowNumbr=(RowNumbr+1)
    wks OpNumbr,@A[RowNumbr],@Assembly
    wks OpName,@B[RowNumbr],@Assembly
    wks OpCost,@C[RowNumbr],@Assembly
    wks OpValue,@D[RowNumbr],@Assembly
    TotalCost=(TotalCost+OpCost)
    ValueAdded=(ValueAdded+OpValue)
    display "{OpNumbr}   {OpName}
{OpCost}   {OpValue} "
  end
  pwks TotalCost,G1,@Assembly
  pwks ValueAdded,G2,@Assembly
  wks HeadTotalCost,G1,Head
  wks BodyTotalCost,G1,Body
  wks TailTotalCost,G1,Tail
  wks HeadTotalValue,G2,Head
  wks BodyTotalValue,G2,Body
  wks TailTotalValue,G2,Tail

  BicTotalCost=(HeadTotalCost+BodyTotalCost+TailT
otalCost)
  TotalValueAdded=(HeadTotalValue+BodyTotalValu
e+TailTotalValue)
  display ""
  display "   Total Cost= {TotalCost}   Value
Added Measure={ValueAdded} "
  display ""
  display " Total cost of the Bicycle : {BicTotalCost}"
  display " Total Value Added Measure :
{TotalValueAdded}"
  display " Hit any key to continue ..~";
Rule 6c
if EconOption=Add_Operation then
  ServeEconOption=Add_Operation
  wks NumbrOfOperation,F1,@Assembly   !Cell F1
stores the Numbr Of operations
  LastOperation=(NumbrOfOperation+1)
  display " You have selected the Add operation
Option. "
  display " The new operation will be added to the
{Assembly} assembly"
  display " line in the order you specify. "
  NewOpNumbr=0
  whiletrue NewOpNumbr<1 or
NewOpNumbr>(LastOperation) then
      reset AskOpNumbr
      Find AskOpNumbr
      NewOpNumbr=(AskOpNumbr)
  end
  reset ReadOpCost
  Find ReadOpCost

!Shift records before adding new information
  offset=(NumbrOfOperation-NewOpNumbr+1)
  LineIndex=(offset)
  whiletrue LineIndex > 1 then
  LineIndex=(LineIndex-1)
    Currline=(LineIndex+1)
    wks OpName, @B[Currline],@Assembly
    wks OpCost, @C[Currline],@Assembly
    wks OpValue, @D[Currline],@Assembly
    nextline=(Currline+1)
    OpNumbr=(nextline-1)   !adjust to the right
operation number
    pwks OpNumbr, @A[Nextline],@Assembly
    pwks OpName, @B[Nextline],@Assembly
    pwks OpCost, @C[Nextline],@Assembly
    pwks OpValue, @D[Nextline],@Assembly
    display " OperationNumbr #{OpNumbr}
Name={OpName} Op_Cost={OpCost}

```
Op_Value={OpValue}"
  end
!Add new record now..
  NewRowNumbr=(NewOpNumbr+1)
  pwks
NewOpNumbr,@A[NewRowNumbr],@Assembly
  pwks
NewOpName,@B[NewRowNumbr],@Assembly
  pwks
NewOpCost,@C[NewRowNumbr],@Assembly
  pwks
NewOpValue,@D[NewRowNumbr],@Assembly
  reset NewOpCost
  reset NewOpValue
  wks
NewOpNumbr,@A[NewRowNumbr],@Assembly
  wks
NewOpName,@B[NewRowNumbr],@Assembly
  wks
SNewOpCost,@C[NewRowNumbr],@Assembly
  wks
SNewOpValue,@D[NewRowNumbr],@Assembly
  display " OperationNumbr #{NewOpNumbr}
Name={NewOpName} Op_Cost={SNewOpCost}
Op_Value={SNewOpValue}"
  NumbrOfOperation=(NumbrOfOperation+1)
  pwks  NumbrOfOperation,F1,@Assembly
  display " Now you can provide despcription for
{NewOpName} and it will"
  display " be entered into the information base "
  display " ( Hit any key to continue ..) ~"
  call edit, "{NewOpName}"
!Add related tools & their safety precaution now..
  whiletrue SelectAddtools<>Quit then
    reset SelectAddtools
    find SelectAddtools
    reset ServeAddTools
    find ServeAddTools
  end
;


Rule 6c1
if SelectAddtools<>Quit then
    ServeAddTools=Add_new_tools_now_to_database
    reset NewToolName
    menu NewToolName,All,tools,TOOLS
    find NewToolName
    ToolName=(NewToolName)
    !append to database the newtool required by this
operation
    whiletrue NewToolName=AddNewTool then
```

```
      reset TempToolName
      find TempToolName
      ToolName=(TempToolName)
      reset NewToolName
    end
    Op_Name=(NewOpName)
    Tools=(ToolName)
    APPEND TOOLS
    call edit,"{ToolName}"

else
    ServeAddTools=did_not_select_to_add_new_tool
!ie. selected to quit..
;


Rule 6d
if EconOption=Delete_Operation then
  ServeEconOption=Delete_Operation
    wks NumbrOfOperation,F1,@Assembly
    LastOperation=(NumbrOfOperation)
    display " You have selected the Delete Operation
Option."
    display " You will have to specify the Operation
number, in terms "
    display " of its order in the assembly line, which you
want to remove"
    display " from the {Assembly} assembly. "
    DelOpNumbr=0
    whiletrue DelOpNumbr<1 or
DelOpNumbr>(NumbrOfOperation) then
        reset AskOpNumbr
        Find AskOpNumbr
        DelOpNumbr=(AskOpNumbr)
    end
!Del records  new information
LineIndex=(DelOpNumbr)
    whiletrue LineIndex<(NumbrOfOperation) then
        LineIndex=(LineIndex+1)   !Add One, to offset
the first row of heading
        Nextline=(LineIndex+1)    !move the rest of the
records one row up...
        wks OpName, @B[Nextline],@Assembly
        wks OpCost, @C[Nextline],@Assembly
        wks OpValue, @D[Nextline],@Assembly
        Currline=(Nextline-1)
        OpNumbr=(Currline-1)
        pwks OpNumbr, @A[Currline],@Assembly
        pwks OpName, @B[Currline],@Assembly
        pwks OpCost, @C[Currline],@Assembly
        pwks OpValue, @D[Currline],@Assembly
        display " OperationNumbr #{OpNumbr}
```

```
Name={OpName} Op_Cost={OpCost}
Op_Value={OpValue}"
    end
    NumbrOfOperation=(NumbrOfOperation-1)
    pwks NumbrOfOperation,F1,@Assembly
    display " Hit any key to continue ..~"
;
Rule 6e
if EconOption=Edit_Operation then
  ServeEconOption=Edit_Operation
    wks NumbrOfOperation,F1,@Assembly
    LastOperation=(NumbrOfOperation)
    display " You have selected to Edit an operaiton in
the {Assembly} assembly."
    display " You will have to specify the operaiton
number of the operation "
    display " which you want to edit. "
    EditOpNumbr=0
    whiletrue EditOpNumbr<1 or
EditOpNumbr>(LastOperation) then
        reset AskOpNumbr
        Find AskOpNumbr
        EditOpNumbr=(AskOpNumbr)
    end
    NewRowNumbr=(EditOpNumbr+1)     !Add One, to
offset first row of heading..
    wks
OldOpName,@B[NewRowNumbr],@Assembly
    wks  OldOpCost,@C[NewRowNumbr],@Assembly
    wks
OldOpValue,@D[NewRowNumbr],@Assembly
    reset ReadOpCost
    Find  ReadOpCost


!UpDate new record now..
    pwks
NewOpName,@B[NewRowNumbr],@Assembly
    pwks
NewOpCost,@C[NewRowNumbr],@Assembly
    pwks
NewOpValue,@D[NewRowNumbr],@Assembly
    reset NewOpCost
    reset NewOpValue
    display " OperationNumbr #{NewOpNumbr}
Name={NewOpName} Op_Cost={SNewOpCost}
Op_Value={SNewOpValue}"
    display " Hit any key to continue ~"
;
```

```
Rule 6z
if EconOption=Edit_Operation then
    ReadOpCost=now
    reset NewOpName
    reset NewOpCost
    reset NewOpValue
    Display " The old Operation Name is {OldOpName}
"
    Find NewOpName    ! the name of the new operation
    Display " The old Operation Cost is {OldOpCost}"
    Find NewOpCost    ! the cost of the new operation
    Display " The old Operation Value is
{OldOpValue}"
    Find NewOpValue    ! the added value for the new
operation
else
    ReadOpCost=now
    reset NewOpName
    reset NewOpCost
    reset NewOpValue
    Find NewOpName    ! the name of the new operation
    Find NewOpCost    ! the cost of the new operation
    Find NewOpValue    ! the added value for the new
operation
;


!_____
_____

ask Assembly : " Select an Assembly of your interest..
";
Choices Assembly: Head,Body,Tail;
ask MainOption : " Select an Option which you want to
perform.. ";
Choices MainOption :
Economic_Analysis,Display_Information;
ask Done : " Do you want to quit ? ";
Choices Done :Yes,No;

ask AskOpNumbr:" Select an operation by typing its
operation Number : 1 to {LastOperation}";
RANGE AskOpNumbr: 1,10;
ask NewOpName : " Type the new Operation name : ";
ask NewOpCost : " Enter the new Operation cost in
dolloar(s) :";
Range NewOpCost: 0,10000;
ask NewOpValue : " Enter the new Operation value in
dollar(s) : ";
Range NewOpValue: 0,10000;
```

ask EconOption : " Menu For Economic Analysis";
Choices EconOption : Display_Operation,Add_Operati
on,Delete_Operation,Edit_Operation,Quit;
ask PickTools : " select a tool from the list for viewing
the tool's safety precautions ";
ask SelectAddTools : " Now input tools that is related
to the operation {NewOpName}";
Choices SelectAddTools :Input_Related_Tool,Quit;
ask NewToolName : "Select a tool which
{NewOpName} requires; select AddNewTool if tool
doesn't exists in menu:";
ask TempToolName : "What is the name of the tool
(less than 9 characters, please!)";

Bibliography

Addis, T. R., *Designing Knowledge-Based Systems*, Prentice Hall, Englewoods Cliffs, NJ, 1985.

Adeli, Hojjat, ed., *Knowledge Engineering, Volume 2: Applications*, McGraw-Hill, New York, 1990.

Adeli, Hojjat, ed., *Knowledge Engineering, Volume I: Fundamentals*, McGraw-Hill, New York, 1990.

Allwood, R. J., *Techniques and Applications of Expert Systems in the Construction Industry*, Halsted Press, NY, 1989.

Amsted, B. H.; P. E. Ostwald; and M. L. Begeman, *Manufacturing Processes*, John Wiley, New York, 1987.

Aoki, Masanao, *Dynamic Analysis of Open Economies*, Academic Press, New York, 1981.

Badiru, Adedeji B., *Project Management Tools for Engineering and Management Professionals*, Industrial Engineering and Management Press, Norcross GA, 1991.

Badiru, Adedeji B., "Artificial Intelligence Applications in Manufacturing," in Cleland, David I. and Bopaya Bidanda, eds., *The Automated Factory Handbook: Technology and Management*, TAB Professional and Reference Books, New York, 1990a, pp. 496–526.

Badiru, Adedeji B., "Strategic Planning for Automated Manufacturing," in Parsaei, H. R., T. L. Ward, and W. Karwowski, eds., *Justification Methods for Computer Integrated Manufacturing Systems*, Elsevier Science Publishers, Amsterdam, the Netherlands, 1990b, pp. 17–39.

Badiru, Adedeji B., "A Systems Approach to Total Quality Management," *Industrial Engineering*, Vol. 22, No. 3, March 1990c, pp. 33–36.

Badiru, Adedeji B., "A Management Guide to Automation Cost Justification," *Industrial Engineering*, Vol. 22, No. 2, Feb. 1990d, pp. 26–30.

Badiru, Adedeji B., "Systems Integration for Total Quality Management," *Engineering Management Journal*, Vol. 2, No. 3, Sept. 1990e, pp. 23–28.

Badiru, Adedeji B. and Gary E. Whitehouse, *Computer Tools, Models, and Techniques for Project Management*, TAB Professional & Reference Books, Inc., Blue Ridge Summit PA, 1990.

Badiru, Adedeji B., *Project Management In Manufacturing and High Technology Operations*, John Wiley, New York, 1988a.

Badiru, Adedeji B., "Expert Systems and Industrial Engineers: A Practical Guide for a Successful Partnership," *Computers & Industrial Engineering*, Vol. 14, No. 1, 1988b, pp. 1–13.

Badiru, Adedeji B., "Successful Initiation of Expert Systems Projects," *IEEE Transactions on Engineering Management*, Vol. 35, No. 3, August 1988c, pp. 186–190.

Badiru, Adedeji B., "Cost-Integrated Network Planning Using Expert Systems," *Project Management Journal*, Vol. 19, No. 2, April 1988d, pp. 59–62.

Badiru, Adedeji B., "State Space Modeling for Knowledge Representation in Project Monitoring and Control," presented at the ORSA/TIMS Fall Conference, Denver, October 1988e.

Badiru, Adedeji B.; Janice Karasz; and Bob Holloway, "AREST: Armed Robbery Eidetic Suspect Typing Expert System," *Journal of Police Science and Administration*, Vol 16, No. 3, September 1988, pp. 210–216.

Badiru, Adedeji B. and Hassan Haideri, "Use of Expert Systems in the Heat Treatment of Steel," presented at the ORSA/TIMS Spring Conference, Washington DC, April 1988.

Badiru, Adedeji B., "Cantor Set Modeling for Manufacturing Knowledge Representation," presented at the ORSA/TIMS Spring Conference, New Orleans, April 1987a.

Badiru, Adedeji B., "Set Theory and Knowledge Base Organization," presented at the ORSA/TIMS Fall Conference, St. Louis, MO, October, 1987b.

Badiru, Adedeji B.; Jan Mathis; and Bob Holloway, "AREST Expert System To Aid Crime Investigations," *AI Interactions*, Texas Instruments Data Systems, Vol. 3, No. 3, November 1987, pp. 5–6.

Badiru, Adedeji B., "Process Capability Analysis on a Microcomputer," *Softcover Software*, Industrial Engineering & Management Press, Norcross GA, 1985, pp. 7–14.

Baker, H., "List Processing in Real Time on a Serial Computer," *Communication of the ACM*, Vol. 21, No. 4, 1978, pp. 280–293.

Barkocy, Brian E. and W. J. Zdeblick, "A Knowledge-Based System for Machining Operation Planning," in *Smart Manufacturing with Artificial Intelligence*, Krakauer, J., ed., First edition, Society of Manufacturing Engineers, Dearborn MI, 1987, pp. 76–88.

Barkovsky, A., "LISP vs PROLOG," *Computers and Electronics*, Vol. 23, No. 1, 1985, p. 71.

Bergstrom, R. P., "AI: Fad with a Future?" *Manufacturing Engineering*, April 1985, p. 65.

Bernold, Thomas and Ulrich Hillenkamp, editors, *Expert Systems in Production and Services*, North-Holland, NY, 1987.

Bharwani, S. S.; J. T. Walls; and M. E. Jackson, "Intelligent Process Development of Foam Molding for the Thermal Protection System (TPS) of the Space Shuttle External Tank," *Proceedings of Third Conference on Artificial Intelligence for Space Applications*: Part I, NASA Conference Publication 2492, Huntsville AL, November 2–3, 1987, pp. 195–202.

Blessing, J. A. and B. A. Watford, "INFMSS—An Intelligent Scheduling System," *Proceedings of the IIE Spring Conference*, May 1987, pp. 476–482.

Bonner, Paul, "University Police Capture Data in Their Multiuser System," *PC WEEK*, July 28, 1987, p. C/4.

Boose, J. H., *Expertise Transfer for Expert System Design*, ed. Gavreil Salvendy, Elsevier Science Publishers, Amsterdam, the Netherlands, 1986.

Boose, J. H., "A Knowledge Acquisition Program for Expert Systems Based on Personal Construct Psychology," *International Journal of Man-Machine Studies*, Vol. 20, 1985, pp. 21–43.

Botten, Nancy A. and Tzvi Raz, eds., *Expert Systems*, Industrial Engineering and Management Press, Norcross GA, 1988.

Bourne, D. A., "CML: a Meta-Interpreter for Manufacturing," *AI Magazine*, Vol. 7, No. 4, 1986, pp. 86–95.

Bourne, D. A. and M. S. Fox, "Autonomous Manufacturing: Automating the Job-Shop," *IEEE Computer*, Vol. 17, No. 9, 1984, pp. 76–86.

Bowen, K. A., "Programming with Full First-Order Logic," *Machine Intelligence*, Vol. 10, J. Hayes, D. Michie, and Y. Pao, eds., Chichester, 1982, pp. 421–440.

Brachman, R. J., "What IS-A Is and Isn't: An Analysis of Taxonomic Links in Semantic Networks," *IEEE Computer*, Vol. 16,. No. 30, 1983.

Brachman, R. J.; R. E. Fikes; and H. L. Levesque, "KRYPTON: A Functional Approach to Knowledge Representation," *IEEE Computer*, Vol. 16, No. 67, 1983.

Bramer, Max, ed., *Practical Experience in Building Expert Systems*, John Wiley, New York, 1990.

Brooks, Rodney A., "Solving the Find-Path Problem by Good Representation of Free Space," *IEEE Transactions on Systems, Man, and Cybernetics*, Vol. SCM-13, No. 3, March/April 1983, pp. 190–197.

Brown, Donald E. and Chelsea C. White, III, *Operations Research and Artificial Intelligence: The Integration of Problem-Solving Strategies*, Kluwer Academic Publishers, Boston, 1990.

Brown, P. F. and S. R. Ray, "Research Issues in Process Planning at the National Bureau of Standards," In *Proceedings of the 2nd International Conference*, April 1987, pp. 111–119.

Bruno, G.; A. Elia; and P. Laface," A Rule-Based System to Schedule Production," *IEEE Computer*, Vol. 17, No. 9, 1986, pp. 32–40.

Buchanan, Bruce G. and Edward H. Shortliffe, eds., *Rule Based Expert Systems: The MYCIN Experiments of the Stanford Heuristics Programming Project*, Addison-Wesley, Reading MA, 1984.

Bullers, William I.; Shimon Y. Nof; and Andrew B. Whinston, "Artificial Intelligence in Manufacturing Planning and Control," *AIIE Transactions*, Vol.12, No. 4, December 1980, pp. 3351–3363.

Bungers, D., "Using Expert Systems for Customer Service of Ford Europe," *Expert Systems and Knowledge Engineering: Essential Elements of Advanced Information Technology*, North-Holland, Amsterdam, the Netherlands, 1986, pp. 215–220.

Chandrasekaran, B., "Design Problem Solving: A Task Analysis," *AI Magazine*, Vol. 11, No. 4, Winter 1990, pp. 59–71.

Chang, T. C. and R. A. Wysk, *An Introduction to Automated Process Planning Systems*, Prentice Hall, Englewoods Cliffs NJ, 1985.

Chang, T. C. and R. A. Wysk, "Integrating CAD and CAM through Automated Process Planning," *International Journal of Production Research*, Vol. 22, No. 5, 1984, pp. 877–894.

Chen, Jen-Gwo, *Prototype Expert System for Physical Work Stress Analysis*, Ph.D. Dissertation, School of Industrial Engineering, University of Oklahoma, Norman OK, 1987.

Chi, M. T. H.; R. Glaser; and E. Rees, "Expertise in Problem Solving," *Advances in the Psychology of Human Intelligence*, Lawrence Erlbaum, Hillsdale NJ, Vol. 1, 1982, pp. 70–75.

Chiesi, H. L.; G. J. Splich; and J. F. Voss, "Acquisition of Domain Related Information in Relation to High and Low Domain Knowledge," *Journal of Verbal Learning and Verbal Behavior*, Vol. 18, 1979, pp. 257–273.

Chorafas, Dimitris N., *Knowledge Engineering: Knowledge Acquisition, Knowledge Representation, the Role of the Knowledge Engineer, and Domains Fertile for AI Implementation*, Van Nostrand, New York, 1990.

Clocksin, W. and C. Emellish, *Programming in PROLOG*, Springer-Verlag, New York, 1984.

Cohen, J., "Describing PROLOG by its Interpretation and Compilation," *Communication of the ACM*, Vol. 28, No. 12, 1985, pp. 1311–1324.

Collins, H. M., *Changing Order: Replication and Induction in Scientific Practice*, Sage, London, 1985.

Colmerauer, A., "PROLOG in 10 Figures," *Communications of the ACM*, Vol. 28, No. 12, 1985, pp. 1296–1310.

Cook, Thomas, "Expert Systems: Panacea or Just a Niche Tools?," *OR/MS Today*, June 1991, p. 6 and p. 8.

Coyne, R. D., "Design Reasoning Without Explanations," *AI Magazine*, Vol. 11, No. 4, Winter 1990, pp. 72–80.

Coyne, R. D. et al, *Knowledge-Based Design Systems*, Addison-Wesley, Reading MA, 1989.

D'Ambrosio, Bruce, "Expert Systems: Myth or Reality," *Byte*, January, 1985, p. 7.

Datar, Neetin N., *A Prototype Knowledge Based Expert System for Robot Consultancy—ROBCON*, MS Thesis, School of Industrial Engineering, University of Oklahoma, Norman OK, 1989.

Datar, Neetin N. and Adedeji B. Badiru, "A Prototype Knowledge Based Expert System for Robot Consultancy—ROBCON," in *Proceedings of the 1988 Oklahoma Symposium on Artificial Intelligence*, University of Oklahoma, Norman OK, November 1988, pp. 51–68.

Davies, B. J. and I. L. Darbyshire, "The Use of Expert Systems In Process Planning," *Annals of CIRP*, Vol. 33, 1984, pp. 303–306.

Davis, R., "Logic Programming and PROLOG: A Tutorial," *IEEE Software*, Vol. 2, No. 5, 1985, pp. 53–62.

Degarmo, E. Paul; T. T. Black; and Ronald A. Kohser., *Materials and Processes in Manufacturing*, 7th ed, Macmillan, New York, 1988.

Dempster, Arthur P., "A Generalization of Bayesian Inference," *Journal of the Royal Statistical Society*, Series B, Vol. 30, No. 2, 1968.

DePorter, Elden L.; J. M. Sepulveda; and Denise F. Jackson, " The Role of Expert Systems in Cybernetic Systems: An Application to Planning and Control of CIM Systems," presented at the ORSA/TIMS conference, St. Louis MO, October 1987.

Dhanushkodi, Satyanarayanan, *An Expert System for Simulation Modeling of Project Networks*, MS Thesis, School of Industrial Engineering, University of Oklahoma, Norman OK, 1989.

Diederich, J.; I. Ruhmann; and M. May, "KRITON: A Knowledge Acquisition Tool for Expert Systems," *International Journal of Man-Machine Studies*, Vol. 27, No. 1, 1987, pp. 29–40.

Dietz, D., "Hybrid Programming Language Eases Applications of Artificial Intelligence," *Defense Electronics*, Vol. 15, No. 10, 1983, pp. 168–177.

Di Piazza, Joseph S. and Frederick A. Helsabeck, "LAPS: Cases to Models to Complete Expert Systems," *AI Magazine*, Vol. 11, No. 3, Fall 1990, pp. 80–107.

Dixon, N., Preconscious Processing, John Wiley, New York, 1981.

Doyle, L. E. et al, *Manufacturing Processes and Materials for Engineers*, 3rd ed, Prentice Hall, Englewood Cliffs, NJ 1985.

Dreyfus, Hubert L., *What Computers Can't Do: A Critique of Artificial Reason*, New York, Harper & Row, 1979.

Duda, R. O.; J. G. Gaschnig; and P. Hart, "Model Design in the Prospector Consultant System for Mineral Exploration," In *Expert Systems in the Micro Electronic Age*, ed. D. H. Michie, Edinburgh University Press, Edinburgh, 1979.

Dutta, Amitava and Amit Basu, "An Artificial Intelligence Approach to Model Management in Decision Support Systems," *IEEE Transactions*, September, 1984, pp. 89–97.

Dym, Clive L. and Raymond E. Levitt, *Knowledge-Based Systems in Engineering*, McGraw-Hill, New York, 1991.

Elithorn, A. and R. Banerji, *Artificial And Human Intelligence*, Elsevier Science Publishers, Amsterdam, the Netherlands, 1984.

Engelmore, Robert and Tony Morgan eds., *Blackboard Systems*, Addison-Wesley, Reading MA, 1988.

Ernst, Christian J., *Management Expert Systems*, Addison-Wesley, Reading MA, 1988.

Esogbue, Augustine O., "Dynamic Programming, Fuzzy Sets, and the Modeling of R&D Management Control Systems," *IEEE Transactions on Systems, Man, and Cybernetics*, Vol. SCM-13, No.1, January/February 1983, pp. 18–30.

Evanson, Steven E., "How to Talk to an Expert," *AI Expert*, February 1988, pp. 36–41.

Feigenbaum, Edward A. and Pamela McCorduck, *The Fifth Generation: Artificial Intelligence and Japan's Computer Challenge to the World*, Addison-Wesley, Reading MA, 1983.

Fisher, E. L., "An AI-Based Methodology for Factory Design," *AI Magazine*, Vol. 7, No. 4, 1986, pp. 72–85.

Ford, F. Nelson, "Decision Support Systems and Expert Systems: A Comparison," *Information and Management*, Vol. 8, 1985, pp. 21–26.

Ford R. D. and B. J. Schroer, "An Expert Manufacturing Simulation System," *Simulation*, Vol. 48, No. 5, May 1987, pp. 193–200.

Fox, M. S. and S. F. Smith, "ISIS: A Knowledge-Based System for Factory Scheduling," *Expert Systems Journal*, Vol. 1, No. 1, 1984, pp. 25–49.

Fox, Mark, et al, "Callisto—An Intelligent System for Managing Large Projects," Research Report, Intelligent Systems Laboratory, Carnegie Mellon University, 1987.

Freedman, R. S. and R. P. Frail, "OPGEN: the Evolution of an Expert System for Process Planning," *AI Magazine*, Vol. 7, No. 5, 1987, pp. 58–70.

Freidland, P., "Acquisition of Procedural Knowledge From Domain Experts," *In Proceeding of the Seventh International Joint Conference on Artificial Intelligence*, 1981, pp. 856–861.

French, S., *Scheduling and Sequencing*, John Wiley, New York, 1982.

Gabriel, R., *Performance and Evaluation of LISP Systems*, MIT Press, Cambridge MA, 1985.

Gaines, B. R., "An Overview of Knowledge Acquisition and Transfer," *International Journal of Man-Machine Studies*, Vol. 27, No. 3, 1987, pp. 453–470.

Gaines, B. R. and M. L. G. Shaw, "Knowledge Engineering Techniques," *Proceedings of AUTOFACT '86*, Society of Manufacturing Engineers, Dearborn MI, 1986, pp. 8–79 to 8–96.

Ganascia, J. G., "Using an Expert System in Merging Qualitative and Quantitative Data Analysis," *International Journal of Man-Machine Studies*, Vol. 20, 1984, pp. 319–330.

Gardner, Howard, *The Mind's New Science*, Basic Books, Inc., New York, 1985.

Garg, C. J. and G. Salvendy, "A Conceptual Framework for Knowledge Elicitation," *International Journal of Man-Machine Studies*, Vol. 27, No. 2, 1987, pp. 521–531.

Gargano, Michael Sylvia Friederich, *Expert Systems Design and Development Using VP-Expert*, John Wiley, New York, 1989.

Geissman, J. R. and R. D. Schultz, "Verification and Validation of Expert Systems," *AI Expert*, Feb. 1988, pp. 26–41.

Gero, John S., "Design Prototypes: A Knowledge Representation Schema for Design," *AI Magazine*, Vol. 11, No. 4, Winter 1990, pp. 26–36.

Gero, John S., ed., *Expert Systems in Computer-Aided Design*, North-Holland, Amsterdam, the Netherlands, 1987.

Gersham, Anatole and Thomas C. Wolf, "Management of User Expectations in a Conventional Advisory System," *IEEE Transactions: Computer Society*, 1985.

Gevarter, W. B., *Artificial Intelligence Expert Systems Computer Vision and Natural Language Processing*, Noyes Publications, Park Ridge NJ, 1984.

Gieszl, L. R., "The Expert Applicability Question," *Proceedings of the Conference on AI and Simulation: Simulation Series*, Vol. 18, No. 3, July 1987, pp. 17–20.

Gilman, Hank, "Detectives On Disks: Law Enforcers Use New Computer Software to Solve Crimes," *Wall Street Journal*, September 11, 1987.

Golden, Bruce L.; Edward A. Wasil; and Patrick T. Harker, eds., *The Analytic Hierarchy Process: Applications and Studies*, Springer-Verlag, New York, 1989.

Grant, T. G., "Lessons for OR from AI: A Scheduling Case Study," *Journal of Operations Research*, Vol. 37, No. 1, 1986, pp. 41–57.

Gray, James F., *Sets, Relations, and Functions*, Holt, Rinehart and Winston, New York, 1965.

Guenthner, Franz, Hubert Lehmann, and Wolfgang Schonfeld, "A Theory for the Representation of Knowledge," *IBM Journal of Research & Development*, Vol. 30, No. 1, January 1986, pp. 39–56.

Hallam, J., "Blackboard Architectures and Systems," in Mirzai, A. R., ed., *Artificial Intelligence: Concepts and Applications in Engineering*, MIT Press, Cambridge MA, 1990, pp. 35–64.

Hamill, Bruce W., "Psychological Issues in the Design of Expert Systems," *Proceedings of the Human Factors Society—28th Annual Meeting*, 1984, pp. 73–77.

Harmon, Paul; Rex Maus; and William Morrissey, *Expert Systems: Tools & Applications*, John Wiley, New York, 1988.

Harmon, Paul and David King, *Expert Systems: Artificial Intelligence in Business*, John Wiley, New York, 1985.

Hartzband, D. J. and F. J. Maryanski, "Enhancing Knowledge Representation in Engineering Databases." *IEEE Transactions*, September, 1985, pp. 39–46.

Hasemer, Tony, *Looking at LISP*, Addison-Wesley, Reading MA, 1984.

Haugeland, John, *Artificial Intelligence, The Very Idea*, Cambridge, MA, MIT Press, 1985.

Hawkins, D., "An Analysis of Expert Thinking," *International Journal of Man-Machine Studies*, Vol. 18, 1983, pp. 1–47.

Hayes, P., "The Logic of Frames," In Metzing, D., ed., *Frame Conceptions and Text Understanding*, de Gruyter, Berlin, 1979, pp. 46–61.

Hayes-Roth, B. et al, "Building Systems in the BB Environment," in Engelmore, Robert and Tony Morgan eds., *Blackboard Systems*, Addison-Wesley, Reading MA, 1988.

Hayes-Roth, Frederick, "The Knowledge-Based Expert System: A Tutorial," *IEEE Transactions*, September 1984, pp. 11–28.

Hayes-Roth, F.; D. A. Waterman; and D. B. Lenat, *Building Expert Systems*, Addison-Wesley, Reading MA, 1983.

Healy, Kathleen Jurica, "Artificial Intelligence Research and Applications at the NASA Johnson Space Center," *AI Magazine*, Vol. 7, No. 3, 1986, pp. 146–152.

Hellerstein, Joseph L.; David A. Klein; and Keith R. Milliken; *Expert Systems in Data Processing: Applications Using IBM's Knowledge Tool*, Addison-Wesley, Reading MA, 1990.

Herrod, Richard A., "AI: Promises Start to Pay Off," *Manufacturing Engineering*, March 1988, pp. 98–103.

Hicks, Richard and Ronald Lee, *VP-Expert for Business Applications*, Holden-Day, Inc., Oakland CA, 1988.

Hink, R. F. and D. L. Woods, "How Humans Process Uncertain Knowledge: An Introduction for Knowledge Engineers," *AI Magazine*, Vol. 8, No. 3, Fall 1987, pp. 41–51.

Hirch, A., "Toolkit Extends the Benefits of LISP-Based Computer to FORTRAN Programming," *Electronic Design*, May 31, 1984, pp. 193–202.

Hoffman, R. R., "The Problem of Extracting the Knowledge of Experts from the Perspective of Experimental Psychology," *AI Magazine*, Vol. 8, No. 2, Summer 1987, pp. 53–67.

Holloway, Bob; Janice Karasz; and Adedeji B. Badiru, "Knowledge Elicitation for Expert Systems in the Law Enforcement Domain," *Journal of Computers & Industrial Engineering*, Vol. 17, Nos. 1–4, 1989, pp. 90–94.

Holtzman, Samuel, *Intelligent Decision Systems*, Addison-Wesley, Reading MA, 1989.

Horowitz, E., *Fundamentals of Programming Languages*, Computer Society Press, Inc., Maryland, 1984.

Howard, Ronald, *Dynamic Probabilistic Systems*, John Wiley, New York, 1971, pp. 949–955.

Ignizio, James P., *Introduction to Expert Systems*, McGraw-Hill, New York, 1990.

Inagaki, S., "Assembly Robot Sensors Designed for Specific Tasks," *Journal of Electronic Engineering*, Tokyo, Japan, Vol. 20, No. 198, 1983, pp. 85–89.

Jackson, Peter, *Introduction to Expert Systems*, 2nd, Addison-Wesley, Reading MA, 1990.

Jindia, A. K., "Expert Systems Remove Repetitive Tedious Work For Customer Order Entry," *Industrial Engineering*, Vol. 22, No. 11, November 1990, pp. 51–53.

Jones, R., "The C Programming Language," *Data Processing*, Vol. 27, No. 10, 1985, pp. 35–38.

Joshi, Ajay P., *PROCESS-Plus: A Prototype Expert System for Generative Process Planning*, MS Thesis, School of Industrial Engineering, University of Oklahoma, Norman OK, 1989.

Joshi, Ajay P.; Neetin N. Datar; and Adedeji B. Badiru, "Knowledge Acquisition and Transfer," in *Proceedings of the 1988 Oklahoma Symposium on Artificial Intelligence*, Norman OK, November 1988, pp. 355–378.

Judd, J. Stephen, *Neural Network Design and the Complexity of Learning*, MIT Press, Cambridge MA, 1990.

Karode, Amol W., *An Integrated Approach for Multiple Knowledge Representation: Hierarchical Blackboard Based Expert Statistical Process Control System*, MS Thesis, School of Industrial Engineering, University of Oklahoma, Norman OK, 1991.

Karp, Richard M. and Michael O. Rabin, "Efficient Randomized Pattern-Matching Algorithms," *IBM Journal of Research & Development*, Vol. 31, No. 2, March 1987, pp. 249–260.

Keene, Sonya E., *Object-Oriented Programming in COMMON LISP: A Programmer's Guide to CLOS*, Addison-Wesley, Reading MA, 1989.

Keller, Brian C. and Thomas R. Knutilla, "U.S. Army Builds An AI Diagnostic Expert System, By Soldiers For Soldiers," *Industrial Engineering*, Vol. 22, No. 9, September 1990, pp. 38–41.

Kernighan, B. and Kitchie, D., *The C Programming Language*, Englewood Cliffs NJ, Prentice Hall, 1978.

Khuzema, K., *An Expert Heuristic Selection System for Project Scheduling*, MS Thesis, School of Industrial Engineering, University of Oklahoma, Norman OK, 1988.

Kidd, A. L., *Knowledge Acquisition for Expert Systems*, Plenum, New York, 1987.

Kinnucan, Paul, "Computers That Think Like Experts," *High Technology*, 1984, pp. 30–42.

Knight, B.; R. Endersby; and V. R. Voller, "The Use of Expert Systems in Industrial Control," *Measurement and Control*, Vol. 17, December 1984, pp. 409–413.

Krag, W. B., "Towards Generative Manufacturing Technology," presented at the 15th Numerical Control Society Meeting and Technical Conference, April 9–13, 1978, pp. 146–159.

Krakauer, Jake, ed., *Smart Manufacturing with Artificial Intelligence*, First edition, Society of Manufacturing Engineers, Dearborn MI, 1987.

Kreutzer, Wolfgang and Bruce J. McKenzie, *Programming for Artificial Intelligence: Methods, Tools, and Applications*, Addison-Wesley, Reading MA, 1991.

Kuipers, B. J., "A Frame for Frames," In Bobrow, G. and A. Collins, eds., *Representation and Understanding*, Academic Press, New York, 1975.

Kumara, Soundar R. T., et al, "Expert Systems in Industrial Engineering," *International Journal of Production Research*, Vol. 24, No. 5, 1986, pp. 1107–1125.

Kumara, Soundar R. T.; R. L. Kashyap; and A. L. Soyster eds., *Artificial Intelligence: Manufacturing Theory and Practice*, Industrial Engineering and Management Press, Norcross GA, 1988.

Kundu, Sukhamay, *Artificial Intelligence*, McGraw-Hill, New York, 1991.

Kusiak, Andrew, "Designing Expert Systems for Scheduling of Automated Manufacturing," *Industrial Engineering*, Vol. 19, No. 7, July 1987, pp. 42–46.

Kusiak, Andrew, ed., *Expert Systems*, Society of Manufacturing Engineers, Dearborn MI, 1988.

Lafrance, M., "The Knowledge Acquisition Grid: A Method for Training Knowledge Engineers," *International Journal of Man-Machine Studies*, Vol 27, No. 1, 1987, pp. 245–255.

Larkin, J.; J. McDermott; D. F. Simon; and H. Simon, "Expert and Novice Performance in Solving Physics Problems," *Science*, 1980, pp. 1335–1342.

Lenat, Douglas and R. V. Guha, *Building Large Knowledge-Based Systems*, Addison-Wesley, Reading MA, 1990.

Liebowitz, Jay, *Introduction to Expert Systems*, Mitchell Publishing, Inc., Santa Cruz CA, 1988.

Liebowitz, Jay and Daniel A. De Salvo, eds., *Structuring Expert Systems: Domain, Design, and Development*, Yourdon Press, Englewoods Cliffs NJ, 1989.

Lin, You-Feng and Shwu Yeng T. Lin, *Set Theory with Applications*, 2nd ed., Mariner Publishing Co., Inc., Tampa FL, 1981.

Linden, E., "Putting Knowledge to Work," *Time Magazine*, March 28, 1988, pp. 60–63.

Lindsey, D. V., " The Probability Approach to the Treatment of Uncertainty in Artificial Intelligence and Expert Systems," In *Proceedings of Uncertainty in Artificial Intelligence and Expert Systems Conference*, George Washington University, Washington DC, 1984.

Loftus, E. F., "Leading Questions and the Eyewitness Reports," *Cognitive Psychology*, Vol. 7, 1975, pp. 560–572.

Lozano-Perez, Tomas, "Automatic Planning of Manipulator Transfer Movements," *IEEE Transactions on Systems, Man, and Cybernetics*, Vol. SCM-11, No.10, Oct 1981, pp. 681–698.

Luger, George F. and William A. Stubblefield, *Artificial Intelligence and the Design of Expert Systems*, Benjamin/Cummings, Redwood City CA, 1989.

MacLennan, B., *Principles of Programming Languages*, Holt, Rinehart and Winston, 1983.

Maher, Mary Lou, "Process Models for Design Synthesis," *AI Magazine*, Vol. 11, No. 4, Winter 1990, pp. 49–58.

Maher, Mary Lou, "Engineering Design Synthesis: A Domain-Independent Representation," *Artificial Intelligence for Engineering Design, Analysis, and Manufacturing*, Vol. 1, No. 3, 1988, pp. 207–213.

Maher, Mary Lou, "HI-RISE: An Expert System for Preliminary Structural Design," In Expert Systems for Engineering Design, M. Rychner, ed., Academic Press, San Diego, CA, 1988, pp. 37–52.

Malmborg, C. J., et al, "A Prototype Expert System for Industrial Truck Type Selection," *Industrial Engineering*, March 1987, pp. 58–64.

Manuel, T., "LISP and PROLOG Machines are Proliferating," *Electronics*, Vol. 56, No.3, November 1983, pp. 132–137.

Marshall, G.; T. J. Barber; and J. T. Boardman, "Methodology for Modelling a Project Management Control Environment," *IEEE Proceeding-D: Control Theory and Applications*, Vol. 134, Part D, No. 4, July 1987, pp. 278–285.

Maus, Rex and Jessica Keyes, *Handbook of Expert Systems in Manufacturing*, McGraw-Hill, New York, 1991.

Mavrovouniotis, Michael L., ed., *Artificial Intelligence in Process Engineering*, Academic Press, New York, 1990.

Mellichamp, J. M. and A. F. A. Wahab, "An Expert System for FMS Design," *Simulation*, Vol. 48, No. 5, May 1987, pp. 201–208.

Mill, F. G. and S. Spraggett, "Artificial Intelligence for Production Planning," *IEE Computer-Aided Engineering Journal*, Vol. 1, No. 4, 1984, pp. 210–213.

Miller, F. D., et al, "ACE: An Expert System for Preventive Maintenance Operations," *Record*, January 1986.

Minsky, M., "A Framework for Representing Knowledge," In Winston, P., ed., *The Psychology of Computer Vision*, McGraw-Hill, New York, 1975, pp. 211–277.

Mirzai, A. R., ed., *Artificial Intelligence: Concepts and Applications in Engineering*, MIT Press, Cambridge MA, 1990.

Mishkoff, Henry C., *Understanding Artificial Intelligence*, Texas Instruments Information Publishing Center, Dallas TX, 1985.

Mittal, S.; B. Chandrasekaran; and J. Sticklen, "Patrec: A Knowledge-Directed Database for a Diagnostic Expert System," *IEEE Transactions*, September 1984, pp. 51–58.

Mittal, S. and C. L. Dym, "Knowledge Acquisition from Multiple Experts," *AI Magazine*, Vol. 6, No. 2, 1985.

Moralee, D. S., "The Use of Knowledge Engineering in an Industrial Research Environment—A Retrospect," *Expert System and Knowledge Engineering*, North-Holland, Amsterdam, the Netherlands, 1986, pp. 101–110.

Murray, Jerome T. and Marilyn J. Murray, *Expert Systems in Data Processing: A Professional's Guide*, McGraw-Hill, New York, 1988.

Nau, S. D. and Tien-Chien Chang, "A Knowledge Based Approach to Generative Process Planning," presented at the symposium of computer-aided and intelligent process planning, ASME Winter Meeting, Miami Beach FL, 1985.

Nau, S. D. and Tien-Chien Chang, "Prospects for Process Selection using Artificial Intelligence," *Computers in Industry*, Vol. 4, 1983, pp. 253–263.

Naylor, Chris, *Build Your Own Expert System*, Halsted Press, New York, 1983.

New York Times, "Setback for Artificial Intelligence," March 4, 1988.

Newell, Allen and Herbert A. Simon, *Human Problem-Solving*, Prentice Hall, Englewood Cliffs NJ, 1972.

Newell, Allen and Herbert A. Simon, "Computer Simulation of Human Thinking," *The RAND Corporation*, April 20, 1961, p. 2276.

Newquist, Harvey P., "The New Crime Stopper's Notebook: The Expert System," *AI Expert*, March 1988, pp. 19–21.

Newquist, III, Harvey P., "Braining the Expert," *AI Expert*, February 1988, pp. 67–69.

Nguyen, Tin A.; W. A. Perkins; T. J. Laffey; and Deanne Pecora, "Knowledge Base Verification," *AI Magazine*, Vol. 8, No. 2, Summer 1987, pp. 69–75.

Nida, K., et al, "Some Expert System Experiments in Process Engineering," *Chemical Engineering Research & Design*, Vol. 64, September 1986.

Nii, H. P., "Blackboard Systems: The Blackboard Model of Problem Solving and the Evolution of Blackboard Architectures," *AI Magazine*, Vol. 7, 1986, pp. 38–53.

Niwa, Kiyoshi, *Knowledge-Based Risk Management in Engineering: A Case Study in Human-Computer Cooperative Systems*, John Wiley, New York, 1989.

Nof, Shimon Y., "An Expert System for Planning/Replanning Programmable Facilities," *International Journal of Production Research*, Vol. 22, 1984, pp. 45–57.

Nowland, Russell, *Development of a Multimedia Expert System for a Design for Manufacturing Information System*, MS Thesis, School of Industrial Engineering, University of Oklahoma, Norman OK, 1989.

Oxman, Steven W., "Expert Systems Represent Ultimate Goal of Strategic Decision Making," *Data Management*, April 1985, pp. 36–38.

Paperback Software International, *VP-Expert Reference Manual*, Paperback Software International, Berkeley CA, 1989.

Parsaye, Kamran; M. Chignell; S. Knoshafian; and H. Wong, *Intelligent Databases: Object-Oriented, Deductive Hypermedia Technologies*, John Wiley, New York, 1989.

Partridge, Derek and Yorick Wilks, eds., *The Foundations of Artificial Intelligence: A Sourcebook*, Cambridge University Press, Cambridge MA, 1990.

Patterson, Dan W., *Introduction to Artificial Intelligence and Expert Systems*, Prentice Hall, Englewood Cliffs NJ, 1990.

Pearl, Judea, *Heuristics: Intelligent Search Strategies for Computer Problem Solving*, Addison-Wesley, Reading MA, 1984.

Pearl, Judea, *Probabilistic Reasoning in Intelligent Systems: Network of Plausible Inference*, Morgan Kaufmann, San Mateo CA, 1988.

Pedersen, Ken, *Expert Systems Programming: Practical Techniques for Rule-Based Systems*, John Wiley, New York, 1989.

Phillips, R. H. and C. B. Mouleeswaran, "A Knowledge Based Approach to Generative Process Planning," In *Proceedings of AUTOFACT 85*, No. 1985, pp. 10.2–10.15.

Pipitone, F., "The FIS Electronics Troubleshooting System," *BYTE*, Vol. 19, No. 7, July 1986, pp. 68–76.

Pohl, I., *A Book on C*, The Benjamin/Cummings Publishing Company, 1984.

Preiss, K. and E. Kaplansky, "Automated Part Programming for CNC Milling by Artificial Intelligence Techniques," *Journal of Manufacturing Systems*, Vol. 4, No. 1, 1987, pp. 51–63.

Prerau, David S., *Developing and Managing Expert Systems: Proven Techniques for Business and Industry*, Addison-Wesley, Reading MA, 1990.

Prerau, David S., "Knowledge Acquisition in the Development of a Large Expert System," *AI Magazine*, Vol. 8, No. 2, Summer 1987, pp. 43–51.

Pulat, P. Simin and A.B. Badiru, "Optimization of Oil Industry Investment Yield," Consulting Working Paper, School of Industrial Engineering, University of Oklahoma, Norman OK, 1990.

Rajaram, N. S., "Expert System Building Tools: Present Trends and Future Needs," *ISA Transactions*, Vol. 26, No. 1, 1987, pp. 53–55.

Rajaram, N. S., "Artificial Intelligence—the Achilles Heel of Robotics and Manufacturing," *Robotics Engineering*, January 1986, pp. 10–15.

Raudsepp, E., "Profile of the Creative Individual," *Creative Computing*, October 1983, pp. 196–209.

Reddy, Y. V. R.; Mark S. Fox; and N. Hasain, "The Knowledge-Based Simulation System," *IEEE Software*, March 1986, pp. 26–37.

Rice, L., "LISP Notes: LISP for MS/DOS and CP/M I/0 and Sorting in LISP," *Access*, Vol. 4, No. 6, 1985, pp. 35–40.

Rich, Elaine and Kevin Knight, *Artificial Intelligence*, 2nd, McGraw-Hill, New York, 1991.

Rifkin, G., "LISP Defends AI Foothold Despite PROLOG Challenge," *Computerworld*, May 27, 1985, pp. 45–48.

Rolston, David W., *Principles of Artificial Intelligence and Expert Systems Development*, McGraw-Hill, New York, 1988.

Roth, F.; Waterman, D.; and Lenat, D., *An Overview of Expert Systems, Building Expert Systems*, Addison-Wesley, Reading MA, 1983.

Saaty, Thomas L., *The Analytic Hierarchy Process*, McGraw-Hill, New York, 1980.

Sagan, Hans, *Advanced Calculus*, Houghton Mifflin, Boston, 1974.

Sathi, A.; Mark S. Fox; and M. Greenberg, "Representation of Activity Knowledge for Project Management," *IEEE Transactions on Pattern Analysis and Machine Intelligence*, Vol. 7, 1985, pp. 531–552.

Schaffer, G. H., "Artificial Intelligence: A Tool for Smart Manufacturing," *American Machinist & Automated Manufacturing*, Vol. 130, No. 8, 1986, pp. 83–94.

Schalkoff, Robert J., *Artificial Intelligence: An Engineering Approach*, McGraw-Hill, New York, 1990.

Schank, Roger C. and R. P. Abelson, *Scripts, Plans, Goals, and Understanding*, Erlbaum, Hillsdale NJ, 1977.

Schank, Roger C. and Peter G. Childers, *The Cognitive Computer*, Addison-Wesley, Reading MA, 1984.

Schindler, Max, "Expert Systems Poised To Reshape Industry," *Electronic Design*, March 19, 1987, pp. 29–32.

Schreiber, R. R., "Quality Control with Vision," *Vision*, Vol. 2, No. 4, 1985, pp. 7–13.

Scown, Susan J., *The Artificial Intelligence Experience: An Introduction*, Digital Equipment Corporation, Maynard MA, 1985.

Sell, Peter S., *Expert Systems—A Practical Introduction*, John Wiley, New York, 1985.

Shafer, Glenn A., *Mathematical Theory of Evidence*, Princeton University Press, Princeton. NJ, 1979.

Shannon, Claude E., "Programming a Computer for Playing Chess," *Philosophical Magazine*, Series 7, Vol. 41, 1950, pp. 256–275.

Shanteau, James, "Psychological Characteristics of Expert Decision Makers," In *Proceedings of the NATO Advanced Research Workshop on Expert Judgment*, Porto, Portugal, 1986.

Sheil, B., "Family of Personal LISP Machines Speeds AI Program Development," *Electronics*, Vol. 56, November 3, 1983, pp. 153–156.

Shirai, Yoshiaki and Jun-ichi Tsujii, *Artificial Intelligence: Concepts, Techniques and Applications*, John Wiley, New York, 1982.

Shoisral, H. "Structures, Meta-Structures, and Expert System Languages," *IEEE Transactions*, 1985, pp. 113–114.

Siddall, James N., *Expert Systems for Engineers*, Marcel Dekker, New York, 1990.

Siegel, P., *Expert Systems—A Non-Programmers Guide To Development And Applications*, TAB Books, Blue Ridge Summit PA, 1986.

Silverman, Barry G., "Critiquing Human Judgment Via Knowledge Acquisition Systems," *AI Magazine*, Vol. 11, No. 3, Fall 1990, pp. 60–79.

Silverman, Barry G., "Expert Intuition and Ill-Structured Problem Solving," *IEEE Transaction on Engineering Management*, Vol. EM-32, No. 1, February 1985, pp. 29–33.

SME, *Tool and Manufacturing Engineers Handbook*, McGraw-Hill, New York, 1976.

Smith, S. F.; M. S. Fox; and P. S. Ow, "Knowledge-Based Factory Scheduling Systems," *AI Magazine*, Vol. 7, No. 4, 1986, pp. 45–61.

Somby, Tom, "OKIE—Expert System for Trouble Shooting Computer Hardware," presented at the Symposium on Artificial Intelligence, University of Oklahoma, Norman OK, November 2–3, 1987.

Sowa, John, ed., *Principles of Semantic Networks*, Morgan Kaufmann, San Mateo CA, 1990.

Sriram, Duvvuru, et al, "Knowledge-Based System Applications in Engineering Design: Research at MIT," *AI Magazine*, Vol. 10, No. 4, Fall 1989, pp. 79–96.

Steele, G., *Common LISP-The Language*, Digital Equipment Corporation, Maynard MA, 1984.

Steele, G. and Sussman, G., "Design of a LISP-Based Microprocessor," *Communications of the ACM*, Vol. 23, No. 11, 1980, pp. 628–644.

Stendel, H. J., "Computer Aided Process Planning: Past, Present and Future," *International Journal of Production Research*, Vol. 22, No. 2, 1984, pp. 253–266.

Stendel, H. J. and L. L. Firchow, "An Expert System for Evaluating and Selecting Computer-Aided Process Planning Systems," *Knowledge Based Systems for Manufacturing*, Vol. 24, 1986, pp. 267–297.

Stevens, John K., "Reverse Engineering The Brain," *Byte*, April 1985.

Sundaram, Deepak, *JUSTEX: An Expert System for the Justification of Advanced Manufacturing Technology*, MS Thesis, School of Industrial Engineering, University of Oklahoma, Norman OK, 1991.

Sundaram, Deepak and Adedeji B. Badiru, "JUSTEX: An Expert System for the Justification of Advanced Manufacturing Technology," in *Knowledge-Based Systems and Neural Networks: Techniques and Applications*, Sharda, Ramesh et al., editors, Elsevier Science Publishing Co., New York, 1991, pp. 89–98.

Sunku, Ravindra, *ROBEX: An Expert System for Manufacturing Robot System Implementation*, MS Thesis, School of Industrial Engineering, University of Oklahoma, Norman OK, 1991.

Sunku, Ravindra and Adedeji B. Badiru, "ROBEX (Robot Expert): An Expert System for Manufacturing Robot System Implementation," *Computers & Industrial Engineering*, Vol. 19, Nos. 1–4, 1990, pp. 481–483.

Szidarovszky, F.; M. E. Gershon; and L. Duckstein, *Techniques for Multiobjective Decision Making in Systems Management*, Elsevier, New York, 1986.

Takeda, Hideaki; Paul Veerkamp; Tetsuo Tomiyama; and Hiroyuki Yoshikawa, "Modeling Design Processes," *AI Magazine*, Vol. 11, No. 4, Winter 1990, 37–48.

Tanimoto, Steven L., *The Elements of Artificial Intelligence: Using Common LISP*, Computer Science Press, New York, 1990.

Taylor, E. C., "Developing a Knowledge Engineering System in the TRW Defense Systems Group," *AI Magazine*, Vol. 6, No. 2, 1985, pp. 58–63.

Taylor, M. M., *The Bilateral Cooperative Model of Reading: A Human Paradigm For Artificial Intelligence*, Elsevier Science Publishers, Amsterdam, the Netherlands, 1984.

Tello, E., "The Languages of AI Research," *PC Magazine*, April 16, 1985, pp. 173–189.

Texas Instruments, "Knowledge-Based Systems: A Step-By-Step Guide To Getting Started," *Proceedings of the Second Artificial Intelligence Satellite Symposium*, Texas Instruments, Dallas TX, 1986.

Thomas, R. M., *Advanced Techniques in AutoCAD*, Sybex, Alameda CA, 1988.

Thompson, Beverly and William Thompson, *Micro Expert*, McGraw-Hill, New York, 1985.

Tou, J. T., "Design of Expert Systems for Integrated Production Automation," *Journal of Manufacturing Engineering*, Vol. 4, No. 2, 1987, pp. 147–155.

Townsend, W. B., "Artificial Intelligence Techniques for Industrial Applications in Shop Scheduling," Masters Thesis, Naval Postgraduate School, Monterey CA, June 1983.

Troxler, Joel W. and Leland Blank, "A Comprehensive Methodology for Manufacturing System Evaluation and Comparison," *Journal of Manufacturing Systems*, Vol. 8, No. 3, 1989, pp. 176–183.

Turban, Efraim, "Expert Systems—Another Frontier for Industrial Engineering," *Computers and Industrial Engineering*, Vol. 10, No. 3, 1986, pp. 227–235.

Tversky, A., and Kahneman, D., "Extensional versus Intuitive Reasoning: The Conjunction Fallacy in Probability Judgment," *Psychological Review*, Vol. 4, 1983, pp. 293–315.

Vandamme, F., "Knowledge Extraction from Experts in View of the Construction of Expert Systems," In *Proceedings of the NATO Advanced Research Workshop on Expert Judgment*, Porto, Portugal, 1986.

Verity, J., "PROLOG vs LISP," *Datamation*, Vol. 30, January 1984, pp. 50–55.

Villa, A., et al, "An Expert Control System for Tool Life Management in Flexible Manufacturing Cells," *Annals of CIRP*, Vol. 34, No. 1, 1985, pp. 87–90.

Walpole, Ronald E. and Raymond H. Myers, *Probability and Statistics for Engineers and Scientists*, 2nd ed., Macmillan, New York, 1978.

Walter, Eric, *Identifiability of State Space Models with Applications to Transformation Systems*, Springer-Verlag, New York, 1982.

Wang, Wally and John Mueller, *Illustrated VP-Expert*, Wordware Publishing, Inc., Plano TX, 1989.

Warren, D. and Pereira, L., "PROLOG—The Language and its Implementations Compared With LISP," *Proceedings of the ACM Symposium of Artificial Intelligence and Programming Languages*, SIGART/SIGPLAN Notices, August 1977, pp. 109–115.

Waterman, D. A., *A Guide to Expert Systems*, Addison-Wesley, Reading MA, 1986.

Waterman, D. A. and F. Hayes-Roth, *An Investigation of Tools for Building Expert Systems*, Rand Corporation, Santa Monica CA, 1982.

Webster, Robin, "Expert Systems on Microcomputers," *Computers and Electronics*, Vol. 23, No. 3, 1985, pp. 69–73, 94–104.

Weill, R. Spur G. and W. Eversheim, "Survey of Computer Aided Process Planning Systems," *Annals of the CIRP*, Vol. 3, No. 2, 1982, pp. 45–56.

Weiss, Sholom and Casimir Kulikowski, *Computer Systems that Learn: Classification and Prediction Methods from Statistics, Neural Nets, Machine Learning and Expert Systems*, Morgan Kaufmann, San Mateo CA, 1990.

Weiss, Sholom M. and Casimir A. Kulikowski, *A Practical Guide to Designing Expert Systems*, Rowman & Allanheld, Totowa NJ, 1984.

Weitz, R., "Technology, Work, and the Organization: The Impact of Expert Systems," *AI Magazine*, Vol. 11, No. 2, 1990, pp. 50–60.

White, A. P., "Inference Deficiencies in Rule-Based Expert Systems," In *Proceedings of the 4th Technical Conference of the British Computer Society Specialist Group on Expert Systems*, Cambridge University Press, 1985.

Winston, P., "The LISP Revolution," *Byte*, Vol. 11, April 1985, pp. 209–217.

Wolfgram, Deborah D.; Teresa J. Dear; and Craig S. Galbraith, *Expert Systems for the Technical Professional*, New York: John Wiley, 1987.

Woods, W. A., "What's Important About Knowledge Representation?" *IEEE Computer*, Vol. 16, No. 22, 1983, pp. 58–70.

Wyland, D., "Software That Learns," *Computerworld*, November 11, 1985, pp. 93–104.

Wynot, M., "Artificial Intelligence Provides Real-Time Control of DEC's Material Handling Process," *Industrial Engineering*, April 1986, pp. 34–44.

Zadeh, Lotfi A., "Fuzzy Logic, Principles, Applications, and Perspectives," public lecture, University of Oklahoma, Norman OK, April 18, 1991.

Zadeh, Lotfi A., "Fuzzy Sets," *Information and Control*, Vol. 8, 1965, pp. 338–353.

Zarri, Gian Piero, "Expert Systems and Information Retrieval: An Experiment in the Domain of Biograhical Data Management," *International Journal of Man-Machine Studies*, Vol. 20, 1984, pp. 87–106.

Zeskind, D., "LISP Processors Speed Development of Artificial Intelligence Applications," *EDN*, Vol. 27, January 6, 1982, pp. 63–70.

Index

430